An Educator's Guide to SPECIAL EDUCATION LAW

Second Edition

Brenda J. Bowlby
Catherine Peters
Martha Mackinnon

Canada Law Book
A Division of the Cartwright Group Ltd.
240 Edward Street, Aurora, Ontario L4G 3S9
www.canadalawbook.ca

Printed in Canada

The publisher, and every person involved in the creation of this publication, disclaims any warranty as to the accuracy, completeness or currency of the contents of this publication. This publication is intended for information purposes only. The publisher is not engaged in rendering legal or other professional advice and this publication should not be relied upon as providing such advice. The publisher, and every person involved in the creation of this publication, disclaims all liability in respect of the results of any actions taken or not taken in reliance upon information in this publication.

Library and Archives Canada Cataloguing in Publication

Bowlby, Brenda J. (Brenda Jean), 1952-

An educator's guide to special education law / Brenda J. Bowlby, Catherine Peters, Martha Mackinnon. – 2nd ed.

(Educators' guides to the law)
Includes bibliographic references and index.
ISBN 978-0-88804-493-8

1. Special education–Law and legislation–Ontario.
I. Peters, Catherine II. Mackinnon, Martha, 1948- III. Title.
IV. Series: Educators' guides to the law

KEO771.4B69 2010 344.713'0791 C2010-903611-5
KF4209.3.B69 2010

This book is dedicated

To my husband, Rick Burgess,
and my daughter, Lindsay Burgess, who,
with love and support, gave me "their time"
to write this book.

BJB

To my family, friends and colleagues, whose support
and encouragement have made this book possible.

CLP

For my family which has always valued education
and law and my work in each; for the students who
have taught me so much; and for the friends who
have cared about me, even through indexing.

MMM

Foreword

Effective special education begins with knowledge. Brenda, Catherine and Martha are provincially well known for their expertise in special education law and its application to the education of children with special needs. Over the years we have come to rely on their expertise not only through their writing, but through their presentations and through their wise counsel. Their experiences in managing the changes in special education legislation and supporting school boards in difficult times are unprecedented. All three have demonstrated sensitivity towards the needs and responsibilities of the boards, and the rights of parents and students.

This update to the first edition of *An Educator's Guide to Special Education* is an essential resource with new chapters on discipline, post-secondary education, and use of advocates and parent representatives. Through their experience in presenting to a wide variety of audiences and sharing expertise that helps to ground daily practice with students and parents, they bring a legal framework together for practical day-to-day use, which helps educators and parents engage in better decision-making processes. As a reader of this book you will come away with a deeper understanding of the legislative requirements and the journey towards effective practice.

As educators, we know and believe that the progress of every child matters. Policies in special education are built on the premise that special education programs and services enable students with special needs to have equitable access to learning and opportunities to pursue and achieve the goals of their educational program. It is the process involved with implementation that makes a belief become a reality for these children. While Ontario educators have long been recognized for their attention and delivery of programs and services that comply with these requirements, an increased public awareness of the accountability structures and fewer resources has made it more difficult.

The creativity of committed teachers, principals and board personnel continues to be exemplary in Ontario. However, the reality of carrying out these responsibilities, heightened accountability, and increased parental and student rights lead educators to seek out resources and the guidance of experts in educational law. The need to be cognizant of the legislative requirements and to be confident that our programs are being delivered within the parameters of the law is essential — hence, the value of *An Educator's Guide to Special Education Law*.

The second edition of *An Educator's Guide to Special Education Law* will give educators the confidence to speak knowledgeably to parents and advocates about programs, services, processes and legislative requirements. This book places a great deal of information in one compact place. The next best thing to having Brenda, Catherine and Martha on the other end of the telephone is having their book on the corner of your desk!

June 2010

Louise Moreau
Superintendent of Special Education

Suzanne Moffatt
Education Officer

Preface

The first edition of this book was written primarily for educators who, on a daily basis, face increasingly complex legal issues in the course of providing education to exceptional pupils and unidentified pupils with disabilities. Our hope was that the book would prove to be useful for parents and others seeking to understand the legal aspects of special education. Through the years since the first edition was written, we understand that those we targeted did find the book to be helpful, as did others, including lawyers and educators engaged in learning about special education as part of a program to obtain additional qualifications.

The second edition retains the goal of the original, which was to provide an overview of the legal framework together with a practical analysis of the legal questions that arise on a day-to-day basis. In respect of the appeal process, we wanted to provide a layperson's overview of how the process works and how hearings unfold, together with some explanation of the manner in which legal issues are handled along the way. Our firm belief was — and remains — that an understanding of the overall legal process will permit better informed decision-making along the way.

Since the publication of the first edition, a number of things have happened: the Ministry of Education issued a new handbook, entitled *Special Education: A Guide for Educators, 2001*; the province's approach to "safe schools" was overhauled to change the underlying principle of discipline from what, rightly or wrongly, was viewed as punishment for "infractions" to discipline as an educational tool for changing inappropriate student behaviours; the parents of children living with autism became active in a significant way, advocating for the educational and treatment rights of their children in every possible forum (including the Special Education Tribunal, the Human Rights Tribunal, the courts — in individual and class actions — and intense political lobbying); the exceptional pupils who benefitted from the special education programs and services provided in elementary and secondary schools through the past decade moved on to post-secondary education. All these developments — along with the growing number of inquiries we were receiving about a second edition — persuaded us that it was now time to revise the first edition of *An Educator's Guide to Special Education Law*.

In response to the developments since the first edition, we have not only updated the text and footnotes to include recent case law and legal developments, we have added additional chapters. Specifically, a new chapter on discipline reviews, in detail, the legal challenges an educator faces when considering discipline for an exceptional pupil; a new chapter on post-secondary education addresses the challenges being faced by colleges and universities in accommodating students with disabilities in the absence of a prescriptive statutory framework; and we have added a chapter on the use of advocates and representatives in order to clarify when parents are entitled to representation and who can provide that representation.We need to acknowledge that the law of Ontario is the focus of this book, because the three of us practice in Ontario. We hope, however, that because of the similarities in special education law and human rights law across Canada, that this book will also be helpful to those living and working in other Canadian jurisdictions.

Finally, two of us wish to express our appreciation for the support from our partners and colleagues at Hicks Morley Hamilton Stewart Storie LLP in our writing and revision of this book. The third expresses the same sentiments to her colleagues at Justice for Children and Youth.

June 2010

Brenda Bowlby
Catherine Peters
Martha Mackinnon

Table of Contents

Foreword v
Preface vii

1 Introduction 1

What is Special Education Law? 1
Bill 82 2
The Current Process 2
Other Legislation 4
Other Issues 4

2 The Legal Framework 7

Introduction 7
Administrative Law 7
Education Law 13
Human Rights Law 16
Child Welfare Law 19
Conclusion 19

3 The Administrator's Framework 21

Introduction 21
The Special Education Plan 22
The Special Education Advisory Committee 33
The Parent Guide 41
Limits on Class Size 42
Policy/Program Memoranda 45

4 Identification and Exceptionality 47

Introduction 47
Categories of Exceptionality 49
To Identify or Not to Identify 55

5 Placement 57

Introduction 57
What is Placement? 57
Standard to be Used in Determining Placements 66
Implementing a Placement 72
Placements Pending an Appeal and Transitional Placements 73
Ministry Directives Regarding Programming 74

6 The Identification, Placement and Review Committee 77

Introduction 77
Establishment of the IPRC 79
Referral of Students to the IPRC 79
Conduct of the IPRC Proceeding 84
Parental Request to Discuss the IPRC's Decision 107
Transition 108
Implementation of the Decision 109

7 The Individual Education Plan 111

Introduction 111
Mandatory Individual Education Plans 112
Optional Individual Educational Plans 113
Development Process 114
Contents of the IEP 116
Timelines for Completion of the IEP 119
Review 120
Ontario Student Record 120

8 Role of Parent Advocates 121

Parents' Rights to be Represented by Advocates 123

Advocates at Informal Meetings ... 123
Advocates at the Identification Placement Review Committee ... 124
Advocates at the SEAB ... 125
Advocates at the Special Education Tribunal ... 125
Competency of Lay Advocates ... 126
Cost of Representation ... 126
Finding Representatives ... 127

9 Alternative Dispute Resolution: Mediation ... 129

Alternate Dispute Resolution: Mediation ... 129
Some Advantages of Mediation ... 130
Mediation and Special Education ... 131
The Mediation Process ... 133
Mediation During Proceedings Before the Special Education Tribunal... 134
Preparation for Mediation ... 134
Concluding Comments ... 134

10 The First Stage of Appeal ... 137

Introduction ... 137
Grounds and Scope of Appeal ... 138
School Board Objection that Appeal Does Not Relate to Identification or Placement ... 139
Timing of the Appeal ... 140
The Notice of Appeal ... 143
Parties to the Appeal ... 144
Setting Up the Special Education Appeal ... 145
Administrative Support for and Expenses of SEAB Members ... 146
The SEAB Meeting ... 146
Decision of the SEAB ... 152
The School Board's Decision ... 153
Implementation of the Board's Decision ... 155

11 The Final Appeal ... 157

Introduction ... 157
The Special Education Tribunal ... 157
Initiating the Appeal: The Who, When, What and How ... 158
Procedural Rules Governing the Tribunal's Processes ... 164
Preliminary Matters ... 165

The Hearing Process 172
Providing Evidence to the Tribunal 176
The Special Education Tribunal's Decision 185
Remedies Available 188
Legal Costs 191
Effect of the Special Education Tribunal's Decision 192

12 The Human Rights Process 193

Introduction 193
Comparing the Special Education and Human Rights Regimes 194
Recent Changes to the Human Rights Process 195
The Human Rights Tribunal of Ontario 196
Representatives 199
Delivery of Filing of Documents 200
Applications, Responses and Replies 203
Intervention by the Commission and Other Affected Persons 216
Early Dismissal and Deferral 220
Expedited Proceedings and Interim Remedies 223
Request for an Order During Proceedings 226
Mediation and Settlements 228
Scheduling the Hearing 230
Pre-Hearing Disclosure 231
The Hearing 234
Decision and Remedies 243
Reconsideration 246

13 Review by the Courts 249

Introduction 249
Review of IPRC and SEAB Decisions 249
The Procedure for Judicial Review 250
The Grounds for Judicial Review of Special Education Tribunal Decisions 255
Grounds for Review of Human Rights Tribunal Decisions 266
Remedies Available on Judicial Review 269
Implementation of the Judicial Review Decision 270

14 Discipline and Other Issues 271

Introduction 271

Human Rights and Discipline 272
Mitigating and Other Factors 274
Recording Consideration of Mitigating and Other Factors 277
Dealing With Students Who Cannot Control Their Actions But Pose a Threat to School Safety 277

15 Post-Secondary Education 281

Introduction 281
Transition to Post-Secondary Education 282
Accommodation in Post-Secondary Education: The Governing Principles 285
How Far is Too Far? The Limits on the Duty to Accommodate 288
The Accommodation Process 295

Index 299

1

Introduction

WHAT IS SPECIAL EDUCATION LAW?

We use the term "special education law" in this book to define the legal rights and obligations surrounding the education of students who are "exceptional"— that is, students whose educational needs are not met by the regular curriculum because of mental and/or physical disabilities or because of the high level of their intellectual needs ("giftedness").

Special education law in Ontario had its genesis in Bill 82[1] in 1980. Bill 82 amended the *Education Act* to incorporate provisions requiring that exceptional students be identified and provided with placements where they can receive appropriate special education programs and services. While the amendments that Bill 82 made to the *Education Act* remain in place today with only minor modifications, special education law has continued to develop, augmented by changes to regulations under the *Education Act*,[2] as well as interpretations of the legislation provided by the Special Education Tribunals and the courts. Human rights and constitutional legislation have also come into play to shape this unique area of law.

In this book, we will review the rights of exceptional students and their parents and the obligations of school boards and the provincial government outlined in the statutory framework that constitutes Ontario's blueprint for special education. In this chapter, we will provide a brief overview of the most recent historical context of today's statutory framework, an overview of the legal process for identification, placement and appeal, and a general outline of the contents of this book.

---

1 *Education Amendment Act, 1980*, S.O. 1980, c. 61.

2 R.S.O. 1990, c. E.2.

BILL 82

Prior to the enactment of Bill 82, children with severe disabilities were often excluded from Ontario's school systems. In some localities, parents set up "schools for the mentally retarded". In some cases, such schools were housed in buildings built for that purpose. In other cases, parents set up "schools" in community spaces or church basements; and in some cases, children with disabilities simply remained at home and received no education or were placed in residential institutions.

Bill 82 was heralded as introducing "universal access" to publicly funded education to all Ontario's children.[3] It came with the recognition that, in order for the right to an education to be meaningful for children with disabilities, special measures would have to be taken where those disabilities interfered with the ability of these children to learn from the normal curriculum. The Bill 82 amendments to the *Education Act* charged the Minister of Education, in the first instance, with the responsibility of ensuring that those measures were taken. Moreover, the Minister was also charged with the responsibility of setting up a process for parents[4] to appeal the appropriateness of special education placements provided for their children.

Bill 82 also imposed on each school board the obligation to provide special education programs and special education services for its exceptional pupils, either directly or through the purchase of service agreements with another school board.[5]

The framework created by Bill 82 was supplemented by a number of regulations and Ministerial policies and directives. This framework, which was introduced in 1980, remains essentially intact today.

THE CURRENT PROCESS

At the outset, school boards were required to phase in special education programs and services over a five-year period[6] and to report to the Minister on

---

[3] The provisions of Bill 82 applied to both the public school boards and Roman Catholic separate school boards. Private or independent schools are not subject to the special education provisions of the *Education Act*.

[4] Throughout this book, the term "parent" includes both parents when they live together or are separated but have joint custody of the student, as well as the custodial parent when the parents are separated. It also refers to the student's legal guardian where a court has made an order naming an individual or individuals as the child's guardian. "Guardian" is defined by s. 1 of the *Education Act* as "a person who has lawful custody of a child, other than the parent of the child". Note that a child aged 18 years or older is an adult and that any guardianship order ceases to have effect once the child reaches the age of majority, unless the basis of the guardianship order is that the individual is not competent.

[5] The language imposing this obligation remains unchanged today and is currently set out in s. 170(1), para. 7 of the *Education Act*.

[6] *Special Education Programs and Services*, R.R.O. 1980, Reg. 274.

their progress. The reporting obligation on the status of school board special education plans continues today.[7]

The process for identifying exceptional students has changed little over the past two decades. School boards are required by regulation[8] to establish at least one Identification, Placement and Review Committee ("IPRC") for the purpose of determining whether students are exceptional.[9] Where a student is determined to be exceptional, the IPRC must use the definitions of exceptionalities that have been prescribed by the Minister.[10] Once a student is identified as exceptional, the IPRC must determine the placement[11] for the student and, thereafter, must review the placement at least annually. This process must be carried out in consultation with parents and all IPRC decisions must be made in the presence of parents. Once a placement is implemented, an Individual Education Plan must be created by school staff, again in consultation with parents.[12]

In accordance with the directive to the Minister of Education to provide a process for parents to appeal the appropriateness of special education placements, parents have been given the right to request a review of the IPRC decision by a tripartite board (a Special Education Appeal Board)[13] comprised of a parent appointee, a school board appointee and a chair selected by the appointees. Following a meeting with all persons who might contribute to the matter, the Special Education Appeal Board must make a recommendation to the school board, which will then reconsider the IPRC's decision.

Should the parents disagree with the school board's decision on placement, the parents are entitled as of right to appeal to the Special Education Tribunal.[14] This tribunal was initially established by the Bill 82 amendments to the *Education Act* and these statutory provisions continue today. The decision of the Special Education Tribunal is final and binding on the parents and the school board, subject only to review by the courts where the tribunal makes a legal error in its process or decision.[15]

Beyond the statutory scheme, parents and school boards are increasingly turning to mediation as an alternative forum for resolving their differences over identification and placement disputes. We have devoted a full chapter to this process because it provides a much more constructive approach to the resolution of disputes between parents and the school board than the appeal process itself.[16]

---

7 See Chapter 3, "The Administrator's Framework".

8 *Special Education Programs and Services*, R.R.O. 1990, Reg. 306.

9 See Chapter 6, "The Identification, Placement and Review Committee".

10 See Chapter 4, "Identification and Exceptionality".

11 See Chapter 5, "Placement".

12 See Chapter 7, "The Individual Education Plan".

13 See Chapter 10, "The First Stage of Appeal".

14 See Chapter 11, "The Final Appeal".

15 See Chapter 13, "Review by the Courts".

16 See Chapter 9, "Alternative Dispute Resolution: Mediation".

OTHER LEGISLATION

Legal recognition of the rights of persons with disabilities has existed in Canada since only 1982. It was in this year that Ontario's *Human Rights Code, 1981*,[17] was proclaimed in force, replacing prior human rights legislation and adding "handicap" as a protected ground. The right to equal treatment under the law for persons with disabilities in the *Canadian Charter of Rights and Freedoms* did not come into force until 1985. It is significant to note that Bill 82, which entrenched in Ontario's *Education Act* the right of students with disabilities to an education in Ontario's schools, was passed in 1980, prior to both of these enactments.

Because human rights law also deals with the rights of persons with disabilities,[18] it was foreseeable that once "handicap"(now "disability") was added as a ground of discrimination, parents of students with disabilities would also access the procedures under the *Human Rights Code*[19] as a means of seeking resolution of disputes involving their children with disabilities.[20] Similarly, the *Canadian Charter of Rights and Freedoms* guarantees equal treatment under the law without discrimination on certain grounds, including mental and physical disability. Both pieces of legislation have played a role in the development of special education law.[21]

OTHER ISSUES

Quite apart from the issues that arise, either in the process of identifying and placing exceptional students or in the special education appeal process, unique challenges arise daily for school staff in attempting to meet the needs of

---

17 S.O. 1981, c. 53; proclaimed in force June 15, 1982.

18 It should be noted that giftedness is not a disability under the *Human Rights Code*; however, where a gifted student also has a disability, such as a learning disability or other physical or mental disability, the Code would have application in respect only of that disability. Similarly, the Code would apply to the behavioural exceptionality only where the student's behavioural problems arise or are perceived to arise from a mental or physical disability.

19 R.S.O. 1990, c. H.19.

20 The earliest special education case to reach a Human Rights Board of Inquiry was *Lanark, Leeds and Grenville Roman Catholic Separate School Board v. Ontario (Human Rights Commission)* (1986), 7 C.H.R.R. D/3546 (Ont. Bd. Inq.), revd 40 D.L.R. (4th) 316, 8 C.H.R.R. D/4235 (Div. Ct.), affd 57 D.L.R. (4th) 479*n*, 10 C.H.R.R. D/6336 (C.A.), where the complaint centred on three students, all identified as "trainable mentally retarded" (now called "developmental disability"), who were enrolled as students in a separate school board, but received most of their education in a school operated by the co-terminus public board of education under a purchase of special education services agreement. Ultimately, the complaint was dismissed by the Divisional Court on the basis of a provision of the *Human Rights Code* that has since been removed.

21 See Chapter 2, "The Legal Framework".

exceptional pupils. This includes making determinations regarding the appropriateness of using discipline to address behavioural issues of exceptional pupils. Dealing with students whose disabilities give rise to violent behaviour or students who are medically fragile can raise challenging legal issues that can, on occasion, involve balancing the rights of the student in question with the rights of others. We will look at these issues in the chapter on discipline.[22]

[22] See Chapter 14, "Discipline and Other Issues".

2

The Legal Framework

INTRODUCTION

Special education law is a unique discipline, drawing on principles derived from a number of separate, overlapping and sometimes competing legal regimes. This complex legal framework provides the context for understanding the structure and functioning of Ontario's special education scheme, which is described in detail in later chapters of this book.

In this chapter, we have described, in general terms, four of the key sources of special education law: administrative law, education law, human rights law and child welfare law.

ADMINISTRATIVE LAW

Special education law is part of the broader discipline of administrative law. Administrative law can be described, in very general terms, as the body of legal principles that regulates the manner in which the government exercises its authority vis-à-vis its citizens. "Government", in this context, includes the Cabinet, government ministries, the Legislature and the judiciary; however, it also covers a wide range of governmental and quasi-governmental decision-makers, boards and tribunals that carry out statutory functions and/or exercise statutory authority to make decisions affecting the lives of members of the public.

The special education regime imposes duties and obligations on a number of different administrative decision-makers. The most important of these are the Minister of Education, school boards and the adjudicative bodies involved in special education decision-making, particularly the Special Education Tribunal.

The Minister of Education

Under the *Education Act*,[1] some very specific obligations are placed on the Minister of Education with respect to special education. Section 8(3) of the *Education Act* sets out the Minister's obligations:

> 8(3) The Minister shall ensure that all exceptional children in Ontario have available to them, in accordance with this Act and the regulations, appropriate special education programs and special education services without payment of fees by parents or guardians resident in Ontario, and shall provide for the parents or guardians to appeal the appropriateness of the special education placement, and for these purposes the Minister shall,
>
> (a) require school boards to implement procedures for early and ongoing identification of the learning abilities and needs of pupils, and shall prescribe standards in accordance with which such procedures be implemented; and
>
> (b) in respect of special education programs and services, define exceptionalities of pupils, and prescribe classes, groups or categories of exceptional pupils, and require boards to employ such definitions or use such prescriptions as established under this clause.

Pursuant to these obligations, the Ministry of Education has established regulations governing the special education process.[2] The Ministry has also developed and implemented a number of guidelines and policy documents, which set out the standards that the Ministry expects school boards to meet in implementing the special education scheme.[3] In addition, the Ministry has developed a complex funding scheme, pursuant to which the funding available

---

1 R.S.O. 1990, c. E.2.

2 *Identification and Placement of Exceptional Pupils*, O. Reg. 181/98; *Special Education Programs and Services*, R.R.O. 1990, Reg. 306; *Special Education Advisory Committees*, O. Reg. 464/97.

3 See, for example, Ontario Ministry of Education and Training, "Special Education Monographs No. 1: The Special Education Appeal Board" (Special Education Branch, March 1985); Ontario Ministry of Education and Training, "Special Education Monographs No. 2: Identification, Placement and Review Committees" (Special Education Branch, October 1985); Ontario Ministry of Education, "Individual Education Plans: Standards for Development, Program Planning and Implementation" (Toronto: The Ministry, 2000), available online at http://www.edu.gov.on.ca/eng/general/elemsec/speced/iep/iep.pdf; Ontario Ministry of Education, *Standards for School Boards' Special Education Plans* (Toronto: The Ministry, 2000); Ontario Ministry of Education, *Special Education: A Guide for Educators* (Toronto: The Ministry, 2001), available online at http://www.edu.gov.on.ca/eng/general/elemsec/speced/guide.html; Ontario Ministry of Education, *The Individual Education Plan (IEP): A Resource Guide* (Toronto: The Ministry, 2004), available online at http://www.edu.gov.on.ca/eng/general/elemsec/speced/guide/resource/index.html; Ontario Ministry of Education, *Incorporating Methods of Applied Behaviour Analysis (ABA) into Programs for Students With Autism Spectrum Disorder (ASD)* (Toronto: The Ministry, 2007), available online at http://www.edu.gov.on.ca/extra/eng/ppm/140.html.

to school boards for special education programs and special education services is determined.[4]

School Boards

School boards are also administrative decision-makers. They, too, have specific obligations with respect to special education under the *Education Act*. In particular, pursuant to section 170(1), para. 7, every school board is required to:

> 7. provide or enter into an agreement with another board to provide in accordance with the regulations special education programs and special education services for its exceptional pupils.

Pursuant to this obligation, school boards must establish and maintain a special education plan, and review the plan annually.[5] Any amendments to the plan must be submitted to the Ministry for review and the Ministry may, at any time, require the school board to make amendments to its special education plan.[6] As well, school boards must report every two years to the Ministry on their provision of special education programs and special education services.[7]

School boards are also required to establish Identification, Placement and Review Committees ("IPRCs") and Special Education Appeal Boards ("SEABs"), consider their recommendations concerning the identification and placement of exceptional pupils and review of identification and/or placement, and make decisions based on those recommendations.[8] This obligation includes an obligation to publish a parent's guide explaining the IPRC and SEAB processes,[9] and an obligation to require the development of an individual education plan ("IEP") where placement in a special education program has been implemented.[10]

The Special Education Tribunal

The Special Education Tribunal is an administrative decision-maker. Under section 57 of the *Education Act*, the Tribunal is given the statutory authority to hold a hearing and decide parents' appeals of school board decisions concerning the identification and placement of exceptional pupils.[11]

---

4 See, for example, *Grants for Student Needs — Legislative Grants for the 2009-2010 School Board Fiscal Year*, O. Reg. 155/09.

5 Regulation 306, s. 2(2) to (4).

6 *Ibid.*, s. 2(4) and (5).

7 *Ibid.*, s. 3. These requirements are discussed further in Chapter 3, "The Administrator's Framework".

8 O. Reg. 181/98.

9 *Ibid.*, s. 13.

10 *Ibid.*, s. 6. For further discussion, see Chapters 6 to 9.

11 *Education Act*, s. 57(3) and (4). For further discussion, see Chapter 11, "The Final Appeal".

Administrative Law Requirements

The principles of administrative law provide an important set of "checks and balances" on the manner in which all the administrative decision-makers identified earlier carry out their functions under the special education scheme. All administrative bodies must conform to certain basic procedural and substantive requirements in carrying out their functions. When they do not, the courts may judicially review their decisions and set their decisions aside or otherwise direct them to comply with their statutory responsibilities.

Administrative law requirements are discussed further in Chapter 13, "Review by the Courts". Some of the basic legal requirements that govern special education decision-makers are outlined here.

The Canadian Charter of Rights and Freedoms

The Ministry of Education, school boards, the IPRC, the SEAB and the Special Education Tribunal are all subject to the *Canadian Charter of Rights and Freedoms*. Their actions, recommendations and decisions must all be consistent with the Charter — where they are not, they will be set aside.

The provision of the Charter that arises most often in the special education context is section 15, the equality rights provision, which states:

> 15(1) Every individual is equal before and under the law and has the right to the equal protection and equal benefit of the law without discrimination and, in particular, without discrimination based on race, national or ethnic origin, colour, religion, sex, age or mental or physical disability.
>
> (2) Subsection (1) does not preclude any law, program or activity that has as its object the amelioration of conditions of disadvantaged individuals or groups including those that are disadvantaged because of race, national or ethnic origin, colour, religion, sex, age or mental or physical disability.

The equality rights guarantee in section 15 is subject to section 1 of the Charter, which provides:

> 1. The *Canadian Charter of Rights and Freedoms* guarantees the rights and freedoms set out in it subject only to such reasonable limits prescribed by law as can be demonstrably justified in a free and democratic society.

During the 1990s, there was considerable debate and litigation over the question of whether or not Ontario's special education regime was consistent with section 15 of the Charter. Groups of parents, aided by some advocacy groups for persons with disabilities, argued that section 15 required a presumption in favour of integrated education. School boards, other groups of parents and the Ministry of Education argued that section 15 required a more individualized approach, involving a consideration in each case of the educational setting in which the student's best interests could be met. This issue was ultimately resolved in the seminal case of *Eaton v. Brant County Board of Education*,[12] in which the Supreme Court of Canada preferred the latter approach and upheld the constitutionality of Ontario's special education scheme.

Since *Eaton*, there have been a number of other examples where the Charter has been invoked to challenge various aspects of the special education regime in Ontario.[13] Of particular note, over the past few years, several Charter challenges have been filed against the Ministry of Education and/or specific school boards regarding the special education programs and services available to children with autism. In the most high profile of these cases to date, *Wynberg v. Ontario*,[14] the Ontario Court of Appeal dismissed a Charter challenge alleging that the Ontario Government's Intensive Early Intervention Program violated the equality rights of children with autism.

Even in the absence of a Charter challenge, administrative bodies are expected to respect "Charter values" in carrying out their statutory functions. Thus, special education decision-makers must be vigilant to ensure that their actions and decisions are consistent with both the Charter and the social values underlying it.

Procedural Fairness and Natural Justice

All administrative decision-makers are required to comply with basic rules of "natural justice" and "procedural fairness". These court-made rules are designed to ensure that persons who may be affected by administrative decisions receive fair treatment. Among other things, these rules require notice of the information being considered by the decision-maker and an opportunity to respond to it. They also require that the decision in question be made by an unbiased and impartial decision-maker.

All the administrative bodies involved in special education decision-making — the Ministry, school boards, IPRCs, SEABs and the Special Education Tribunal — are bound by these court-made procedural rules. The specific procedural rules that are applicable will vary from case to case, depending on, among other things, the statutory and regulatory requirements, the decision-maker involved, the decision under consideration and the tribunal's own procedural choices.[15]

---

12 (1997), 142 D.L.R. (4th) 385, [1997] 1 S.C.R. 241.

13 See, for example, *Adler v. Ontario* (1996), 140 D.L.R. (4th) 385, [1996] 3 S.C.R. 609; *Concerned Parents for Children with Learning Disabilities Inc. v. Prince Albert (Various Boards of Education)* (1998), 27 C.P.C. (4th) 304, 82 A.C.W.S. (3d) 41 (Sask. Q.B.).

14 (2006), 269 D.L.R. (4th) 435, 40 C.C.L.T. (3d) 176 (Ont. C.A.), leave to appeal to S.C.C. refused 276 D.L.R. (4th) vii, [2007] 1 S.C.R. xvi.

15 *Baker v. Canada (Minister of Citizenship and Immigration)* (1999), 174 D.L.R. (4th) 193 at pp. 210-214, [1999] 2 S.C.R. 817.

In addition to the court-made rules of natural justice and procedural fairness, some administrative decision-makers are governed by the *Statutory Powers Procedure Act* ("*SPPA*"),[16] which sets out a statutory template for tribunals to follow in establishing their own procedural rules. In the special education context, the Special Education Tribunal is governed by the *SPPA* and has developed Rules of Procedure to govern its proceedings.

When an administrative body does not comply with the procedural rules applicable to it — whether the court-made rules of "procedural fairness" and "natural justice" or its own procedural rules — its decisions can be overturned by a court. Accordingly, it is necessary both to understand the basic procedural rules and to ensure that they are followed, in order to immunize the decision from judicial intervention.

Review of Administrative Decisions

An administrative decision-maker may be given the statutory authority to exercise a discretion or to hold a hearing, adjudicate factual and legal issues and reach a decision on a matter. An example of discretionary authority is the school board's discretion to accept or reject the recommendations of the SEAB with respect to identification and/or placement.[17] An example of adjudicative authority is the Special Education Tribunal's statutory authority to hear and decide special education appeals under section 57 of the *Education Act*.

The courts generally defer to the decisions of administrative bodies; however, the degree of deference will depend on a number of factors. These factors include the statutory and regulatory requirements, the decision-maker involved, the nature of the decision in question and the tribunal's expertise.[18] Where deference is at its highest, the administrative decision will only be set aside when it is "unreasonable"; where deference is at its lowest, the decision will be set aside when it is "incorrect".

Conclusion

The three broad categories of administrative review discussed earlier provide the context within which all the various administrative bodies involved in the special education scheme carry out their statutory functions. They inform both the procedures followed and the decisions made by these bodies. As such, they comprise an important part of the legal framework for special education in this province.

---

16 R.S.O. 1990, c. S.22.

17 O. Reg. 181/98, s. 30.

18 *Dunsmuir v. New Brunswick* (2008), 291 D.L.R. (4th) 577, [2008] 1 S.C.R. 190, at para. 64.

EDUCATION LAW

Special education law is also part of the discipline of education law. Education law is part of the broader discipline of administrative law; however, education law is also its own unique discipline, and the source of many important legal principles applicable to the public education system. These principles are an important part of the legal framework within which special education decisions are made.

Constitutional Requirements

Our Constitution protects both denominational, separate and dissentient school rights and minority language instruction rights in certain contexts.

Section 93 of the *Constitution Act, 1867* preserves denominational, separate and dissentient school rights that existed at the time of Confederation:

> 93. In and for each Province the Legislature may exclusively make Laws in relation to Education, subject and according to the following Provisions: —
>
> (1) Nothing in any such Law shall prejudicially affect any Right or Privilege with respect to Denominational Schools which any Class of Persons have by Law in the Province at the Union:
>
> (2) All the Powers, Privileges, and Duties at the Union by Law conferred and imposed in Upper Canada on the Separate Schools and School Trustees of the Queen's Roman Catholic Subjects shall be and the same are hereby extended to the Dissentient Schools of the Queen's Protestant and Roman Catholic Subjects in Quebec:
>
> (3) Where in any Province a System of Separate or Dissentient Schools exists by Law at the Union or is thereafter established by the Legislature of the Province, an Appeal shall lie to the Governor General in Council from any Act or Decision of any Provincial Authority affecting any Right or Privilege of the Protestant or Roman Catholic Minority of the Queen's Subjects in relation to Education:
>
> (4) In case any such Provincial Law as from Time to Time seems to the Governor General in Council requisite for the due Execution of the Provisions of this Section is not made, or in case any Decision of the Governor General in Council on any Appeal under this Section is not duly executed by the proper Provincial Authority in that Behalf, then and in every such Case, and as far only as the Circumstances of each Case require, the Parliament of Canada may make remedial Laws for the due Execution of the Provisions of this Section and of any Decision of the Governor General in Council under this Section.

These rights are further reinforced in section 29 of the Charter, which provides:

> 29. Nothing in this Charter abrogates or derogates from any rights or privileges guaranteed by or under the Constitution of Canada in respect of denominational, separate or dissentient schools.

The Charter also protects the right of certain Canadian citizens to have their children educated in English or French, where that language is the minority language in the province in which they reside:

> 23(1) Citizens of Canada
> (a) whose first language learned and still understood is that of the English or French linguistic minority population of the province in which they reside, or
> (b) who have received their primary school instruction in Canada in English or French and reside in a province where the language in which they received that instruction is the language of the English or French linguistic minority population of the province,
>
> have the right to have their children receive primary and secondary school instruction in that language in that province.
>
> (2) Citizens of Canada of whom any child has received or is receiving primary or secondary school instruction in English or French in Canada, have the right to have all their children receive primary and secondary school instruction in the same language.
>
> (3) The right of citizens of Canada under subsections (1) and (2) to have their children receive primary and secondary school instruction in the language of the English or French linguistic minority population of a province
> (a) applies wherever in the province the number of children of citizens who have such a right is sufficient to warrant the provision to them out of public funds of minority language instruction; and
> (b) includes, where the number of those children so warrants, the right to have them receive that instruction in minority language educational facilities provided out of public funds.[19]

Like any form of publicly funded education, special education programs and services must be provided in a way that is consistent with and respectful of these important constitutional rights.[20] In other words, special education programs and services must be available in both the English and French languages, at both public and separate school boards.

---

[19] Section 59 of the *Constitution Act, 1982* provides that s. 23(1)(*a*) will only come into force in Quebec where proclamation is authorized by the legislative assembly or government of Quebec. That authorization has never been given. Accordingly, s. 23(1)(*a*) is not in force in the Province of Quebec.

[20] In Ontario, this principle is reinforced in the *Education Act*, s. 1(4) and (4.1), which provides:

> 1(4) This Act does not adversely affect any right or privilege guaranteed by section 93 of the *Constitution Act, 1867* or by section 23 of the *Canadian Charter of Rights and Freedoms*.
>
> . . . .
>
> (4.1) Every authority given by this Act, including but not limited to every authority to make a regulation, decision or order and every authority to issue a directive or guideline, shall be exercised in a manner consistent with and respectful of the rights and privileges guaranteed by section 93 of the *Constitution Act, 1867* and by section 23 of the *Canadian Charter of Rights and Freedoms*.

Other Statutory Requirements

Quite apart from the constitutional requirements with respect to education that are described earlier in this chapter, the *Education Act* and other applicable legislation impose a wide variety of obligations on school boards. A full discussion of all of these requirements is beyond the scope of this work; however, some examples that will be relevant to special education include the following:

- the establishment of the school calendar[21] and the school day;[22]
- class size requirements;[23]
- enrolment limitations in special education classes;[24]
- compulsory school attendance requirements and resident pupil requirements;[25]
- requirements with respect to transportation of students;[26]
- requirements governing the holding of school board meetings and the keeping of school board records;[27]
- restrictions on the use and disclosure of information in the Ontario School Record;[28]
- requirements governing access to and the collection, use and disclosure of students' personal information under the *Municipal Freedom of Information and Protection of Privacy Act*;[29]
- the provincial code of conduct and requirements concerning behaviour, discipline and safety in the schools;[30] and
- *Occupational Health and Safety Act*[31] requirements with respect to persons working on school property.

In providing special education programs and services to exceptional pupils, school boards must comply not only with the specific requirements of the special education regime, but also with the myriad obligations and requirements listed above.

---

21 *School Year Calendar, Professional Activity Days*, R.R.O. 1990, Reg. 304.
22 *Operation of Schools — General*, R.R.O. 1990, Reg. 298, s. 3.
23 *Education Act*, s. 170.1; *Class Size*, O. Reg. 399/00.
24 Regulation 298, ss. 30 and 31.
25 *Education Act*, ss. 18 to 49.2.
26 *Ibid.*, s. 190.
27 *Ibid.*, ss. 200 to 209; *Electronic Meetings*, O. Reg. 463/97.
28 *Ibid.*, s. 266.
29 R.S.O. 1990, c. M.56.
30 *Education Act*, ss. 300 to 316; Regulation 298, s. 23.
31 R.S.O. 1990, c. O.1.

HUMAN RIGHTS LAW

Special education law is also subject to the discipline of human rights law. The Ontario *Human Rights Code*[32] prohibits discrimination in the provision of services (including educational services) on the basis of disability. The term "disability" is broadly defined in section 10(1) of the Code as follows:

> "because of disability" means for the reason that the person has or has had, or is believed to have or have had,
>
> (a) any degree of physical disability, infirmity, malformation or disfigurement that is caused by bodily injury, birth defect or illness and, without limiting the generality of the foregoing, includes diabetes mellitus, epilepsy, a brain injury, any degree of paralysis, amputation, lack of physical co-ordination, blindness or visual impediment, deafness or hearing impediment, muteness or speech impediment, or physical reliance on a guide dog or other animal or on a wheelchair or other remedial appliance or device,
>
> (b) a condition of mental impairment or a developmental disability,
>
> (c) a learning disability, or a dysfunction in one or more of the processes involved in understanding or using symbols or spoken language,
>
> (d) a mental disorder, or
>
> (e) an injury or disability for which benefits were claimed or received under the insurance plan established under the *Workplace Safety and Insurance Act, 1997*.

Most students identified as "exceptional pupils"— with the exception of those who are gifted — will have a "disability" for the purpose of this definition; however, not every difference in treatment with respect to these students that is related to the disability will constitute discrimination. Rather, as the Supreme Court of Canada recognized in the *Eaton*[33] case, in some cases, differences in treatment will be necessary and appropriate in order to ensure equal treatment of persons with disabilities:

> The principal object of certain of the prohibited grounds is the elimination of discrimination by the attribution of untrue characteristics based on stereotypical attitudes relating to immutable conditions such as race or sex. In the case of disability, this is one of the objectives. The other equally important objective seeks to take into account the true characteristics of this group which act as headwinds to the enjoyment of society's benefits and to accommodate them. Exclusion from the mainstream of society results from the construction of a society based solely on "mainstream" attributes to which disabled persons will never be able to gain access. Whether it is the impossibility of success at a written test for a blind person, or the need for ramp access to a library, the discrimination does not lie in the attribution of untrue characteristics to the disabled individual. The blind person cannot see and the person in a wheelchair needs a ramp. Rather, it is the failure to make reasonable accommodation, to fine-tune society so that its structures and assumptions do not result in the relegation and banishment of disabled persons from participation, which results in discrimination against

---

[32] R.S.O. 1990, c. H.19 (the "Code"), ss. 1 and 11.

[33] *Eaton v. Brant County Board of Education* (1997), 142 D.L.R. (4th) 385, [1997] 1 S.C.R. 241, at para. 67.

> them. The discrimination inquiry which uses "the attribution of stereotypical characteristics" reasoning as commonly understood is simply inappropriate here. It may be seen rather as a case of reverse stereotyping which, by not allowing for the condition of a disabled individual, ignores his or her disability and forces the individual to sink or swim within the mainstream environment. It is recognition of the actual characteristics, and reasonable accommodation of these characteristics which is the central purpose of s. 15(1) in relation to disability.

Although the above statements were made in the context of the equality rights provisions of the Charter, they apply equally under the Code. Where the treatment of a student with a disability gives rise to an inference of discrimination — which is the case where a student's disability interferes with the student's capacity to benefit from the regular curriculum or regular instruction — the Code imposes on the school board a duty to accommodate the pupil to the point of undue hardship.[34]

"Accommodation" and "undue hardship" are very complex legal concepts; a full discussion of these concepts is beyond the scope of this chapter. For present purposes, it will suffice to note that the Supreme Court of Canada has emphasized the need to accommodate persons with disabilities, in order to increase the inclusiveness of our social institutions.[35]

Section 14(1) of the Code also provides for the implementation of a "special program", which is "designed to relieve hardship or economic disadvantage or to assist disadvantaged persons or groups to achieve or attempt to achieve equal opportunity or that is likely to contribute to the elimination of [discrimination]".

The special education regime is, at its essence, a form of legislated "special program" for students with disabilities. The regime recognizes that, without accommodation, students with disabilities would have a lesser ability to profit from the service of education than their non-disabled peers. They would, to use the language of *Eaton*, be left to "sink or swim" in the mainstream environment. In response to this problem, the Legislature established a process for identifying students with special educational needs, and determining the placement that will best serve those needs. The placement — and the special education programs and services provided in the placement — are all means of accommodating the special needs arising from the student's disability.

The Human Rights Tribunal of Ontario has stated:[36]

> [T]he statutory scheme for special education has as its central purpose the accommodation of children with special needs, including those with disabilities, so that they are able to receive the benefits of education available to others (see *Eaton*, para. 68). With respect to the provision of education services to children

---

34 *Human Rights Code*, ss. 11 and 17.

35 *British Columbia (Public Service Employee Relations Commission) v. B.C.G.S.E.U.* (1999), 176 D.L.R. (4th) 1, [1999] 3 S.C.R. 3, at para. 68.

36 *Campbell v. Toronto District School Board*, 2008 HRTO 62, at para. 42.

with disabilities, therefore, it has the same goal as the *Code*. In the words of the Board, "special education is all about finding the appropriate accommodation for students with disabilities."

Thus, it can be seen that the special education regime parallels the requirements of the Code in several significant respects. In addition, the implementation of the special education regime can be reviewed under the Code, to ensure that the standards of the Code are maintained.[37] Thus, the Code is an important part of the legal framework governing Ontario's special education scheme.

Humans rights litigation is becoming increasingly common in special education matters. Human rights issues can be, and often are, raised in the course of proceedings before special education decision-makers. As the *Eaton* case demonstrates, the Special Education Tribunal has been interpreting and applying human rights legislation in the course of its decision-making for many years. Any lingering doubt about the Tribunal's authority to consider human rights legislation was removed in 2005, when the Supreme Court of Canada confirmed that administrative tribunals are generally presumed to have the power to interpret and apply general statutes, such as human rights legislation, in the course of carrying out their statutory mandate.[38] Accordingly, human rights issues are now raised quite commonly in proceedings before the Tribunal.

At the same time, human rights complaints have become increasingly common as a means of challenging various aspects of special education decision-making. Until June 30, 2008, exceptional pupils (or, more often, their parent(s) or guardian(s)) who felt that a school board's special education decision-making was inconsistent with the *Human Rights Code* could file a human rights complaint with the Ontario Human Rights Commission. In most cases, the commission would investigate the complaint and, sometimes after a delay of several years, make a decision as to whether or not there was sufficient evidence of an infringement of the *Human Rights Code* to warrant a hearing before the Human Rights Tribunal of Ontario. As a result, however, of amendments to the Code that took effect on July 1, 2008, a pupil or his/her parent(s) or guardian(s) can now file a human rights application directly with the Human Rights Tribunal of Ontario. The Tribunal was also given extensive new powers to manage the cases before it.[39] It is reasonable to expect that the

37 Section 47(2) of the Code provides:

> 47(2) Where a provision in an Act or regulation purports to require or authorize conduct that is a contravention of Part I, this Act applies and prevails unless the Act or regulation specifically provides that it is to apply despite this Act.

38 *Tranchemontagne v. Ontario (Disability Support Program, Director)* (2006), 266 D.L.R. (4th) 287, [2006] 1 S.C.R. 513.

39 See Chapter 12, "The Human Rights Process", and Brenda J. Bowlby, Daniel Michaluk and Jennifer Wootton Regan, *An Educator's Guide to Human Rights*, 2nd ed. (Aurora: Canada Law Book, 2009), another publication in the "Educator's Guides to the Law" series of which this book is a part.

availability of this more streamlined and expeditious process for litigating human rights disputes will increase the incidence of special-education-related human rights litigation in the future.

The special education regime under the *Education Act* and the *Human Rights Code* provides overlapping remedial avenues for pupils (or their parent(s) or guardian(s)) who wish to allege that special education decision-making is inconsistent with the Code. Although both these avenues are available, there are arguments available to a school board to prevent duplicative litigation.[40] Thus, in many cases, pupils (or their parent(s) or guardian(s)) will not be permitted to litigate in both forums at the same time or to relitigate the same issues a second time in the alternate forum.

CHILD WELFARE LAW

Finally, special education law has important links to the discipline of child welfare law. Although parents generally have the right to make important life decisions on their child's behalf, including schooling decisions, the courts retain a general supervisory jurisdiction to intervene to ensure that the child's best interests are protected.[41] In the *Eaton* decision, the Supreme Court of Canada held that the essence of the identification and placement process under the *Education Act* is to determine the educational "best interests" of the child from the child's own perspective.[42] While parental preference will ordinarily be given some weight, it will not always be determinative of the issue.[43]

CONCLUSION

As the preceding discussion illustrates, special education law draws upon and is influenced by a vast body of overlapping — and sometimes competing

---

40 For example, s. 45.1 of the *Human Rights Code* allows the Human Rights Tribunal of Ontario to dismiss an application in whole or in part where it is of the opinion that another proceeding has appropriately dealt with the substance of an application. This provision could be used in a case where the Special Education Tribunal has already considered the matter, including any human rights issues, in order to obtain a full or partial dismissal of a parallel human rights application. There are also a variety of common law doctrines — such as abuse of process and the rule against collateral attack, the details of which are beyond the scope of this discussion — which may be available in order to prevent duplicative litigation and/or forum shopping. See *Campbell v. Toronto District School Board*, *supra*, footnote 36, for a case in which the Human Rights Tribunal of Ontario applied abuse of process doctrine to preclude the relitigation of issues that had already been determined by the Special Education Tribunal.

41 See, for example: *Eve (Re)* (1986), 31 D.L.R. (4th) 1, [1986] 2 S.C.R. 388; *B. (R.) v. Children's Aid Society of Metropolitan Toronto* (1995), 122 D.L.R. (4th) 1, [1995] 1 S.C.R. 315.

42 (1997), 142 D.L.R. (4th) 385, [1997] 1 S.C.R. 241, at para. 77.

43 *Eaton*, *supra*, at para. 79.

— legal principles. This complex legal framework lies beneath many of the specific legislative and court-made requirements comprising the special education regime, which are discussed in the upcoming chapters of this book.

3

The Administrator's Framework

INTRODUCTION

The *Education Act*,[1] regulations and Ministry directives, including Policy/Program Memoranda and Standards, impose on school boards specific requirements concerning the manner in which special education programs and services are planned for and delivered to exceptional students. These requirements create a framework based on which a school board, its superintendents, principals and teachers will carry out the school board's obligations under the *Education Act* in respect of its exceptional students.

Generally, the obligations imposed on administrators by the various statutory, regulatory and Ministry directives are summarized in Policy/Program Memorandum No. 11.[2] This "PPM" notes the requirement that school boards have in place the early identification of children's learning needs by way of "procedures to identify each child's level of development, learning abilities, and needs" and that school boards must "ensure that educational programs are designed to accommodate these needs and to facilitate each child's growth and development".

In the first instance, the school board must set out, in a Special Education Plan ("SEP"), an outline of the special education placements and the special education programs and services it will be providing for its exceptional pupils. This plan is subject to review by the Minister of Education, who may require that the school board amend the plan. This

---

1 R.S.O. 1990, c. E.2, s. 170(1), para. 7.

2 Ontario Deputy Minister of Education, "Policy/Program Memorandum No. 11: Early Identification of Children's Learning Needs" (Toronto: Ministry of Education, 1982), available online at http://www.edu.gov.on.ca/extra/eng/ppm/11.html.

document will also serve to inform parents and the public about the manner in which the board is carrying out its special education responsibilities.[3]

In order to ensure that school boards receive input from parents of exceptional pupils in developing and delivering special education programs and services, each school board is required to establish a Special Education Advisory Committee ("SEAC") comprised of representatives of parent advocate groups together with trustees.[4]

To ensure that parents are fully informed as to their rights in the identification and placement process, school boards must produce a Parent Guide that details the process whereby students are identified and placed and parental rights to appeal identification and/or placement.[5]

In planning for special education classes, limits are placed on maximum class sizes, based on the exceptionality with which each class is designed to deal.

Two other critical parts of the "Administrator's Framework" are the Identification Placement and Review Committee (dealt with in Chapter 6, "The Identification, Placement and Review Committee") and the Individual Education Plan (dealt with in Chapter 7, "The Individual Education Plan").

In this chapter, we will canvas the legal obligations underlying the creation and review of the SEP and the operation of the SEAC. We will also outline the obligation of a school board to create a Parent Guide. Finally, we will describe the maximum limits on the size of special education classes established for particular exceptionalities.

THE SPECIAL EDUCATION PLAN

Historical Context: The Multi-Year Plans

When Bill 82[6] ushered in Ontario's present scheme of special education in 1980, some school boards already had relatively sophisticated arrays of special education services and programs in place. Others did not.

In recognition of the disparity in the level of special education programs and services available at school boards throughout Ontario prior to 1980, Bill 82 provided for a five-year "phase-in" period. The deadline by which all school boards were expected to have put the necessary special education programs and services in place to meet the needs of their exceptional pupils was September 1, 1985. (In the case of special education programs and services for the "trainable retarded" designation, the target date was December 31, 1985.)[7]

---

3 *Special Education Programs and Services*, R.R.O. 1990, Reg. 306.
4 *Education Act*, s. 57.1.
5 *Identification and Placement of Exceptional Pupils*, O. Reg. 181/98.
6 *Education Amendment Act, 1980*, S.O. 1980, c. 61.
7 *Special Education Programs and Services*, R.R.O. 1980, Reg. 274.

During the phase-in period leading up to the full implementation date, each school board was required to prepare and file, annually, a "multi-year plan" outlining the blueprint for proceeding to put into place the special education programs and services that would be needed to comply with its statutory obligation to provide special education programs and services for all its exceptional pupils by the target date.[8] The culmination of this process of preparing and filing multi-year plans was the preparation and filing of a SEP for the 1985-1986 school year, which disclosed all the special education programs and services that the school board had put into place to address the needs of the school board's exceptional pupils.[9]

Following the filing of the 1985-1986 SEP, each school board was required to file a report on its special education programs and services, commencing in 1987 and every two years thereafter. At first, no policy or directive specified the form or contents of a school board's special education plans; however, in 1999, the Ministry of Education required school boards to submit a full new SEP instead of a biannual report and stipulated the criteria that would be used to review the plans.[10] In addition, in any school year during which the SEP was amended, the plan was to be submitted to the Minister for review on or before July 31st of that school year.[11]

Current Requirements

In the Fall of 2000, the Ministry of Education issued a new policy document, entitled "Standards for School Boards' Special Education Plans" (the "*Standards*").[12] This policy set out precise requirements for SEPs and advised school boards of the standards against which their SEPs would be measured. While the policy does not have the force of law, the Minister does have the power to "require a board to amend its special education plan in a manner that the Minister considers necessary so as to ensure that the board provides special education programs and special education services that meet the current needs of the exceptional pupils of the board".[13] The *Standards* reflect what the Minister considers to be necessary to meet the current needs of exceptional students and the Minister may require boards to amend their SEPs to comply with them.

---

8 During this period, students were entitled to receive only those special education programs or services that, under the terms of the multi-year plan, had been put into place at the particular point in time: *Dolmage v. Muskoka Board of Education* (1985), 15 D.L.R. (4th) 741, 49 O.R. (2d) 546 (Div. Ct.).

9 Regulation 306.

10 Ontario Ministry of Education, "Memorandum to Directors of Education Re: Report to the Minister/Annual Review of Special Education Plans" (Toronto: Queen's Printer for Ontario, 2000).

11 Regulation 306, s. 2(4).

12 Ontario Ministry of Education, *Standards for School Boards' Special Education Plans* (Toronto: The Ministry, 2000).

13 Regulation 306, s. 2(5).

The issuance of the *Standards* marks a change in the role and function of the SEP. Previously, the SEP was primarily a reporting document that allowed the Minister to monitor the manner in which each board was providing special education programs and services for its exceptional pupils. The *Standards* contemplate, however, that the purpose of the SEP is not only to inform the Minister, but also the public, about the manner in which the school board is carrying out its special education responsibilities. Each school board must make its SEP available to the public and inform the public how to access the document. When the school board maintains an Internet website, the board must include information on how the SEP may be accessed. It is not necessary for the board to include the SEP on the website, but the Ministry encourages that this be done.[14]

Maintenance and Review of the SEP

The SEP, as a plan of the board, is subject to the ultimate approval of and adoption by resolution of the board of trustees.

School boards are required to keep their SEPs current. In addition to ongoing review of SEPs, which may result in *ad hoc* amendments, each school board must annually review its SEP. This review must be completed by July 31st of each year[15] and the SEP must be amended to ensure that it continues to address the needs of the school board's exceptional pupils. Review of the SEP will normally fall, in the first instance, to special education staff, although the SEAC will also play a role in ensuring that the SEP is maintained and updated.[16]

The *Standards* impose an obligation on school boards to "consult" with members of the community, including parents of children who are receiving special education programs and services and school councils, as part of the process of developing and modifying their SEPs.[17]

Ministerial Review of SEPs and Amendments to SEPs

It is the responsibility of the Minister of Education to ensure that all exceptional children in Ontario have available to them appropriate special education programs and services without payment of fees.[18] In order to carry out this statutory mandate, the Minister has been given a broad power of review and the power to require school boards to amend their SEPs where the Minister is of the view that the plans are deficient. Specifically, the Minister may require a school board to amend its SEP "in a manner that the Minister considers necessary so as to ensure that the board provides special education

14 The *Standards*, *op. cit.*, footnote 12, at p. 17.
15 R.R.O. 1990, Reg. 306, s. 2(3).
16 *Special Education Advisory Committees*, O. Reg. 464/97.
17 The *Standards*, *op. cit.*, footnote 12, at p. 4.
18 *Education Act*, s. 8(3).

programs and special education services that meet the current needs of the exceptional pupils of the board".[19]

In order to facilitate the Minister's ongoing review of SEPs, each board is required to forward any amendments it has made to its SEP to the Minister of Education for review. Amendments include any modifications, addition or deletion of programs, services and/or personnel (*i.e.*, positions) approved by the board following a review of the special education plan.[20] Any amendment made in the preceding 12 months must be submitted to the Minister by July 31st of each year.[21]

Every two years, a school board must submit to the Minister a report on the provision by the school board of special education programs and special education services. This report must be prepared in accordance with procedures stipulated by the Minister and approved by the board of trustees. As already noted, the deadline for submission of the first report was May 15, 1987. Reports have been required every two years since the first report.[22] As also noted, in 1999, the Ministry of Education required school boards to submit a full new SEP that complied with stipulated criteria.[23] The Minister requires that SEPs comply with the *Standards* it has specified as a matter of policy.

Contents of the Special Education Plan

The SEP must disclose the methods by which a school board will comply with its obligation under s. 170(1), para. 7 of the *Education Act* to "provide or enter into an agreement with another board to provide in accordance with the regulations special education programs and special education services for its exceptional pupils".

A "special education program" is defined as "an educational program [in respect of an exceptional pupil] that is based on and modified by the results of continuous assessment and evaluation and that includes a plan containing specific objectives and an outline of educational services that meets the needs of the exceptional pupil".[24]

"Special education services" are defined as "facilities and resources, including support personnel and equipment, necessary for developing and implementing a special education program".[25]

Implicit in the requirement that the school board disclose the methods it will use to comply with its obligation to provide special education services and programs for its exceptional pupils is a requirement that the school board will

---

19 Regulation 306, s. 2(5).
20 *Ibid.*, s. 2(2).
21 *Ibid.*, s. 2(4).
22 *Ibid.*, s. 3.
23 *Education Act*, s. 170(1), para. 7.
24 *Ibid.*, s. 1(1).
25 *Ibid.*

also disclose the various placements in which these special education services and programs will be provided. Accordingly, the SEP must also set out the range of placements that the school board will make available for its exceptional pupils. The Ministry of Education has made this one of the standards with which a school board must comply in its SEP.[26]

Standards for Special Education Plans

The *Standards* provide a very detailed set of requirements of what must be included in each school board's SEP. Indeed, the *Standards* go beyond a requirement that certain information be contained in the SEP and reflect an expectation that each board will have set up certain mechanisms, procedures and policies as a precondition to meeting the *Standards* for the SEP. Thus, the *Standards* not only require that descriptions of policies and procedures be included in the SEP, but actually dictate the policies and procedures that must be put into place by the school board in order to comply with the *Standards*.

We have summarized here the requirements imposed on school boards by the *Standards*.

The School Board's Consultation Process

The *Standards* contemplate the existence in each school board of a process for public consultation, undertaken with the assistance of the Special Education Advisory Committee ("SEAC"),[27] to allow the school board to receive continuous feedback on special education issues from the community. This process must be described in the SEP. The SEP must also describe how the school board ensures the SEAC's involvement in the annual plan review; describe majority and minority reports that have been received from the SEAC together with the school board's response to those reports; state how community members, and particularly parents of children receiving special education programs and services, are given an opportunity to provide input (including timelines and methods for providing opportunities); and include a summary of the feedback received from the community. Finally, the SEP must set out the results of any internal or external reviews of the school board's special education programs and services undertaken in the prior or current school year and list any planned reviews.

Special Education Programs and Services

The School Board's General Model for Special Education

The SEP must include a detailed outline of the school board's general philosophy and service-delivery model for the provision of special education

[26] The *Standards*, *op. cit.*, footnote 12, at p. 9.

[27] See the discussion about this statutory Committee later in this chapter, under the heading "The School Board's Special Education Advisory Committee".

programs and services. The SEP must comply with the *Canadian Charter of Rights and Freedoms*, the Ontario *Human Rights Code*,[28] the *Education Act* and regulations[29] and must include a statement confirming this.

Roles and Responsibilities

The SEP must include a description of the roles and responsibilities of the Ministry of Education, the school board, the SEAC, principals and teachers, parents or guardians and students.[30]

Early Identification Procedures and Intervention Strategies

School boards have long been required by Policy/Program Memorandum No. 11, "Early Identification of Children's Learning Needs",[31] to put into place "procedures to identify each child's level of development, learning abilities and needs and to ensure that educational programs are designed to accommodate these needs and to facilitate each child's growth and development".[32] The *Standards* require that the SEP must explain these procedures in detail, including an outline of the school board's guiding principles or philosophy, the types of assessment tools/strategies used to gather information on students for the purpose of developing educational programs and the types of early intervention strategies used to support students before they are referred to an Identification, Placement and Review Committee ("IPRC").

The SEP must also set out the role of teachers and parents in early identification, as well as the school board's policies and procedures on screening, assessment, referral, identification and program planning for students who may be in need of special education programs and services. In addition, the SEP must disclose the school board's procedures for notifying parents that their child is having difficulty; procedures for referring children for assessment and the manner in which parents will be notified about and be involved in this process; and procedures for notifying parents that their child might be referred to an IPRC or might be provided with special education programs and services without a referral to an IPRC.

Finally, the SEP must include a statement that "these procedures are a part of a continuous assessment and program planning process which should be initiated when a child is first enrolled in school or no later than the beginning of a program of studies immediately following Kindergarten and should continue throughout a child's school life".[33] While not required, in order to facilitate a successful school beginning, many school boards meet

---

28 R.S.O. 1990, c. H.19.

29 Regulation 306; O. Reg. 181/98; O. Reg. 464/97.

30 See Appendix A of the *Standards*, *op. cit.*, footnote 12, which sets out in detail the information necessary to meet this requirement.

31 Ontario Deputy Minister of Education, *op. cit.*, footnote 2.

32 *Ibid.*, at p. 1.

33 *Ibid.*, at p. 6.

with parents to discuss special needs and possible interventions even before a child enrolls, especially where the needs are quite significant.

The IPRC Process and Appeals

The SEP must set out a description of the school board's IPRC process and include a copy of the school board's Parent Guide. In addition, the SEP must set out statistics concerning the number of IPRC referrals, reviews and appeals within the school board during the previous school year.

Educational and Other Assessments

The SEP must set out the types of educational assessment tools used within the school board and, for each assessment tool, must set out the qualifications of staff administering the tool and the legislation governing the staff (*e.g.*, *Education Act*, *Regulated Health Professions Act, 1991*,[34] *Health Care Consent Act, 1996*,[35] and other applicable legislation). In addition, for each assessment tool, the SEP must include the average waiting time for assessments and the criteria for managing waiting lists; an acknowledgement that requirements for obtaining parental consent are met prior to conducting the assessment; an explanation of how assessment results are communicated to parents; a description of the protocols in place for sharing information with staff and outside agencies; and an explanation of how the privacy of information is protected.

Specialized Health Support Services in School Settings

The *Standards* require that the SEP disclose information on each type of specialized health support service that is provided to the school board's students (*i.e.*, nursing, occupational therapy, physiotherapy, nutrition, speech and language therapy, speech correction and remediation, administering of prescribed medications, catheterization, suctioning, lifting and positioning, assistance with mobility, feeding, toileting and others). This information must be set out under stipulated headings that include the following:

- agency or position of person who performs the service (*i.e.*, Community Care Access Centre, board staff, parent, student);
- eligibility criteria for students to receive the service;
- position of person who determines eligibility to receive the service and the level of support;
- criteria for determining when the service is no longer required; and
- procedures for resolving disputes about eligibility and level of support (if any).

---

[34] S.O. 1991, c. 18.

[35] S.O. 1996, c. 2, Sch. A.

Categories and Definitions of Exceptionalities

The categories and definitions of exceptionalities prescribed by the Minister in accordance with his or her authority under section 8(3) of the *Education Act*[36] must be set out in the SEP. In addition, the SEP must describe the ways in which the IPRC applies the categories and definitions when making identification and placement decisions.

Special Education Placements Provided by the School Board

The SEP must describe how the SEAC is involved in providing advice on the range of placements offered by the school board.

In addition to setting out the range of placement options available for each category of exceptionality, the SEP must set out the admission criteria and the admission process for each placement option. As well, a description of the process for determining the level of support provided in each placement and the school board's criteria for assigning intensive support for students who are in need of a great deal of assistance must be set out in the SEP. The alternatives provided when the needs of a student cannot be met within the range of placements and how those options are communicated to the parents must also be disclosed in the SEP.

Reflecting the IPRC's obligation to consider a regular class placement prior to considering placement of an exceptional pupil in a special education class,[37] the *Standards* require that the SEP acknowledge that a regular class placement for an exceptional student is the first option considered by an IPRC. Further, the SEP must set out the different ways in which a student can be integrated into the regular classroom when regular class placement can meet the student's needs. The SEP must also list the criteria used to determine whether or not there is a need to change a student's placement.

Finally, the SEP must set out maximum class size for each type of special education class.

Provincial Demonstration Schools in Ontario

The *Standards* set out information[38] on the programs and services offered by the Provincial and Demonstration Schools and require this information to be included in each school board's SEP. In addition, the SEP must set out, by program, the number of students who are otherwise qualified to be resident pupils[39] and who are attending Provincial and Demonstration schools.

36 See Chapter 4, "Identification and Exceptionality".

37 O. Reg. 181/98, ss. 17(1) and 23(6).

38 The *Standards*, *op. cit.*, footnote 12, at Appendix E.

39 A person is qualified to be an elementary resident pupil from September 1st when the person is aged six years to the end of June in the year in which the person reaches 21 years of age, the person resides in the jurisdiction of the school board and the person's parent or guardian is a tax supporter of the school board. A person is qualified to be a secondary resident pupil when the person and the person's parent or guardian live in the jurisdiction of the board or the person is an owner or tenant

Information must also be provided on how transportation is provided for students to and from Provincial and Demonstration Schools.

Special Education Staff

The *Standards* include a form[40] that must be included in the SEP, which sets out information on the types of staff (teachers, educational assistants, other professional resource staff and paraprofessional staff) involved in providing special education programs and services.

Staff Development

The SEP must make reference to the school board's plans for the professional development of its special education personnel, including the overall goal of these plans. The SEP must set out specifics on courses, in-service training and other types of professional development activities provided by the board for its staff, together with an outline of the manner in which staff members are trained on legislative requirements and Ministry policy. In addition, the SEP must set out how the board makes its staff aware of the SEP and of professional development opportunities.

The *Standards* impose an obligation on school boards to seek input from staff and to consult the SEAC in creating professional development plans. The SEP must disclose how this obligation has been met.

Finally, the SEP must outline details of the board's budget allocation for staff development in special education, together with any cost-sharing arrangements with other ministries or agencies for staff development.

Equipment

The SEP must include an explanation of how the school board determines student needs for individualized equipment and the criteria for purchasing individualized equipment. In addition, the manner of allocation of the board's budget for equipment must be set out in the SEP.

Accessibility of School Buildings

The *Standards* contemplate that school boards will develop a multi-year capital expenditure plan for improving accessibility to their buildings and facilities, including schools, school grounds and administrative offices. The

---

of residential property separately assessed in the jurisdiction of the board and lives in the jurisdiction of the board, or where the person is over the age of 18 years and has lived in the jurisdiction of the board for the 12 preceding months. At the secondary school level, a resident pupil may also be a student who would otherwise be a resident pupil of another board, but who is enrolled in a secondary school under "open access" or pursuant to an agreement for the provision of education services between the board providing the services and the board where the student would otherwise have been a resident pupil (*Education Act*, ss. 33, 36 and 37). A secondary student is entitled to attend a secondary school or secondary schools without payment of fees for a maximum of seven years (*Education Act*, s. 33).

40 The *Standards*, *op. cit.*, footnote 12, at Appendix F.

SEP must include a summary of this multi-year capital expenditure plan, including an outline of the resources that are dedicated to providing barrier-free access in future years. Further, the SEP must report on the board's progress in implementing the capital expenditure plan and include a statement advising how the public can obtain a complete copy of the multi-year capital expenditure plan.

Transportation

The *Standards* stipulate that certain students are eligible to receive transportation, including: students in special education programs (whether in special education classes or regular classes); students in educational programs in care, treatment and correctional facilities and in Provincial and Demonstration Schools; and students requiring transportation to attend summer school programs.

The SEP must also describe the process used by the school board to decide whether it is in the best interests of a student with special needs to be transported with other children or transported separately. As well, the SEP must set out the criteria for determining safety that are used in the board's tendering process in selecting transportation providers for exceptional students.

The School Board's Special Education Advisory Committee

The *Standards* require the school board to outline, in its SEP, the manner in which the SEAC has fulfilled its responsibilities as outlined in the Regulation.[41]

The SEP must include the names of SEAC members and indicate the basis of their memberships on SEAC — whether they are trustees or representatives of parent associations. If the latter, then the names of the associations with which they are affiliated must be set out. In addition, a contact address, telephone number and/or e-mail address for each member must be set out. Where applicable, the SEP must indicate that the SEAC includes membership representing Native students. The SEP must set out the process for selecting SEAC members as well as the meeting times and locations of the SEAC.

The SEP must describe how the SEAC has fulfilled its responsibilities during the school year in which the plan was developed and must set out the documentation provided by the school board to the SEAC to enable it to fulfil its responsibilities.

Finally, the SEP must set out the ways in which members of the public, including parents, can make their views known to the SEAC.

---

41 O. Reg. 464/97. See the discussion under heading "The Special Education Advisory Committee", for discussion of SEAC.

Co-ordination of Services with Other Ministries or Agencies

The *Standards* contemplate that the school board will have developed strategies to ensure a smooth transition for students with special needs who are entering or leaving a school. The SEP must disclose specific details of the planning that is done in advance for students with special needs who are arriving at one of the board's schools from other programs, including pre-school programs (whether nursery, speech and language programs, or programs for the deaf), care, treatment and correctional programs, and programs provided by other boards of education.

The school board must indicate in its SEP whether it is the board's policy or practice to accept assessments of incoming students from the program that the student has been attending or whether the board requires its own assessment of incoming students. Where the board does its own assessment, the estimated waiting time for completing the assessment must be set out in the SEP.

For students leaving to attend other programs offered by other school boards or by care, treatment or correctional facilities, the school board must detail in its SEP the way in which it shares information about the departing students.

Finally, the school board must identify in the SEP the position of the board employee who is responsible for ensuring the successful transition of students who are leaving the board to transfer into other programs or who are being admitted to the board from other programs.

Addressing Placements for Persons Not Enrolled as Students

Although not referenced in the *Standards*, school boards are required by regulation to address, in their SEP placements, two categories of students who are not actually attending schools.[42]

School boards are required to ensure that the SEP provides for the enrolment and placement of each student with a developmental disability who is qualified to be a "resident pupil"[43] of the school board and is attending a day nursery, licensed under the *Day Nurseries Act*[44] in a program for children with developmental disabilities.

Similarly, SEPs must make provision for the enrolment and placement of certain persons under the age of 21 years who are qualified to be resident pupils of the school board and who reside in licensed facilities, such as a hospitals, group homes, institutions or young offenders' facilities within the jurisdiction of the school board where no educational program is provided by the Ministry

---

42 R.R.O. 306, ss. 4 and 5.
43 See discussion in footnote 39.
44 R.S.O. 1990, c. D.2.

of Education or the Ministry of Correctional Services.[45] In this case, the school board must make provision in its SEP for the enrolment and placement of each person under the age of 21 years who resides in the licensed facility and who is qualified to be a resident pupil or would be qualified to be a resident pupil if the person's parents were to reside within the area of jurisdiction of the board. Accordingly, a public school board would not be required to include provision in its SEP for a students aged 16 or older who are living independently and are separate school supporters or students living with parents who are separate school supporters and vice versa.

THE SPECIAL EDUCATION ADVISORY COMMITTEE

In order to ensure that parents have input into the school board's special education planning process, the *Education Act* requires each school board to create a Special Education Advisory Committee ("SEAC").[46] School authorities, other than those established on lands owned by the Crown in right of Canada or Ontario or an agency of either and that are exempt from taxation for school purposes, are also required to establish a SEAC.[47]

The SEAC is charged with the responsibility of making recommendations to the board "in respect of any matter affecting the establishment, development and delivery of special education programs and services for exceptional pupils of the board".[48] The SEAC is also obliged to participate in certain school board functions relating to special education, which will be discussed under the heading "Role of the SEAC".

The special education issues on which the Special Education Advisory Committee is expected to advise school boards includes the following:

- philosophy and goals;
- organizational structures;
- policies and procedures;
- role of personnel;
- delivery of systems;
- staffing (teaching, administration, professional support, paraprofessional support);
- program development (types, location);
- identification of special needs assessment;
- transportation policies/practices;
- special needs;
- interaction with other board committees in related areas;
- any other matter in special education.[49]

---

45 R.R.O. 1990, Reg. 306, s. 5.
46 *Education Act*, s. 57.1(1).
47 O. Reg. 464/97, s. 3; *Education Act*, s. 68.
48 O. Reg. 464/97, s. 11(1).

Parents are represented on the SEAC by "local associations". A "local association" is defined as "an association or organization of parents that operates locally within the area of jurisdiction of a board and that is affiliated with an association or organization that is not an association or organization of professional educators but that is incorporated and operates throughout Ontario to further the interests and well-being of one or more groups of exceptional children or adults".[50]

Role of the SEAC

The SEAC is given a general power to make recommendations to a school board "in respect of any matter affecting the establishment, development and delivery of special education programs and services for exceptional pupils of the board".[51] These recommendations may be presented to the board of trustees. Before the board or a committee of the board makes any decision on the recommendation — whether to accept the recommendation with or without amendments, to reject the recommendation or send the matter back to the SEAC — the board of trustees, or the committee, first must provide the SEAC with "an opportunity . . . to be heard".[52] This requirement can be met by providing the opportunity for one or more representatives of SEAC to present the recommendation in person, together with supporting submissions, to the board or a committee. Alternatively, the recommendation might be forwarded by the SEAC, together with a written submission explaining the purpose of the recommendation. The SEAC might be "heard" by way of a written submission where the circumstances legitimately preclude the opportunity to make submissions personally or where the recommendation is expected to be agreed to by the board or committee. In some cases, the SEAC may decide that the recommendation is sufficiently straightforward that no personal presentation is required.

In addition to its authority to make recommendations on special education programs and services, the SEAC plays a significant role in the review of the SEP and in the part of the annual budget process that relates to special education.[53]

---

49 This list appears in the "Special Education Information Handbook 1984" (Toronto: The Ministry, 1984). This "Handbook" was replaced in 2001 by "Special Education, A Guide for Educators", (Ontario: The Ministry, 2001), which can be found on-line at http://www.edu.gov.on.ca/eng/general/elemsec/speced/guide.html. While the list set out above does not appear in the new guide, these issues do arise necessarily in considering the establishment, development and delivery of special education programs and services.

50 O. Reg. 464/97, s. 1.

51 *Ibid.*, s. 11(1).

52 *Ibid.*, s. 11(2).

53 *Ibid.*, s. 12.

School boards are specifically directed to ensure that the SEAC is given the opportunity to "participate" in the school board's annual review of its SEP.[54] This does not mean that the SEAC may direct that the board make amendments to its plan; however, the SEAC may recommend changes to the SEP during the review process and, as noted previously, the board is obliged to provide an opportunity to the SEAC to be heard on this issue before it accepts, rejects or makes some other decision on the recommendation. The *Standards*[55] require that a description of any majority or minority reports from the SEAC concerning the board's SEP that have been received from SEAC members must be included in the SEP. Moreover, any motions or recommendations from the SEAC related to the school board's approval of the SEP must be submitted to the Ministry of Education with the SEP.[56]

School boards must also ensure that their SEACs have the opportunity to "participate" in the school board's annual budget process of preparing estimates of revenues and expenditures as that process relates to special education.[57] This means that the school board must provide, at the very least, an opportunity for the SEAC to be heard on any recommendations it makes on budget issues that touch on special education programs and services before any final decisions are made on special education expenditures. Indeed, the entitlement to "participate" in budget decisions suggests that the SEAC should be involved actively in the special education budget process, which might be achieved through meaningful consultation in the budget planning process.

In addition, a school board must provide its SEAC with the opportunity to review the financial statements that it prepares annually for submission to the Ministry of Education, as those financial statements relate to special education.[58] This will allow the SEAC's participation in the budget process to be more meaningful.

Composition of the SEAC

SEACs are composed, generally, of representatives of local associations and trustees. In addition, where the school board or school authority has entered into an agreement with the Crown or a band or council of the band — as defined by the *Indian Act*[59] — or an educational authority authorized by the federal government to provide education for Native students, persons must also be appointed to represent Native interests.[60]

---

54 *Ibid.*, s. 12(1).
55 *Op. cit.*, footnote 12, at p. 4.
56 *Ibid.*, at p. 17.
57 O. Reg. 464/97, s. 12(2); *Education Act*, s. 231.
58 O. Reg. 464/97, s. 12(3); *Education Act*, s. 252.
59 R.S.C. 1985, c. I-5, s. 2(1).
60 *Education Act*, s. 188.

School Board SEACs

School board SEACs are comprised of:

- *Representatives of Local Associations*: There must be one representative from each of up to 12 local associations that operate within the school board's jurisdiction. Where there are more than 12 local associations operating within the school board's jurisdiction, the board must select the 12 local associations that will be represented on the SEAC.[61] No criteria are imposed on the school board in making this selection, but a selection of local associations that represent a broad spectrum of exceptionalities will result in a more credible SEAC than will a narrower selection of local associations representative of only a few exceptionalities.
  Once the school board has selected the local associations, it is up to each local association to nominate the person who will represent the local association on the SEAC; the school board must appoint the local association's nominee to the SEAC. In addition, an "alternative" member must be nominated by the local association and appointed by the school board.[62] Nominees for SEAC membership and alternates selected by local associations must be qualified to vote for trustees of the board (*i.e.*, they must have directed their taxes to the board, be at least 18 years of age[63] and a Canadian citizen)[64] and they must be resident in the area of the school board's jurisdiction.[65] A local association may not nominate a person to the SEAC — either as a member or as an alternate — who is an employee of the school board.[66]
- *Board of Trustees*: From amongst its own members, the board of trustees is required to appoint three trustees to the SEAC, unless the board of trustees is comprised of fewer than 12 trustees. In the latter case, the number of trustees to be appointed to the SEAC is 25% of the total number of trustees rounded down to the nearest whole number. Where a board is limited to fewer than three members on the SEAC, the board must also appoint an alternate member for each member it appoints to the SEAC.[67]
- *Representatives of Interests of Native Students*: Where a school board has entered into an agreement to provide accommodation, instruction

---

61 O. Reg. 464/97, s. 2(1)(*a*), (2) and (3).
62 *Ibid.*, s. 2(1)(*b*).
63 *Education Act*, ss. 58.6, 58.7 and 58.9; *Municipal Elections Act, 1996*, S.O. 1996, c. 32, Sch.
64 *Education Act*, ss. 1(10) and 58.9.
65 O. Reg. 464/97, s. 5(1).
66 *Ibid.*, s. 5(3).
67 *Ibid.*, s. 2(1)(*c*), (*d*) and (4).

and special services to Native students and a trustee has been appointed to the school board's board of trustees to represent the interests of Native students,[68] the SEAC must include one person to represent the interests of Native students. Where more than one trustee has been appointed to represent the interests of Native students, the SEAC must include two persons to represent the interests of Native students. In addition, alternates are to be appointed for each person appointed to the SEAC to represent the interests of Native students. In each case, the representatives and alternates must be nominated by the band councils with whom the school board has entered into the agreement. The board of trustees must appoint the persons nominated by the band council.[69] A person nominated by the band council need not be qualified to vote for trustees of the school board nor must the person reside in the area of the school board's jurisdiction to be eligible to be nominated and appointed to the SEAC.[70]

- *Additional Members*: The board of trustees may appoint an unlimited number of additional members to the SEAC who are not representatives of local associations or trustees of the board or members of any other committee of the school board. Examples might include representatives of medical associations, or associations that do not meet the definition of "local association". Employees of the board are not eligible to be appointed as members of the SEAC and additional members must be eligible to vote for trustees of the school board and must reside in the area of the jurisdiction of the board.[71] The Regulation does not limit the ability of additional members to vote on SEAC motions or otherwise participate fully in the SEAC.

School Authority SEACs

In the case of school authorities, SEAC representatives are to be comprised of the following:

- *Local Associations*: Two representatives must be appointed from amongst all the local associations that operate locally within the area of jurisdiction of the board. Where there are more than two local associations within the area of jurisdiction of the board, the local associations should agree on the two persons they will nominate as their representatives and the school authority must appoint these nominees. In addition, two alternates nominated by the local

---

68 *Education Act*, s. 188; *First Nations Representation on Boards*, O. Reg. 462/97.

69 O. Reg. 464/97, s. 4.

70 *Ibid.*, s. 5(2).

71 *Ibid.*, ss. 2(1)(*f*), (5), 5(1) and (3).

associations must be appointed by the school authority; however, where no local associations have been established in the area, the school authority must appoint two persons as SEAC members and two persons as alternates who are not trustees or employees of the board. The persons appointed to the SEAC, whether as representatives of local associations or otherwise, must be qualified to vote for trustees of the school authority and must be resident of the area of the jurisdiction of the school authority.[72]

- *Board of Trustees*: One trustee must be appointed as a member of the SEAC, together with one alternate.[73]
- *Representatives of the Interests of Native Students*: Where the school authority has entered into an agreement to provide accommodation, instruction and special services to Native students, and one trustee has been appointed as a trustee to the board of the school authority to represent the interests of Native students, one person nominated by a band council must be appointed by the school authority to the SEAC. Where two trustees or more have been appointed to the school authority to represent the interests of Native students, two persons nominated by the band council (or band councils) must be appointed to the SEAC.[74]

Term of Office of SEAC Members

Members of the SEAC are appointed for a term of office that corresponds with the three-year term of office of the board of trustees. Members are appointed following the election of a new board and membership in the SEAC continues until a new board is organized following an election.[75]

A SEAC member (or alternate) is deemed to "vacate" his or her position when he or she:

- is convicted of an indictable offence;
- is absent from three consecutive regular SEAC meetings without the authorization of a SEAC resolution that has been entered in the minutes (provided that, in the case of the alternate, he or she had notice of the meeting); or
- no longer holds the qualifications to be appointed to the committee (*e.g.*, he or she ceases to be a member of the local association that nominated him or her or moves away from the area over which the school board/school authority has jurisdiction).[76]

---

72 *Ibid.*, ss. 3(1)(*a*), (*b*), (2) and 5.
73 *Ibid.*, s. 3(1)(*c*) and (*d*).
74 *Ibid.*, ss. 3(1)(*e*) and 4.
75 *Ibid.*, s. 6.
76 *Ibid.*, s. 7(1) and (2).

Where a member or alternate vacates his or her position on the SEAC, either by way of resignation or because he or she is deemed to have vacated his or her position, the school board must appoint a qualified replacement for the remainder of the vacating member's term. The process that the board followed in the first instance in appointing the member or the alternate who has vacated his or her position must be followed by the board in appointing a replacement. For example, where the member or alternate who vacates his or her position is the representative of a local association, then the local association must nominate the person whom the board will appoint as a replacement.[77] Where the member or alternate is deemed to have vacated his or her position as a consequence of being convicted of an indictable offence, his or her replacement cannot be named until either the time for taking an appeal from the conviction has passed and no appeal has been taken or, where an appeal is taken, until the final determination of the appeal. Where the appeal is successful and the conviction is quashed, the member or alternate is deemed not to have vacated his or her seat.[78]

Role of SEAC Alternates

Where a member cannot attend a meeting, the member is obliged to advise his or her alternate. Once notified that the member for whom he or she is appointed cannot attend a meeting, the alternate is obliged to attend the SEAC meeting and act in the place of the member.[79]

As well, where a member has vacated his or her position and the position has not yet been filled, the alternate, if any, is authorized to act in the member's place on the SEAC.[80]

Since SEAC meetings are open meetings, alternates are able to attend SEAC meetings as observers when not acting in place of a member. Although alternates may not participate in a meeting unless acting in place of an absent member, it is prudent for them to attend as many meetings as possible in order to keep abreast of the business being conducted at the SEAC, so that the alternates could participate more meaningfully if they were called on to attend in place of absent members.

---

77 *Ibid.*, s. 8.

78 *Ibid.*, s. 7(4).

79 *Ibid.*, s. 9(9) and (10). While not specified in the regulation, it may be inferred that the alternate would also act in place of a SEAC member who has a conflict of interest. This might occur in circumstances where a parent who is a SEAC member has an exceptional student enrolled with the board and is appealing a placement issue. In such circumstances, the SEAC member could be in a conflict of interest when the SEAC deals with any matters that touch on the issues between the parent and the board.

80 *Ibid.*, s. 8(3).

Conduct of SEAC Meetings

A majority of the SEAC's members (or alternates attending on their behalf) constitutes a quorum.[81] The SEAC must meet at least 10 times a year and may meet by teleconference, in accordance with the board's policy on teleconferencing.[82]

At the first meeting of the SEAC following its appointment, the members must elect a chair and a vice-chair from among their membership. The chair will preside at all meetings, assisted by the vice-chair, except in cases where the chair is absent. In that event, the vice-chair will preside at the meeting. Should both the chair and the vice-chair be absent from a meeting, the members present would be required to select a chair for that meeting.[83]

Decisions of the SEAC are made based on a vote of the majority of the members present. Every member (or alternate sitting in the member's place), including the chair, has one vote. In the event of a tie vote, the motion is lost.[84]

Support for the SEAC

A school board is required to provide the SEAC with the administrative support, including personnel and facilities, that the school board considers necessary for the proper functioning of the committee. This will include secretarial support and professional support from the school board's special education experts. It will also mean providing technical support in the form of both equipment and personnel in order to allow meetings to be held by way of teleconferencing or videoconferencing.[85] This is particularly important in the case of school boards with geographic jurisdiction over large areas where members may be able to attend meetings only when they are able to do so through electronic means.

Beyond administrative assistance, the school board is obliged to educate all SEAC members and their alternates about the role of the SEAC and the school board in relation to special education and about the special education policies of both the Ministry of Education and the school board. Specifically, the school board is required to provide to the SEAC members and their alternates "information and orientation" on these matters.[86]

---

81 *Ibid.*, s. 9(1) and (8).

82 Section 208.1 of the *Education Act* permits the government to make regulations respecting the conduct of electronic meetings by boards. *Electronic Meetings*, O. Reg. 463/97, has been introduced under this section. This regulation requires each school board to develop and implement a policy providing for the use of electronic means for the holding of meetings of the board and committees of the board. Members who participate in a meeting in accordance with this policy will be deemed to be present at the meeting.

83 O. Reg. 464/97, s. 9(3), (4), (5) and (6).

84 *Ibid.*, s. 9(1), (2) and (7).

85 *Ibid.*, s. 10(1).

86 *Ibid.*, s. 10(2).

THE PARENT GUIDE

A guide specifically designed to explain the special education process to parents must be prepared and made available to parents by every school board. The Parent Guide must include the following information:[87]

- An explanation of the function of the IPRC where a student is referred to the IPRC for the purposes of identification and placement in the first instance or for review of identification and/or placement.
- An outline of the procedures that the IPRC must follow, as set out in O. Reg. 181/98, together with an outline of any procedures established for the IPRC by the school board respecting the identification and placement of exceptional students.
- An explanation of the IPRC's duty, both to describe the student's strengths and needs and to include in its statements of decision the categories and definitions of any exceptionalities identified by the IPRC.
- An explanation of the function of a Special Education Appeal Board ("SEAB") and the right of a parent to appeal decisions of the IPRC to an SEAB.
- A list of those parent organizations of which the school board is aware that are "local associations" — that is, associations or organizations of parents that operate locally within the board's jurisdiction and are associated with incorporated associations or organizations that operate throughout Ontario to further the interests and well-being of one or more groups of exceptional children or adults.[88]
- A list of the names, addresses and telephone numbers of the provincial and demonstration schools in Ontario.
- An indication of the extent to which the school board provides special education programs and special education services and the extent to which it purchases those programs and services from another school board.
- An explanation that no IPRC placement can be implemented unless either a parent has consented to the decision in writing or the time limit for filing an appeal in respect of the decision has expired and no appeal has been filed or, if an appeal were filed, the appeal has been abandoned.

A sample Parent Guide is attached to the *Standards* and the guide prepared by the school board must also contain the information set out in this sample.[89]

---

[87] O. Reg. 181/98, s. 13.

[88] O. Reg. 464/97, s. 1.

[89] The *Standards*, *op. cit.*, footnote 12, at Appendix B.

Copies of the Parent Guide prepared by the school board must be made available at each school in the board's jurisdiction and at the board's head office. In addition, the board must provide a copy of its Parent Guide to the Ministry of Education.[90]

Where a principal refers a pupil to the IPRC for the first time, either on the request of the parent or at the principal's initiative, the principal must provide a copy of the Parent Guide to the parents within 15 days after notifying the parents of the student's referral to the IPRC.[91]

Where a parent or pupil requests the school board to provide a copy of the Parent Guide in a Braille, large print or audio-cassette format, the school board must supply the guide in that format.[92]

LIMITS ON CLASS SIZE

In setting up special education classes, school administrators must be mindful of limits that have been placed by the "Operation of Schools" regulation on the maximum number of students who can be placed in specific special education classes.[93] It is noteworthy that much of the language of this regulation regarding class size was drafted prior to the establishment of the scheme for special education set out elsewhere in the *Education Act* and regulations; as such, it initially did not reference specific "exceptionalities", but rather referenced specific disabilities[94] for which the class was established. Although the regulation has been subject to some amendment — *e.g.*, to replace references to the "trainable retarded" and "educable retarded" with "developmental disability" and "mild intellectual disability", respectively — certain other references in the regulation do not coincide with defined exceptionalities.

The regulation commences with a preamble that makes clear that the maximum enrolment in any special education class is dependent on the exceptionalities of the students in the class along with the special education services available to the teacher of the class. The regulation then proceeds to set maximum upper limits on the number of students in those classes that are specifically designated to deal with specific exceptionalities or disabilities:

- The maximum size for classes for students who are "emotionally disturbed or socially maladjusted" is eight pupils.[95] (Note: There is no specific reference to the "behaviour" exceptionality in the regulation.)

---

90 O. Reg. 181/98, s. 13(2).

91 *Ibid.*, s. 14(6).

92 *Ibid.*, s. 13(3).

93 *Operation of Schools — General*, R.R.O. 1990, Reg. 298, s. 31.

94 See Chapter 4, "Identification and Exceptionality", for definitions of exceptionalities.

95 Regulation 298, s. 31(*a*).

- The maximum class size for a special education class for autistic or aphasic students is six students.[96]
- A class designated for students who are deaf is limited in size to a maximum of 10 students.[97] The maximum size of a special education class for children with hearing impairment — which corresponds to the current "hard of hearing" exceptionality — who are younger than compulsory school age is eight students.[98] Otherwise, a special education class for students who have hearing impairments is limited to 12 students.[99]
- A special education class for students with "speech and language disorders" can have a maximum of 10 students.[100] While there is no such exceptionality, language impairment and speech impairment are two exceptionalities that are recognized in the Ministry's definitions.
- The maximum size for a class of students with "severe learning disabilities" is eight students.[101] There is no limit on a special education class for students whose learning disabilities are not "severe". Where a special education class for "aphasic" students is established, the size is limited to six students.[102]
- The maximum size for a special education class designated for students with a "mild intellectual disability" is 12 students in the primary division and 16 students in the junior and intermediate divisions.[103]
- A special education class established for students identified with "developmental disability" has a size limit of 10 students.[104]
- The maximum size for a class of gifted students in elementary school is 25 students.[105] There is no limit on the number of grade levels that can be included in the class. There are no limits imposed on the size of any gifted class that might be established at the secondary level.[106]
- The maximum size of a special education class established for students with "orthopaedic or other physical handicaps" is 12 students.[107]

---

[96] *Ibid.*, s. 31(*f*).
[97] *Ibid.*, s. 31(*b*).
[98] *Ibid.*, s. 31(*a*).
[99] *Ibid.*, s. 31(*c*).
[100] *Ibid.*, s. 31(*b*).
[101] *Ibid.*, s. 31(*a*).
[102] *Ibid.*, s. 31(*f*).
[103] *Ibid.*, s. 31(*d*).
[104] *Ibid.*, s. 31(*b*).
[105] *Ibid.*, s. 31(*e*).
[106] It should be noted that the limits imposed on the size of regular classes do not apply to classes for exceptional students: *Class Size*, O. Reg. 118/98, s. 3(1), definition "class".
[107] Regulation 298, s. 31(*c*).

- The maximum size for a class established for blind students is 10 students.[108] Where a class is established for students with limited vision — now "low vision" — the size is limited to 12 students.[109]
- The maximum class size for a special education class established for students with "multiple handicaps for whom no one handicap is dominant" — now "multiple exceptionalities" — is six pupils.[110]
- Where a special education class is established for students with different exceptionalities, the maximum class size is 16 students.[111]
- Where students with exceptionalities are placed in regular classes, the normal class-size limits will apply.[112]

A current trend in special education is to establish self-contained classes with names such as "Associated Class", "Structured Teaching Class", "General Skills Class" or "Essential Skills Class", which are not specifically designated for a particular disability or exceptionality, but rather are designed to provide specific types of assistance and learning environments for students who may have different exceptionalities. Consequently, students with different exceptionalities may be placed in the same class. In such a case, as long as there is sufficient support in the form of "special education services"— which might include education assistants and/or child and youth workers — such a class may have an enrolment of up to 16 students,[113] even where, at a particular point in time, all the students in the class happen to have the same exceptionality. The key consideration will be whether the class has been established to deal with the needs of one particular exceptionality or whether the intention is that the class will be for students with different exceptionalities who would benefit from the particular curriculum, learning environment and supports offered in the class. In the latter case, the maximum enrolment can be up to 16 students, provided that sufficient special education services supports are provided to the teacher to permit instruction that benefits all the students in the class.[114]

[108] *Ibid.*, s. 31(*b*).
[109] *Ibid.*, s. 31(*c*).
[110] *Ibid.*, s. 31(*f*).
[111] *Ibid.*, s. 31(*g*).
[112] *Education Act*, s. 170.1.
[113] Regulation 298, s. 31(*g*).
[114] Where parents view this trend as simply a way to increase class size, save money and reduce the needed supports, however, they may challenge the authority of a school board to re-name self-contained classes in order to avoid the class size protections in s. 31 of Regulation 298. Where all of the students in a class frequently have the same exceptionality, the school board's conduct may be open to challenge with skepticism.

POLICY/PROGRAM MEMORANDA

The Ministry of Education issues Policy/Program Memoranda ("PPM") from time to time that provide further direction and guidance to school boards on various issues.[115] A number of these PPMs deal specifically with or touch indirectly on special education issues, including the following:

- PPM 8: "Learning Disabilities";[116]
- PPM 11: "Early Identification of Children's Learning Needs";[117]
- PPM 59: "Psychological Testing and Assessment of Pupils";[118]
- PPM 76C: "Alternative Educational Programs and Services for Deaf, Blind, and Deaf-Blind Exceptional Pupils";[119]
- PPM 81: "Provision of Health Support Services in School Settings";[120]
- PPM 89: "The Residential Demonstration Schools for Students with Learning Disabilities: General Information and Details of the Referral Process";[121]
- PPM 140: "Incorporating Methods of Applied Behaviour Analysis (ABA) into Programs for Students with Autism Spectrum Disorders (ASD)";[122]

---

[115] These PPMs may be found on line at http://www.edu.gov.on.ca/extra/eng/ppm/ppm.html.

[116] Ontario Deputy Minister of Education, "Policy/Program Memorandum No. 8: Learning Disabilities" (Toronto: Ministry of Education, 1982), available online at http://www.edu.gov.on.ca/extra/eng/ppm/8.html.

[117] Ontario Deputy Minister of Education, *op. cit.*, footnote 2.

[118] Ontario Deputy Minister of Education, "Policy/Program Memorandum No. 59: Psychological Testing and Assessment of Pupils" (Toronto: Ministry of Education, 1982), available online at http://www.edu.gov.on.ca/extra/eng/ppm/59.html.

[119] Ontario Deputy Minister of Education, "Policy/Program Memorandum No. 76C: Alternative Educational Programs and Services for Deaf, Blind, and Deaf-Blind Pupils" (Toronto: Ministry of Education, 1991), available online at http://www.edu.gov.on.ca/extra/eng/ppm/76c.html.

[120] Ontario Deputy Minister of Education, "Policy/Program Memorandum No. 81: Provision of Health Support Services in School Settings" (Toronto: Ministry of Education, 1984), available online at http://www.edu.gov.on.ca/extra/eng/ppm/81.html.

[121] Ontario Deputy Minister of Education, "Policy/Program Memorandum No. 89: The Residential Demonstration Schools for Students with Learning Disabilities: General Information and Details of the Referral Process" (Toronto: Ministry of Education, 1990), available online at http://www.edu.gov.on.ca/extra/eng/ppm/89.html.

[122] Ontario Deputy Minister of Education, "Policy/Program Memorandum No. 140: Incorporating Methods of Applied Behaviour Analysis (ABA) into Programs for Students with Autism Spectrum Disorders (ASD)" (Toronto: Ministry of Education, 2007), available online at http://www.edu.gov.on.ca/extra/eng/ppm/140.html.

- PPM 145: "Progressive Discipline and Promoting Positive Student Behaviour".[123]

[123] Ontario Deputy Minister of Education, "Policy/Program Memorandum No. 145: Progressive Discipline and Promoting Positive Student Behaviour" (Toronto: Ministry of Education, 2009), available online at http://www.edu.gov.on.ca/extra/eng/ppm/145.html.

4

Identification and Exceptionality

INTRODUCTION

Given that the *Education Act*[1] establishes a statutory right for all school-aged children to an education,[2] the rationale for the provision of special education is that, for some students, access to the education to which they have a right is not possible without modifications to the regular curriculum and/or program. So, in order to ensure that all students have an equitable opportunity to learn, the Ministry of Education's "Policy/Program Memorandum No. 11"[3] directs school boards to have procedures in place to identify each student's level of development, learning abilities and needs from the time the student is first enrolled in school. This policy of early identification ensures that educational programs are designed to accommodate each student. The process results in the identification of students who are called "exceptional pupils" under the *Education Act*. An "exceptional pupil" is defined as:[4]

> a pupil whose behavioural, communicational, intellectual, physical or multiple exceptionalities are such that he or she is considered to need placement in a special education program.

With the exception of the "gifted" exceptionality, there is significant overlap between the concept of an "exceptional pupil" under the *Education Act* and a student with a "disability" under the *Human Rights Code*.[5] A student with a disability is entitled to be accommodated and to receive educational

1 R.S.O. 1990, c. E.2.

2 *Education Act*, s. 1, definition "exceptional pupil".

3 Ontario Deputy Minister of Education, "Policy/Program Memorandum No. 11: Early Identification of Children's Learning Needs" (Toronto: Ministry of Education, 1982), available online at http://www.edu.gov.on.ca/extra/eng/ppm/11.html.

4 *Education Act*, s. 1.

5 R.S.O. 1990, c. H.19, s. 10(1), definition "disability".

services free of discrimination because of disability. "Exceptional" students are exceptional because, for reasons generally related to one or more disabilities, they have specific educational needs that can only be met by placement in a special education program. This point was underlined by the Special Education Tribunal in a case where a parent sought an identification of "exceptional, physical" for her child based on the child's environmental sensitivities. Rejecting the appeal, the Tribunal stated:[6]

> The principal issue in the appeal regarding the child born in 1983's possible identification as "exceptional", is whether or not the child's apparent sensitivity to environmental conditions significantly interferes with the child's ability to learn or the child's capacity to function in school. In its examination of the appellants' case, the Tribunal is unable to find any convincing evidence that the child is so affected.

It is true that not every student who has a disability requires special education. For example, a student may have a physical disability for which he or she requires use of a wheelchair, but not require a special education program in order to benefit from the regular curriculum. Further, a student who is identified as "gifted" does not have a disability, but qualifies for special education.

For students with disabilities that interfere in their ability to benefit from the regular curriculum as presented in the regular classroom, however, the purpose of special education is to provide the accommodations that will permit those students with the same opportunities to benefit from education as are provided to their non-disabled peers.

School boards are required to both provide appropriate special education programs for exceptional students and accommodate the needs of students with handicaps where those handicaps preclude the student from accessing education in the normal course. This book focuses on the provision of special education under the statutory regime of the *Education Act*. School boards are also subject to the *Human Rights Code*;[7] however, in carrying out its obligations under the *Education Act* to provide appropriate special education programs and services to exceptional students, a school board will generally also comply with its statutory obligations under the *Human Rights Code* as well.[8]

---

6 *S. & Carlton Board of Education* (1993-04-02), File No. 18 (Ont. Spec. Ed. (Eng.) Trib.), at p. 21.

7 See Brenda J. Bowlby, Daniel Michaluk and Jennifer Wootton Regan, *An Educator's Guide to Human Rights*, 2nd ed. (Aurora: Canada Law Book, 2009), another publication in the "Educator's Guides to the Law" series of which this book is a part.

8 *Eaton v. Brant County Board of Education* (1997), 142 D.L.R. (4th) 385, [1997] 1 S.C.R. 241; *Campbell v. Toronto District School Board*, 2008 HRTO 62. Both statutes are more likely to be followed where the spirit of each and the goal of educating all students is considered.

This chapter will canvass the specific exceptionalities that will apply when a student is "identified".

CATEGORIES OF EXCEPTIONALITY

The categories of exceptionality recognized in the *Education Act* are:

- behaviour;
- communication;
- intellectual;
- physical; and
- multiple.[9]

The Minister of Education has been directed by s. 8(3)(*b*) of the *Education Act* to,

> (b) in respect of special education programs and services, define exceptionalities of pupils, and prescribe classes, groups or categories of exceptional pupils, and require boards to employ such definitions or use such prescriptions as established under this clause.

The Minister has, for some of the categories listed above, defined additional subcategories. For each category or subcategory, the Minister has prescribed an outline of the characteristics, from an educational perspective, which will define the exceptionality. The definitions originally provided by the Minister[10] were updated in 1999.[11] Because the wording of the definition of each exceptionality is critical in determining whether or not a student falls within that exceptionality, we have set out the precise language from the Ministry of Education document that establishes the definition.

Behaviour

Not every incident of inappropriate behaviour indicates a behavioural exceptionality. The key will be whether or not the behavioural problems interfere in the student's ability to learn.[12] The specific definition that the Minister of Education has given to the exceptionality of "behaviour" is as follows:[13]

---

9 See *Education Act*, s. 1(1), definition "exceptional pupil".

10 Ontario Ministry of Education, *Special Education Information Handbook* (Toronto: The Ministry, 1981).

11 Ontario Ministry of Education, *Standards for School Boards' Special Education Plans* (Toronto: The Ministry, 2000), at Appendix D (the "*Standards*").

12 In *S. & Peel District School Board* (2007-02-12), File No. 58b (Ont. Spec. Ed. (Eng.) Trib.), the Special Education Tribunal found that, although the student had been diagnosed with ADHD, OCD and ODD, the child displayed none of the criteria set out in the Ministry definition and that a designation of "behavioural" neither reflected the child's needs nor was in his best interests.

13 The *Standards*, *op. cit.*, footnote 11, at p. 32, at Appendix D. Parents frequently

A learning disorder characterized by specific behaviour problems over such a period of time, and to such a marked degree, and of such a nature, as to adversely affect educational performance, and that may be accompanied by one or more of the following:

(a) an inability to maintain interpersonal relationships;
(b) excessive fears or anxieties;
(c) a tendency to compulsive reaction;
(d) an inability to learn that cannot be traced to intellectual, sensory or other health factors, or any combination thereof.

Communication

Communication exceptionalities include a wide range of special needs, including deafness and hearing impairments, learning disabilities and speech disorders. Autism is also usually characterized as a communication exceptionality. Accordingly, the Minister has defined several subcategories for this category. The definition of each subcategory follows.

Autism

Pervasive developmental disorder and autism are characterized by difficulty with communication and interactional skills, often accompanied by difficulty relating to others and adapting to the environment. The Ministry's definition of the exceptionality of autism is as follows:[14]

A severe learning disorder that is characterized by:

a) disturbances in:
   - rate of educational development;
   - ability to relate to the environment;
   - mobility;
   - perception, speech, and language;

b) lack of the representational symbolic behaviour that precedes language.

The Ontario Ministry of Education has provided a much fuller description of the characteristics of autism in "Special Education Monographs No. 4: Students With Autism".[15]

Deaf and Hard-of-Hearing

A unique feature about special education for young children with hearing difficulties is that, "[a] hearing-handicapped child who has attained the age of

---

suggest that their children would not have behavoural issues if the underlying disability were properly addressed. For example, students with learning disabilities may display behaviours that adversely affect their educational performance, yet the appropriate identification may be a "learning disability" and not "behaviour" — compare with the diagnoses described in the previous footnote.

14 *Ibid.*

15 Ontario Ministry of Education, "Special Education Monographs No. 4: Students With Autism" (Special Education and Provincial Schools Branch, 1990), available online at http://www.edu.gov.on.ca/eng/general/elemsec/speced/monog4.html.

two years may be admitted to a special education program for the hearing-handicapped."[16] This provision is relatively dated and may reflect a time when most children with hearing disabilities were enrolled in schools for the deaf.

The current definition of the exceptionality is as follows: "An impairment characterized by deficits in language and speech development because of a diminished or non-existent auditory response to sound."[17]

Language Impairment

This subcategory of the communication exceptionality is defined as follows:[18]

> A learning disorder characterized by an impairment in comprehension and/or use of verbal communication or the written or other symbol system of communication, which may be associated with neurological, psychological, physical, or sensory factors, and which may:
> a) involve one or more of the form, content, and function of language in communication; and
> b) include one or more of the following:
> - language delay;
> - dysfluency;
> - voice and articulation development, which may or may not be organically or functionally based.

Speech Impairment

The educational exceptionality of speech impairment is defined as follows:[19]

> A disorder in language formulation that may be associated with neurological, psychological, physical, or sensory factors; that involves perceptual motor aspects of transmitting oral messages; and that may be characterized by impairment in articulation, rhythm, and stress.

Learning Disability

The definition of learning disability is as follows:[20]

> A learning disorder evident in both academic and social situations that involves one or more of the processes necessary for the proper use of spoken language or the symbols of communication, and that is characterized by a condition that:
> a) is not primarily the result of:
> - impairment of vision;
> - impairment of hearing;
> - physical disability;

---

16 *Operation of Schools — General*, R.R.O. 1990, Reg. 298, s. 30.
17 The *Standards*, *op. cit.*, footnote 11, at p. 32, at Appendix D.
18 *Ibid.*
19 *Ibid.*, at p. 33.
20 *Ibid.*

- primary emotional disturbance;
- cultural difference; and

b) results in a significant discrepancy between academic achievement and assessed intellectual ability, with deficits in one or more of the following:
- receptive language (listening, reading);
- language processing (thinking, conceptualizing, integrating);
- expressive language (talking, spelling, writing);
- mathematical computations;

c) may be associated with one or more conditions diagnosed as:
- a perceptual handicap;
- a brain injury;
- minimal brain dysfunction;
- dyslexia;
- developmental aphasia.

Policy/Program Memorandum No. 8, which was revised in 1982, sets out a requirement that children be assessed for learning disabilities in their language of instruction.[21] This PPM also notes that where the student's language is other than English or French, a "reasonable delay in language based aspects of assessment" should be considered. The PPM requires that assessment of learning disabilities be based on some or all of the following:[22]

1. continuous educational assessment;
2. detailed health assessment (hearing, vision, physical and neurological);
3. psychological assessment;
4. language assessment;
5. social/family history;
6. assessment of observed behaviours in a variety of settings.

Intellectual

The intellectual category has been broken down into three subcategories: giftedness, mild intellectual disability and developmental disability.

Giftedness

The definition of this subcategory of intellectual is as follows:

> An unusually advanced degree of general intellectual ability that requires differentiated learning experiences of a depth and breadth beyond those normally provided in the regular school program to satisfy the level of educational potential indicated.[23]

It has been traditional for school boards to determine whether or not a student is gifted through standardized testing to determine the student's I.Q. As time has gone on, other criteria have been added — *e.g.*, strengths in areas

---

21 Ontario Deputy Minister of Education, "Policy/Program Memorandum No. 8: Learning Disabilities" (Toronto: Ministry of Education, 1982), available online at http://www.edu.gov.on.ca/extra/eng/ppm/8.html.

22 *Ibid.*.

23 The *Standards*, *op. cit.*, footnote 11, at p. 33, at Appendix D.

other than I.Q., creativity, demonstration of task commitment and perseverance and an academic assessment that the student is several years or grades above his/her peers. The Special Education Tribunal has made clear that all criteria must be considered and that I.Q. testing cannot be used as the final determinant when other criteria point to the student being gifted.[24]

Mild Intellectual Disability

The definition of mild intellectual disability is as follows:[25]

> A learning disorder characterized by:
> a) an ability to profit educationally within a regular class with the aid of considerable curriculum modification and supportive services;
> b) an inability to profit educationally within a regular class because of slow intellectual development;
> c) a potential for academic learning, independent social adjustment, and economic self-support.

Developmental Disability

This exceptionality is defined as follows:

> A severe learning disorder characterized by:
> a) an inability to profit from a special education program for students with mild intellectual disabilities because of slow intellectual development;
> b) an ability to profit from a special education program that is designed to accommodate slow intellectual development;
> c) a limited potential for academic learning, independence, social adjustment, and economic self-support.[26]

The Special Education Tribunal has made the following comments regarding the difference between Developmental Disability and Mild Intellectual Disability:

> There is a significant difference in these definitions. Students with an identification of "Mild Intellectual Disability" have the potential for academic learning, independent social adjustment, and economic self-support. Students identified as having a developmental disability are described as having limited potential for academic learning, independent social adjustment and economic self-support. It follows that a student identified with a Mild Intellectual Disability would have programming that would foster the potential for academic

---

24 *B. & Upper Canada District School Board* (2001-09-24), File No. 28 (Ont. Spec. Ed. (Eng.) Trib.). In this case, the board had a "cut-off" I.Q. score of 130 in determining giftedness. The student's score fell below this level, despite several attempts at testing his I.Q.; however, in circumstances where the student had done very well in Education Quality and Accountability Office testing and where the parent provided evidence that the student's brother was gifted and there was a significant family history of giftedness, the Tribunal found the student to be gifted.

25 The *Standards*, *op. cit.*, footnote 11, at p. 33, at Appendix D.

26 *Ibid.*, at p. 34.

> learning, independent social adjustment and economic self-support as compared to a life skills program that would be less rigorous and more practical.[27]

Where a question arises whether a student should be identified as having a developmental disability or mild intellectual disability, however, the Tribunal has usually recommended that parents agree to a psychological assessment in order to make a final determination on the issue.[28] In one case, pending this assessment, the Tribunal directed that the student simply be identified as Exceptional with an Intellectual disability.[29]

Physical

The physical category of exceptionality is broken into two subcategories: physical disability; and blind and low vision.

Physical Disability

The definition of the physical disability exceptionality is as follows:[30]

> A condition of such severe physical limitation or deficiency as to require special assistance in learning situations to provide the opportunity for educational achievement equivalent to that of pupils without exceptionalities who are of the same age or developmental level.

Blind and Low Vision

This subcategory is defined as follows: "A condition of partial or total impairment of sight or vision that even with correction affects educational performance adversely."[31]

Multiple

The definition of multiple exceptionalities is as follows:[32]

> A combination of learning or other disorders, impairments, or physical disabilities, that is of such nature as to require, for educational achievement, the services of one or more teachers holding qualifications in special education and the provision of support services appropriate for such disorders, impairments, or disabilities.

---

27 *D. & Windsor Essex Catholic District School Board* (2003-09-30), File No. 38 (Ont. Spec. Ed. (Eng.) Trib.), at p. 23.

28 *D. & Windsor Essex Catholic District School Board, supra*; *I. & Toronto District School Board* (2005-11-17), File No. 46c (Ont. Spec. Ed. (Eng.) Trib.).

29 *I. & Toronto District School Board, supra.*

30 The *Standards*, *op cit.*, footnote 11, at p. 34, at Appendix D.

31 *Ibid.*

32 *Ibid.*

The Special Education Tribunal has made clear that, when a student is identified as having "Multiple Exceptionalities", all the specific exceptionalities must be defined.[33]

TO IDENTIFY OR NOT TO IDENTIFY

It is becoming more common for school boards to simply provide students who have exceptionalities with individual education plans along with the services and programs they need, without referring the student to the Identification, Placement and Review Committee ("IPRC") process. Generally, this appears to be limited to students who do not require special education class placements.

Quite apart from any pedagogical considerations or system-wide administrative issues,[34] it should be first noted that the identification and placement of students through the IPRC process under the *Education Act* is not discretionary. Section 8(3) requires that the Minister of Education to ensure that "all exceptional children in Ontario" have appropriate special education programs and services made available to them "in accordance with this Act". Moreover, the Minister is required to define exceptionalities and require school boards to use these definitions.[35] The Act therefore contemplates that all exceptional pupils will be identified, utilizing the process set out in the Act and Regulations. In one case, where a school board wished to do away with any identification for a student, but wished to continue to provide an IEP, the Special Education Tribunal appeared to be of the view that, where a student requires an IEP and accommodations to deal with the student's needs, the student should be identified appropriately.[36]

Second, it should be noted that students who have been identified through the formal IPRC process during their elementary and secondary years may find it easier to obtain disability services when they move on to post-secondary education. Where they are able to take an identification with them, the nature of the needs they have will be much clearer to the disabilities services offices of the colleges or universities that they wish to attend and it may be unnecessary for them to provide proof that they have a disability that requires accommodation.[37]

---

[33] *D. & Windsor Essex Catholic District School Board*, *supra*, footnote 27.

[34] For example, the identification and annual review processes ensure that information is collected in order to make regular assessments about programming and services for the student. The identification process also triggers transition plans for older students and produces the kind of documentation that may be necessary to inform the Special Education Advisory Committee and review the Special Education Plan.

[35] *Education Act*, s. 8(3).

[36] *S. & Peel District School Board* (2007-02-12), File No. 58b (Ont. Spec. Ed. (Eng.) Trib.).

The problem that does arise with those few parents who view the identification of their children as imposing a "stigma" should be acknowledged. It is often easier for school staff to "compromise" with these parents by simply avoiding the identification process and providing the student with an individual education plan and the services/programming the student needs; however, ultimately, it may not be beneficial to the student to refrain from identifying the student. Therefore, the issue becomes one of educating the parents rather than avoiding the requirements of the *Education Act*.

A further problem can arise where identification is dependent on a psychological or medical assessment and parents have refused to co-operate, either in consenting to or obtaining the assessment or in providing a copy of the assessment, when it exists. In this case, it may be necessary to use a partial identification. For example, as previously noted, in one appeal, where one of the issues was whether the student was properly identified with "developmental disability" or a "mild intellectual delay", the existing psychological assessment was quite old and was, therefore, considered to be not sufficiently reliable to permit a determination. In this case, the Special Education Tribunal limited the identification of the student to "exceptional with an Intellectual exceptionality" and recommended that a new psychological assessment be completed and that the matter then be referred back to the IPRC for a more specific identification.[38]

[37] See Chapter 15, "Post-Secondary Education", for further discussion regarding the transition of exceptional students into post-secondary education.

[38] *I. & Toronto District School Board*, *supra*, footnote 29.

5

Placement

INTRODUCTION

Over the years, placement has proved to be a significant source of litigation between parents and school boards, not only in cases before the Special Education Tribunal, but also in cases before the Human Rights Tribunal and the courts under the *Human Rights Code*[1] and the *Canadian Charter of Rights and Freedoms*. The decisions arising in these various venues have defined the standards that educators must apply in making placement decisions.

To complicate matters, placement is not defined in the legislation, although the legislation seems to suggest that placement is distinguishable from special education services and programs. Under Ontario's scheme, a school board's decisions on a student's "placement" can be appealed by parents, but "special education services" and "special education programs" alone cannot; however, recent decisions of the Special Education Tribunal have made clear that special education programs and services cannot be separated from placement.

In this chapter, we will consider the meaning of placement, examine the relationship between placement and special education programs and services and review the standards that are to be used in making placement decisions.

WHAT IS PLACEMENT?

In normal usage, "placement" means a situation, site or location. The usage of the word in the context of special education does not generally extend to a specific geographic location (*e.g.*, a particular school); rather, placement is a description of a generic setting (or settings) where the appropriate special education programs and services can be delivered to the student.

---

1 R.S.O. 1990, c. H.19.

While the *Education Act*[2] defines "special education programs"[3] and "special education services",[4] it contains no definition of "placement". The Ministry of Education, however, has stated that the range of options to be considered by IPRCs include regular class with support, regular class with resource assistance, regular class with withdrawal assistance, special education class with partial integration, special education class full-time. Provincial demonstration schools are also noted as a placement option, although application must be made for admission to this placement.[5]

In the first two decades following the introduction of special education into Ontario's *Education Act*, there was a firm belief by educators that special education programs and services were to be regarded as separate from placement. This belief was fostered by the language of the *Education Act* itself, as well as the regulations dealing with IPRCs. The Act, itself, and the current regulation, as did the regulation that preceded it, appear to make a clear distinction between placement and special education programs/services:

- Section 8(3) of the *Education Act* requires the Minister of Education to ensure that all exceptional students in Ontario have "appropriate special education programs and special education services", but the section deals quite distinctly with placement, by requiring the Minister to "provide for the parents or guardians to appeal the appropriateness of the special education placement".[6]
- Section 11(1), para. 5 of the *Education Act* empowers the Minister of Education to make regulations respecting special education programs and services, while para. 6 empowers the Minister to make regulations governing procedures for parent appeals of "identification and placement of exceptional pupils in special education programs".

---

2 R.S.O. 1990, c. E.2.

3 "Special education program" means "in respect of an exceptional pupil, an educational program that is based on and modified by the results of continuous assessment and evaluation and that includes a plan containing specific objectives and an outline of educational services that meets the needs of the exceptional pupil": *Education Act*, s. 1(1), definition "special education program".

4 "Special education services" means "facilities and resources, including support personnel and equipment, necessary for developing and implementing a special education program": *Education Act*, s. 1(1), definition "special education services".

5 Ontario Ministry of Education, Special Education: A Guide for Educators (Toronto: The Ministry, modified March 16, 2009), at pp. D10-D11, available online at http://www.edu.gov.on.ca/eng/general/elemsec/speced/guide.html.

6 The subsection reads: "The Minister shall ensure that all exceptional children in Ontario have available to them, in accordance with this Act and the regulations, appropriate special education programs and special education services without payment of fees by parents or guardians resident in Ontario, and shall provide for the parents or guardians to appeal the appropriateness of the special education placement."

- O. Reg. 181/98[7] permits the IPRC to make decisions on placement, but limits the IPRC to making recommendations on special education programs and services.[8] Similarly, the regulation provides for parent appeals of IRPC decisions on placement, but not on IPRC recommendations on special education programs and services.[9]

Similarly, the *Education Act* provides, in s. 57(3), that:

> 57(3) Where a parent or guardian of a pupil has exhausted all rights of appeal under the regulations in respect of the identification or placement of the pupil as an exceptional pupil and is dissatisfied with the decision in respect of the identification or placement, the parent or guardian may appeal to a Special Education Tribunal for a hearing in respect of the identification or placement.

The section makes no reference to an appeal of special education programs or services.

The Special Education Tribunal, however, made clear from the outset that the determination of placement must include some consideration of the programs and services that will be delivered in the placement. In *D. & Muskoka Board of Education*,[10] the first decision by the Tribunal made during the "phase-in" period,[11] the following comment was made:[12]

> While the nature and content of the program that is provided to an exceptional pupil pursuant to a placement may be considered in order that the rationale for the placement can be understood, opinions in respect of the course content, the staffing allocated to the program, the adequacy of a teacher's capabilities to communicate in sign language, and the means by which the program could or should be enhanced or improved, tend to obscure those other matters that have to be considered in trying to decide whether a placement that has been recommended is right or wrong.

The Tribunal's decision was reviewed by the Ontario Divisional Court, which commented as follows:[13]

> In considering the placement of a child in the phase-in period, the first step is to ascertain the needs of the child. This must include a consideration of such things as the nature and content of the programme and the services required to accomplish this purpose. When turning to placement, one must be sought which is suitable to the needs of the pupil. In doing so, however, it is essential to consider what programmes and services are available and perhaps even the degree of availability.

---

7 *Identification and Placement of Exceptional Pupils*, O. Reg. 181/98.

8 *Ibid.*, s. 16(1).

9 *Ibid.*, s. 26(1).

10 (1984-02-28), File No. 1 (Ont. Spec. Ed. (Eng.) Trib.), affd 15 D.L.R. (4th) 741, 49 O.R. (2d) 546, *sub nom. Dolmage v. Muskoka Board of Education* (Div. Ct.).

11 See Chapter 3, "The Administrator's Framework".

12 *D. & Muskoka Board of Education*, *supra*, footnote 10, at p. 9.

13 *Ibid.* (Div. Ct.), at p. 750.

These comments were made in the context of a case that arose during the "phase-in" period, which lasted from 1980 to September 1, 1985. They continue to have application to the extent that they suggest that a consideration of placement includes a consideration of the programs and services that are provided in the particular placement.[14]

The Tribunal has made clear that it considers special education programs and services to be intertwined with placement and that it will consider programs and services to be part of the placement where it feels that such consideration is necessary in order to determine an appropriate placement:[15]

> It is the view of the Tribunal that appropriate programs and services are interconnected with the issue of placement. Inclusion of students who have special education needs into the regular classroom requires that appropriate programming and services be put into place to ensure that those needs are met. This is contrasted with a special education placement where the services and programs are built into the placement itself. A regular class placement can only be considered when the services and program are identified.

The Tribunal has, therefore, stated that in a regular class, the special education services and programs that will form part of the placement must be defined as part of the placement.[16]

In the case of special education placement, while the Tribunal has noted that services and programs generally are defined by the special education placement, the Tribunal has also made clear that when considering a special class placement, it will consider special education programs and services delivered in the special education class as part of the placement where it is necessary to do so in order to determine a placement that meets the educational needs of the student:[17]

> Because of the intertwining of placement and program in the autism program, the Tribunal believes that it is necessary to hear the case on appeal in order to understand the student's needs and the proposed placement. The Tribunal needs to determine if the placement [in a special education class with partial integration] can be tailored to meet the student's needs and strengths.

---

14 We expect that this consideration will become increasingly important in the larger classes authorized for students with different exceptionalities — see *Operation Of Schools — General*, R.R.O. 1990, Reg. 298, s. 31(*g*); *J.K. & The Toronto District School Board* (2009-03-12), File No. 2008-04 (Ont. Spec. Ed. (Eng.) Trib.).

15 *I. & Toronto District School Board* (2005-11-17), File No. 46c (Ont. Spec. Ed. (Eng.) Trib.), at p. 22. See also *W. & Limestone District School Board* (2005-12-15) File No. 50 (Ont. Spec. Ed. (Eng.) Trib.); *D. & Toronto District School Board* (2002-12-24), File No. 30 (Ont. Spec. Ed. (Eng.) Trib.); *L. & Le Conseil scolaire de District Catholique du Centre-Est de l'Ontario* (2001-11-02), File No. 29 (Ont. Spec. Ed. (Fr.) Trib.); and *L. & Conseil des écoles catholiques de langue française du Centre-Est de l'Ontario* (2004-12-02), File No. 42 (Ont. Spec. Ed. (Fr.) Trib.).

16 *I. & Toronto District School Board*, *supra*.

17 *T. & Peterborough, Victoria, Northumberland, Clarington Catholic DSB* (2006-09-14), File No. 56 (Ont. Spec. Ed. (Eng.) Trib.).

Generically, placements can extend from a "regular class placement with monitoring" to full-time placement in a provincial or demonstration school, to a whole range of placements in between.[18] Some of the placements in between include the following:[19]

- "Regular class with indirect support": the student is in a regular class and support is provided to the classroom teacher by way of consultation from experts in providing programming for the student;
- "Regular class with resource assistance": the student is in a regular class, but is provided with direct assistance from a special education teacher, either on a one-on-one basis in the regular class or as part of a small group;
- "Regular class with withdrawal assistance": the student spends more than 50% of the school day in a regular class and is withdrawn from the regular class for the balance of the time to work with a special education teacher, either individually or as part of a group, usually in a special education resource room.
- "Special education class with partial integration": the student spends more than 50% of the school day in a special education class and is integrated in a regular class for less than 50% of the day.
- "Full time special education class": the student is placed, full-time, in a special education class.[20]

---

18 Ontario Schools for the Blind and Deaf are generally referred to as "provincial schools". They include: The W. Ross Macdonald School (blind and deaf-blind students), The Sir James Whitney School (deaf students) and The Ernest C. Drury School (deaf students). See Ontario Deputy Minister of Education, "Policy/Program Memorandum No. 1: Ontario Schools for the Blind and Deaf as Resource Centres" (Toronto: Ministry of Education, 1986), available online at http://www.edu.gov.on.ca/extra/eng/ppm/1.html. Demonstration schools are also provincially operated schools that are geared to students with severe learning disabilities who require the facilities of a residential school. There are three demonstration schools in Ontario: Robarts School, the Sagonaska School and the Trillium School. School boards can refer students to a demonstration school upon the recommendation of an IPRC; however, decisions regarding admission are made by the Provincial Committee on Hearing Disabilities. Where the school board or parents (or the student, if aged 18 years or more) disagree with the Committee's decision and request an appeal, the Director of the Special Education and Provincial Schools Branch will appoint a review committee to hear the appeal. See Ontario Deputy Minister of Education, "Policy/Program Memorandum No. 89: The Residential Demonstration Schools for Students with Learning Disabilities: General Information and Details of the Referral Process" (Toronto: Ministry of Education, 1990), available online at http://www.edu.gov.on.ca/extra/eng/ppm/89.html.

19 The placements are set out, as of the date of writing, on the Ministry of Education's web page on "The Identification, Placement and Review Committee", http://www.edu.gov.on.ca/eng/general/elemsec/speced/identifi.html.

20 A continuing question is the extent to which the placement of a student identified as having both a behaviour exceptionality and a learning disability in a self-contained

Placements can also include various combinations or permutations of the above placements. For example, a student in a special education class might be withdrawn for a portion of each day for one-on-one support with a special education teacher or aide; a student might spend half the day in a regular class with support and the other half in a resource class where he or she receives either one-to-one instruction or instruction in a small group. A regular classroom or special education class placement might involve modification of the regular curriculum for the student or the creation of an alternative curriculum.

In one appeal to the Special Education Tribunal, the school board did not offer self-contained gifted classes at the secondary level, which was the placement being sought by the parents for their gifted son; however, the school board did congregate gifted students in certain regular university-stream grade 9 classes and provided them there with a differentiated gifted program in that context; the Special Education Tribunal ordered placement in a gifted congregated (cluster) program.[21]

In addition, in at least one case, the Tribunal has approved a placement of home instruction.[22] "Home instruction" was defined in the school board's Special Education Plan to mean a modified school day with individual instruction that could be carried out in a location other than a school. This case involved an exceptional student, diagnosed with autism, who displayed outbursts of very aggressive behavior that prompted the school board to conclude that special education services could not be provided for him at a school. The specific placement proposed was modified home instruction, which would be provided in one of the school board's buildings with full-time support educational aide. A home instruction teacher would provide seven hours per week to assist with the academic program. The principal of the secondary school that the student would have otherwise attended was to be responsible for supervising the placement.

A good example of the manner in which the Tribunal has considered programs and services as part of the placement is *R. & Carleton Roman Catholic Separate School Board.*[23] In this case, the Ontario Special Education (English) Tribunal found that the placement of a student identified as gifted did not meet the student's needs. The reasons for this were, first, that the frequency and intensity of special education activities designed and provided for the student were insufficient to meet the needs of someone with his level of giftedness; second, the nature of the special education placement did not address the discrepancy between the achievement level customarily expected

---

behaviour class is a different placement than a placement in a self-contained learning disability class and is, therefore, appealable.

21 *Y. & X.X. District School Board* (2002-02-18), File No. 31 (Ont. Spec. Ed. (Eng.) Trib.).

22 *E. & Dryden Board of Education* (1998), File No. 24 (Ont. Spec. Ed. (Eng.) Trib.).

23 (1988-12-16), File No. 17 (Ont. Spec. Ed. (Eng.) Trib.).

of a student of his age and what he was capable of doing; and third, there was a lack of school board impetus in coming to grips with and managing the student's case. The Tribunal determined that the student's needs would be best met in a congregated class comprised of his gifted peers and ordered a placement in a congregated class. Since the school board did not have such a class, it was directed to purchase the placement from its co-terminus board.

There have been other cases where the Tribunal considered programs and services to be part of a particular placement and has given directions with respect to programs or services to be provided in that particular placement:

- In *S. & Carlton Board of Education*,[24] the Tribunal ordered that all future Individual Education Plans include a statement that the student was described by a physician as being environmentally sensitive.
- In *O. & The Wentworth County Board of Education*,[25] the student was identified as deaf. The appeal involved the decision by the school board to maintain the student's placement in a regular class with resource withdrawal, but to replace the resource teacher, who had been fluent in cueing, and to provide an aide fluent in cueing in the resource classroom, as well as in the regular class. The Tribunal ordered that the student continue in a regular class for about 50% of the day with a cueing aide, but that the school board provide a teacher of the deaf for the balance of the day and ensure that an effective mechanism was established to co-ordinate the various aspects of the student's program and provide for continuous assessment of the student and evaluation of his program.

The cases listed above were all decided prior to the replacement of the original regulation governing IPRCs and Special Education Appeal Boards ("SEABs") with O. Reg. 181/98. The current regulation requires IPRCs to "consider whether placement in a regular class, with appropriate special education services . . . would meet the pupil's needs".[26] This provision makes clear that the IPRC must consider special education programs and services that could be provided in the placement.[27]

Some of the cases in which the Tribunal has made orders on placement that include directions on services and/or programs to be provided as part of the particular placement are set out below:

- In *D. & Windsor Essex Catholic District School Board*,[28] parents appealed an IPRC placement decision for their child who had been identified with multiple exceptionalities. The IPRC's placement

[24] (1993-04-02), File No. 18 (Ont. Spec. Ed. (Eng.) Trib.).
[25] (1987-06-05), File No. 12 (Ont. Spec. Ed. (Eng.) Trib.).
[26] O. Reg. 181/98, s. 17(1).
[27] *Ibid.*, s. 16.
[28] (2003-09-30), File No. 38 (Ont. Spec. Ed. (Eng.) Trib.).

decision was "Regular Class/Resource Assistance" and included a recommendation that the child "Continue in present placement with Resource Support as deemed appropriate by school personnel". The parents appealed this decision on the basis that the decision was neither clear or specific enough to permit them to make an informed decision about the placement. The Special Education Tribunal rejected the board's objection that the parents were seeking to appeal services and program that were not appealable. The Special Education Tribunal held that, in this case, the issue of appropriate program was intertwined with the issue of placement, such that if the special education program provided to the student were inappropriate, then the placement would also be inappropriate.

- In *I. & Toronto District School Board*,[29] the Special Education Tribunal ordered, as part of the placement, that an educational assistant be provided for a minimum of 50% of the student's time in the regular class and that "a co-ordinated intensive mathematics and language program, planned, implemented and evaluated by a teacher with special education qualifications . . . be delivered by withdrawal support."
- In *W. & Limestone District School Board*,[30] the Special Education Tribunal decided that it had jurisdiction to deal with an appeal by a father regarding the provision of an American Sign Language ("ASL") interpreter in the regular class placement. This case was somewhat unique, insofar as the parents of the child were not in agreement on the placement. The mother wished that the child — who was identified as exceptional, deaf and hard of hearing — continue in the placement of Regular Class with Withdrawal, so that the child could work with a teacher of the deaf and hard of hearing, while the father, who was deaf himself, wanted the placement to be changed to Regular Class with Resource Support (and no withdrawal) and a full time ASL interpreter.
- In *T. & Peterborough, Victoria, Northumberland, Clarington Catholic District School Board*,[31] the Special Education Tribunal ordered not only that the school board place the student in a special education class with partial integration, but made specific orders regarding the development of an IEP "with appropriate measurable communication and academic goals"; that the board work with the appellant and consultants from the Geneva Centre to develop and implement behaviour strategies that allowed the student to learn within the autism program; that there be an increase of the amount of time the student spent with the speech and language pathologist to compensate

---

29 (2005-11-17), File No. 46c (Ont. Spec. Ed. (Eng.) Trib.).

30 (2005-12-15) File No. 50 (Ont. Spec. Ed. (Eng.) Trib.).

31 (2006-09-14), File No. 56 (Ont. Spec. Ed. (Eng.) Trib.).

for the time the student had spent at home on suspensions from the board and that a Transition plan be created for the student. In this case, it appears that the student had lost considerable time from school through suspensions and an expulsion for behaviours associated with the student's diagnosis; while there had been some home instruction, the services of the speech and language teacher for which SIP funds had been provided were not part of the home instruction.

- In *C. & Toronto District School Board*,[32] the Special Education Tribunal confirmed the IPRC's change of placement from Regular Class to a Special Education Class designed in a middle school setting, but also ordered that the placement include "[i]ntegration to further develop the child's social skills"; that "[t]hese opportunities should occur during non-academic activities to the greatest extent possible, so that the child can interact with other children in the school"; and "[d]irect consistent teaching of an augmentative communication system to help the child learn a system to communicate [the child's] needs independently." There was no disagreement by the school board during the hearing about the appropriateness of including the programming and services in the placement, but the parent had expressed a specific concern about integration and the teaching of an augmentative communication system.[33]

While the Special Education Tribunal has heard appeals based on services or programming, it has distinguished between appeals on placement where special education services and programming are intertwined with the placement and appeals that are "primarily or exclusively focused on such matters as programming, services, class size, the provision of educational assistant support, staff qualifications, and so on"[34] or on the experience or expertise of staff.[35] The Special Education Tribunal has indicated that it does not have jurisdiction to deal with appeals that are made for the purpose of seeking orders on such issues.[36] These issues do not relate to the determination or definition of the placement, but rather relate to the actual delivery of services, which is a matter for the school board to deal with in accordance with its obligations under the *Education Act* and regulations.

The issue of whether Intensive Behavioural Intervention ("IBI") is either considered a placement or a special education service or program for students with autism was dealt with by the Special Education Tribunal in a series of

32 (2006-10-02), File No. 55 (Ont. Spec. Ed. (Eng.) Trib.).

33 *C. & Toronto District School Board*, *supra*, at p. 15.

34 *W.F. & The Ottawa Catholic School Board* (2008-05-26), File No. 2008-02 (Ont. Spec. Ed. (Eng.) Trib.).

35 *L. & Conseil des écoles catholiques de langue française du Centre-Est de l'Ontario* (2004-12-02), File No. 42 (Ont. Spec. Ed. (Fr.) Trib.).

36 *Ibid.*, and *W.F. & The Ottawa Catholic School Board*, *supra*, footnote 34.

appeals involving students with autism. IBI is a program of therapy, developed by Dr. Ivor Lovaas in the early 1990s, based on applied behaviour principles articulated by B.F. Skinner and delivered by a trained therapist under the supervision of a clinical psychologist. The Tribunal made clear that IBI is neither education nor an educational service or placement. The Tribunal pointed out that education is delivered under the direction of a teacher.[37] The Tribunal drew a distinction between IBI and applied behavioural principles and noted that teachers do receive training in applied behaviour principles in teacher's college and regularly use them in classroom instruction.[38]

STANDARD TO BE USED IN DETERMINING PLACEMENTS

The only guidance provided by the *Education Act* for measuring the adequacy of a placement is found in section 8(3). This section requires the Minister to "provide for the parents or guardians to appeal the *appropriateness* of the special education placement" (emphasis added).

This somewhat imprecise language was considered by a court in an application for judicial review of the first Tribunal decision. In *Dolmage v. Muskoka Board of Education*,[39] the Divisional Court stated as follows:

> I cannot help but think that the language of s. [8(3)] should not be read in any more absolute sense than the words reasonably require. To do so would ignore the practicalities previously adverted to. The idea of an "appropriate" special education programme, and the "appropriateness" of the placement of the pupil, surely involves the idea of suitability, and is not to be confused with a placement which amounts to perfection.

The court's comments are still applicable today.

---

37 *C. & Simcoe County District School Board* (2003-09-15), File No. 34 (Ont. Spec. Ed. (Eng.) Trib.), affd 197 O.A.C. 331, 139 A.C.W.S. (3d) 681, *sub nom. Clough v. Simcoe County District School Board* (Ont. S.C.J. (Div. Ct.)); *C. & Dufferin-Peel Catholic District School Board* (2003-09-18), File No. 35 (Ont. Spec. Ed. (Eng.) Trib.); *T. & Simcoe County District School Board* (2004-05-28), File No. 41 (Ont. Spec. Ed. (Eng.) Trib.); *W. & Simcoe County District School Board* (2004-05-27), File No. 40 (Ont. Spec. Ed. (Eng.) Trib.). As well, see Ontario Deputy Minister of Education, "Policy/Program Memorandum No. 140: Incorporating Methods of Applied Behaviour Analysis (ABA) into Programs for Students with Autism Spectrum Disorders (ASD)" (Toronto: Ministry of Education, 2007), available online at http://www.edu.gov.on.ca/extra/eng/ppm/140.html, gives direction to school boards regarding the use of Applied Behavioural Analysis and calls for closer ties between school boards and agencies in the community that specialize in autism.

38 The Ontario Ministry of Education has also issued "Policy/Program Memorandum 140", *ibid.*, which gives directions to school boards on "Incorporating Methods of Applied Behaviour Analysis (ABA) into Programs for Students with Autism Spectrum Disorders (ASD)" and requires each school board to provide an Applied Behaviour Analysis ("ABA") program.

39 (1985), 15 D.L.R. (4th) 741 at p. 749, 49 O.R. (2d) 546 (Div. Ct.).

In the first two decades following the introduction of special education into the statutory scheme for education in Ontario,[40] disputes over the standard to be used for measuring placement arose most often in the context of parents seeking "integrated" placements for their severely developmentally disabled children. The litigation resulting from these disputes has involved both the *Human Rights Code* and the *Canadian Charter of Rights and Freedoms* and has resulted in decisions that have served, finally, to define the criteria to be used by school boards in making placement decisions.

A review of the historical context gives focus to the criteria that are currently used to determine the appropriateness of a special education placement.

Historical Context: The Integration Movement

Bill 82[41] was introduced at a time when children with severe developmental disabilities (then referred to as "trainable retarded" or "trainable mentally retarded") were excluded from the mainstream of education in Ontario. Indeed, it was heralded as legislation that established universal access to all Ontario students. It did so by incorporating into the *Education Act* a definition of "exceptional pupil", which included all students, including those identified as "trainable retarded", and by removing admissibility requirements that had applied to these students.[42] It also required all school boards to provide — either directly or through purchase of services from other school boards — special education programs and services for their exceptional students.

Bill 82 removed a number of barriers that had existed for students with developmental disabilities in accessing the education system, but it also required that segregated schools and classes be provided for "trainable retarded pupils".[43] While a few school boards in Ontario — primarily Roman Catholic separate school boards — put fully integrated placements into place, the requirement that separate facilities be created and maintained for "trainable retarded pupils" was seen by many as a big step forward from the days when youngsters with severe developmental delays were excluded, for the most part, from the educational system. Prior to Bill 82, when a student was not in one of the few school board jurisdictions where educational services were being provided by the local board, the only educational services available were provided by local parent groups (*e.g.*, local Associations for the Mentally Retarded, now called Associations for Community Living), sometimes in special schools, or sometimes in settings such as church basements.

40 See Chapter 1, "Introduction".

41 *Education Amendment Act, 1980*, S.O. 1980, c. 61.

42 Anne Keeton Wilson, *A Consumer's Guide to Bill 82: Special Education in Ontario* (Toronto: OISE Press, 1983), at p. 9.

43 In fact, the manner of the funding at the time encouraged the use of specialized settings, particularly in respect of students with developmental disabilities.

The movement towards integration of all students into regular classes was occurring across Canada and the United States, driven, in a large part, by parent advocacy groups. Further, at the point Bill 82 was introduced in 1980, a debate was underway amongst academics in the education community over the issue of "segregated"[44] placements versus "integrated" placements, especially in respect of students with developmental disabilities. In Ontario, those spearheading the integration movement turned to legal forums to push for fuller integration of students identified as "trainable retarded", often supplying counsel for parents, to represent them to fight for full regular class placements for their children.

Initially, parents and their advocates seeking to achieve fuller integration for children with developmental delays in the education system focused on the Special Education Tribunal. The Tribunal heard appeals from a number of parents of students with developmental delays seeking to have their children placed in regular classes instead of segregated classes, usually based on the argument that their children had the same right to be in the regular class as non-disabled children; however, early on, the Tribunal made clear that it would examine the circumstances of each individual child and make decisions on placement issues based on the educational needs and best interests of the individual child rather than on philosophical views. The comments of one Tribunal summarized the approach taken by all:[45]

[44] At the time, the word "segregated" was used to denote a placement outside the regular class in a special education class that might be located in regular school or in a school for the "trainable retarded" (now, "developmentally disabled").

[45] As it turned out, in almost all of these cases, the Tribunal decided that the needs of the student required placement in a self-contained class. In *L. & York Region Board of Education* (1985-09-10), File No. 7 (Ont. Spec. Ed. (Eng.) Trib.), the Tribunal rejected placements in both a "class for the trainable retarded" (supported by the school board) or the regular class requested by the parents and ordered placement in a "class for multi-handicapped pupils". In *F. & Nipissing Board of Education* (1986-07-18), File No. 9 (N.E. Reg. Spec. Ed. (Eng.) Trib.), the IPRC's determination of placement in a class for the trainable retarded was upheld, rejecting the parents' position that the student should be re-identified as "educable" and placed in a regular classroom with a teacher's aide for 50% of the day with remaining time spent with a speech pathologist and occupational therapist or, alternatively, in a basic learning skills program in a neighbourhood school. In *M. & Brant County Board of Education* (1986-07-17), File No. 11 (Ont. Spec. Ed. (Eng.) Trib.), the Tribunal upheld the IPRC's determination of placement in a "school for trainable retarded pupils", rejecting the parents' proposed placement in a grade 8 class in the student's neighbourhood school "with an individually adapted curriculum and the support of a teacher's aide" or, alternatively, a "trainable retarded class" in a public school. In *R. & York Board of Education* (1986), File No. 10 (Ont. Spec. Ed. (Eng.) Trib.), the Tribunal confirmed the IPRC's determination of placement in a "primary, self-contained class for slow learners", with a direction that the fullest possible opportunities for integration be provided and rejected the parents' argument of placement in an age-appropriate class in the neighbourhood school with a diagnostician and resource teacher's assistance in the classroom or resource withdrawal, or a teacher's aide.

> It is the firm opinion of this Tribunal that the wholesale integration of exceptional pupils into regular classes, solely on the basis of philosophical principle, untempered by due and informed consideration of each individual situation, is directly counter to the best interests of all pupils. Further, it is the conviction of the Tribunal that the assumption of rigid, doctrinaire positions on the issue, not only threatens the very future of integration as a desirable practice, but specifically, in cases such as the child's, serves only to erode the good will and reason that must obtain if all parties are to act in the child's best interests.[46]

In the meantime, advocates for integration sought other avenues to pursue fuller integration for children with developmental delays, including making complaints to the Ontario Human Rights Commission and bringing actions in the courts under the *Canadian Charter of Rights and Freedoms.*

The case that finally determined the issue, however, started with an appeal of placement to the Special Education Tribunal. *E. v. Brant County Board of Education,*[47] began with an appeal of the placement of Emily Eaton. The appeal focused directly on the issue of self-contained (segregated) class versus integrated placement in a regular class. Emily had no established communication system and, additionally, had severe developmental delays including a severe intellectual handicap. She had originally been placed in a regular kindergarten class and then in a regular grade 1 class with a full-time aide. At the end of her grade 1 year, the IPRC recommended that Emily be placed in a self-contained class. Her parents appealed, resulting in a stay of placement in the regular class, so that, by the time the case reached the Tribunal, Emily was in the regular grade 2 class. At the hearing, the parents squarely put their arguments in support of a fully integrated placement on the footing of equity principles under the *Human Rights Code* and the *Canadian Charter of Rights and Freedoms.* They argued that a placement outside the regular class discriminated against Emily on the basis of her disability and violated her equality rights under the Charter. The Tribunal heard evidence that:

- In the grade 2 class, Emily often fell asleep and this falling asleep seemed to be her way of shutting down when she was over-stimulated.
- Emily would on occasion vocalize in a loud and disturbing way until she was taken out into the hall, where her aide would walk her up and down the hall, an activity that she appeared to enjoy.
- During group activities, the other children were increasingly interacting with the aide instead of Emily, despite the aide's efforts — in short, Emily's interaction with her peers was limited.
- If not watched carefully, Emily would put small things in her mouth.

---

46 *R. & York Region Board of Education*, *supra*, at p. 26.

47 *E. & Brant County Board of Education* (1993-11-19), File No. 19 (Ont. Spec. Ed. (Eng.) Trib.), appn for judicial review dismissed 71 O.A.C. 69 *sub nom. Eaton v. Board of Education (Brant County)*, revd 123 D.L.R. (4th) 43, 27 C.R.R. (2d) 53 (Ont. C.A.), revd 142 D.L.R. (4th) 385, [1997] 1 S.C.R. 241.

The Tribunal concluded that the regular class placement was not meeting Emily's needs and stated:[48]

> [T]he nature and extent of immediate adult intervention and care essential to meet the student's profound intellectual, physical and emotional needs even minimally, has the counter-productive effect of isolating the student, of segregating the student in the theoretically integrated setting.

The test that the Tribunal applied in upholding the decision of the IPRC on placement was: what placement best met Emily Eaton's special needs?[49]

The parents brought an application for judicial review of the Tribunal's decision to the Ontario Divisional Court, which dismissed the application. The parents appealed to the Court of Appeal, where they were successful in getting the decision of the Tribunal quashed.

The Court of Appeal held that the normal placement for a student is in the regular class and that the reason Emily was excluded from the regular class was because she had a disability. The Court of Appeal found that this was discriminatory, unless her parents consented to the placement outside the regular class, and concluded that, since the *Education Act* did not include a presumption in favour of the regular class, the *Education Act* was contrary to section 15 of the Charter. The Court of Appeal held that section 15 of the Charter required that all reasonable efforts should be made to integrate the disabled into the regular class. The court stated: "In short, the Charter requires that, *regardless of its perceived pedagogical merit*, a non-consensual exclusionary placement be recognized as discriminatory and not be resorted to unless alternatives are proven inadequate" (emphasis added).[50]

The school board appealed to the Supreme Court of Canada, which reversed the Court of Appeal's decision and restored the decision of the Special Education Tribunal. While the Court of Appeal had focused on the location of the placement (*i.e.*, a regular class versus a "segregated" class), the Supreme Court of Canada focused on the pedagogical reasons for the placement. The Supreme Court of Canada recognized that the pedagogical principles underlying the placement in a special class were directed towards ameliorating those disadvantages that prevented Emily from benefiting from an education in a regular class. The Supreme Court of Canada stated:[51]

> In some cases, special education is a necessary adaptation of the mainstream world which enables some disabled pupils access to the learning environment they need in order to have an equal opportunity in education. While integration should be recognized as the norm of general application because of the benefits it generally provides, a presumption in favour of integrated schooling would work to the disadvantage of pupils who require special education in order to achieve equality. Schools focussed on the needs of the blind or deaf and special education

---

48 *E. & Brant County Board of Education*, *supra*, (Ont. Spec. Ed. (Eng.) Trib.), at p. 44.
49 *Ibid.*, at p. 38.
50 *Ibid.* (C.A.), at p. 65.
51 *Ibid.*, at para. 69.

> for students with learning disabilities indicate the positive aspects of segregated education placement. Integration can be either a benefit or a burden depending on whether the individual can profit from the advantages that integration provides.

The Supreme Court of Canada went on to say:[52]

> A decision-making body must determine whether the integrated setting can be adapted to meet the special needs of an exceptional child. Where this is not possible, that is, where aspects of the integrated setting which cannot reasonably be changed interfere with meeting the child's special needs, the principle of accommodation will require a special education placement outside of this setting. For older children and those who are able to communicate their wishes and needs, their own views will play an important role in the determination of best interests. For younger children, and those like Emily, who are either incapable of making a choice or have a very limited means of communicating their wishes, the decision-maker must make this determination on the basis of the other evidence before it.

As a result, while consideration must be given to whether an exceptional pupil's needs can be met in a regular class, the educational needs of the student must be given a primary focus in determining placement. Where reasonable modifications cannot be made to a regular class placement to make that placement work, a placement outside the regular class will not be discriminatory, as long as the placement is in the student's best interests.

The Supreme Court of Canada also confirmed the standard of review adopted by the Tribunal in determining appeals on placement — namely, which placement meets the pupils' best interests.[53]

The Regulatory Standard

Immediately prior to the release of the Supreme Court of Canada's decision in the *Eaton* case, the Ontario government established a new test that IPRCs must consider in making placement decisions:[54]

> 17 (1) When making a placement decision . . . the committee shall, before considering the option of placement in a special education class, consider whether placement in a regular class, with appropriate special education services,
>
> (a) would meet the pupil's needs; and
>
> (b) is consistent with parental preferences.
>
> (2) If, after considering all of the information obtained by it or submitted to it under section 15 that it considers relevant, the committee is satisfied that placement in a regular class would meet the pupil's needs and is consistent with

---

52 *Ibid.* (S.C.C.), at para. 77.

53 This standard was reconfirmed by the Ontario Divisional Court in *Pokonzie v. Board of Education (Roman Catholic Separate) of Sudbury District* (1997), 104 O.A.C. 367, 75 A.C.W.S. (3d) 469.

54 O. Reg. 181/98, s. 17 and see also s. 23(6). It should be noted that this regulation had been drafted prior to the decision of the Supreme Court of Canada and, in fact, was put before the Supreme Court of Canada as part of the Ministry of Education's case.

parental preferences, the committee shall decide in favour of placement in a regular class.

The requirements set out in this provision meet the standards imposed by the Supreme Court of Canada in the *Eaton* case. It should be noted that, while parent wishes must be considered, those wishes are not determinative of what the placement will be. This is in keeping with the Supreme Court of Canada's view that the IPRC has the authority to make the final decision on placement, based on the "best interests of the student" test.

IMPLEMENTING A PLACEMENT

Once a placement has been determined, it cannot be implemented by a school board unless one of the following events occurs:

- the parent has given written consent to the placement;
- the parent has failed to appeal a placement decision by the IPRC within 30 days of receipt by the parent of notice of the decision;[55]
- where the parent has appealed to an SEAB, the parent has failed to appeal a placement decision by the school board, following the receipt of the recommendations of the SEAB, within 30 days of receipt by the parent of notice of the decision;[56] or
- where the parent has appealed to the Special Education Tribunal, the parent has abandoned the appeal or the appeal has been dismissed.[57] The decision of whether or not the appeal has been abandoned will be made by either the Tribunal or the Secretary of the Tribunal.

Where a school board is able to implement a placement, it must do so as soon as possible after the occurrence of the event that permits the school board to proceed to make the placement.[58] Where the parent has not consented to the placement, written notice must be provided by the school board of the implementation of the placement.[59]

Where the Tribunal orders a placement different than that argued for by either of the parties to the appeal — as was the case in *O. & The Wentworth County Board of Education*[60] and *L. & York Region Board of Education*[61] — the placement ordered by the Tribunal must be implemented.[62]

---

55 See Chapter 6, "The Identification, Placement and Review Committee".
56 See Chapter 10, "The First Stage of Appeal".
57 O. Reg. 181/98, ss. 20(1), 25(1) and 31(1).
58 *Ibid.*, ss. 20(2) and 25(2).
59 *Ibid.*, ss. 20(3) and 25(3).
60 (1987-06-05), File No. 12 (Ont. Spec. Ed. (Eng.) Trib.).
61 (1985-09-10), File No. 7 (Ont. Spec. Ed. (Eng.) Trib.).
62 *Education Act*, s. 57(4).

PLACEMENTS PENDING AN APPEAL AND TRANSITIONAL PLACEMENTS

Placements Pending an Appeal

When a student is already in a special education placement and the parents are appealing the decision, the pre-existing placement continues during the period of the appeal, unless the parties agree otherwise or unless the appeal is abandoned. This is the case whether the appeal is to the SEAB or the Tribunal.

An interesting situation arises where the IPRC decision being appealed from relates to the transition from elementary school to secondary school. It is often the case that a placement that exists at the elementary school level is not provided at the secondary school level, in which case an issue can arise regarding where the student is placed during the "stay of placement" while the parent's appeal is determined by the Special Education Tribunal: Does the student remain in the elementary school placement (with appropriate adjustments to reflect a grade 9 curriculum)? This situation has arisen in at least one case where the parents of a gifted student appealed his change of placement for his grade 9 year from a self-contained gifted class to a placement in a regular class with enrichment. No gifted classes existed at his secondary school. The board offered him the opportunity of remaining at the elementary school, but with a grade 9 teacher, or moving to secondary school with the offered placement. The Special Education Tribunal's view on this situation was that neither of these two opportunities was appropriate, but that a third option was — the third option being a placement in a cluster of 3 to 15 gifted grade 9 and 10 students whose core subjects were provided at an enriched level in classes filled by other students who had to apply to gain entry.[63] The Special Education Tribunal made the point that, since the student's peers had moved on, keeping him in elementary school meant that he was no longer with his peers. The Special Education Tribunal made clear its view that, where the student is moving to secondary school and a similar placement to the student's last elementary school placement does not exist, during any "stay of placement" pending an appeal on a change of placement, a placement in a secondary school must be found that is as close as possible to the elementary school placement that the student is leaving.

Further, some parents of exceptional students prefer their children to remain in the elementary school environment, which is much less "hectic" and more structured than that of a secondary school; however, grade placement — that is, promotional decisions — are to be made by the principal[64] and are usually distinct from placement decisions, such that the promotion of a student — even where the parent has appealed the placement of a student

---

63 *Y. & X.X. District School Board* (2002-02-18), File No. 31 (Ont. Spec. Ed. (Eng.) Trib.).

64 *Education Act*, s. 265(g).

because the parent does not wish the student to leave elementary school and move to secondary school — is not generally a proper subject matter for appeal. The promotion of a student from elementary school to secondary school has been at the heart of several appeals to the Tribunal;[65] in fact, it is generally regarded as important for a student to remain with his/her age appropriate peers.[66]

Transitional Placements

No student can be denied an education program pending a meeting of the IPRC or a decision under section 9 of O. Reg. 181/98. In such a case, the program provided must be appropriate to the pupil's apparent strengths and needs. It must also be consistent with the principles underlying section 17 of O. Reg. 181/98, discussed previously under the heading "The Regulatory Standard"; that is, consideration must first be given to a regular class placement and a placement outside the regular class may only be made where a placement in a regular class with appropriate special education services would not meet the student's needs. Parental preferences should be considered by the principal in determining a transitional education program. Appropriate education services must be provided to meet the student's apparent need.[67]

MINISTRY DIRECTIVES REGARDING PROGRAMMING

While programming for identified students is generally left to school boards to develop based on current pedagogical principles and curriculum directives, the Ontario Ministry of Education has issued directives in the form of Policy/Program Memoranda ("PPMs") for certain exceptionalities:

- PPM 8: "Learning Disabilities";[68]
- PPM 76C: "Alternative Educational Programs and Services for Deaf, Blind, and Deaf-Blind Exceptional Pupils";[69]

---

65 *M. & Simcoe County Board of Education* (1993-04-02), File No. 17 (Ont. Spec. Ed. (Eng.) Trib.); *I. & Timmins Board of Education* (1997-05-09), File No. 23 (Ont. Spec. Ed. (Eng.) Trib.).

66 *T. & Peterborough, Victoria, Northumberland, Clarington Catholic District School Board* (2005-07-25), File No. 45 (Ont. Spec. Ed. (Eng.) Trib.).

67 O. Reg. 181/98, s. 9.

68 Ontario Deputy Minister of Education, "Policy/Program Memorandum No. 8: Learning Disabilities" (Toronto: Ministry of Education, 1982), available online at http://www.edu.gov.on.ca/extra/eng/ppm/8.html.

69 Ontario Deputy Minister of Education, "Policy/Program Memorandum No. 76C: Alternative Educational Programs and Services for Deaf, Blind, and Deaf-Blind Pupils" (Toronto: Ministry of Education, 1991), available online at http://www.edu.gov.on.ca/extra/eng/ppm/76c.html.

- PPM140: "Incorporating Methods of Applied Behaviour Analysis (ABA)[70] into Programs For Students With Autism Spectrum Disorders (ASD);[71]
- For exceptional students who are suspended or expelled, PPM 141: "School Board Programs For Students On Long-Term Suspension"; PPM 142: "School Board Programs For Expelled Students".[72]

---

70 The Ministry distinguishes between Applied Behavioural Analysis principles, which are based on general principles developed by B.F. Skinner, and IBI therapy, developed by Dr. Ivor Lovass. The latter, which is based on ABA principles, is a therapy delivered by therapists under the direction of a clinical psychologist to children with autism. The Ontario (English) Special Education Tribunal noted, in *C. & Simcoe County District School Board* (2003-09-15), File No. 34 (Ont. Spec. Ed. (Eng.) Trib.), affd 197 O.A.C. 331, 139 A.C.W.S. (3d) 681, *sub nom. Clough v. Simcoe County District School Board* (Ont. S.C.J. (Div. Ct.)), that IBI is not education. The Tribunal also noted that ABA principles are taught in teacher's college and are incorporated into the practice of teaching.

71 *Op. cit.*, footnote 37.

72 Ontario Deputy Minister of Education, "Policy/Program Memorandum No. 141: School Board Programs for Students on Long-Term Suspension" (Toronto: Ministry of Education, 2007), available online at http://www.edu.gov.on.ca/extra/eng/ppm/141.html, and Ontario Deputy Minister of Education, "Policy/Program Memorandum No. 142: School Board Programs for Expelled Students" (Toronto: Ministry of Education, 2007), available online at http://www.edu.gov.on.ca/extra/eng/ppm/142.html. See also *Suspension and Expulsion of Pupils*, O. Reg. 472/07.

6

The Identification, Placement and Review Committee

INTRODUCTION

The responsibility for identifying a student as an exceptional pupil and determining a placement rests, in the first instance, with the Identification, Placement and Review Committee (the "IPRC"). In this chapter, we discuss the composition of the IPRC, the scope of its powers, the manner in which it carries out its responsibilities and the implementation of the IPRC's decision.

ESTABLISHMENT OF THE IPRC

Every school board is required to establish at least one committee for the identification and placement of exceptional pupils.[1] No upper limit is placed on the number of IPRCs that a school board may establish; nor is there any definition of the types of IPRCs that may be set up. Therefore, school boards have flexibility in setting up IPRCs to meet their needs. A school board may decide to establish IPRCs that are dedicated to dealing with only elementary or secondary school students; alternatively, IPRCs may be established to deal solely with the students who reside in a particular geographic area. A separate IPRC may be established for each school or for a group of schools. IPRCs may also be established to deal with particular exceptionalities. Such an IPRC could be composed of members who have expertise in a particular exceptionality, in order to permit more in-depth recommendations to be made about the special education programs and services that might be appropriate in a particular case.

Each IPRC must consist of three or more members. It is mandatory that at least one member of the committee be either:

- a principal employed by the school board;

[1] *Identification and Placement of Exceptional Pupils*, O. Reg. 181/98, s. 10.

- a supervisory officer employed by the board; or
- a supervisory officer employed by another school board whose services are provided under a Minister-approved agreement with another school board.[2]

This mandatory appointee may designate another person to act in his or her place. It is not necessary to obtain the school board's approval for such a designation. The only limitation on this power to designate a replacement is that the person designated must also be either a principal or supervisory officer employed by the school board or a supervisory officer employed by another school board whose services are provided under a Minister-approved agreement with another school board.[3]

In appointing the other members of an IPRC, a school board is limited only in that the school board may not appoint one of its trustees to sit on an IPRC.[4] While, normally, the balance of the committee will be made up of teachers, special education consultants or other special education professionals employed by the school board, a school board is not limited to appointing employees of the school board. It may be helpful, in some circumstances, to appoint outside professionals, such as medical doctors, social workers, psychologists or counsellors to an IPRC;[5] however, where a school board appoints a non-employee to an IPRC, parental consent (or the consent of the student if aged 16 years or older) is necessary in order for the non-employee to have access to the student's personal information.[6]

A chair must be appointed for each IPRC and the manner of selection of the chair is left to the school board to determine in its discretion.[7] The school

---

2 *Ibid.*, s. 11(1) and (2).

3 *Ibid.*, s. 11(3) and (4).

4 *Ibid.*, s. 11(5).

5 The appointment of an external professional may increase parental confidence in the process where non-employees are viewed as more neutral than school board staff.

6 *Municipal Freedom of Information and Protection of Privacy Act*, R.S.O. 1990, c. M.56 ("*MFIPPA*"), ss. 32 and 54.

7 O. Reg. 181/98, s. 10. Provincial schools are schools operated by the Ministry of Education, rather than a single school board. Children attending these schools are expected to return to their home school board after two years — or in exceptional circumstances, three — at a provincial school. It makes sense that the transition back to the local school board should be as seamless as possible. Similar reasoning might apply to children returning to a local school from a treatment program; however, a treatment program is a program, not a school, and there is no authority for a treatment program to hold an IPRC review, even though the education component of the treatment program is delivered by teachers who are employees of the school board. Instead, the Ministry's guidelines for funding approval provide that it is a mutual responsibility between the facility that provides the treatment and the school board that provides the education to "plan and co-ordinate [the] transition process from facility's educational program to community schools": Ontario Ministry of Education, *Guidelines 2005-06: For Approval of Educational*

board may direct that the principal or supervisory officer whom it appoints to the committee also serve as the chair of the committee or it may delegate the responsibility for the selection of the chair for each IPRC to a supervisory officer or a principal. A further option would be for the school board to direct that the committee itself agree on a chair. Since the opportunity to sit as chair can provide an opportunity for leadership experience, the school board may decide that, rather than establishing a permanent chair, the position will be rotated amongst the members of the committee. Whatever procedure a school board decides to use to select an IPRC chair, that procedure should be set out in a board policy.[8]

REFERRAL OF STUDENTS TO THE IPRC

First, it should be noted that the process for identification and placement under the *Education Act*[9] and regulations is intended to apply only to "pupils" of the school board. While some school boards have conducted IPRCs for children prior to their enrolment with the board, the IPRC has no jurisdiction to identify or determine placement for a child who is not enrolled with the school board, with the exception of students who are transferring from a provincial school (see the discussion later in this chapter).

As a practical matter, the issue of whether or not the IPRC has jurisdiction to make determinations about a child prior to the child's enrolment with the school board arises only when the parents and school board disagree on the IPRC's decision on either identification or placement. In this event, parents will not have the right under the *Education Act* or regulations to appeal placement. Beyond this, there are good reasons for a school board to wait until after the student is enrolled before conducting an IPRC meeting. An IPRC will not have access to all the information that it requires to make a properly informed decision before the student is enrolled. For example, there will be no observations available from the board's teachers, because they will have had no opportunity to work with the student or conduct any education assessment. The IPRC will be totally reliant on the information provided by the parent and persons who have been working with the child up to that point (*e.g.*, professionals and/or early childhood educators), none of whom will fully

---

Programs for Pupils in Government Approved Care and/or Treatment, Custody and Correctional Facilities (Toronto: The Ministry), available online at http://www.edu.gov.on.ca/eng/general/elemsec/speced/facilitiesamount/index.html. As a result, where formal IPRC determinations are not authorized, it may still be necessary to hold a meeting, which would do many of the same things as an IPRC.

8 Presumably a school board will establish one policy that covers the jurisdiction of IPRCs, the procedure for selecting an IPRC chair and any other procedures that the board has determined will be followed by IPRCs, pursuant to the board's authority under s. 12(1) of O. Reg. 181/98.

9 R.S.O. 1990, c. E.2.

understand the way the board delivers special education to its exceptional students.

This does not mean that parents and the principal or the school board's special education staff cannot meet to discuss a child's needs prior to the child's enrolment with the school board or that the child will be denied appropriate programming and services pending the IPRC's initial identification and placement decision. In fact, as discussed in Chapter 5, "Placement", a principal is required to provide transitional education programming and services appropriate for the student's apparent strengths and needs, pending a meeting or a decision of the IPRC.[10] Therefore, advance meetings with parents who are proposing to enrol students with special needs that will require special education supports should be encouraged, in order to obtain as much information as possible to plan for the education programming and services that will be provided to the student pending the IPRC's first meeting and decision; however, the first IPRC meeting should not be scheduled either prior to the student's enrolment or so soon after enrolment that staff do not have sufficient time to make the observations and perform the assessments necessary to adequately inform the IPRC in its decision making. In the interim, appropriate supports must be provided.

There are two different routes by which a student who has not previously been identified as an exceptional pupil may be referred to an IPRC. There is also a separate route of referral to an IPRC for students who are transferring into a school board from a demonstration school. In addition, once a student has been identified and placed by an IPRC, there are several routes by which a student's identification or placement can be referred back for review by an IPRC.

Referral of a Student Who Has Not Been Identified as Exceptional

(a) Referral by Principal

A principal of a school at which a student is enrolled may decide to refer the student to an IPRC to determine whether or not the student should be identified as an exceptional pupil and, if so, what the placement of the student should be. This route will generally be used where the student's teacher(s), in consultation with the principal, have determined that the student appears to have an exceptionality that has not been formally identified and that the student would benefit from special education programs or services.[11]

---

[10] O. Reg. 181/98, s. 9.

[11] O. Reg. 181/98, s. 14(1)(*a*). It is not necessary to identify a student as exceptional before providing special education programs and services to the student. In the absence of a formal identification, the school board is precluded from claiming additional funding on the student's behalf. In addition, a number of other consequences may flow from a decision not to identify the student. For example,

In this process, the principal must provide the student's parents with written notice of the referral of the student to the IPRC.[12] It should be noted that, whenever a written communication must be provided to a parent (or to the student), the parent (or student) may require the school board representative providing the communication to use Braille, large print or audio-cassette format for the communication.[13]

Within 15 days of the date on which the principal gave written notice of referral to the parents, the principal must provide to the parents a written statement setting out approximately when the principal expects the IPRC to meet to discuss the pupil. Along with this written statement, the principal must also send a copy of the Parent Guide (see Chapter 3, "The Administrator's Framework").[14] It is wise for a principal to reference, in the written statement, that the Parent Guide has been provided for two reasons: first, reference to the guide in the written statement will act as a reminder to send the guide and, second, reference in the written statement will serve as confirmation that a copy of the guide has, in fact, been provided.

---

there will be no obligation to obtain or consider assessment data regarding the student's strengths and needs, to prepare an Individual Education Plan or to develop a Transition Plan for a student over 14 years of age with respect to post-secondary activities (see also Chapter 7, "The Individual Education Plan", for further discussion of these requirements). There will be no requirement for annual reviews and the parents will not have a right to appeal school board decisions; however, where the parents do not wish the student to be identified, where there is no dispute as to needs and how the needs will be met and where no additional funding hinges on the identification, some school boards will agree not to identify the student. Even in the absence of a formal identification, the school board is obliged to provide "reasonable accommodation" to a student whose disability precludes the student from benefiting from the normal curriculum delivered in the normal manner. In almost every case, reasonable accommodation in such circumstances would look like the special education programs and services that the student would receive if he or she were identified. See Chapter 1, "Introduction". Where there is disagreement, the rights of both the school and the student can be fully protected and documented in the formal identification system. This will be particularly important for students who had no control over whether or not they were identified early in their schooling, but who seek accommodation in post-secondary education.

12 *Ibid.*, s. 14(1)(*a*). Throughout this chapter, a "parent" means either parent, where they live together or have joint custody of the student, the custodial parent where the parents are separated, or the legal guardian of a student under the age of 18 years. Where the student is 18 years of age or older, the word "parent" should be read to mean the student, since, at 18 years of age, the student is, legally, an adult. It should be noted, however, that notices that are to be sent to parents are also to be sent to students 16 years or older. Indeed, students aged 16 or older have the right to be equal participants at an IPRC.

13 *Ibid.*, s. 4. This same provision applies to any communication that must be provided to parents or students under the regulation.

14 *Ibid.*, s. 14(6).

(b) Request for Referral by Parent

Alternatively, a parent may ask the principal to refer the student to an IPRC. This request must be made in writing and, on receipt, the principal must refer the student to an IPRC.[15]

Within 15 days of receiving the parents' request for referral, the principal must provide the student's parents with a written statement acknowledging receipt of their request and advising approximately when the principal expects the IPRC will meet to discuss the student. A copy of the Parent Guide must also be sent to the parents.[16]

Referral from a Demonstration or Provincial School

Where an exceptional pupil has been enrolled in a demonstration or provincial school[17] and a decision is made that the student will leave the demonstration school and enrol in a school within the jurisdiction of a school board of which the student is a "resident pupil", the superintendent of the demonstration school must notify the director of education of the school board (or the secretary or equivalent in a school board that does not have a director).[18]

On receipt of the notice from the demonstration school, the director of education (who will presumably delegate this responsibility to a supervisory officer or special education administrator) must ensure that the student is referred to the school board's IPRC or, if more than one IPRC has been established by the school board, to the IPRC that is most "appropriate" for the student.[19] Which IPRC is the most "appropriate" IPRC will depend on the manner in which the school board has set up its IPRCs. When IPRCs are set up by geographic area, the IPRC that deals with students from the area in which the student resides or in which he or she would likely attend school will be the most appropriate.

When IPRCs have been established to deal with particular exceptionalities, then the IPRC that deals with the exceptionality of the student who is leaving the provincial or demonstration school may be the most appropriate.

There is an obligation on both the director of education of the board and the superintendent of the demonstration school to use their best efforts to ensure that the IPRC meets as soon as possible after the decision is made to

---

15 *Ibid.*, s. 14(1)(*b*). Although some school boards have developed a practice of not referring students in junior kindergarten or kindergarten to an IPRC or of waiting until a student is in grade 3, these limitations are not found in the legislation or any regulation. A parental request must lead to an IPRC for a student of any age.

16 *Ibid.*, s. 14(6).

17 See Chapter 5, "Placement", at footnote 18.

18 O. Reg. 181/98, s. 14(2).

19 *Ibid.*, s. 14(3) and (5).

move the student from the demonstration or provincial school to a school within the jurisdiction of the school board where the student is a "resident pupil".[20] There is no requirement that the student must be enrolled with the school board prior to the meeting of the IPRC and it makes sense that the IPRC determination respecting placement be made in such a case before the student is actually moved from the provincial or demonstration school to the school that the student will attend.[21]

Within 15 days of receipt of the notification from the demonstration school that the student will be leaving the demonstration school to enter a school within the jurisdiction of the school board, the director of education of the school board must provide the student's parent with a copy of the notice received from the demonstration school, a copy of the Parent Guide and a written statement that indicates approximately when the IPRC is expected to meet for the first time to discuss the student.[22]

Referral for Review

Where a student has been previously identified as an exceptional pupil, the student's identification and/or placement must be referred back to an IPRC for review at least once in each school year. In fact, a responsibility is imposed upon the director of education of the school board to ensure that a review is held at least once in each school year, *unless* there has been an IPRC review held during the school year *or* the parents of the pupil have provided written notice to the principal dispensing with the annual review.[23]

Usually, school boards have policies about annual reviews that require the principal at the school where the student is receiving his or her special education program to refer the student to the committee each year; however, the principal may refer the student back to an IPRC at any time, on written notice to the student's parents.[24]

Alternatively, the student's parents may require the student to be referred back to the IPRC by providing a written request to the principal;[25] however,

---

20 *Ibid.*, s. 14(4).

21 Similar reasoning might apply to children returning to school from a treatment program, especially where the education at the treatment facility was provided by the school board to which the student is returning. While the benefits of information-sharing are similar, a treatment facility is not a school, so the regulatory provisions governing provincial schools do not apply. Rather the obligation to share information is set out in the funding requirements for treatment facilities, which impose a mutual responsibility on both school board and treatment provider to "plan and co-ordinate [the] transition process from facility's educational program to community schools": Ontario Ministry of Education, *op. cit.*, footnote 7.

22 *Ibid.*, s. 14(7).

23 *Ibid.*, s. 21(4)(*b*).

24 *Ibid.*, s. 21(1)(*a*).

25 *Ibid.*, s. 21(1)(*b*).

time constraints are imposed on the parents in making this request. A parent may not request a referral for review before a placement has been in effect for three months and may not make a request for review more often than once in every three-month period.[26] A parent's only possible avenue to avoid these time constraints would be to persuade the principal, whose referral powers are unlimited, to request an earlier review. There is, however, no obligation on the principal to accede to the parent's request when the request is made sooner than three months after the last review or placement change.

Where the student is receiving his or her special education program from another school board under an agreement permitted by section 170(1), para. 7 of the *Education Act*, the student's review will be conducted by an IPRC of the school board that is providing the special education program. This review may be initiated in one of three ways:

- by referral from the principal of the school that is providing the special program;
- by written request of the parent to the principal; or
- by written request of the director of education of the school board that is providing the special program to the principal.[27]

In each case where the student is referred back to an IPRC for review and the school board has established more than one IPRC, the principal must determine the IPRC that is most appropriate to conduct the review, having regard to the expertise and specific mandate of the various IPRCs.[28] In this respect, administrative procedures may be established by the school board to direct a principal in making this determination. Further, the principal must provide the parent with a written statement of the approximate time when the review meeting will take place.[29]

CONDUCT OF THE IPRC PROCEEDING

The regulation that governs IPRCs sets out some rules concerning the manner in which the IPRC is to carry out its mandate, but leaves many of the procedural details to be determined by the school board or the IPRC itself.[30] While the IPRC is not subject to the rigorous procedural obligations of the *Statutory Powers Procedure Act* ("*SPPA*"),[31] the IPRC is obliged to comply with the basic tenets of procedural fairness in dealing with parents and

26 *Ibid.*, s. 21(2).
27 *Ibid.*, s. 21(1) to (4).
28 *Ibid.*, s. 22(1).
29 *Ibid.*, s. 21(5).
30 *Ibid.*, s. 12.
31 R.S.O. 1990, c. S.22. The *SPPA* is a code of minimum procedural rules applicable to administrative decision-makers that exercise a "statutory power of decision".

students.[32] Parents must be provided with all information that the IPRC intends to consider in making its decision and are entitled to attend, with a representative or advocate, all meetings of the IPRC where there are discussions about their child or where decisions are being made about their child.[33] Parents and students 16 years of age or older may be present at and participate in all discussions about the student. They are also entitled to be present when the IPRC makes its decision on identification and placement.

Consistency in Membership of IPRC

The need to ensure consistency in membership of the IPRC making the decision on a particular student arises from the principle of fairness. When an IPRC meets more than once to make an initial identification and placement decision or to conduct a review of placement and one of the decision-makers does not participate in all of the meetings, the perception — and reality — may be that he or she will not be capable of making a fully informed decision.

Therefore, it will be important to ensure that those IPRC members who make the determinations in each case have participated throughout all stages of that case. This means that, where the IPRC will not complete its deliberations in one meeting, the composition of the IPRC dealing with a particular student should be fixed as of the first meeting concerning the student. No new members may be added to the IPRC until the process involved with that student is completed, including any requests by the parent to meet to discuss the IPRC's decision.[34] When the IPRC begins its process and a member is unable to attend a subsequent meeting, that member should not participate in further deliberations of the committee in respect of that particular referral. It is not appropriate to substitute committee members once the IPRC has begun to consider a matter.

---

32 While the IPRC is charged with making decisions, it would appear that it does not exercise a "statutory power of decision" within the meaning of the *SPPA*. The Ontario Divisional Court has found that very specific statutory language is required to create a "statutory power of decision": see *Polten v. University of Toronto* (1975), 59 D.L.R. (3d) 197, 8 O.R. (2d) 749 (Div. Ct.). Among other things, the statute must require the tribunal to hold a hearing. The language of O. Reg. 181/98 requires the IPRC to collect information and to meet and discuss, which falls short of the requirement to hold a hearing. Although the common law duty of fairness can also impose an obligation to hold a hearing, which would bring the *SPPA* into play, it would be unlikely that the circumstances in any case before an IPRC would raise this obligation. Nevertheless, the common law does impose obligations of procedural fairness, which will be outlined in this chapter.

33 O. Reg. 181/98, ss. 5 and 15(8).

34 See discussion here under the heading "Parental Request to Discuss the IPRC's Decision".

Participants in an IPRC Meeting

The necessary participants in an IPRC meeting will include a parent of the student, the student (when the student is aged 16 years or older) and the referring principal.

Ontario Regulation 181/98 gives the parent of the student who is referred to the IPRC and the student, when he or she is 16 years of age or older, the right to attend and participate in all IPRC discussions about the student and the right to be present when the IPRC's identification and placement decisions are made.[35] This imposed transparency in decision-making may limit the candour with which IPRCs discuss particular situations, especially in those rare situations where there are hostile feelings between the parents and school board staff; however, the intent behind this provision is to encourage school board staff to form a partnership with parents so that parents are included in the process right through to the final decision and to promote open communication between parents and school staff.

While a student who is under the age of 16 years is not given a right of participation under the *Education Act* or its regulations, the Supreme Court of Canada has recognized that for "older children and those who are able to communicate their wishes and needs, their own views will play an important role in the determination of best interests".[36] Accordingly, an IPRC may also permit a student younger than 16 years to attend and participate in a meeting.

It is important to note that the parental/student right to attend and participate in discussions extends only to those situations where members of the IPRC are meeting as a committee. It would not appear that the provision precludes individual members of the IPRC from holding discussions about administrative matters related to setting up meetings.[37]

There may be an issue about which a parent has party status, where a student's parents are separated or divorced. In this situation, normally the parent with whom the student resides (the "custodial parent")[38] has the right to make decisions respecting the student's schooling.[39] Only a custodial parent has the right to be notified of a referral to an IPRC or a request to review identification and placement, to participate in the IPRC process and to receive IPRC decisions; however, where a separation agreement or a court order gives

---

35 O. Reg. 181/98, s. 5.

36 *Eaton v. Brant County Board of Education* (1997), 142 D.L.R. (4th) 385, [1997] 1 S.C.R. 241, at para. 77.

37 O. Reg. 181/98, s. 5.

38 Where parents separate, the "custodial parent" will be the parent who has been awarded custody by a court order or, where there is no court order but the child lives with one of the parents with the consent or acquiescence of the other, the parent with whom the child resides is the custodial parent: *Children's Law Reform Act*, R.S.O. 1990, c. C.12, s. 20(4).

39 *Children's Law Reform Act*, s. 20(4).

joint custody to parents, both parents will continue to have the right to make decisions about the student and to participate in IPRC meetings.

Even where parents are separated and one has custody of the student, a court order or separation agreement may give limited rights to the non-custodial parent to have a say in the student's schooling. In any event, the non-custodial parent will continue to have the right to be given information about the education of the student and, accordingly, the school will be obliged to provide information to the non-custodial parent on request.[40] Where the custodial parent agrees or where the IPRC believes the non-custodial parent has relevant information to contribute and his or her presence would contribute to a better determination of identification and placement, the non-custodial parent may attend IPRC meetings.

Where a dispute arises between separated parents concerning the rights of each to provide input into the student's schooling, the principal may request a copy of any court order or the portion of the separation agreement that outlines the custodial arrangements.

The principal who referred the student is entitled to participate in the IPRC proceedings, although he or she may delegate a vice-principal or teachers more familiar with the student to act in his or her stead. In the case of a student being transferred to the school board from a demonstration school, the superintendent of the demonstration school that initiated the process and the director of education of the school board to which the student is being transferred would both be entitled to participate in the IPRC process; however, in the latter circumstance, it is likely that responsibility for dealing with the process of the transfer, including attendance at IPRC meetings, would be delegated to another official — in the case of the superintendent of the provincial or demonstration school, the principal of that school, and in the case of a director of education of the receiving school, a superintendent or special education administrator.

As well, the student's teachers will often be participants. Consultants and other professionals who have worked with the student may also participate in IPRC proceedings.

Where a school board provides special education programs to a student of another school board under an agreement for purchase of services entered into pursuant to section 170(1), para. 7 of the *Education Act*, the student's identification and placement will be reviewed by an IPRC of the school board that is providing the special program. In such a case, in addition to the other usual participants — parents/student, principal, teachers — the school board providing the special education program must invite a representative of the purchasing board to be present at and participate in all committee discussions

---

[40] Where a custody order is made under the *Divorce Act*, R.S.C. 1985, c. 3 (2nd Supp.), s. 16, similar principles apply.

about the student and to be present when the IPRC makes decisions about the identification or placement of the student.[41]

IPRC Meetings

Procedures

Ontario Regulation 181/98, which requires the establishment of IPRCs, imposes few requirements for the conduct of IPRC meetings. A school board may develop additional procedures to be followed by the IPRC, but may not mandate any procedures that are in conflict with those set out in the regulation. It is, in fact, quite appropriate for a school board to establish a policy that sets out the procedures to be followed in conducting IPRCs and IPRC reviews. This will help to ensure consistency in the conduct of IPRCs across the school board. Items that can be included in a policy on IPRC procedures include: the quorum for the IPRC where the number of committee members is greater than three; the forms to be used by all IPRCs and review IPRCs; and the format of their meetings.

The Ministry of Education's resource document, *Special Education: A Guide for Educators, 2001*,[42] provides a number of helpful suggestions for school boards in formulating their IPRC procedures.

The Ministry of Education suggests that school boards may find it useful to design a form to record the IRPC's decision.[43] In any event, an IPRC must issue a statement of decision and this written statement must record at least the following information:

- whether or not IPRC has decided to identify the student as exceptional;
- where the student is identified as exceptional, the category/definition of exceptionality or exceptionalities that have been identified;
- a description of the exceptional student's strengths and needs;
- the IPRC's placement decision, where the student is exceptional;
- the IPRC's recommendations regarding a special education program and special education services, if any;
- the IRPC's reasons for placing the student in a special education class, where that is the IPRC's decision;
- the name, date of birth and grade of the student;
- the names of the committee members present;
- the names of other persons present, including the parent, the parent's representatives, if any, any other persons who present information

---

41 O. Reg. 181/98, s. 22(2).

42 Ontario Ministry of Education, *Special Education: A Guide for Educators, 2001* (Toronto: The Ministry, 2001), at pp. D1 to D18, available online at http://www.edu.gov.on.ca/eng/general/elemsec/speced/guide.html.

43 *Ibid.*, at p. D12.

on behalf of the parents, all school board staff who present information or participate in the discussion, and any persons from outside the school board who present information or participate in the discussion;

- a list of the documents considered by the IPRC;
- a space for parents to sign when they agree with the IPRC's decision on exceptionality and on placement; and
- the process available to the parents when they do not agree with the IPRC's decision.

In addition, in the case of a review IPRC, the form could include:

- where the decision is to change identification, the reasons for that decision; and/or
- where the decision is to change placement, the reasons for that decision.[44]

The school board may also determine, in its policy dealing with IPRC procedures, the format for providing notice to parents and the procedures to be followed in sending out the notice. When parents in all areas of the school board are treated in the same manner, this may substantially reduce the possibility of a perception by some parents that they have been treated inequitably in comparison with other parents with whom they have compared notes. An exception exists, of course, for the parent who wishes and is entitled to receive notices in Braille or on audiotape.[45]

The school board may also determine the procedures to be used by the IPRC in decision-making — *e.g.*, consensus, majority or unanimity. Any decision reached by the IPRC must be consistent with the school board's Special Education Plan.[46]

Beyond any procedures set out in the regulation or mandated by the school board, each IPRC has an inherent power to determine its own processes. The exercise of this power must not result in conflict with those requirements imposed by the regulation or by the school board or with the basic tenets of fairness to the persons who are entitled to participate in the meetings. A fair opportunity must be given to the parents, the principal and teachers to provide information; however, the IPRC may direct any person who has become repetitious in providing information to move on to a new point. Moreover, if the tenor of the meeting were to become heated, then the chair could recess the meeting for a few minutes or longer in order to allow emotions to subside. Where a person presenting information becomes abusive and the person is not a necessary participant (the parent and the principal are both necessary participants), the person may be directed to leave the meeting.

---

44 *Ibid.* See also O. Reg. 181/98, ss. 18 and 23.

45 O. Reg. 181/98, s. 4.

46 *Ibid.*, s. 12.

It is prudent, however, to warn the person first that, if the person were not to change his or her conduct, then he or she would be asked to leave the meeting. If one of the necessary parties to the IPRC meeting were to become verbally abusive towards others, then the committee could consider giving a warning to the person that the meeting will be adjourned unless the conduct that prompts the warning ceased. If the conduct were to continue, then the IPRC chair could adjourn the meeting. In short, the IPRC is entitled to insist that all participants treat each other with respect and civility.

Notice

An effort should be made to set up IPRC meetings at a time most convenient to all parties. Through this process, participants will typically know the date of the meeting; nevertheless, written notice of every IPRC meeting, including the date, time and place of the meeting, should be provided to any person who has a right to attend the meeting. In the case of the parents and student (if aged 16 or older), notice must be given at least 10 days in advance of the IPRC's meeting;[47] however, a parent may agree to an earlier meeting. A copy of the notice should also be given to the principal. In the case of a student transferring from a demonstration school, the superintendent of the demonstration school that initiated the process should be given notice, as well as the director of education of the school board to which the student is being transferred — *i.e.*, the school board that has established the IPRC. In the case of an IPRC review of a student to whom a special education program is being provided under a purchase of services agreement, the director of education of the purchasing board should be provided with notice.

There is no specified method of delivery of the notice and, accordingly, as an alternative to regular mail, the notice may be delivered personally, by courier or by facsimile. Electronic mail is also a possibility, although proof of delivery to the intended recipient may be troublesome; for this reason, e-mail should be used with caution.

When the notice is sent by mail, it will be deemed to be received by the person to whom it is addressed on the fifth day after the day on which it is mailed, unless the fifth day is a school holiday within the meaning of the regulation that defines school holidays; in this latter case, the date of deemed delivery will be the next day that is not a school holiday.[48] The notice must be

47 *Ibid.*, s. 5(5).

48 *Ibid.*, s. 3; *School Year Calendar, Professional Activity Days*, R.R.O. 1990, Reg. 304, as currently written, defines "school holidays", at s. 4, as being every Saturday and Sunday; Canada Day (where the school is open in July); Labour Day; Thanksgiving; the school break over Christmas and New Year's Day; Family Day, March break, Good Friday, Easter Monday and Victoria Day. The summer vacation period is not designated by the regulation as a school holiday; however, it was not likely the intent of the Ministry that the summer vacation period would be treated as other than a "school holiday" for the purposes of O. Reg. 181/98. Accordingly,

received by the parent 10 days in advance of the meeting date. Accordingly, where it is to be sent by mail, it must be sent by at least the 15th day preceding the day on which the meeting is to be held.

The notice may indicate that the meeting may proceed in the absence of the addressee of the notice. For example, the letter setting out the notice of time, date and location of the IPRC meeting might include the statement: "Please note that the IPRC's meeting to discuss [student] may proceed in your absence, should you not attend at the appointed time and place." The school board, however, should demonstrate some flexibility in altering the date and time of the meeting when parents advise, after receiving the notice, that they cannot attend at the appointed date and time, particularly when the parents have not been consulted in setting the date and time for the meeting.[49]

Agenda

The IPRC is responsible for setting the agenda for each meeting. A meeting will normally start with a statement of welcome to the participants, introductions and a short statement of the purpose of the meeting. The matters that should be canvassed through the process include:

- the strengths and needs of the student;[50]
- the definition or definitions of any exceptionalities that the student may have; and
- placement.

---

until the matter is clarified by way of an amendment to the regulation, a school board should carefully consider the position it will take where a time limit expires during the summer vacation period.

[49] As a practical matter, where a parent misses the IPRC meeting that the parent wished to attend, the parent is not without recourse. The parent may request a meeting to discuss the decision — see the discussion here under the heading, "Parental Request to Discuss the IPRC's Decision" — or may refuse to consent to the placement decided by the IPRC in the parent's absence and initiate an appeal of the IPRC's decision (see Chapter 10, "The First State of Appeal"). Alternatively, the parent may request a new IPRC meeting after three months have elapsed — see the discussion under the heading entitled "Review of an Identified Student's Identification and Placement". Accordingly, an IPRC may wish to adjourn a meeting that the parent fails to attend where it is known that the parent did wish to be present.

[50] In at least one case, a Special Education Tribunal ("SET") has accepted jurisdiction to hear an appeal on placement based on the failure of an IPRC either to discuss the student's needs and list them on the IPRC decision form or to discuss the services needed to meet those needs: *D. & Toronto District School Board* (2002-12-24), File No. 30 (Ont. Spec. Ed. (Eng.) Trib.). The SET stated in this case that "[t]he Tribunal agrees with the parents that the needs of the child and appropriateness of the placement are an integral part of an IPRC decision and that needs and services should be discussed at an IPRC before a placement decision can be made".

The agenda should ensure that all these matters are canvassed and that an opportunity is provided to the parents/student, if participating, to provide input in the discussion.

On the issue of special education services and programs, it is to be remembered that the IPRC not only has the jurisdiction to make recommendations about special education programs and services, but must do so where the parent makes a requests that the IPRC do so.[51] In addition, the IPRC is required to consider whether or not a student's needs can be met in a regular class with "appropriate special education services" that would meet the student's needs, before the IPRC considers placing the student in a special education class.[52] Further, the Tribunal has stated that, where a student's placement is to be in a regular class, the special education services and programs to be provided to the student in the regular class placement must be identified, since those services and programs serve to define the placement. The Tribunal has stated that, consequently, parents must be supplied with sufficient information about the services and program to be provided to the student in the proposed placement to permit them to make an informed decision about whether or not to accept the placement.[53]

All of this means that an IPRC that is determining or reviewing placement will almost always have to consider — and, therefore, discuss — the services and programs that are appropriate to meet the student's needs.[54] It is, therefore, important that the agenda reflect this.

"Pre-IPRC" Meetings

It is now common for schools to work through the decisions that will be reached at the formal IPRC meeting in "pre-IPRC" meetings where those decisions are likely to be uncontroversial. These "pre-IPRC" meetings take the form of case conferences held in advance of the formal IPRC meeting. This

51 O. Reg. 181/98, s. 16(1).

52 *Ibid.*, s. 17.

53 In *D. & Windsor Essex Catholic District School Board* (2003-09-30), File No. 38 (Ont. Spec. Ed. (Eng.) Trib.), a case involving a student identified with multiple exceptionalities, the Tribunal found that the IPRC's decision of "Regular Class with Resource Assistance" with a recommendation of "Resource Support as deemed appropriate by school personnel" was lacking in enough clarity and detail to permit the parents to make an informed decision about whether or not the proposed placement would meet the needs of the student.

54 In *D. & Toronto District School Board* (2002-12-24), File No. 30 (Ont. Spec. Ed. (Eng.) Trib.), the SET granted leave to appeal on the basis of the parent's objection that the IPRC had declined to discuss either the student's needs or the services to be provided to the student. The SET stated that, while the IPRC may only make decisions regarding identification and placement, the issue of appropriate programs and services is interconnected with the issue of placement and that the consideration of appropriate services is, therefore, a necessary part of the IPRC's decision.

process makes a great deal of sense, since these "pre-IPRC" meetings permit issues to be worked out in advance of the formal IPRC meeting. In this case, the formal IPRC meeting is usually quite short, since all issues and decisions have been worked out in advance. There is nothing in the regulations that precludes this process, as long as it is made clear to the parents that these "pre-IPRC" meetings are part of the IPRC process, the parents are invited to participate in all of these pre-IPRC meetings and all the information and issues that the IPRC is required to consider are considered (including an opportunity for parents to discuss them), either in the "pre-IPRC" meeting or at the IPRC meeting itself.

Parent Representatives

Some parents and students over 16 years may wish to bring along a representative to IPRC meetings. They are specifically given the right to have a representative present at any IPRC discussions about the student, either to speak on their behalf or simply to be present to provide support.[55] Parents and students over 16 years also have a right to have a representative present to support them when the IPRC makes its decision. Students who are 16 years of age or older are entitled to their own representative, separate from any representative their parents might have.

The choice of who will act as the representative of the parents or student rests with the parents or student; their choice may include legal counsel, a representative of a parent advocacy group or a friend. The presence of counsel or a parent advocate can, on occasion, introduce a note of adversity to the process or otherwise impose a filter on direct dialogue between the committee members and the parents; however, at the same time, some parents can feel overwhelmed by the number and expertise of school board staff and believe that bringing legal counsel or a parent advocate will provide protection for them. Parents will be less likely to feel the need for protection provided by representatives when they are encouraged to feel that their views and information are respected as much as the views and information provided by school board staff. A genuinely respectful IPRC climate will go a long way to reduce parental perceptions that formal representation is necessary in order to be heard at an IPRC.

On the other hand, discouraging the attendance of persons on whom parents may feel dependent to ensure the enforcement of their rights can only serve to alienate the parents and create an atmosphere of distrust. It is wise, therefore, that any discussion with parents and students about the possible presence of representatives acknowledge the legal right to representation.

---

[55] O. Reg. 181/98, s. 5(3).

Adjournments

Generally, the date and time of an IPRC meeting will be set in consultation with parents. Where that is not possible, as much advance notice as possible should be provided to parents. After the notice of the IPRC meeting has been sent out, there may be occasions where either school staff or a parent may seek an adjournment of the meeting. Such requests may be made in advance of the IPRC meeting or at the meeting itself.

The request for an adjournment should be directed to the chair of the IPRC. Where school board policy so provides, decisions on adjournment requests may be made by the chair of the IPRC alone. In the absence of a school board policy that gives the chair the authority to decide adjournment requests, the IPRC may determine its own procedure and may assign to the chair the responsibility to make decisions on adjournment requests. Otherwise, all members of the IPRC should be involved.

Assuming that the request for an adjournment is made in good faith and for legitimate reasons, the adjournment will normally be agreed to by the IPRC; however, if adjournment requests become excessive or agreement on a mutually acceptable meeting time is not forthcoming, then the IPRC may proceed to set a date and time that appears to be the most reasonable in the circumstances and to send notice, well in advance of the meeting, to all participants. In this situation, care should be taken *not* to set the meeting at a time and date on which it is known the parent will not be able to attend.

Closed Meetings

The question of whether or not an IPRC meeting should be "closed" only becomes an issue where persons other than those directly interested (*i.e.*, custodial parents, the student, school staff involved with the student and members of the IPRC) seek to attend the meeting. The issue may arise where a non-custodial parent seeks to attend and the custodial parent objects. While a non-custodial parent may have information to contribute to a meeting, he or she does not have the same rights as a custodial parent to be present throughout the IPRC's discussions.

The school board may set out procedural rules about who may or may not attend IPRC meetings, provided that the rights of persons who are entitled to attend are respected. Should the school board not establish any such rules, then the IPRC itself may determine who may and may not attend a meeting.

The IPRC has the power to control its own process and may exclude any person from attending the meeting where it deems it appropriate to do so. Moreover, in light of the fact that the student's personal information will be disclosed during the meeting, the requirements of the *MFIPPA* would likely require the IPRC to exclude persons, other than school board staff, the parent and the student, from the meeting unless the parent (or student, if aged 16 or older) has consented to the presence of the person.

Information to be Considered

An IPRC that has received a referral is obliged to consider certain information in its deliberations.

The IPRC must obtain and consider an educational assessment of the student.[56] This assessment will normally be prepared by the student's teachers and any special education teachers who have worked with the student. In the case of a student who is just entering the school system from a program outside the school system, information should be obtained from the educators and staff involved in that program. Parental consent will usually be required before the program will release information.

The IPRC must consider any information about the student submitted to it by a parent or, where the student is 16 years of age or older, by the student. In addition, the IPRC must consider any other information that is provided to it that it considers relevant.[57] This includes any information provided by teachers, consultants and other school board personnel who have interactions with the student, as well as information from persons who have provided information to the IPRC at the suggestion of the parents. The IPRC is not limited to information that others choose to provide about the student; it may actively seek out any other information that it considers might be relevant,[58] subject only to obtaining any written consents that may be required (e.g., as in the case of medical or psychological information).

While the IPRC may not have the power to compel attendance at its meetings by way of summons, the IPRC may invite the attendance of persons who may provide relevant information that might assist the IPRC in its deliberations. This will include any teachers, consultants and other professionals (*e.g.*, psychologists, speech and language pathologists, or occupational therapists) who have worked with the student. In the case of a student entering

56 *Ibid.*, s. 15(1).

57 *Ibid.*, s. 15(6) and (7). Information is relevant when it is specific to the student and helps the IPRC to understand the student's strengths and needs. On occasion, parents may object to information on the basis that the information either is not relevant or is prejudicial — for example, information that a student with a behavioural exceptionality has engaged in violent conduct outside the school. The test of relevance will be whether or not the information relates to the student and assists in the determination of identification and/or placement. Where parents argue that information should not be considered or received because of its prejudicial effect, the IPRC must balance the degree of relevance of the information with the degree of the prejudice inherent in the information. When the information would be of minimal assistance only in making a decision on identification or placement, the IPRC may decide not to consider the information.

58 *Ibid.*, s. 15.

the school system for the first time, it may also include early childhood educators or others who have worked with the student up to that point in time. Such persons may decline to attend an IPRC meeting without parental consent and it is wise to secure parental consent before inviting them.

The IPRC must obtain and consider a health assessment of the pupil by a qualified medical practitioner and/or a psychological assessment, where the IPRC is of the view that a health or psychological assessment is necessary in order to make a correct decision on identification or placement.[59] The IPRC may request that parents obtain the assessment from a doctor or psychologist who has been treating the student or may suggest that the student be seen by a different doctor or psychologist;[60] however, this requirement is subject to parental consent and specifically makes the IPRC's obligation to obtain an assessment subject to the *Health Care Consent Act, 1996*.[61] This Act requires the consent of the student, when the student is capable of understanding the nature of the assessment and the implication of the consent, and if not, then the consent of the parent, to undergo the health assessment.[62] Consent to the disclosure of the assessment to the IPRC may be assumed where the parent agrees to co-operate in obtaining the assessment in the first instance, although the doctor/psychologist may require written consent of the parent (or adult student) prior to providing the assessment directly to the school board.

Where the student is under 16 years of age and the parents consent, the IPRC may interview the student. Parents have the right to be present during the interview.[63] A student who is 16 years of age or older is entitled to attend and participate in IPRC meetings and, accordingly, the regulation does not extend any authority to the IPRC to interview a student who is 16 years of age or older. Presumably, where a student aged 16 or over attends an IPRC meeting, the IPRC may engage the student in discussion sufficient to obtain the information that the IPRC would obtain in an interview. The IPRC probably does not have the power to compel the student to attend, even when the student is 16 years of age or older. As a result, should the student refuse to attend, the IPRC would be obliged to forego this potentially valuable source of information.

In a review case, any individual education plans ("IEPs") (see Chapter 7, "The Individual Education Plan") that have been previously prepared for the

---

59 *Ibid.*, s. 15(2) and (3).

60 While the regulation is silent on the issue of who pays for the assessment, the requirement in s. 8(3) of the *Education Act* that special education services and programs will be made available without payment of fees makes clear that the school board will be responsible to pay for any health or psychological assessments required by and provided to the IPRC; however, the school board would not be responsible to pay the costs of any assessments obtained by a parent for submission to the IPRC, in the absence of any request by the IPRC at the school.

61 S.O. 1996, c. 2, Sch. A.

62 *Health Care Consent Act, 1996*, ss. 4, 10 and 20.

63 O. Reg. 181/98, ss. 5, 15(4) and (5).

student would seem an obvious and relevant source of information; however, the IPRC may consider the student's progress with reference to the student's IEP *only* with the written permission of a parent or the student, where the student is 16 years of age or older.[64] Where parents (or the student) withhold permission, the IPRC would still be able to consider the student's progress based on the reports of teachers, the principal and/or consultants.

The Ontario Student Record ("OSR") may also contain information relevant to the IPRC's deliberations, including report cards, testing results or, in the case of a student who is being referred in the anticipation of an identification of a "behavioural" exceptionality, records detailing conduct by the student that bear on the identification. The *Education Act* specifically limits access to information contained in the OSR to supervisory officers, the principal and teachers of the school attended by the student and the parents of a student under the age of 18 years or the student, if 18 years or older, except where a parent or pupil who is of an age to control his or her own documents, consents to the disclosure.[65] Accordingly, members of the IPRC who are supervisory officers or the principal or teachers at the school attended by the student may have access to the documents in the OSR; however, the provisions of the *Education Act* appear to preclude access by any other members of the IPRC, even when they are school board employees, unless written consent is given by a parent or the pupil, if of an age to control his or her own OSR documents. Normally, such consent will be readily forthcoming from parents and no issue will arise.

When an issue does arise with respect to the disclosure of OSR documents, it would appear that the *MFIPPA* provides a solution that permits the

---

[64] *Ibid.*, s. 23(2).

[65] *Education Act*, s. 266. This section, which provides that the right of the student to control his or her own information does not arise until the student is no longer a minor — *i.e.*, has reached age 18 (as *per* the *Age of Majority and Accountability Act*, R.S.O. 1990, c. A.7) — is not consistent with O. Reg. 181/98 or with the *MFIPPA*. O. Reg. 181/98 accords students aged 16 full participatory rights in the special education process. Section 54 of the *MFIPPA* designates 16 years as the age at which persons may exercise rights in respect of their personal information, which includes the contents of the OSR; this includes the right to consent to disclosure of the information. Section 53 of the *MFIPPA* provides that the Act overrides the confidentiality provisions of any other act, and s. 52 makes the Act applicable to every document in the custody of a school board, including the OSR. As a result, it is at least arguable that, where students aged 16 and 17 consent, OSR documents can be disclosed; however, the matter is not entirely clear since s. 266(2) of the *Education Act* imposes a strict prohibition on the disclosure of OSR documents and specifically defines the limited circumstances in which OSR documents may be disclosed (see footnote 68, *infra*); those circumstances do not include the consent of a student aged 16 or 17 years. Accordingly, it is also arguable that parental consent is still a prerequisite to disclosure of any OSR documents for a 16 or 17 year old student to persons other than the student's principal, teachers and supervisory officers. Indeed, it may be necessary to obtain the consent of both the parent and the student, if aged 16 or 17 years, to disclosure of OSR documents in such a case.

disclosure of documents to all IPRC members who are school board employees, even when they are not teachers or the principal of the school attended by the student or supervisory officers of the school board. The *MFIPPA* permits the disclosure of documents containing "personal information" (which includes OSR records) to employees of the school board who need the information in the performance of their duties where the disclosure of the information is "necessary and proper in the discharge of the [school board's] functions".[66] In permitting disclosure in these circumstances, *MFIPPA* specifically overrides any statutory confidentiality provisions that otherwise apply to documents containing personal information.[67] As a consequence, it has been suggested that, to the extent that the IPRC considers any OSR record to be relevant to its deliberations (excepting only the IEP, which, as noted previously, cannot be considered by the IPRC without parental consent), all members of the IPRC who are employees of the school board may be able to access information from the OSR without requiring the consent of a parent/pupil.[68]

---

66 *MFIPPA*, s. 32(*d*). The identification and placement of exceptional pupils falls within the "necessary and proper discharge" of a school board's functions.

67 Section 52 of the *MFIPPA* makes the Act applicable to any record in the custody of a school board and s. 53 provides that the Act prevails over the "confidentiality" provisions in any other Act (a "confidentiality override"), unless that Act specifically provides otherwise. Since the *Education Act* does *not* provide otherwise, the confidentiality provisions of s. 266 of the *Education Act* in respect of the OSR are overridden and must be read subject to the *MFIPPA*.

68 A countervailing argument might be made that the "confidentiality override" provisions of the *MFIPPA* do not override s. 266(2) of the *Education Act*. This section stipulates that OSR documents are "privileged" and that, without parental permission, OSR documents may only be used by supervisory officers and the principal or teachers of the school that the student attends and are not admissible in any legal proceeding. The thrust of the argument is that s. 266(2) is not a "confidentiality" provision; however, in two companion Investigation Reports issued on September 6, 1996, the Information and Privacy Commissioner Ontario held that s. 266 of the *Education Act* is a "confidentiality provision" and is subject to the "confidentiality override" provisions of the *MFIPPA*: see *A Regional Police Services Board (Re)*, 1996 CanLII 7762 (Ont. I.P.C.), and *A Separate School Board (Re)*, 1996 CanLII 7763 (Ont. I.P.C.). In addition, several arbitration boards have decided that, despite s. 266 of the *Education Act*, information and documents from the OSR can be disclosed in arbitration proceedings. Some of these decisions have been based on the "confidentiality override" provisions of the *MFIPPA*, while others have been based on fairness considerations. In several of these cases, however, measures were put in place to ensure that disclosure was limited to arguably relevant documents. See *Hastings and Prince Edward District School Board and O.S.S.T.F., District 29 (Willock) (Re)* (2000), 62 C.L.A.S. 193 (P. Knopf); *Windsor Board of Education and O.S.S.T.F., District 1 (Re)* (unreported, June 12, 1995, Ont. Ed. Rel. Comm., J.W. Samuels, File No. 587); *Toronto District School Board and O.S.S.T.F. (Thomson) (Re)* (2005), 144 L.A.C. (4th) 232, 83 C.L.A.S. 218 (Whitaker); *Toronto District School Board and E.T.F.O. (Brown) (Re)* (2006), 154 L.A.C. (4th) 103, 87 C.L.A.S. 183 (Herlich). See *Ontario Public School Authority and O.S.S.T.F., District 57 (Dunning) (Re)* (2000), 62 C.L.A.S.

In the event that any member of the IPRC is not an employee of the school board, written permission of the parent (or student, if aged 18 years or older) must be obtained before this IPRC member may review an OSR record.[69] Normally, consent to disclosure will be readily provided so that no issue about OSR documents arises; however, where written consent is not forthcoming, the IPRC must decide whether or not the record must be considered in order to make its decision. If it were determined that the OSR record were necessary, then the non-employee member of the IPRC would be obliged to refrain from participating for the remainder of the case. Similarly, it should also be noted that, where a non-employee is attending the IPRC meeting — for example, a child care worker who has worked with the student — consent to disclosure of OSR documents or information from the documents should be obtained when such documents and/or information are to be discussed while these non-employees are present at the meeting. In the absence of consent, the non-employee should be asked to leave the meeting while information from OSR documents is being discussed.

Where the IPRC does obtain or receive information relating to the student, the chair of the IPRC must provide the information to the parent of the pupil and, where the student is 16 years of age or older, to the student "as soon as possible after the chair . . . obtains [the] information".[70] This includes any information about the student provided to an individual member of the IPRC. (For example, a former teacher of the student may provide information about his or her experiences with the student to the chair of the IPRC).

Before any steps are taken by the IPRC or any school board employee on behalf of the IPRC to collect information about the student, the requirements of the *MFIPPA* should be considered. This Act operates to limit the collection of information about a student to circumstances where express authority has been given by the student's parent or by the student, when aged 16 or older, where the collection has been expressly authorized by a statute, or where the collection is "necessary to the proper administration of a lawfully authorized activity".[71] Collection of information by the IPRC pursuant to section 15 of O. Reg. 181/98[72] constitutes a collection under the authority of a statute. Beyond this, any information that the IPRC actively solicits outside an IPRC meeting from persons not employed by the school board (*e.g.*, former teachers or professionals no longer employed by the school board who previously worked

133 (Roberts), which addressed the same issue under the companion statute applicable to provincial institutions, the *Freedom of Information and Protection of Privacy Act*, R.S.O. 1990, c. F.31. The matter has not yet been considered in depth by the courts.

69 *Education Act*, s. 266(2).

70 O. Reg. 181/98, s. 15(8) and (9).

71 *MFIPPA*, s. 28(2).

72 This section requires the IPRC to collect an educational assessment and a health assessment or psychological assessment where, in the judgment of the IPRC, the assessment is necessary to make a determination on identification or placement.

with the student), may be properly collected only where the information is relevant to the identification or placement of the student and is necessary for the purpose of determining identification or placement.[73] Where the IPRC does collect information about the individual from sources outside the school board without the consent of the parent or student aged 16 or older, the *MFIPPA* requires the school board to send to the parent, or to the student aged 16 or older, a written notice of the collection; this written notice must set out the legal authority for the collection,[74] the principal purpose for which the information will be used (*i.e.*, for the determination or review of identification and/or placement), and the title, business address and telephone number of the employee of the institution who can answer questions about the collection of the information.[75]

Record of the Proceedings

It is important for the IPRC to maintain a record of its proceedings. Should the parents appeal the IPRC's decision, it will be necessary to forward the record, together with a statement of its decision, to a Special Education Appeal Board ("SEAB").[76]

A record of the IPRC's proceedings will include any written documents generated by the IPRC. This will include the notice of the hearing, the agenda, any letter requesting a health or psychological assessment and the written statement of decision, together with copies of all documents that the IPRC has received. The notes of individual committee members do not form part of the record, unless the member is charged with making notes on behalf of the IPRC. Should the IPRC ask a secretary to attend and make notes for the committee, these notes would form part of the record.

The record will include any report, assessment or other document that is presented by any party or that the IPRC might request or obtain in the course of its deliberations with respect to a particular student. This includes any document that has been obtained from the OSR. It should be noted that, while an SEAB will not be able to require that OSR records be produced without parental permission or the permission of a student aged 18 years or older,[77] the SEAB will be entitled to receive copies of all documents that form part of the IPRC's record, including records and assessments from the OSR. It will be important, therefore, that school board staff ensure that all relevant

[73] The authority for collection in this case is O. Reg. 181/98, s. 10, which requires school boards to establish IPRCs to make determinations on identification and placement of exceptional pupils.

[74] In the case of an IPRC's collection of information, see O. Reg. 181/98, s. 15 and, in the case of a review committee, see s. 27.

[75] *MFIPPA*, s. 29(2). In the case of collection of information by the IPRC, this person would be the chair of the IPRC.

[76] O. Reg. 181/98, s. 27(6).

[77] See footnote 57.

documents from the OSR are produced to the IPRC before it reaches its decision, so that a complete record has been compiled in the event of an appeal to a SEAB. Where parents do not consent to the production of OSR documents before the IPRC and OSR documents are not produced,[78] then the IPRC should, in its decision, carefully set out all information supplied by the teachers and principal, which may include information from OSR documents.

A form such as that suggested under the heading "Procedures" can be used to keep track of the proceedings in each case. The easiest way to keep track of documents is to number them consecutively as they are received by the IPRC and maintain a list of the documents, setting out a brief description of each document by its assigned number.

Electronic Recording of Meetings

Since no formal written record (such as a court transcript) of IPRC meetings is created, an issue can arise in conducting an IPRC meeting as to whether the meeting may be recorded by any participant. While people like recordings as a way to ensure clarity as to what was said, some people view the issue of electronic recording as a violation of their privacy rights. To others, a request to electronically record a meeting suggests a degree of mistrust of the process. Many people prefer not to be electronically recorded and, as a result, the recording of the proceedings can inhibit full and frank discussion, either because of natural reticence or because of a fear that taped comments might subsequently be played out of context or, worse, electronically altered.

The issue of whether IPRC meetings may be electronically recorded may be dealt with in a policy of the school board dealing with IPRC procedures. For example, the policy might permit the electronic recording of IPRC proceedings subject to defined conditions. Conditions might include the following: that all participants must first agree to be electronically recorded; that the process of electronically recording the meeting will not interfere with or interrupt the meeting; that the person who seeks to electronically record the meeting will be responsible for the cost of recording the meeting and will provide a copy of the electronic record to the IPRC (in which case, the electronic record becomes part of the IPRC's record).

Where the school board decides that, generally speaking, meetings should not be electronically recorded, it should make exceptions in appropriate circumstances. For example, where a parent has a disability that precludes him or her from making notes of the meeting, the parent might be permitted to audiotape the proceeding. Conditions similar to those set out here previously may be imposed in these circumstances, where appropriate.

---

[78] See the discussion here under the heading "Information to be Considered", for a discussion of the disclosure of OSR documents where parents do not consent.

Where the issue of electronically recording an IPRC meeting has not been dealt with in a school board policy, the matter is left to be determined by each IPRC on a case-by-case basis. In this situation, the IPRC has the authority to determine whether or not it will permit the electronic recording to occur. Each case will be different and the decision whether to permit the electronic recording should be made based on the circumstances of each individual case. Where the members of the IPRC themselves are not opposed to being electronically recorded, the IPRC may canvass the other participants to obtain their views on being electronically recorded. This input, while not required, [79] will allow the IPRC to consider, before it makes a decision on the issue, whether or not permitting the electronic recording of the meeting might generate a discomfort level for some participants that would inhibit their participation in the meeting and, therefore, undermine the IPRC process. Where the IPRC does permit a participant to electronically record the meeting, the IPRC may impose conditions, including a requirement that the IPRC be provided with a copy of the electronic recording or that the making of the recording must not disrupt the IPRC process.

As noted previously, there will be exceptional circumstances where the IPRC should permit an electronic recording to be made of the meeting. Again, conditions may be imposed on the granting of the request to electronically record the meeting, even where unusual circumstances justify the request. One condition that should always be imposed is that the IPRC be given a copy of the electronic recording.

The IPRC's Decision

Parents and the student (if aged 16 or older) and their representatives are entitled to be present when the IPRC makes its decisions on identification and placement.[80] This right exists whether the IPRC is dealing with a student who has not previously been identified as exceptional, a student who is being transferred from a demonstration school or with a review of a student's identification and/or placement.

The Supreme Court of Canada has made clear that the IPRC must ensure that its determinations are made "from a subjective, child-centred perspective, one that attempts to make equality meaningful from the child's point of view

---

79 Ontario Ministry of Education and Training, "Special Education Monographs No. 2: Identification, Placement and Review Committees" (Special Education Branch, October 1985), suggests that there is a legal risk to a chairperson to allow a person to tape record an IPRC meeting unless every person present gives written permission. It is the writers' view that this statement is not accurate, since the IPRC does have authority over its own processes and there is no individual common law or statutory privacy right that would override the IPRC's right to permit or even direct a meeting to be electronically recorded.

80 O. Reg. 181/98, s. 5(1)(*b*).

as opposed to that of the adults in his or her life".[81] In addition, an IPRC's decision must be consistent with the school board's Special Education Plan.[82]

Identification and Placement

In the case of a student who has not previously been identified as exceptional, the IPRC's mandate is to decide whether or not the student should be identified as exceptional. Where the IPRC decides that the student is exceptional, it must then determine which category or definition of exceptionality as defined by the Minister of Education applies to the student.[83]

Once the student is identified as exceptional, the IPRC must determine what the placement of the student should be. In making this determination, the IPRC must first consider whether or not a placement in a regular class with appropriate special education services would "meet the pupil's needs" and be "consistent with parental preferences" before it considers the option of placement in a special education class.[84]

The IPRC *must* decide in favour of a regular class placement for the student when, after considering all the relevant information it has obtained, it is satisfied that placement in a regular class "would meet the pupil's needs and is consistent with parental preferences".[85] This does not mean that the IPRC must decide in favour of special class placement where it is satisfied that a regular class placement would meet the student's needs, but the student's parents prefer a special class placement; nor is the IPRC bound to decide in favour of a regular class placement where it concludes that the student's needs could *not* be met there with appropriate special education services, while parental preference is for the regular class placement. An IPRC decision that does not reflect parental preferences, however, should be made carefully, recognizing that the outcome of a decision that is not reflective of parental preferences may be appealed by the parents.

It is often difficult to separate placement from the special education services and programs that a student may require. The IPRC is permitted to discuss proposals for special education services and programs for the student and *must* discuss proposals for special education services and programs where

---

81 *Eaton v. Brant County Board of Education* (1997), 142 D.L.R. (4th) 385, [1997] 1 S.C.R. 241 ("*Eaton*"), at para. 77. The school board, the IPRC, the Special Education Appeal Board and the Special Education Tribunal are equally bound by this direction of the Supreme Court of Canada.

82 O. Reg. 181/98, s. 12(2).

83 *Ibid.*, s. 18. See Chapter 4, "Identification and Exceptionality".

84 O. Reg. 181/98, s. 17(1). The IPRC may consider the following range of placements: a regular class with indirect support, a regular class with resource assistance, a regular class with withdrawal assistance, a special education class with partial integration or a special education class full-time: Ontario Ministry of Education, *op. cit.*, footnote 42, at pp. D10 to D11. See also Chapter 5, "Placement".

85 O. Reg. 181/98, s. 17(2).

the parent or student (aged 16 years or older) requests it to do so; however, while the IPRC may discuss special education services or programs, it may not make decisions about the services and programs to be provided — rather, it is limited to making recommendations that it will set out in its "statement of decision".[86]

Once the IPRC has reached its decision, the chair of the committee is obliged, "as soon as possible" to send a written statement of the decision to the parents of the student and to the student, if 16 years of age or older; to the principal who made the referral, where the referral was made by a principal; and to the director of education of the school board that established the IPRC.[87]

The IPRC's written statement of decision must indicate whether or not the student has been identified as an exceptional pupil and, if so, must include the following:

- a description of the student's strengths and needs as assessed by the committee;
- the categories and definitions of any exceptionalities identified by the committee, based on the categories and definitions established by the Minister of Education;
- the IPRC's decision on placement;
- the IPRC's recommendations, if any, on the special education services and programs that would be appropriate to provide to the student;
- when the recommended placement includes placement in a special education class, the reasons for that decision.[88]

While not required, where the IPRC's decision does not accord with parental preferences, it may be wise for the IPRC to record the reasons for its disagreement with the parents' wishes. This will provide parents with written insight on the IPRC's reasoning and will also make clear that consideration has been given to the parents' views.

Student Transferred from a Demonstration or Provincial School

Where the IPRC is considering a student who is being transferred from a demonstration school, there will be no need to make a determination that the student is exceptional in the first instance, since the student will already have been identified. The IPRC is still obliged to consider the categories and definitions of exceptionality that apply to the pupil; however, the main focus of the IPRC's deliberations will be on placement.

86 *Ibid.*, s. 16.
87 *Ibid.*, s. 18.
88 *Ibid.*

As in the case of a student who has not been previously identified, when considering placement for a student transferred from a provincial or demonstration school, the IPRC must first consider the option of placement in a regular class with appropriate special education services. Again, only where the IPRC concludes that such a placement would not meet the student's needs or where the parents would prefer a special education class placement, may the IPRC consider a placement other than a regular class placement.[89]

When the IPRC has reached its decision, the chair of the committee is obliged, "as soon as possible" to send a written statement of the decision to the parents of the student and to the student, if 16 years of age or older, and to the director of education of the school board that established the IPRC.[90]

The written statement must include the same points, listed here under the heading "Identification and Placement", that the IPRC must address where the student is already enrolled with the school board.[91]

Review of an Identified Student's Identification and Placement

Where the IPRC is charged with reviewing the identification or placement of an identified exceptional pupil, the committee must decide whether it is satisfied with the identification and placement of the student or whether either or both should be changed.[92]

When reviewing placement, where the student is in a regular class placement and the IPRC wishes to consider the option of special class placement, it must first determine that the regular class placement, with appropriate special education supports, is *not* meeting the student's needs. The IPRC must also consider the parents' views on the student's placement.[93]

Where the IPRC determines, on review, that it is satisfied with the identification and placement, it is required "as soon as possible" to send a written statement of confirmation of the student's identification and placement to a parent of the student and to the student, if aged 16 or older; to the principal of the school where the pupil's special education program is being provided; to the director of education of the school board that is providing the special education program; and, in the case where the special education program is being purchased by another board, to the director of education of the purchasing board.[94]

Where the IPRC decides that identification or placement or both should be changed, it is required, "as soon as possible", to provide written notification

89 *Ibid.*, s. 17.
90 *Ibid.*, s. 18.
91 *Ibid.*
92 *Ibid.*, s. 23.
93 *Ibid.*, s. 23(6).
94 *Ibid.*, s. 23(3).

to the same individuals listed above. In this case, however, the written statement must also set out the following:

- Whether the committee considers that the student should continue to be identified as an exceptional pupil and, if not, the reasons for this determination.
- Where the committee considers that the student should continue to be identified as exceptional, then the written statement must set out the following:
  - the committee's description of the student's strengths and needs;
  - the categories and definitions of any exceptionalities identified by the committee, and, where these are changed from the prior identification, the reasons for the changed determination;
  - the committee's decision on placement and, where this represents a change from the prior placement, the reasons for the changed placement; and
  - when the placement includes a special class placement, the reasons for this placement, whether or not this represents a change of placement.[95]

Recommendation that a Student Aged 21 Years or Older Remain in School

A "resident pupil" is entitled to attend an elementary school without payment of fees until the student reaches 21 years of age.[96] Where the student has completed elementary school, the student may attend secondary school without payment of fees for seven or more years.[97] Section 49.2 of the *Education Act* permits a school board to direct a student, in certain circumstances, to enrol in a continuing education course or class operated by the school board. Students who are subject to this direction are those who have attended one or more secondary schools for seven or more years or who have not attended school for four or more years after the end of the calendar year in which they turned 16, or who are going to reach the age of 21 years of age by December 31st in the school year.[98] This provision will not apply to an "exceptional pupil" where an IPRC recommends to a school board that an "exceptional pupil" who is 21 years of age or older remain in a secondary day program.[99] Such students are exempted from the application of section 49.2.

---

95 *Ibid.*, s. 23(4) and (5).

96 *Education Act*, ss. 32 and 33.

97 *Ibid.*, s. 38.

98 *Ibid.*, s. 49.2(1) and (2), and *Grants for Student Needs — Legislative Grants for the 2008-2009 School Board Fiscal Year*, O. Reg. 85/08.

99 O. Reg. 181/98, s. 16(3).

Should the IPRC decline to make such a recommendation, there is no right of appeal.[100]

PARENTAL REQUEST TO DISCUSS THE IPRC'S DECISION

Once the IPRC has rendered its decision and advised the parents of the decision in writing, the parent(s) may request a meeting with the IPRC to discuss the decision. This request must be in writing and must be delivered to the principal (or the director of education when the student is coming from a demonstration school) within 15 days of the day on which the parent receives the IPRC's statement of decision or, in the case of a review, the IPRC's confirmation of identification and placement.[101] Where the fifteenth day is a school holiday as defined in Regulation 304,[102] the time limit will be extended on a day-by-day basis to the next day that is not a school holiday. Where the statement of decision or confirmation is sent by ordinary mail to the parent, the parent is deemed to have received the statement on the fifth day following the date of mailing (or, if the fifth day is a school holiday, the next day that is not a school holiday) and the 15 days starts to run from that date.[103] Otherwise, the time frame for the parent's request starts to run on the actual date of delivery of the statement of decision or confirmation. It is important, therefore, that a record be kept of the manner of delivery of the statement of decision or confirmation and the date it is either mailed or actually delivered.

In the case of a referral of a student to the IPRC by a principal, the parent's request must be delivered to the principal. In the case of the transfer of a student from a demonstration school, the request must be forwarded to the director of education of the school board to which the student is being transferred.[104] In the case of a review of identification and/or placement, the parent's request to discuss the IPRC's decision must be sent to the principal of the school at which the student's special education program is provided.[105]

While an IPRC may refuse to deal with a request to discuss a statement of decision or confirmation that is received after the time limit has expired, an IPRC is not precluded from meeting with the parents to discuss a statement of decision or confirmation where the request to do so is received out of time — indeed, doing so might assist in avoiding an appeal by the parents; however, when an IPRC or a school board decides that the IPRC will accept late requests to discuss statements of decision or confirmation, guidelines should

[100] Where a school board has failed to include appropriate transition plans in the Individual Education Plan, it may be more likely to approve continued special education for exceptional students who are 21 or older.

[101] O. Reg. 181/98, ss. 19 and 24.

[102] *School Year Calendar, Professional Activity Days*, R.R.O. 1990, Reg. 304.

[103] O. Reg. 181/98, s. 3.

[104] *Ibid.*, s. 19.

[105] *Ibid.*, s. 24.

be established to determine the circumstances in which this will occur in order to ensure consistency in dealing with parents. For example, a late request might be accepted where the parent is able to establish to the satisfaction of the school board that the post office delivered the statement more than five days after it was mailed or where an exceptional circumstance precluded the parent from forwarding the request in a timely manner (*e.g.*, this might include a death or serious illness in the family or absence of the family due to vacation). Where the IPRC does decide that it will meet with parents who have made a request outside the statutory timelines, the IPRC should set out in writing that it is agreeing to meet with the parents "without prejudice" to the fact that the parents did not request the meeting within the required timelines. This will make clear that the IPRC is not waiving the statutory timelines should the parents subsequently attempt to appeal, relying on the fact that the IPRC did meet with them despite the late request.

On receipt of the request, the principal or director of education, as the case may be, must arrange for the IPRC to meet "as soon as possible" with the parent. Where the student, aged 16 or older, wishes to attend, the student must be included in the meeting. The principal or director of education should also be included in the meeting.[106]

Following the meeting between the IPRC and the parent (and the student, if aged 16 or older), the chair of the IPRC must, "as soon as possible", send a written notice to each individual who was originally entitled to receive a copy of the statement of decision or confirmation. The notice must state whether or not the IPRC has made any changes to its decision as a result of the meeting. Where the IPRC has decided to make changes, it must reissue the statement of decision or confirmation and set out written reasons for the changes. The reissued statement and written reasons must be sent out with the notice of changes.[107]

TRANSITION

Where a student who is not in a special education placement has been referred to an IPRC for a determination on identification, the pupil must be provided with a program that is appropriate to the pupil's apparent strengths and needs, together with appropriate special education services, pending the IPRC's decision. Unless the student's needs cannot be met in the regular class with appropriate special education services, the program must be provided in the regular class.[108] Similarly, a student transferring from another school board, who was identified while enrolled with the other school board, must be provided with an appropriate program and appropriate special education services pending a meeting with an IPRC of the new school board. Again,

[106] *Ibid.*, ss. 19 and 24.
[107] *Ibid.*
[108] *Ibid.*, s. 9.

where appropriate special education services would permit the student's needs to be met in a regular class, this interim placement will be appropriate and should be provided where regular class is the parent's preferred placement.

IMPLEMENTATION OF THE DECISION

Where an IPRC has made a placement decision, the school board may not implement the placement unless the parent of the student consents, in writing, to the placement or the time-period for the filing of a notice of appeal to an SEAB has expired without a notice of appeal being filed; however, upon parental consent being given or the time limit for appeal expiring without any notice of appeal being filed, the placement must be implemented "as soon as possible".[109]

Where the school board implements a placement decision of an IPRC without written consent of the parents (*i.e.*, after the expiry of the time period for filing an appeal), the school board must give written notice of the implementation to a parent of the pupil.[110]

The prohibition on changing a student's placement unless the parent has consented or the time to appeal the IPRC's decision has elapsed can prove to be troublesome for the party — whether the parent or the school board — who holds a strong belief that the existing placement is not in the student's best interests. The placement in place at the point an appeal is launched is effectively "stayed" pending completion of the appeal process; that is, it cannot be changed pending the completion of the appeal without the consent of the parent, unless the appeal were abandoned. An additional problem can arise where the stay is still in place at the point the student is eligible to be promoted from grade 8 to grade 9. Secondary schools are very different places from elementary schools and, often, the same special programs are offered in a very different manner in secondary schools than in elementary schools. It should be noted, first, that the stay of placement does not prevent promotion of the student from one grade to another. This may mean that, of necessity, the placement will have to be changed in some respects, but the school board is obliged to attempt to ensure that the placement in the new grade will be as close as possible to the "stayed" placement.

Where an appeal is launched that results in a stay of placement, the best solution will be for the school board and the parent to attempt to reach agreement on a temporary interim placement pending the completion of the appeal. Such agreement might be "without prejudice" to the position taken by either party in the appeal.

---

[109] *Ibid.*, ss. 20(1) and (2), 25(1) and (2).

[110] *Ibid.*, ss. 20(3) and 25(3).

7

The Individual Education Plan

INTRODUCTION

An Individual Education Plan ("IEP") is a written plan setting out the educational goals and expectations as well as the special education programs and services to be provided to a student who has been identified as exceptional and the methods by which the student's progress will be assessed.[1]

Prior to 1998, there was no specific legislative, regulatory or ministerial stipulation of what an IEP must contain, beyond the reference in section 1(1) of the *Education Act*[2] to such a plan under the definition of "special education programs":

> "special education program" means, in respect of an exceptional pupil, an educational program that is based on and modified by the results of continuous assessment and evaluation and that includes a plan containing specific objectives and an outline of educational services that meets the needs of the exceptional pupil.

In 1998, further requirements for the IEP were spelled out in section 6(3) of O. Reg. 181/98:

> The individual education plan must include,
> (a) specific educational expectations for the pupil;
> (b) an outline of the special education program and services to be received by the pupil; and
> (c) a statement of the methods by which the pupil's progress will be reviewed.

The regulation also requires, at section 6(4), that, for exceptional students aged 14 years or older (other than gifted students), the IEP must include "a plan for transition to appropriate post-secondary school activities, such as work, further education and community living".

1 *Identification and Placement of Exceptional Pupils*, O. Reg. 181/98, s. 6(3).
2 R.S.O. 1990, c. E.2.

In addition, the Ministry of Education has now developed several special education resource documents with which school boards are required to comply in developing IEPs.[3] In 2000, the Ministry released *Individual Education Plans: Standards for Development, Program Planning, and Implementation*[4] (the "*IEP Standards*"), which sets out the Ministry's current policy on IEPs. The requirements that the *IEP Standards* impose in the creation of IEPs are quite detailed and, therefore, in this chapter, we will include only a brief summary of the most important requirements. In 2004, the Ministry released *The Individual Education Plan (IEP): A Resource Guide*,[5] which, as the name implies, is intended as a guide only. Educators who are charged with the responsibility of developing IEPs should make reference to both these Ministry documents.

This chapter will review the requirements of IEPs imposed by O. Reg. 181/98 and Ministry policies.

MANDATORY INDIVIDUAL EDUCATION PLANS

An IEP must be developed for a student who has been identified as exceptional when the placement decision is implemented. This is so whether the placement decision is that of an Identification, Placement and Review Committee ("IPRC") — either in the first instance or on a review of placement — or a decision of the school board following a recommendation from a

---

3 The Ministry may have been responding to parental concerns that many IEPs lacked specificity and were not responsive.

4 (Toronto: The Ministry, 2000), available online at http://www.edu.gov.on.ca/eng/general/elemsec/speced/iep/iep.html. The Ministry apparently intends school boards to comply with the *IEP Standards*, as it has a monitoring power and refers to the *IEP Standards* in every curriculum document; however, there is no express regulatory authority for enforcing compliance with the *IEP Standards*. The "Introduction" section of the *IEP Standards* states that the Ministry will conduct a review of IEPs from randomly selected school boards to assess compliance with the articulated standards and require school boards whose IEPs do not comply with the standards to amend their practices. A copy of the school board's IEP form must be included in the board's special education plan and the Minister is authorized to require a board to amend its special education plan as the Minister determines necessary: *Special Education Programs and Services*, R.R.O. 1990, Reg. 306, s. 2(5).

5 Ontario Ministry of Education, *The Individual Education Plan (IEP): A Resource Guide* (Toronto: Ministry of Education, 2004), available online at http://www.edu.gov.on.ca/eng/general/elemsec/speced/guide/resource/index.html. This document is an updated version of the Ministry's resource document that was originally introduced in 1998: Ontario Ministry of Education and Training, *Individual Education Plan (IEP) Resource Guide* (Toronto: The Ministry, 1998), available online at http://www.edu.gov.on.ca/eng/general/elemsec/speced/iepeng.pdf. It also replaces the discussion of IEPs in Ontario Ministry of Education, *Special Education: A Guide for Educators* (Toronto: The Ministry, 2001), available online at http://www.edu.gov.on.ca/eng/general/elemsec/speced/guide.html.

Special Education Appeal Board or of a decision of the Special Education Tribunal.[6]

In any of these cases, the school board is required to "promptly" notify the principal of the school where the student's special education program is to be provided of the need to develop an IEP for the student. The principal is charged with the responsibility of ensuring that the IEP is developed and that it is done in consultation with the parent and, where the student is aged 16 years or older, in consultation with the student.[7]

There are circumstances, which will be discussed under the heading "Optional Individual Education Plans", in which an IEP may be developed for a student who has not been identified as exceptional; however, where the school board wishes to claim additional funding in relation to the needs of a student who has not been identified but who is receiving special education programs and services, an IEP must be developed for the student.[8]

OPTIONAL INDIVIDUAL EDUCATION PLANS

IEPs can also be developed for students who are receiving special education programs or services, but who have not been formally identified and for whom no additional funding is sought. In fact, many school boards in Ontario develop IEPs to guide the special education programs and services for large numbers of students who have special needs, but who have never undergone a formal IPRC process.[9]

---

6 O. Reg. 181/98, s. 6(1).

7 *Ibid.*, s. 6(2).

8 Ontario Ministry of Education, *Special Education Funding Guidelines: Special Equipment Amount (SEA) and Special Incidence Portion (SIP), 2008-09* (Toronto: The Ministry, 2008), available online at http://www.edu.gov.on.ca/eng/funding/0809/speced.pdf; *Grants For Student Needs — Legislative Grants for the 2009-2010 School Board Fiscal Year*, O. Reg. 155/09.

9 Although this practice is common, students with special needs who are not formally identified as exceptional do not have access to the full panoply of rights available under the statutory scheme. The practice also seems inconsistent with a school board's obligations with respect to early identification: see Ontario Deputy Minister of Education, "Policy/Program Memorandum No. 11: Early Identification of Children's Learning Needs" (Toronto: Ministry of Education, 1982), available online at http://www.edu.gov.on.ca/extra/eng/ppm/11.html. Thus, there are negative aspects associated with this practice. It may also create issues for identified students going on to post-secondary education who may need to access assistance from the disability services office in the college or university they are attending. Many students find it much easier to access these services when their exceptionalities have been properly identified prior to their departure from secondary school. See Chapter 15, "Post-Secondary Education". In fact, an argument is made by Justice for Children and Youth that, where a student is exceptional, the student has the right to be identified as exceptional and a parent's wishes should not interfere with the child's legal right to identification and accommodation.

DEVELOPMENT PROCESS

Legal Responsibility

The development of the IEP and its compliance with provincial standards are the principal's responsibility.[10] Therefore, the principal has the authority to decide what should be included in the IEP; however, this is subject to the requirements set out in the legislation and Ministry policy.

A principal may designate a vice-principal or teacher to act on his or her behalf in co-ordinating and overseeing the development of the IEP; however, the ultimate responsibility for the IEP will remain with the principal. As a result, the principal is required to provide his or her assurance that the IEP is appropriate to the student's strengths and needs and meets the requirements of the *IEP Standards* by signing the IEP.[11]

Development Team

The "team" who will develop an IEP will be designated by the principal and, in addition to the principal (or vice-principal), may include the student's teachers, special education consultants and other professionals who work with the student. All school board team members who are involved in the development of the IEP must be identified in it. Collectively, they must have knowledge of the Ontario curriculum, have knowledge of the student and, where possible, experience teaching the student, have knowledge of the special education strategies and resources available in the school board, and be qualified to provide or supervise the provision of special education programs and services to meet the needs of the student.[12]

Information

The *IEP Standards* impose on the principal an obligation to ensure that information from a variety of sources is considered in developing a student's IEP. This will include information in the Official Student Record — including report cards and past IEPs — classroom observation, current work of the student, information from the student, the parent, school and board staff who have worked with the student and, where the parent consents (or information and privacy legislation permits), from outside professionals and paraprofessionals who have done assessments, performed diagnostic tests or otherwise worked with the student. The IEP must include a list of the information sources used in its development and updating.[13]

---

10 See *IEP Standards*, *op. cit.*, footnote 4, at section 10, "Staff Involvement in the Development of the IEP".

11 *Ibid.*

12 *Ibid.*

13 *Ibid.*, section 11, "Information Sources".

Consultation

In developing the IEP, the principal is required to consult with the parent and the student, in the case of a student who is 16 years of age or older. In the case of a student for whom a transition plan is required,[14] the principal must also consult with such community agencies and post-secondary institutions as the principal considers appropriate in the process of completing the transition plan portion of the IEP.[15]

Parent and Student

In the case of the identification of the student in the first instance or a review situation where there is likely to be a disagreement over placement, the principal's consultation with the parent (and student, if aged 16 or older) will normally take place following the IPRC process. Where the placement is a continuing one and there is ongoing agreement on the student's special education program and the special education services to be provided to the student, the consultation process is likely to be much more informal and may even be part of the "pre-IPRC" process of discussion between the school and the parents.

Since the principal has a legal duty to consult when developing a student's IEP, the principal should, during the process of developing the plan, seek input from parents and students over the age of 16 years and give fair consideration to any suggestions made by the parent/student.

While consultation is not defined, the presentation to a parent of an IEP for approval — in what appears to be a full and final form — might not be perceived by the parent to be consultation, particularly where the principal declines to make any changes to the IEP after the parent/student has reviewed the form. Thus, the IEP form given to the parents for their input should not be signed by the principal, since this would suggest finality; marking the form as "draft" would also be helpful. The principal is not obliged to accept every suggestion provided by the parent or student. Indeed, the principal may decide to incorporate none of the parent/student suggestions into the IEP; however, in doing so, the principal must give due consideration to what the parent/student has had to say during the consultation process and the principal should have a legitimate reason for dismissing any parental/student suggestions that are not used. In such a case, it is prudent for the principal to ensure that his or her reasons have been clearly communicated to the parent/student. An open discussion and exchange of ideas will provide at least an opportunity for parents and students to feel that they have been consulted, even where the principal does not agree with all of their ideas.

---

[14] See O. Reg. 181/98, s. 6(4), (5) and (6). See also the discussion later in this chapter, under the heading "Transition Plans".

[15] *Ibid.*, s. 6(7).

Finally, it is important to note that a parent's refusal to "sign" the IEP does not mean that the IEP cannot be "finalized". A parent's right is only to be consulted and a parent cannot dictate what goes into — or is left out of — an IEP.

Transition Plans

For exceptional students who are 14 years of age or older — other than those students identified as exceptional solely on the basis of giftedness — the IEP must include a plan for the transition of the student to "appropriate post-secondary school activities, such as work, further education or community living". The principal is required to "consult with such community agencies and post-secondary educational institutions as he or she considers appropriate".[16]

Documentation of Consultations

The IEP must include a form documenting the date and the outcome of each consultation.[17] The parent and student (if aged 16 or older) must be asked to sign the form and indicate whether they were consulted in the development of the IEP, whether they declined the opportunity to be consulted and whether they received a copy of the IEP. Any comments they provide must be noted on the form.[18]

IPRC and Special Education Tribunal Recommendations

In developing the IEP, the principal is required to take into consideration any recommendations of the IPRC or Special Education Tribunal regarding special education programs or services.[19]

CONTENTS OF THE IEP

The contents of the IEP are dictated generally by section 6(3) of O. Reg. 181/98 and, in detail, by the *IEP Standards.* Generally, the IEP must include:

- a statement of the specific educational expectations for the pupil;

---

16 *Ibid.*, s. 6(4), (5) and (7). Additional information regarding the transition planning process can be found in the Ministry of Education's resource document, *Transition Planning: A Resource Guide, 2002* (Toronto: The Ministry, 2002), available online at http://www.edu.gov.on.ca/eng/general/elemsec/speced/transiti/transition.html.

17 *IEP Standards*, *op. cit.*, footnote 4, at section 8, "The Transition Plan".

18 *Ibid.*, section 9, "Parent/Student Consultation".

19 *Ibid.*, section 5, "Special Education Strategies, Accommodations, and Resources" and section 11, "Information Sources". These requirements arise from O. Reg. 181/98, s. 6(6)(*b*).

- an outline of the special education program and services to be received by the pupil; and
- a statement of the methods by which the pupil's progress will be reviewed.

As noted previously, the regulation also requires that, where the student is 14 years of age or older — except in the case of a student who is identified solely as gifted — the IEP "must include a plan for transition to appropriate post-secondary school activities, such as work, further education and community living".[20]

There is much additional information that must be included in order to meet the *IEP Standards*, which we have summarized below:[21]

- *Reason for developing an IEP* — The IEP must state the reason it is being created — *e.g.*, because the student was identified as exceptional or to support a funding claim or because the unidentified student requires special education programs or services.[22]
- *Student Profile* — The student's basic profile will include the student's full name; gender; date of birth; student identification number; current school year; name of the school and principal; date of the student's most recent IPRC and the student's exceptionality or exceptionalities; the IPRC's most recent placement decision; the student's current grade and/or special class placement; the subjects or courses to which the IEP applies; relevant medical conditions; relevant assessment data; and elementary school program exemptions or secondary school compulsory course substitutions.[23]
- *The Student's Strengths and Needs* — The IEP must include a description of the strengths and needs of the student. Where the student has been identified by the IPRC, this description must be based on and consistent with the description of strengths and needs provided by the IPRC. Where the student has not been identified, the description of strengths and needs must be based on appropriate educational, psychological and/or health assessments, as well as on observations of the student.[24]
- *The Special Education Program* — Where a student is working on unmodified provincial curriculum expectations at the regular grade level, the IEP need not set out the student's learning expectations. In

[20] O. Reg. 181/98, s. 6(4) and (5).

[21] The summary is taken from the *IEP Standards*, *op. cit.*, footnote 4, under the heading "Standards for Development and Program Planning". The list that follows is not intended to be exhaustive. Other IEP requirements arising from the *IEP Standards* are mentioned elsewhere in this chapter. Please see the *IEP Standards* for the full list of requirements.

[22] *Ibid.*, section 1, "Reasons for Developing an IEP".

[23] *Ibid.*, section 2, "Student Profile".

[24] *Ibid.*, section 3, "The Student's Strengths and Needs".

this case, the IEP will indicate that fact and will set out the student's current level of achievement. In other cases, a student's program will include three components: an assessment of the student's current level of achievement; annual goals for the student; and the learning expectations that meet the unique educational needs of the student. In instances where the student is working on learning expectations that are alternative to the provincial curriculum, the student's level of achievement will be based on a description of progress towards those learning expectations. Where the student's learning expectations are based on modifications to the provincial curriculum, the student's level of achievement will be based on the letter grade or mark as reported on the student's provincial report card.
Where the student's learning expectations are modified from the provincial curriculum in any respect or are alternative expectations, the IEP must set out annual goals for the student, based on what the student can reasonably be expected to achieve by school year end. Similarly, where the student is working on modified expectations or alternative expectations, the IEP must set out learning expectations that describe the specific knowledge and skills that the student will be expected to demonstrate during the school year in order to progress from the student's current level of achievement to achieve the annual goals.[25]

- *Special Education Strategies, Accommodations and Resources* — The IEP must set out the individualized teaching strategies, individualized accommodations and resources that will be provided to facilitate the student's learning. This includes an identification of teaching staff and non-teaching staff (including professional and paraprofessional special education support staff) who will be working with the student, the services that will be provided and the frequency of contact with the student. Individualized equipment to be used with the student must also be set out in the IEP.[26]
- *Assessment, Evaluation and Reporting* — The IEP must describe the methods that will be used to measure the student's achievement, including any accommodations made to regular classroom assessment procedures for the student — *e.g.*, administering tests individually or providing additional time to complete assignments. Since the progress of exceptional students must be reported to parents with the same frequency as for other students, the IEP must indicate the dates on which evaluations will be completed (at least once every reporting period) and the format to be used to report student progress to parents.[27]

---

25 *Ibid.*, section 4, "The Special Education Program".
26 *Ibid.*, section 5, "Special Education Strategies, Accommodations and Resources".
27 *Ibid.*, section 6, "Assessment, Evaluation, and Reporting".

- *Provincial Assessments* — The IEP must set out the testing accommodations that will be provided to the student to facilitate the student's participation in provincial assessments of student achievement; however, any such accommodations cannot impact the level or content of the assessment, performance criteria of the assessment or the reliability or validity of the assessment. Moreover, accommodations must comply with policies of the Education Quality and Accountability Office and the Ministry of Education. In those rare cases where it is determined that a provincial assessment is not appropriate for the student, the IEP must include a statement explaining the reasons for this and identify the applicable Ministry or EQAO policy under which the exemption arises.[28]
- *Transition Plan* — As has been noted, for identified students — other than those students identified solely as gifted — aged 14 years or older, the IEP must include a transition plan that addresses the student's transition from school into post-secondary activities that are appropriate for the student. Such activities include "work, further education and community living". The plan must set out goals for the transition that are specific, realistic and build on the student's identified strengths, needs and interests. Persons involved in providing assistance in the transition process must be identified and timelines must be included.[29]

TIMELINES FOR COMPLETION OF THE IEP

The IEP must be completed within 30 days of the student's placement in a special education program.[30] The *IEP Standards* say that for this purpose, "placement" means "one of the following":

- the first day of attendance in a new special education program, whether specified in an IPRC decision or provided by the school board without formal identification;
- the first day of a new school year or semester in which the student continues in a placement confirmed by an IPRC review; or
- the first day of enrolment in a special education program resulting from a change of placement.[31]

---

[28] *Ibid.*, section 7, "Provincial Assessments".

[29] *Ibid.*, section 8, "The Transition Plan". See also *Transition Planning: A Resource Guide, 2002*, *op. cit.*, footnote 16.

[30] O. Reg. 181/98, ss. 6(8) and 7(7).

[31] *IEP Standards*, *op. cit.*, footnote 4, section 12, "Date of Completion of the IEP".

The *IEP Standards* do not address timelines for an IEP required because of a change of identification, although if the change of identification involves a new placement, then an IEP will be required.

Both the date on which the student begins the placement and the date on which the IEP is completed must be recorded in the IEP. A copy must be sent to the parent of the student and the student (if aged 16 years or older).[32]

REVIEW

The IEP is often referred to as a "living document". It must be reviewed by the principal in order to determine whether or not it should be updated each time there is a change in placement and each time an existing placement is confirmed through the regular review process or through an appeal.[33] The *IEP Standards*, however, impose a much more detailed process of monitoring, which requires the assigned staff member to develop and implement the IEP in carrying out certain co-ordination activities. This includes establishing a plan for evaluating and monitoring the progress made by the student in achieving the learning expectations set out in the IEP.[34]

Where, through the process of regular evaluation and monitoring, it is identified that adjustments are needed in the student's special education program — either because the student is not progressing towards his or her goals or is exceeding the learning expectations identified in the IEP — the IEP must be adjusted. Where these adjustments require significant changes to the learning expectations set out in the IEP, the parent and student, if aged 16 years or older, must be consulted prior to the changes being made.[35]

ONTARIO STUDENT RECORD

The IEP is to be kept in the Ontario Student Record unless the parent of the student has objected in writing.

---

32 O. Reg. 181/98, ss. 6(8) and 7(7).

33 *Ibid.*, s. 7(1) and (2).

34 *IEP Standards*, *op. cit.*, footnote 4, under the heading "Standards for Implementation and Review".

35 *Ibid.*

8

Role of Parent Advocates

Since the first edition of this book, there have been several developments with respect to the use of representatives in special education matters. More law schools offer a course in education law. More lawyers have attended training sessions on special education issues. Paralegals are now required to be licensed by the Law Society of Upper Canada, as lawyers have always been. While there is a growing number of "lay" advocates (*i.e.*, non-lawyers or non-paralegals) who may have some practical or personal experience with the special education system, legal limits have been placed on the ability of such lay advocates to provide advice on the law or make submissions on the law on behalf of parents.[1]

---

1 The *Law Society Act*, R.S.O. 1990, c. L.8, prohibits the provision of legal services by any person who is not licensed by the Law Society of Upper Canada unless the requirement to be licensed is specifically exempted by Law Society by-laws. Section 1(5) of the Act defines the provision of legal services as follows: "[A] person provides legal services if the person engages in conduct that involves the application of legal principles and legal judgment with regard to the circumstances or objectives of a person." Section 1(6) stipulates that giving a person advice with respect to the legal interests, rights or responsibilities of the person or of another person, and representing a person in a proceeding before an adjudicative body are activities that are included in this definition. By-law 4, s. 30(1), para. 5 exempts from the requirement to be licensed any person:

i. whose profession or occupation is not and does not include the provision of legal services or the practice of law,
ii. *who provides the legal services only occasionally*,
iii. who provides the legal services only for and on behalf of a related person, within the meaning of the *Income Tax Act* (Canada), a friend or a neighbour, *and*
iv. *who does not expect and does not receive any compensation, including a fee, gain or reward, direct or indirect, for the provision of the legal services.* [emphasis added]

It is an offence for a person other than a licensed lawyer or paralegal to provide legal services unless the person falls within one of the exemptions stipulated in the By-Law. In other provinces, the provision of legal services by qualified and regulated legal professionals is similarly governed by statutes.

Most parents feel deeply invested in the education of their children who have special educational needs. The need that some parents feel to have the assistance of an advocate when dealing with the school or the school board comes directly from the perception that the relationship between parents and the school or school board has disintegrated into a "we/them" situation, in which the school has all the power and the parent is not being heard. Such parents often feel relatively less powerful than the educators and school board officials with whom they are dealing and may want advocacy support in an effort to level the playing field. Some parents may feel that school staff do not understand enough about their child's particular exceptionality and needs or the way the exceptionality is manifested, and may seek an "expert" advocate to help them explain to the relevant educators what they know about their child. Some parents may be exhausted and emotional from advocating for their children in the health care and social services systems and feel they need an education advocate who can remain calmer than they themselves can. They may have had a bad experience in a previous school or school board and may have difficulty trusting the current situation. They may feel the need for an advocate who understands human rights and education law in order to assist them in situations where they feel that their child's rights are being ignored. Many of these parents feel they cannot afford a lawyer and the legal aid certificate system is not available to any parent, no matter how economically disadvantaged, to help them retain a lawyer.

As a result, a variety of types of lay advocates (*i.e.*, non-lawyers or non-paralegals) have emerged. There are advocates with no particular training or expertise who simply provide emotional support for parents or serve as witnesses to the process so that parents feel more equal to educators. There are advocates with training or experience in specific disabilities who may have information about effective programs and strategies. There are advocates, perhaps with mediation or negotiation training, who can listen effectively to help parents express their concerns and wishes as well as hearing the school's concerns and wishes. There are advocates who feel they have learned so much from navigating the special education system on behalf of their own children that they can help other parents, either as no-cost volunteers or as money-earning ventures. There are advocates, with a variety of backgrounds and expertise, who have taken training with the Ontario Association of Education Advocates and are members of the Association. While the Association provides useful training, it does not have regulatory power, cannot set uniform standards of practice and cannot discipline members who do not measure up to the Association's non-binding standards.

Apart from lay advocates who are untrained in the law, there are licensed legally trained practitioners. These are paralegals[2] and lawyers who must have

[2] Unfortunately, no college offers a course in education law or special education at this time. Courses in advocacy are available.

specific qualifications in order to be able to practice and who must abide by professional standards of practice and conduct; however, the vast majority of lawyers practising in the education field in Ontario represent school boards or teacher federations and would consider it a potential conflict of interest to represent parents or students. While there are lawyers who are competent and willing to represent parents and students, they may be difficult to find, even for families that can afford to retain legal counsel.

PARENTS' RIGHTS TO BE REPRESENTED BY ADVOCATES

The Ministry of Education has recognized the role of lay advocates in its *Shared Solutions* document, a resource for reducing conflict:[3]

> All parents have the right to advocate for their child. Parents may wish to work with a parent advocate if they are unfamiliar with school board processes, or if their child's needs are complex, or if they feel that the intervention of a third party might be helpful. A parent advocate may accompany the parents to meetings to help them express their concerns. Parent advocates may be people with training in advocacy or may have some special education experience, possibly gained as an advocate for their own children. Parent advocates have a role to play in special education in Ontario; they can help improve communication between parents and educators and prevent or limit the scope of a potential conflict.
>
> Advocacy for a student with special education needs works best when the parent or parent advocate:
>
> - has proven relationship/communication skills and/or an existing positive working relationship with educators;
> - is familiar with how special education programs and services are designed and provided;
> - is familiar with special education policy/legislation;
> - is familiar with the school system in which the student is registered.

ADVOCATES AT INFORMAL MEETINGS

Sometimes, parents want to bring advocates to help them with such things as their consultation in the development of an Individual Education Plan or in putting their views across in case conferences. Parents have no legal entitlement to representation in these activities, which are not hearings or appeals. The decision as to whether to permit additional advocacy support will be up to school administration.

It may be useful to consider the reason for the desire for an advocate. Resources that help parents feel more comfortable may also help school staff. Where the parent seeks to bring a lay advocate who has some expertise to offer regarding the student's exceptionality, the school board may want to consider

---

[3] Ontario Ministry of Education, *Shared Solutions — A Guide to Preventing and Resolving Conflicts Regarding Programs and Services for Students with Special Education Needs* (Toronto: The Ministry, 2007), available online at http://www.edu.gov.on.ca/eng/general/elemsec/speced/shared.html, at p. 27.

permitting the advocate to attend informal meetings. Alternatively, where the lay advocate is able to help the parent focus and articulate his/her views, this can assist, particularly where the lay advocate brings a more objective view to the process than that of which the parent is capable.

Where the parent seeks to have a lawyer or paralegal attend such meetings, however, there is a risk that the dynamics of the meeting may be impacted by a shift in focus to legal issues instead of pedagogical issues. Parents do not have a right to bring legal counsel to informal meetings and may do so only when the school board agrees. School board decisions on whether or not the parents will be permitted to bring their lawyer to an informal meeting are best made on a case-by-case basis. Where the school board does agree to permit the parents to bring their own lawyer, normally, the school board will want its own legal counsel to attend.

In the, hopefully, rare event that a lay advocate accompanying a parent to an informal school meeting acts in a manner that is disruptive of the proceedings and/or abusive towards to school staff,[4] a school may prohibit the attendance of that individual at future informal meetings.

ADVOCATES AT THE IDENTIFICATION PLACEMENT REVIEW COMMITTEE

Regulation 181/98, the regulation governing Identification, Placement and Review Committees ("IPRCs"), specifies that a parent and student over 16 may have a representative to speak on their behalf or otherwise support them.[5] "Representative" is not defined, but would seem to include all of the types of advocates described above, including lawyers and paralegals. Since the IPRC is a committee rather than an adjudicative body and since the focus of the IPRC is usually pedagogical in nature, it is not usual for legal issues to be discussed or argued at IPRC meetings.[6] Consequently, unless a legal issue arises during the course of the IPRC in connection with which the lay advocate either advises the parent or makes submissions on the parent's behalf, no question will normally arise respecting the ability of the lay advocate to represent the parent at the IPRC meeting.

4 Unfortunately, there have been cases where lay advocates working with parents have been disrespectful and even abusive towards school staff. To say the least, such behaviour can serve only to exacerbate any rifts that have been developing in the parent/school relationship. It is important for such lay advocates to understand that they are obliged to comply with the Provincial Code of Conduct, which requires that all persons in the school community act with civility and respect towards each other and that they are not helping their "clients" with such conduct.

5 *Identification and Placement of Exceptional Pupils*, O. Reg. 181/98, s. 5.

6 Occasionally, there may be differences of opinion about the relevance of information that one of the participants wants to provide to the IPRC. Sometimes, there are also disagreements about whether something is a program or service and can, therefore, be the subject of an IPRC recommendation.

ADVOCATES AT THE SEAB

The provisions of Reg. 181/98 relating to a Special Education Appeal Board ("SEAB") do not specify the right to a representative; however, because the SEAB is dealing with an appeal from a decision made by an IPRC where the parent had the right to a representative before the IPRC, it follows that the parent would likely be entitled to have a representative before the SEAB. This would, however, be a decision to be made by the SEAB.

ADVOCATES AT THE SPECIAL EDUCATION TRIBUNAL

It is clear that the Special Education Tribunal ("the Tribunal") is an adjudicative body. Therefore, in jurisdictions such as Ontario where legal restrictions apply regarding who can provide legal services, only licensed legal practitioners and those specifically permitted to provide "legal services" may "represent" school boards and parents and make presentations on their behalf at the hearing.[7]

The Tribunal has specifically noted this restriction in its Rules of Procedure. The Rules of Procedure distinguish between "representatives", who are defined as "either a lawyer or a licensed paralegal, appointed by a Party to represent the Party in the Appeal",[8] and "advocates" or "advisers", who are not licensed legal practitioners. Only those advocates who are volunteers — family, friends and neighbours — may appear before the Tribunal to present the parent's case. Paid lay advocates have no status to represent a family before the Tribunal and no standing to assist parties in representing themselves. Rule 3.1 of the Tribunal's Rules of Procedure defines an "advocate" as a friend, family member, or neighbour who accompanies and helps the party on a volunteer basis (*i.e.*, no payment of fee, directly or indirectly).

The Tribunal has indicated that it does not expect that all parties will be represented by counsel or a lay advocate, but does encourage them to communicate their representation plans to the Tribunal.[9]

Where the Tribunal determines that a lay advocate or adviser is not competent to represent or advise a party properly or does not appear to understand the duties and responsibilities involved in acting for a party at a hearing, or is refusing to comply with those duties or responsibilities, the

---

7 See footnote 1.

8 Rules of Procedure, Special Education (Ontario) Tribunal ("Rules of Procedure"), rule 3.14, available online at http://www.oset-tedo.ca/eng/pdfs/rules.pdf.

9 The Tribunal's Form A, "Notice of Appeal", and Form B, "Response to Notice of Appeal", ask the parties to state whether or not they will be represented: see http://www.oset-tedo.ca.

Tribunal may exclude the advocate from the hearing.[10] In contrast, the Tribunal may not exclude a lawyer who is representing a party or advising a witness.

COMPETENCY OF LAY ADVOCATES

Since the Tribunal has said that it will exclude advocates who are not competent to represent a party, it is useful to consider the Tribunal's description of competent representation:[11]

> A competent representative is a person who is knowledgeable about special education legislation as well as the Tribunal process. In addition to ensuring that the parents are prepared for the hearing, understand the Tribunal's procedures, and are ready to present their case to the Tribunal, the representative's work can consist of helping the parents to:
>
> - determine what outcome (remedy) will best meet the student's needs, that is, the way the parents want the Tribunal to change or modify the school board's identification and/or placement decision;
> - identify what evidence should be presented to the Tribunal;
> - prepare the opening and closing statements and decide on questions to ask witnesses called to give evidence;
> - prepare and organize the documents to be submitted as evidence, such as by selecting those that are relevant and organizing them in a logical way (*e.g.*, in a tabbed binder);
> - select their witnesses and help prepare them for the hearing by, for example, discussing with them what they might be asked at the hearing;
> - decide whether the student will be present at the hearing;
> - prepare the student, if needed, to give evidence to the Tribunal.

COST OF REPRESENTATION

The Tribunal does not arrange or pay for representation for parties. The Tribunal cannot order one party to pay for representation for the other party, nor does it determine or comment on the qualifications or expertise of the representative chosen by a party. School boards are almost always represented by lawyers. Many parents choose to or feel compelled to represent themselves.[12]

---

10 *Statutory Powers Procedure Act*, R.S.O. 1990, c. S.22, s. 23; rule 10.7. See also the discussion of competency, later in this chapter.

11 Ontario Special Education Tribunal, "Information for Parties" (Toronto: The Tribunal, 2008), available online at http://www.oset-tedo.ca/eng/pdfs/information09.pdf.

12 While the Tribunal cannot make an order requiring one party to pay for the representation of another party, proceedings in which one party is unrepresented may be less efficient and more frustrating for the party that is represented by counsel. As a result, in the interests of an effective resolution, school boards may consider whether, in specific, very challenging or complicated cases, it is in the

FINDING REPRESENTATIVES

Parents often find a representative through a referral from other parents or from the various advocacy organizations for exceptional children. Low-income parents can approach a community-based legal clinic for information or referrals. School boards can help parents by suggesting such outside sources of help.

---

boards' own best interests to provide funding for counsel for an unrepresented parent.

9

Alternative Dispute Resolution: Mediation

INTRODUCTION

The normal litigation processes in Canada are based on an "adversarial model" in which the parties to a dispute attempt to convince a decision-maker that one of them should "win" the dispute. Alternative Dispute Resolution ("ADR") is a term that encompasses the various processes used to resolve disputes outside the normal litigation routes, including processes that are non-adversarial in nature.

The Ontario Ministry of Education has encouraged special educators to consider approaches designed to avert conflicts that end up in litigation. In 2007, the Ministry issued *Shared Solutions: A Guide to Preventing and Resolving Conflicts Regarding Programs and Services for Students With Special Education Needs*,[1] which provides an overview of techniques that can be used to avoid conflicts in the first place and resolve disputes before adversarial proceedings begin.

In this chapter, we will focus on one of the best-known ADR processes: mediation. Specifically we discuss some advantages of mediation — both in general and, more specifically, in the special education context.

Mediation is assuming an increasingly central role in the special education appeal process. As will be discussed later in this chapter, the Special Education Tribunal now routinely offers mediation to parties prior to hearing an appeal; however, it is not necessary for an appeal to be launched in order to access mediation. When the parents and school board agree, a mediator can be brought in prior to an appeal being made — and increasingly, Special

1 Ontario Ministry of Education, *Shared Solutions: A Guide to Preventing and Resolving Conflicts Regarding Programs and Services for Students With Special Education Needs* (Toronto: The Ministry, 2007), available online at http://www.edu.gov.on.ca/eng/general/elemsec/speced/shared.pdf.

Education Appeal Boards are taking a mediation approach in their meetings with the parties.

SOME ADVANTAGES OF MEDIATION

It is now widely recognized that the litigation process is fundamentally ill-suited for achieving a lasting and mutually satisfactory resolution of many kinds of disputes.

Because of its adversarial nature, litigation can cause or exacerbate animosity between the parties. This can be very harmful where the parties need to maintain an ongoing relationship.

Litigation also focuses, almost exclusively, on the enforcement of legal rights. Some types of disputes, although framed in terms of competing legal rights, have more to do with emotional reactions, personal interests, relationship issues, value judgments, broader policy considerations and other factors. Although litigation provides a forum for the parties to determine their respective legal rights, it often results in "winner takes all" outcomes that do not address these deeper concerns. Accordingly, litigation can sometimes result in "lose-lose" situations, where even the party who "wins" will not be truly satisfied with the outcome of the proceedings.

Moreover, litigation is a time-consuming and expensive process. Parties who expend considerable time and resources seeking a determination of their legal rights, only to find that the end result does not really address the interests that led them to commence the litigation, often feel that they have "lost" more than they have "won" through the litigation process.

Mediation is a process whereby the parties to a dispute enlist the assistance of a third party to endeavour to resolve outstanding issues without the necessity for litigation. Through mediation, the parties are encouraged and assisted to focus less on the enforcement of legal rights and more on identifying and addressing the interests underlying the dispute.[2] From the perspective of the parties, the goal of the process is to find a "win-win" resolution that — where necessary or desirable — will preserve their relationship.

Mediation is a very low-risk method of dispute resolution. The process is entirely voluntary and consensual.[3] The mediator cannot make decisions that

---

2 The interest-based model of mediation is generally utilized in the context of the special education decision-making; however, as discussed further in Chapter 12, "The Human Rights Process". Where mediation arises in the context of a human rights proceeding, the Human Rights Tribunal of Ontario will use a rights-based approach to mediation. Under a rights-based approach, greater emphasis is placed on the legal rights of the parties and what they might expect to achieve in the event of litigation.

3 It is widely recognized that mediation is unlikely to be successful unless the parties agree to mediation and accept the involvement and assistance of the mediator. Accordingly, mediation is generally only attempted where all the parties to a dispute agree to participate.

are binding on the parties.[4] In the vast majority of cases, the parties and the mediator will enter into an agreement protecting matters discussed in the mediation from disclosure in the event that the matter proceeds to litigation. Mediation gives the parties the opportunity to work together with the mediator to reach a resolution of the dispute themselves — an opportunity that may not be available if formal litigation were to ensue. As a result, participants usually have very little to lose — and a great deal to gain — by agreeing to mediation.

Mediation is also an extremely flexible method of dispute resolution. Mediation provides the parties with an opportunity to be creative in finding a resolution to their dispute. The parameters of the resolution are not limited by the possible outcomes of litigation; they are only limited by the imagination of the parties. Mediation can take place at any time — before proceedings are commenced, after proceedings are commenced but before a hearing begins, or at any time up to the release of the final decision by the decision-maker.[5]

Finally, mediation is usually less time-consuming and less expensive than formal litigation. Even where the mediation is lengthy, the time and expense associated with mediation will usually still be less than the time and expense associated with formal litigation — and, where the mediation results in a settlement, the results will usually be more palatable to all concerned.

MEDIATION AND SPECIAL EDUCATION

Special education disputes involve both ongoing relationships and a wide range of "non-legal" issues. As a result, these disputes are often very difficult to resolve "successfully" through formal litigation.

The focus of the special education process should always be on the best interests of the student. The student's parents and the educators who work with the student every day are in a much better position to identify and work towards those best interests than an external tribunal and, indeed, conflict and litigation can be destructive to the student's best interests.

The home-school/parent-teacher relationship is fundamental to the special education process. A positive and co-operative relationship between the student, his or her parents, school board personnel and school staff is an essential component of a successful ongoing educational experience for a

4 The parties may decide to give the mediator the power to make binding decisions. In such a case, the mediation is usually called "mediation-arbitration" (commonly referred to as "med-arb") and the mediator is more properly referred to as a "mediator-arbitrator".

5 Notably, a school board's decision in response to a recommendation by the Special Education Appeal Board is not considered a "final" decision, because it can be appealed to the Special Education Tribunal. As a result, mediation can usefully occur after this decision has been made.

student with special needs.[6] Both school boards and parents should give careful consideration to the impact that litigation may have on this relationship — and on the educational and emotional well-being of the student.

Special education disputes cannot and should not be viewed merely as contests between competing legal rights. Rather, these disputes usually occur when the parents and school officials have conflicting views about the educational approach that will best serve the student's special needs. Differing medical diagnoses, pedagogical theories, religious or social values and perceptions of events often underlie disputes between parents and school officials about the appropriateness of identification and/or placement decisions. The kind of "all or nothing" outcomes generated by litigation will usually do little to resolve these differing views. As a result, even where one party "wins" the litigation, ongoing disputes may occur about the implementation of the decision.

Mediation may assist to address parental concerns that the parents are not on a level playing field with school officials. The mediator is not another person sent by the school board to "make the parents understand". Rather, the mediator will help both the school board and parents to understand each other; however, the perception of a power imbalance will not be easily changed where the school board brings to the mediation a contingent of staff who have all been involved in the case. The parents, who will often attend without any support from an advocate or lawyer, may feel overwhelmed in a situation in which they are significantly "outnumbered" by school board staff. School boards should consider these dynamics in determining who participates in the process on their behalf.

Mediation can occur at any point in the special education decision-making process. It can take place even before the parents have appealed to the Special Education Tribunal, on the understanding that the parents could still appeal if mediation were not successful; however, to date, it has been more common for the parties to wait until an appeal has been filed with the Tribunal before exploring the prospect of mediation. While an appeal to the Tribunal is pending, the school board retains the right to change its decision on identification and/or placement in accordance with an agreement with the parents.[7] This gives the parties an incentive to engage in ongoing efforts to resolve their differences and thereby avoid the need for a hearing before the Tribunal. Mediation is widely perceived as a very valuable tool to assist the parties in achieving this end.

---

6 This consideration is especially important where the student will remain in the school system.

7 *Identification and Placement of Exceptional Pupils*, O. Reg. 181/98, s. 31(2). See also the discussion in Chapter 10, "The First Stage of Appeal".

THE MEDIATION PROCESS

Mediation can occur only where both parties agree to engage in the process and to the selection of a mediator. Both parties should keep in mind that the mediator's role — even when the mediator is an expert in special education — is not to select a "winner", but to assist them in resolving their dispute. At any point during the mediation, either party may walk away.

Mediation is a confidential process and all documents submitted and statements made during the mediation are confidential and without prejudice.[8] Any documents shared at the mediation are to be returned or destroyed at the end of the mediation and cannot be used by the opposing party in evidence before the Tribunal or in any other proceeding.[9]

The mediator will determine the process that will be followed at the mediation. As a result, the details of the mediation process can vary considerably from case to case. Often, the mediator will begin the session with introductions and some introductory remarks designed to describe the process that will be followed and the ground rules that will govern the mediation — *e.g.*, that all parties must treat each other with courtesy and respect, that disruptive behaviour will not be tolerated, that information exchanged must be kept confidential and the like. Following these introductory remarks, the mediator will usually ask each party for an outline of their position and the outcome they would like to achieve through mediation.[10] The mediator may ask the parties to provide this information around a common table or the mediator may split up the parties and discuss this information with each of them privately. In either case, once the parties have outlined their position, the mediator will virtually always split up the parties and work with them separately from that point onwards. Where the parties are able to reach a resolution, the mediator will encourage them to prepare an agreement in writing reflecting that resolution before leaving the mediation and may assist the parties as appropriate in formulating the terms of that agreement.

Ideally, the parties will be able to resolve all of the issues between them on the day scheduled for the mediation. Where they do not, the mediator will usually give the parties a reasonable opportunity to continue their settlement discussions when the mediator believes that doing so will be fruitful in reaching a settlement.

---

[8] See, for example, the Ontario Special Education (English) Tribunal Rules of Procedure, rule 9.3.

[9] Rule 9.4.

[10] Where the parents are unrepresented, the mediator may help them to articulate their position.

MEDIATION DURING PROCEEDINGS BEFORE THE SPECIAL EDUCATION TRIBUNAL

The Special Education Tribunal's Rules of Procedure provide an opportunity for the parties to engage in mediation during the course of proceedings before the Tribunal.[11] When an appeal is filed with the Tribunal, the Tribunal will offer mediation services at the time of the initial conference call.[12] Although the Tribunal will make this inquiry, the parties are under no obligation to agree to mediation. As previously noted, the process is entirely voluntary.

Where the parents and the school board agree to mediation prior to the appeal proceeding to the Tribunal, the mediation will be conducted by a member of the Tribunal. The Tribunal member who conducts the mediation will not participate in the hearing of the case.[13] The parties will typically be asked to set aside a full day for the mediation, on the understanding that a full day may not be necessary. The Tribunal will determine a date and a location for the mediation, usually in consultation of the parties, and will notify the parties accordingly.

The Tribunal will encourage the parties to complete their settlement discussions on the day of the mediation. The mediator may allow the parties to continue their discussions for a reasonable period after the mediation; however, where the parties' settlement discussions become unduly protracted or unproductive, the Tribunal has the authority to decide to proceed with the appeal.[14]

Where the parties are not able to resolve the issues between them at the mediation, the mediator is required to prepare a Mediator's Report listing the outstanding issues and any agreements reached by the parties concerning scheduling matters. A copy of the Mediation Report is to be provided to the Tribunal and to the parties.[15] The hearing will then proceed and no reference may be made to any information disclosed during the mediation, except with the prior consent of the parties.[16]

PREPARATION FOR MEDIATION

The Ministry of Education has provided some useful suggestions for preparing for mediation in its resource document, *Special Education: A Guide for Educators, 2001*:[17]

---

[11] Rule 9.

[12] Rule 9.1.

[13] *Ibid.*

[14] Rule 9.7.

[15] Rule 9.5.

[16] Rule 9.6.

[17] Ontario Ministry of Education, *Special Education: A Guide for Educators*

- Recognize that mediation is not a win/lose situation. Its success requires both parties to attempt in good faith to reach a mutually satisfactory conclusion. A willingness to consider other points of view, to compromise, and to focus on the critical issues are the hallmarks of successful mediation. Even if the mediation does not achieve agreement on the critical issues, it may have succeeded in clarifying the outstanding problems and the parties' positions on those problems.
- Focus on the child's needs, not on finding fault, blaming, making accusations, or dwelling on past conflicts.
- Clearly outline your position or view of the issues in dispute. Where possible, try to isolate the various issues and determine which of those issues are most important to you and in which areas you can be somewhat flexible.
- Determine what you want to propose to the other party. Develop a list of alternatives or options that could be offered to settle the dispute. Decide the order of importance of these alternatives or options.
- Be willing to consider both short-term and long-term solutions. Some matters may be addressed on a short-term or even experimental basis. An agreement to meet at a later date to evaluate and modify the results may be necessary.
- Prepare for the mediation by asking others to review your position, objectives, and possible solutions. Consider whether it would be easier for you to undertake mediation if you have an adviser or representative with you.[18]

CONCLUDING COMMENTS

Given the potential benefits of mediation, both parents and school board officials should at least consider mediation during the special education decision-making process. A private resolution that addresses the parties' underlying interests and concerns will almost invariably do more to preserve and strengthen the home-school relationship and thereby ensure that the student's educational best interests are served than any litigated outcome. Moreover, even where a resolution is not achieved, mediation can assist in clarifying the issues between the parties and/or reducing the number of issues to be litigated.

(Toronto: The Ministry, 2001), available online at http://www.edu.gov.on.ca/eng/general/elemsec/speced/guide.html.

[18] *Ibid.*, at p. D34.

10

The First Stage of Appeal

INTRODUCTION

A two-stage appeal process is provided under Ontario's special education scheme for parents who disagree with decisions on identification or placement. The first stage of appeal, which is a relatively informal process, is provided for in a regulation[1] under the *Education Act*. The final stage of appeal, an appeal to a Special Education Tribunal, involves a formal hearing governed by the *Statutory Powers Procedure Act*[2] ("*SPPA*"), and is enshrined in the *Education Act*.[3]

Only a parent has a right to trigger the first stage of appeal. Neither the student[4] nor the principal[5] is given the right to appeal the Identification, Placement and Review Committee's decision.

This first stage of appeal is actually a two-step process. The first step involves an *ad hoc* committee called a Special Education Appeal Board ("SEAB"), which is established when the school board receives a written

1 *Identification and Placement of Exceptional Pupils*, O. Reg. 181/98. The Minister of Education is required, under s. 8(3) of the *Education Act*, R.S.O. 1990, c. E.2, to "provide for the parents or guardians to appeal the appropriateness of the special education placement". For this purpose, s. 11(1), para. 5 of the Act empowers the Minister to make regulations, subject to the approval of the Lieutenant Governor, which set out "governing procedures with respect to parents or guardians for appeals in respect of identification and placement of exceptional pupils in special education programs" (s. 11(1), para. 6).

2 R.S.O. 1990, c. S.22.

3 *Education Act*, s. 57. See Chapter 11, "The Final Appeal".

4 The failure of the regulation to give a right of appeal to the student may not be consistent with the *Canadian Charter of Rights and Freedoms*. It is likely that in a Charter challenge, a court would find that a student who has withdrawn from his/her parents' control or who has reached the age of majority has the right to appeal decisions that so directly affect him or her.

5 See Chapter 11, "The Final Appeal", under the heading "Initiating the Appeal: The Who, When, What and How", for further discussion of this issue.

notice of appeal from the parent.[6] The SEAB proceeds in the manner of a consultation, holding a "meeting", rather than a hearing. The SEAB makes recommendations to the school board that, in the second step of the process, decides the outcome of the appeal.

GROUNDS AND SCOPE OF APPEAL

Regulation 181/98 provides that a parent may appeal to an SEAB the following decisions of the IPRC:[7]

> (a) [an IPRC] decision . . . that the pupil is an exceptional pupil;
> (b) [an IPRC] decision . . . that the pupil is not an exceptional pupil; or
> (c) [an IPRC] decision . . . on placement of the pupil.

As discussed in Chapter 5, "Placement", the Special Education Tribunal has made clear that, where special education programs and services are intertwined with the issue of the placement, special education programs and services can be appealed.

A parent may appeal where the parent disagrees with one or more of the decisions of the IPRC.[8] There are no limitations on the reasons for disagreement that a parent may assert in an appeal.

Exceptionality Appeals

The provision of the *Education Act* that requires the Minister to establish a process for parents to appeal "the appropriateness of the special education placement" does not actually make any mention of a process to appeal "exceptionality" or "identification".[9] The *Education Act*, however, does contemplate that the decision on the identification or placement of the pupil as an exceptional pupil may be appealed by a parent to the Special Education Tribunal after "all rights of appeal under the regulations in respect of the identification or placement of the pupil as an exceptional pupil" have been exhausted.[10]

As noted here under the heading "Grounds and Scope of Appeal", parents are given a right to appeal a finding that their child is or is not exceptional. Notably, the language of the regulation does not specifically indicate that the

---

6 In this chapter, "parent" means a parent with custody rights and includes a legal guardian of a student. When issues arise between parents with joint custody or joint decision-making power in education and health matters, the parents should be advised to seek clarification in the courts.

7 O. Reg. 181/98, s. 26(1).

8 *Ibid.*, s. 26(4). As discussed further in this chapter, while the IPRC may make recommendations regarding programs and services, those recommendations are not decisions and cannot be appealed.

9 *Education Act*, s. 8(3). It is this provision that directs the Minister to establish the appeal process in O. Reg. 181/98.

10 *Ibid.*, s. 57(3).

right of a parent to appeal a decision that a student is exceptional includes the right to challenge the categories and definitions of the exceptionality determined by the IPRC; however, as a practical matter, Special Education Tribunals have dealt with appeals where the parents were appealing the category or definition of the exceptionality.

Placement Appeals

As noted in Chapter 5, "Placement", a determination of placement will usually involve a consideration of the special education programs and services that will be delivered in the placement. Although Regulation 181/98 defines the right of parental appeal in a manner that suggests that special education programs and special education services cannot be the subject of an appeal, the Special Education Tribunal has made clear that in a regular class placement, the services and programs to be provided to the student in that placement are part and parcel of the placement. The Tribunal has also indicated that, even in a special class placement, there will be instances where the special education services and programs provided are sufficiently intertwined with the placement that an appeal of placement can involve the services and programs delivered as part of the placement.[11]

There are limits, however, to what can be considered to be "placement" and, therefore, subject to appeal. Technically, placement does not include the specific school at which the placement will take place. Placement does not include a specifically named teacher or aide.[12] Placement does not include a decision as to whether particular activities will occur on Tuesday or Wednesday. IBI therapy has been found not to be a placement or a special education program or service.[13]

School Board Objection that Appeal does not Relate to Identification or Placement

School boards do not have any statutory or regulatory authority to refuse to deal with a parent's appeal on the basis that the issue that the parent is seeking to appeal is not "appealable". This is a decision that must be left, ultimately, to the Special Education Tribunal.

---

11 For a detailed discussion and references to decisions of the Special Education Tribunal, see Chapter 5, "Placement".

12 In *O. v. Wentworth County Board of Education* (1987-06-05), File No. 12 (Ont. Spec. Ed. (Eng.) Trib.), the parents sought to have their deaf student's program delivered by a teacher fluent in cueing rather than by a special education teacher with the assistance of an educational assistant fluent in cueing, as the board proposed to do. The Tribunal, in dismissing the parents' appeal, actually directed a placement for the pupil different from the one determined by the IPRC.

13 *C. v. Toronto District School Board* (2006-10-02), File No. 55 (Ont. Spec. Ed. (Eng.) Trib.).

This is confirmed by Regulation 181/98, which provides for the first level of appeal of an IPRC decision. Regulation 181/98 provides that a special education appeal board "shall not reject or refuse to deal with" an appeal on the basis that the notice of appeal filed by the parent is deficient or fails to properly state the subject of the appeal.[14] In short, technical deficiencies are not to be used to defeat the parent's right to appeal, either by the school board or the SEAB.

However, it is entirely appropriate for the school board to raise the "objection" at the SEAB that the parent's appeal is not proper. The SEAB must hear the appeal and should express an opinion on the school board's objection in its decision. If the SEAB were to indicate in its decision that the issue raised was not appealable, but the parent nevertheless appealed to the Special Education Tribunal, the objection could be raised by the school board again before the Tribunal. The Tribunal will almost always deal first with the issue of whether or not the appeal is proper, since it cannot deal with a matter that is beyond its jurisdiction.[15]

TIMING OF THE APPEAL

A parent who wishes to appeal the IPRC's decision on identification and/or placement resulting from an initial IPRC or a review IPRC must do so by providing written notice to the secretary of the school board (usually, the director of education). This notice of appeal must be received by the secretary within a fixed time frame.[16] The particular time frame applicable in any case depends on whether or not the parent has requested a follow-up meeting with the IPRC to discuss its decision.

Where no follow-up meeting with the IPRC is requested by the parent to discuss the IPRC's decision, the parent must file the notice of appeal within 30 days of receiving the statement of decision of the IPRC.[17]

Where a follow-up meeting is requested by the parent to discuss the IPRC's decision, the parent must file the notice of appeal within 15 days of receiving the IPRC's statement as to whether it has made any changes to its original decision as a result of the meeting.[18] Regulation 181/98 provides that, where the final day on which anything must be done is a "school holiday within the meaning of Regulation 304", the final day is extended to the next day that is not a school holiday. Therefore, if the day on which the appeal must be received by the secretary of the school board were to fall on a day that is a

---

14 O. Reg. 181/98, s. 26(5).

15 The only exception to this will be where the nature of the appeal is such that the Tribunal feels that it needs to hear the facts underlying the appeal in order to be able to determine whether the issue is appealable.

16 O. Reg. 181/98, s. 26.

17 *Ibid.*, s. 26(2)(*a*) and (3)(*a*).

18 *Ibid.*, s. 26(2)(*b*) and (3)(*b*).

"school holiday", then the time limit would be deemed to be extended to the next day that was not a school holiday "within the meaning of Regulation 304".[19]

School holidays are defined by regulation[20] to include the following: every Saturday and Sunday, Canada Day where the school is open during July, Labour Day, Thanksgiving Day, the 14 consecutive days over Christmas during which the school is closed, Family Day, the five days of March break week, Good Friday, Easter Monday and Victoria Day.[21] The summer break period is not specifically listed as school holidays, with the result that a question has arisen as to whether or not days in July (with the exception of Canada Day "when school is open during July") and August count[22] for the purposes of determining the final day for doing anything that must be accomplished with a specific time limit. This issue is particularly important when considering the time limits that parents have for filing an appeal, the time limits a school board has for responding to a notice of appeal and the time limits by which a SEAB must commence its meeting, when the final day would otherwise fall during the summer vacation period.[23]

In determining whether or not the summer vacation period falls within the definition of "school holidays, it is important to note that Regulation 304 sets out a list of "school holidays", but does not stipulate that this list is exhaustive. Rather, Regulation 304 sets out specific dates on which schools will be closed during periods when schools are otherwise open. While the regulation does not specifically designate the summer break period as school holidays, it makes clear that the summer period is a period when school is not open. Therefore, it is sensible to consider that the summer vacation period is, by inference from Regulation 304, a period of school holidays. In considering the timing of SEAB meetings that would otherwise have to be commenced over the summer, it makes sense to draw this inference, since teachers are not available during the summer vacation period and therefore, cannot be expected to attend SEAB meetings conducted during the summer. This means that the very

---

19 *Ibid.*, s. 2.

20 *School Year Calendar Professional Activity Days*, R.R.O. 1990, Reg. 304.

21 *Ibid.*, s. 2(4).

22 It should be noted that the Ministry of Education takes the view that July and August are not part of the school year and so, are not designated as school holidays and do not count for deadline purposes. This interpretation, however, does appear to be at odds with Regulation 304 and the wording of s. 2 of O. Reg. 181/98.

23 The problem arises because many IPRC meetings are held in late May and June, which means that the time limits for filing and/or processing of appeals would end during summer months if the summer vacation period were not considered to be summer holidays. In any event, since many schools are closed during July and August, and since many parents rely on schools to forward their communications to the main administration building, it may be prudent to ensure that mail addressed to the school is picked up and opened in the summer and that a notice be placed on the main entrance to the school advising parents how to get in touch with school board administration during the summer months in which the school is closed.

people needed to provide information to the SEAB would not be available to meet with the SEAB. It cannot have been the intention of the Minister of Education, who issued Regulations 304 and 181/98, that SEAB meetings would proceed in the absence of teachers who may have useful information to contribute. It is the view of the authors, therefore, that a reasonable argument can be made that the summer vacation period should be considered to be school holidays; however, the Tribunal has also made clear that, where the parties agree that a SEAB will proceed during the summer, it should proceed as agreed.[24]

If the parent were to send the notice of appeal by mail, then the notice would be deemed to be received on the fifth day after it had been mailed, unless the fifth day were a school holiday. As noted earlier, in that event, it would be deemed to have been received on the next following day that is not a school holiday.[25]

A school board is not obliged to consider an appeal that has not been filed by a parent in a timely fashion. On the other hand, the parent's source of information about the time limit is likely to be the school board's own "Parent Guide" or the documents provided by the IPRC. Where there has not been clear communication to the parent of the timelines, it may appear to be unduly technical for the school board to rely on the time limits to deny an appeal, particularly where the parent is late only by a day or two.[26] Accordingly, some school boards include a statement advising parents of their appeal rights — including the applicable timelines — in the IPRC's Statement of Decision or in a covering letter with the Statement of Decision.

Where there has been clear communication of timelines to the parents and the parents fail to send the notice of appeal in a timely fashion, a school board may, nevertheless, decide to waive the time limits in any particular case. A school board is under no obligation to waive time limits and should recognize that, if it were to waive time limits, it would be establishing a precedent for future cases. Accordingly, before waiving the timelines, a school board should carefully consider whether or not there are legitimate circumstances that led to the delay in filing the notice of appeal that would justify an exercise of its discretion to waive the time limits in the particular case. Where there are legitimate circumstances justifying waiver of the time limits, careful note of the circumstances should be made so that they are available for future reference.[27]

---

24 *I. v. Toronto District School Board* (2004-12-03), File No. 46a (Ont. Spec. Ed. (Eng.) Trib.). On the other hand, where necessary staff is available, appeals should not be delayed to the following school year as continuity of placement within a school year is generally in the student's best interests.

25 O. Reg. 181/98, s. 3.

26 *I. v. Toronto District School Board*, *supra*, footnote 24. In this case, the parent was not provided with a copy of the Parent Guide in a timely fashion and missed the timelines; therefore, the Tribunal held that it would be unduly technical to hold the parent to the timelines set out in O. Reg. 181/98.

27 As a practical matter, it should be noted that parents who have missed the timelines

In addition, it would be prudent for the school board to state in a written communication to the parents that the waiver of time limits is on a "without prejudice" basis.

THE NOTICE OF APPEAL

The parents' notice of appeal must set out the issue being appealed (*i.e.*, identification, placement, or both) and must include a statement setting out the nature of the disagreement.[28] This should include an explanation of why the parents disagree with the decision.

As previously noted, the parents' notice of appeal cannot be rejected by a SEAB for deficiency simply because the notice of appeal fails to indicate which of the decisions (*i.e.*, identification or placement) the appeal deals with or because it fails to set out the nature of the disagreement. Similarly, the SEAB may not refuse to deal with an appeal for the reason that the parents have not accurately set out the subject of disagreement in the notice of appeal.[29] The purpose behind this is to ensure that the parents' appeal is dealt with on the merits, rather than on technical deficiencies in the manner in which the notice of appeal has been drafted. On the other hand, it is important that both the SEAB and the school board understand the precise nature of the parents' disagreement. This will permit the SEAB to conduct the appeal in a focused manner and will allow the school board to address the parents' disagreement directly. Should the deficiency in the parents' statement of the nature of the disagreement become a problem for either the SEAB or the school board, the SEAB may direct the parents to provide a further and more clear statement of the issue being appealed, adjourn the meeting to permit this to occur, and reconvene the meeting at a mutually convenient time for all parties.[30] Alternatively, the SEAB may, through questions of the parents, clarify the parents' position during the course of the meeting.

---

but are determined to appeal may do so after the passage of three months, by exercising the parents' right to refer the matter back to the IPRC after the placement has been in effect for three months and appealing the IPRC's decision at that point — see O. Reg. 181/98, s. 21(2); however, should the decision of the IPRC that the parents failed to appeal in a timely manner involve a new placement, the school board would be able to put the new placement into effect — see O. Reg. 181/98, s. 25(1). Accordingly, where the school board does agree to a late appeal proceeding, it may wish to make clear that it does so on the understanding that the placement directed by the IPRC will be put into effect in the interim.

28 O. Reg. 181/98, s. 26(4).

29 *Ibid.*, s. 26(5).

30 While s. 28(2) of O. Reg. 181/98 requires that the meeting of the SEAB commences within 30 days after the chair is selected, there is no requirement in the regulation regarding the period within which the meeting must be concluded. Therefore, so long as the SEAB commences a meeting within 30 days, it may continue the meeting over whatever period it deems appropriate. It is only when the meeting is concluded that the time frame for issuing a decision commences.

PARTIES TO THE APPEAL

Generally, the parties to an appeal are referred to as the "appellant" (the party initiating the appeal) and the "respondent" (the party responding to the appeal). Although the "appeal" to an SEAB is much less legalistic than most appeals, the notion of "appellants" and "respondents" still applies.

In the case of a special education appeal, the appellant will be the parents or guardian of the student whose identification and/or placement is the subject-matter of the appeal, except where the student is an adult. The right to appeal IPRC decisions on identification and/or placement is not extended to students (although they may certainly participate at SEAB meetings); however, a school board may wish to be very cautious before refusing to proceed with an appeal filed by a 16- or 17-year-old student living independently.[31]

Generally, the principal of the school in which the pupil is placed is a respondent. In most cases, it was the principal who referred the pupil to the IPRC in the first instance. The "designated representative" of the school board in which the pupil is placed is also a respondent to the appeal. As was described in Chapter 6, "The Identification, Placement and Review Committee", the "designated representative" of a board is defined to be the director of education or, where there is no director of education, the secretary of the board.[32] The director of education will normally delegate this responsibility to a supervisory officer of the board — usually a superintendent or administrator with responsibility for special education.

Where the student is enrolled with another school board that is purchasing the special education programs and services from the school board that the student attends, the designated representative of the school board that is purchasing the special education program also has a right to participate in the appeal.[33] The purchasing school board is not, strictly speaking, either a respondent or an appellant, although it does have an interest in the proceeding, given that it is purchasing services for the student who is the subject of the appeal.

---

31 A prudent school board will be even more cautious in light of the expanding rights of students living independently. A school board's decision may also take into account the student's exceptionality and any relationship between that exceptionality and the capabilities of the student, even when the student is living with parents or in foster care.

32 O. Reg. 181/98, s. 1(1).

33 *Ibid.*, s. 28(5).

SETTING UP THE SPECIAL EDUCATION APPEAL BOARD

The SEAB is comprised of three members, including a member appointed by the school board, a member appointed by the parents, and a chair. The chair is usually appointed by the other two members.[34]

The school board in which the student is placed must appoint its member to the SEAB within 15 days of the day[35] on which the secretary of the board receives the parents' notice of appeal. This appointee cannot be an employee of the school board making the appointment (or, where the placement arises by way of a purchase of services, an employee of the school board purchasing the services) or an employee of the Ministry of Education. There is no prohibition, however, against appointing an employee of another school board. It will be important that the SEAB include a member who understands the perspective of the school board. Accordingly, the school board's appointee to the SEAB often will be a supervisory officer of another school board or a retired supervisory officer of the school board making the appointment.

The school board may not appoint a person who has had any prior involvement in the matter. This would include an outside consultant, such as a psychologist, who assessed the student for the school board.

The parents must appoint a member to the SEAB within 15 days of receipt of the notice of appeal by the secretary of the school board. As with the school board appointee, the parents' appointee cannot be an employee of the school board (or of the purchasing board, where applicable) or an employee of the Ministry of Education. Nor can the parents appoint a person who has had any prior involvement in the matter. A person who has had prior involvement would include either parent or a representative of a support or advocacy group who provided support or advice to the parents through the IPRC process.

The chair is selected jointly by the school board and parents' appointees to the SEAB. Normally the appointees will each consult with the party who appointed her or him in making this selection. As with the other SEAB members, the chair may not be an employee of the school board (or the purchasing board) or of the Ministry of Education, or have had any prior involvement in the matter. The chair must be appointed within 15 days of the later of the date of the appointment by the school board of its appointee and the date of appointment by the parents of their appointee. If the two appointees were unable to agree on a chair, then the local district manager of the Ministry of Education would be charged with appointing the chair.

---

[34] *Ibid.*, s. 27.

[35] *Ibid.*, s. 27(2). Where the final day for doing anything under O. Reg. 181/98 falls on a school holiday as defined in s. 2(4) of Regulation 304, the time is extended to the next day that is not a school holiday: O. Reg. 181/98, s. 2.

ADMINISTRATIVE SUPPORT FOR AND EXPENSES OF SEAB MEMBERS

Administrative support for the SEAB in the form of secretarial and administrative services is to be provided by the school board.[36] This includes typing services and any other administrative assistance that the SEAB may require, such as co-ordinating meetings, arranging locations and sending out notices for the chair.

The travel expenses incurred by SEAB members to attend meetings with the parties — or meetings amongst the SEAB members themselves — are to be reimbursed in accordance with the policies established by the school board for reimbursing trustees for travel expenses.[37] Depending on the particular school board's policy, this might be based on actual out-of-pocket expenses or on a per-kilometre allowance between the SEAB member's residence and the place of the meeting.

Where the school board has established a policy that reimburses trustees for other out-of-pocket expenses reasonably incurred in carrying out their duties, SEAB members may claim similar reimbursement.[38]

THE SEAB MEETING

The SEAB does not proceed by way of a "hearing", but rather holds a meeting to which all persons are invited who, in the opinion of the SEAB chair, might have something relevant to contribute. This meeting must be conducted in an informal manner.[39] The SEAB has no power to compel attendance of witnesses, nor does it have the power to administer oaths or affirmations to witnesses. Like the IPRC, the SEAB must comply with basic elements of procedural fairness; however, the SEAB is not subject to the *SPPA* or the more

---

36 *Ibid.*, s. 27(7).

37 *Ibid.*

38 It is noteworthy that the legislation and regulations are silent on the issue of whether or not the chair and nominees may be paid and, if so, by whom. Under the "arbitration model", where the parties to the arbitration each appoint a nominee and the nominees choose a chair, each party is responsible to pay the fees of his or her nominee and each party is responsible to pay half the fees of the chair. In the case of an SEAB, the parents will normally be able to secure an appointee through a local association, which will not charge a fee. The school board will be responsible for fees, if any, charged by its appointee. (Where the school board appoints a supervisory officer from another school board, fees are not likely to be an issue.) The issue of fees is more likely to arise in the case of a chair. In such a case, it is appropriate that the school board pay these costs — indeed, this may be necessary to secure the appointment of a chair in whom both parties have confidence. Where the appointment of a chair is contingent on the payment of a fee to the chair, an understanding should be reached between the school board and the parents about who will pay the fee *before* the SEAB meets.

39 O. Reg. 181/98, s. 28(2).

stringent elements of fairness applicable to a statutory adjudicator.[40] Required elements of fairness may include the following:

- The parents and appropriate representatives of the school board must receive notice of the meeting in accordance with the regulation.[41]
- Although it is unlikely that the SEAB will receive information in the absence of either party, should this occur, the SEAB should ensure that any such information is shared with the parents and with the representatives of the school board in order to provide each party with the opportunity to rebut any information with which that party disagrees.
- The SEAB must be "unbiased" in carrying out its duties. In this respect, the regulation sets out limitations, as previously referred to, on who is qualified to sit as a member of the SEAB; however, all properly qualified members of the SEAB must also conduct themselves in a way that is free from actual bias or a reasonable apprehension of bias.

Location and Timing of the SEAB Meeting

Responsibility for arranging the SEAB meeting rests with the chair of the SEAB. This responsibility can be carried out with the assistance of administrative staff provided by the school board.[42] The meeting must commence within 30 days[43] following the day on which the chair of the SEAB was "selected"; however, with the written consent of the parents and the "designated representative" of the school board,[44] the meeting may be scheduled to commence on a date beyond the 30-day period.[45]

Given the nature of the proceeding, it is assumed that an effort will be made to find a date for the meeting that is mutually convenient for all parties. Where this proves to be impossible, however, and an agreement to postpone the meeting beyond the 30 days cannot be reached, the chair of the SEAB may be left with no alternative but to select a date within the 30 days that conveniences the greatest number of participants, including the other two members of the SEAB.

The location of the meeting must be at a convenient place for all parties.[46] The meeting might be held in a school or the school board's offices; however, particularly where there is some tension between school board staff and the parents, it may be wise to consider a more "neutral" location, such as a meeting

---

40 These requirements are discussed further in Chapter 11, "The Final Appeal".
41 O. Reg. 181/98, s. 28(1).
42 *Ibid.*, ss. 27(7) and 28(1).
43 *Ibid.*, s. 28(2).
44 See the discussion in this chapter under the heading "The Notice of Appeal".
45 *Ibid.*, s. 28(2) and (3).
46 *Ibid.*, s. 28(2).

room in an outside facility. The school board would be responsible to pay the costs of such outside meeting facilities.

Notice of the Meeting

The chair of the SEAB is responsible to provide notice of the hearing to the parents and, where the student is 16 years of age or older, to the student as well. No notice is required to be given to the school board under O. Reg. 181/98, although the dictates of fairness may require that the school board be given notice. Moreover, providing notice to the school board reduces the appearance — that might otherwise arise — that the chair is communicating "informally" with the school board "behind the scenes".

The notice must be received by the parents and, where entitled, the student, at least 10 days in advance of the meeting.[47]

Participants in the Meeting

Participants at the SEAB's meeting will include the parties: the parents, the student, if aged 16 or older, and the staff designated by the school board to represent the school board at the SEAB meeting. In addition, the chair of the SEAB must invite any person who he or she believes may be able to contribute information with respect to the matters under appeal. This includes any persons who the chair concludes may be able to contribute information or who the chair is persuaded, either by one of the other appointees or by a party, may be able to contribute in some other way to the meeting. It is to be noted, however, that the chair is not obliged to invite a person to attend unless the chair personally believes that the person will be able to contribute information that, presumably, is relevant to the issues before the SEAB.[48]

The regulation does not speak to the right of parties to bring "witnesses" along to provide information to the SEAB, but as long as the information that these witnesses may provide is helpful or relevant to the SEAB, there is no doubt that their participation will be welcomed. The SEAB does have an inherent power to control its own process, which means that the SEAB may limit the number of witnesses, or the amount of time that each takes to provide information. Moreover, where a witness is not providing relevant information, the participation of that witness may be limited.

A measure that the SEAB may take to better order its process and avoid adjournments is to request the parties to provide to the SEAB — and exchange with each other — a list of the "witnesses" and documents they intend to bring to the SEAB meeting, including a brief indication of the information that each witness will provide. This will better enable the parties to prepare, which should result in a more efficient and effective SEAB process.

---

[47] *Ibid.*, s. 5(5). See Chapter 6, "The Identification, Placement and Review Committee", for a discussion on the requirements of giving notice.

[48] *Ibid.*, s. 28(4).

The fact that the regulation that governs the SEAB requires that its meeting be "informal"[49] may suggest that it is not anticipated that any party to the SEAB will be represented by counsel or another representative at the meeting. Whether a party will be permitted to bring counsel or a representative will be a matter to be determined by the SEAB in each case. It is noted, however, that parents do have the right to bring a representative to the IPRC and, accordingly, it seems likely that an SEAB would permit a parent to bring counsel or a representative to a meeting, although the SEAB may reserve the right to limit the involvement of the counsel or representative in the meeting.

IPRC Record

The SEAB must be provided, prior to the commencement of its meeting, with a copy of the IPRC decision being appealed together with the "record" of the IPRC proceeding. This record will include not only a statement of the decision reached by the IPRC but, as well, any reports, assessments or other documents received by the IPRC.[50] This would appear to include documents from the Ontario Student Record ("OSR") if they were considered by the IPRC. Such documents arguably must be provided to the SEAB members whether or not written permission has been provided by the parents or student, if aged 18 or older, for the disclosure of the records.[51]

---

49 *Ibid.*, s. 28(2).

50 *Ibid.*, s. 27(6). See also the discussion in Chapter 6, "The Identification, Placement and Review Committee", under the heading "Information to be Considered".

51 It is a basic rule of statutory interpretation that a regulation cannot overrule, specifically contradict or conflict with a statute. Section 266 of the *Education Act* prohibits an Official Student Record ("OSR") from being produced without parental permission in proceedings other than as specifically permitted by the section. It might be argued, therefore, that O. Reg. 181/98, s. 27(6), which requires any document received by the IPRC to be forwarded to the SEAB, applies only to non-OSR documents unless a parent consents in writing to the production; however, it may also be argued that s. 266(7) of the *Education Act* permits the Minister to override the necessity for parental written permission in respect of the compilation and delivery of information contained in the OSR. This, combined with the power of the Minister to promulgate regulations, arguably permits the Minister to direct that OSR records be disclosed to the SEAB if those documents were to form part of the record of the IPRC used in reaching its decision. In addition, it may be argued that once documents become part of the IPRC's record, they are part of a separate record to which the terms of s. 266 do not apply. It should be noted that, while s. 266 of the *Education Act* stipulates 18 years as the age at which a student gains control over his or her OSR, the *Municipal Freedom of Information and Protection of Privacy Act*, R.S.O. 1990, c. M.56 ("*MFIPPA*"), s. 54(*c*), sets 16 years as the age at which students gain the right to control their personal documents, which would include OSR documents.

Conduct of the Meeting

Normally, an SEAB meeting will commence with an introduction by the chair of the members of the SEAB and a request that the parents and school board representatives introduce themselves. SEAB meetings at a Roman Catholic school board may open with a prayer.

As noted, the SEAB's meeting is to be conducted in an informal manner. The process envisioned by the regulation resembles the "inquisitorial" model of adjudicative decision-making, as opposed to the "adversarial" model. Under the adversarial model, the adjudicator does not determine which witnesses will be called and is not responsible for eliciting evidence from the witnesses who are called. Rather, the adjudicator listens while the parties present the information that they think is important. Under the inquiry (or "inquisitorial") model, the adjudicator plays a much more active role in determining which witnesses will be called and what evidence will be elicited. Since the SEAB operates on the latter model, it is to be expected that, led by the chair, there will be questions and discussion between the SEAB and the parties or other persons contributing information to the meeting.

It is traditional in an appeal that the appealing party takes the position that the decision that is the subject of the appeal is wrong and the responding party takes the position that the decision is right. In the case of an appeal from an IPRC's decision, the parents will be saying that the IPRC's decision is wrong and, in most cases, the school board representatives will be supporting the decision of the IPRC. (On occasion, the principal may also disagree with the IPRC's decision on identification and/or placement, in which case, the principal is not bound to support the IPRC's decision, but may put forward his or her own views on the decision.) Accordingly, the meeting should normally commence with the parents (or the parents' counsel or representative) explaining why the parents believe that the IPRC's decision is wrong. In support of this position, the parents may bring along anyone who the parents feel will be able to provide information relevant to the matters under appeal. As long as the chair is of the opinion that these people may contribute relevant information to the meeting, they will be permitted to participate. The parents may also submit any new documentary information not already presented to the IPRC that the parents feel supports their position. Documents presented to the IPRC will form part of the IPRC's record, which is forwarded to the SEAB before the meeting.

Following the parents' presentation, the school board's staff will present its position to the SEAB. This presentation may involve an explanation by the IPRC chair or another representative of the IPRC's proposed placement (*e.g.*, a superintendent), together with the information that formed the basis for the IPRC's decision. This will likely include the observations of teachers or consultants who have been involved with the student. In addition, the school board's staff may wish to bring others to the SEAB who might contribute to the discussion, including psychologists, social workers or other professionals. Should there be any additional documents that do not form part of the IPRC's record but that might assist the SEAB in its deliberations, these documents may be introduced by the school board; however, this will not include copies of the student's IEPs or OSR documents where there is no written consent of the parent (or student, if aged 18 or over).[52]

After the school board has presented its case, the parents should be given an opportunity to respond. At that point, any other persons who the chair of the SEAB feels might contribute information should be questioned or invited to speak.

Should either the parents or the school board introduce new information at the meeting that takes the other side by surprise, it may be necessary for the party caught by surprise to request an adjournment in order to have an opportunity to deal with and respond to the new information. The SEAB may grant the adjournment where it is of the view that the adjournment is necessary in order to permit the information to be dealt with properly.

The meeting of the SEAB will continue until the SEAB is "satisfied that the opinions, views and information that bear on the appeal have been sufficiently presented to it".[53] While the regulation governing the procedure of the SEAB appears to contemplate that the meeting will be completed in one day, this may not be possible where the chair determines that other people, not present, may have relevant information to contribute. Where it is necessary that the meeting continue on another day, every effort should be made to ensure that the continuation be scheduled at a mutually convenient time for the parties and the SEAB during the 30-day period following the selection of the chair, unless there is agreement to schedule the continuation date beyond the 30-day period. In this case, the agreement should be confirmed in writing. The date for continuation of the meeting should be determined prior to the adjournment of the meeting, so that everyone leaves the meeting with knowledge of the continuation date. Notice of a continuation date should be sent to the parents, with a copy to school board officials — if possible, at least 10 days in advance of the continuation date.

---

52 Section 266(2) of the *Education Act* precludes the introduction of OSR documents in any proceeding (including, presumably, an SEAB meeting) and s. 266(10) imposes a requirement to preserve secrecy in respect of the contents of the OSR, *except* where the disclosure of information contained in OSR documents is required in the performance of an employee's duties. It will be difficult for school board staff to justify their views as to identification or the appropriate placement for a student without reference to information contained in the OSR; however, it is arguable that the verbal disclosure to the SEAB of information that might be contained in OSR documents falls within the exception in s. 266(10), which permits disclosure of information in the performance of an employee's duties, even though the documents themselves cannot be put before the SEAB.

53 O. Reg. 181/98, s. 28(6).

DECISION OF THE SEAB

At the end of the meeting process, the SEAB has only two options: the SEAB may agree with the IPRC, in which case the SEAB will recommend that the IPRC decision be implemented; or, alternatively, the SEAB may disagree with the IPRC and make a recommendation to the school board about the student's identification and/or placement.[54] While the IPRC is specifically given the power to make "recommendations regarding special education programs and special education services",[55] the same power is not extended to the SEAB.

The three members of the SEAB have only three days following the end of the meeting to decide whether they agree or disagree with the IPRC, unless the parents and school board agree to a longer period. When they disagree, they must also decide within the three-day period about the recommendations they will make to the school board on identification and/ or placement.[56] While it is to be expected that the three members will attempt to achieve unanimity, this may not be possible. Two members may agree with one dissenting. In such a case, the dissenting member will issue his or her own conclusion and reasons for reaching this conclusion. This dissenting or minority view will be forwarded to the school board along with the majority view. It is possible that the three members of the SEAB will be able to reach agreement on the final decision, but not on the recommendations regarding identification or placement, resulting in two or even three sets of recommendations, all of which will be forwarded to the school board. There is no provision in the regulation that requires the chair's view to prevail.

As noted, the three members of the SEAB must reach their decision within three days (or such longer period as the parents and board may agree to) following the end of the SEAB meeting. A written statement of the SEAB's recommendation — or recommendations, where multiple recommendations are reached[57] — must be sent to:[58]

---

54 *Ibid.*

55 *Ibid.*, s. 16(2).

56 *Ibid.*, s. 28(6).

57 While the SEAB must reach its decision within three days as provided by s. 28(6) of O. Reg. 181/98, the requirement to send out a "written statement of its recommendations" is found in s. 29, which does not contain a time limit and makes no reference to s. 28(6). A question arises whether or not the three-day limit in s. 28(6) also requires the SEAB to send out its recommendations and reasons in writing within that very short time frame. The Ministry takes the position that, since the manner in which the SEAB shows it has reached its decision within the three-day limit is by sending out its written statement of recommendations, it is an implicit requirement that the SEAB's written statement be sent out within the three-day time frame. Because the time frame is such a short one, it may be difficult for an SEAB to provide meaningful reasons within this short time frame and, accordingly,

(a) a parent of the pupil;
(b) where the pupil is 16 years of age or older, the pupil;
(c) the chair of the committee;
(d) the principal of the school in which the pupil is placed;
(e) the designated representative of the board in which the pupil is placed; and
(f) in the circumstances described in subsection 28(5), the designated representative of the board that is purchasing the special education program.

The written statement must include written reasons for the SEAB's recommendations. As noted, where the SEAB has not reached unanimity in its decision, a separate written statement will normally be prepared by any member who does not agree with the chair, within the same time frame applicable to the majority decision.

THE SCHOOL BOARD'S DECISION

Once the SEAB has released its written statement, the matter must be put to the school board's trustees to determine what action will be taken by the school board with respect to the recommendations.

Within 30 days after receiving the SEAB's written statement, the school board must consider the SEAB's recommendations and decide what action to take with respect to the student.[59]

Although there is no statutory or regulatory requirement that the school board provide an opportunity for parents to be "heard" before it makes its decision, common law requirements of fairness dictate that an individual whose rights are to be determined by a statutory decision-maker has a right to be heard by the decision-maker before the decision is made. Since school board staff will likely present their views to the school board on whether or not the SEAB's recommendations should be adopted, fairness would require that the parents also be given an opportunity to put forward their positions on the SEAB's recommendations and on the position of school board staff on the recommendations. This may be accomplished by providing the parents with a written outline of the position of school board staff on the recommendations and extending to parents the opportunity to make either an oral presentation or a written submission before the school board makes its decision on the SEAB's recommendations.

Whether the parents are to be given an opportunity to make an oral submission or a written submission, they should be given reasonable notice of the date of the school board's meeting (*i.e.*, sufficient notice to permit them to respond) and of the opportunity to make a written or oral submission. Where the opportunity being provided is to make a written submission, a date by

---

the parties should be prepared to agree to extend this time frame where additional time is required.

58 O. Reg. 181/98, s. 29.

59 *Ibid.*, s. 30(1).

which the written submission must be in the hands of the secretary of the board for distribution to trustees should be stated in the notice.

The school board, in making its decision, may adjourn to "the committee of the whole board", and then to a closed session to consider the SEAB's decision;[60] however, for the final decision of the school board to be effective, the school board must, in open session, adopt the resolution of "the committee of the whole board" with respect to the student.

It is important to note that the school board is not obliged to adopt the recommendations of the SEAB, even where there is unanimity amongst the members of the SEAB. Nor is the school board bound by the limitations imposed on the SEAB to agree or disagree with the IPRC on the issues of identification or placement. The school board may go beyond the issue of placement and identification and may make a decision that involves special education programs and services.[61] This flexibility will often enable school boards and parents to reach an agreement in order to resolve the issues between them and avoid further litigation.

Once the school board reaches its decision, that decision must be communicated in writing to each of the persons who received notice of the SEAB's decision. The notice to the parents of the school board's decision must include an explanation of the parent's right to appeal the board's decision to a Special Education Tribunal pursuant to s. 57 of the *Education Act*. A paragraph such as the following would achieve this:

> If you disagree with this decision of the Board on the identification or placement of your child, you have the right, under s. 57 of the *Education Act*, to appeal to a Special Education Tribunal for a hearing in respect of the identification or placement of your child. You may initiate the appeal by forwarding to the Secretary of the Special Education Tribunal a written notice that you wish to appeal the Board's decision on identification and/or placement, together with a statement of the grounds on which you are appealing the decision. This notice may be sent to the Secretary at the following address.

The address, telephone number and fax number of the Secretary, Special Education Tribunal should be set out in the letter.[62]

---

60 A board of trustees constituted as the board must always sit in open session. A committee of the board may sit in closed session in limited circumstances that include the disclosure of personal information about a student of the board: *Education Act*, s. 207.

61 O. Reg. 181/98, s. 30(2).

62 The Tribunal's contact information is currently available at http://www.oset-tedo.ca/eng/contact.html. The Tribunal can move at any time so it is wise, prior to sending out this letter to parents, to verify the Tribunal's address.

IMPLEMENTATION OF THE BOARD'S DECISION

The school board may implement the decision it has reached on the SEAB's recommendation only on the occurrence of one of the following events:

- a parent of the pupil consents in writing to the school board's decision;
- 30 days have elapsed from the day the parent receives (or is deemed to have received) notice of the board's decision *and* no appeal to the Special Education Tribunal has been commenced by the parent within this 30-day period;[63] or
- an appeal to the Special Education Tribunal is dismissed or abandoned.[64]

Neither the regulation nor the *Education Act* define when an appeal to the Special Education Tribunal is deemed to be abandoned and, accordingly, this will be determined by the Secretary of the Special Education Tribunal (or the Chair of the Tribunal, where the Tribunal has been constituted) on a case-by-case basis. One would expect a finding of abandonment to be made where the parent has failed to respond to the Secretary of the Tribunal even after a warning has been given that continued failure to respond will result in a finding that the appeal has been abandoned.

The school board has the discretion, in accordance with an agreement with the parents, to change any decision it has reached following its consideration of the SEAB's recommendations, but may only do so within the 30-day period following the parents' receipt of the school board's decision in the first instance or while an appeal to the Special Education Tribunal is pending.[65] This will permit continuing dialogue between school board staff and parents in an effort to resolve the differences between them. Where an appeal is pending to the Special Education Tribunal, the fact that the school board can change its decision will facilitate the mediation of the dispute between parents and the school board by an outside third party who may be able to assist the parents and the school board in finding a resolution which both are prepared to live with. Mediation at this stage is becoming more common across the province and is discussed further in Chapter 9, "Alternative Dispute Resolution: Mediation".

Where the school board does change its decision, notice of the new decision must be given in writing to each of the persons who received notice of the school board's first decision on the matter. The notice to the parents

---

63 Note that, if the notice were sent by mail, then it would be deemed to be received on the fifth day after the notice had been sent.

64 O. Reg. 181/98, s. 31.

65 *Ibid.*

of the new decision must include the explanation of the parents' right to appeal the new decision to the Special Education Tribunal.[66]

[66] *Ibid.*, s. 30(3).

11

The Final Appeal

INTRODUCTION

When the student's parents or guardian remain dissatisfied with the identification or placement decision made by the school board after the appeal to the Special Education Appeal Board ("SEAB"), there is a final avenue of appeal available to the parents. The *Education Act*[1] provides for a final appeal level of identification and/or placement decisions to the Special Education Tribunal (the "Tribunal").

The right of appeal to the Tribunal is set out in section 57(3) of the *Education Act*, which provides:

> 57(3) Where a parent or guardian of a pupil has exhausted all rights of appeal under the regulations in respect of the identification or placement of the pupil as an exceptional pupil and is dissatisfied with the decision in respect of the identification or placement, the parent or guardian may appeal to a Special Education Tribunal for a hearing in respect of the identification or placement.

This chapter focuses on the considerations involved in initiating and defending an appeal to the Tribunal and on the procedures followed by the Tribunal once the appeal has been filed.

THE SPECIAL EDUCATION TRIBUNAL

The *Education Act* authorizes the Lieutenant Governor in Council to establish one or more Special Education Tribunals.[2] Pursuant to this power, the Lieutenant Governor in Council has established a Special Education Tribunal (English) and a Special Education Tribunal (French).

Each Tribunal consists of a chair — so designated by the Order-in-Council appointing him or her — along with a roster of additional panel members. The Chair may designate one of the other members of the Tribunal as vice-chair of

---

1 R.S.O. 1990, c. E.2.

2 *Ibid.*, s. 57(1).

the Tribunal, who may exercise the powers of the chair in the absence of the chair.[3] All members of the Tribunal are appointed by the Lieutenant Governor in Council for a fixed period of time, which may be extended on renewal of the appointment for one or more further periods of time.

The roster of Tribunal members varies from time to time, since appointments are time limited and may or may not be renewed. Members are appointed by the government of the day and traditionally have strong backgrounds in special education, either as former special educators, as parent advocates or as academics involved in teacher training.

Hearing panels are comprised of three members of the Tribunal, one of whom will act as the chair of the panel. Panels are selected from the roster by the chair or vice-chair on an ad hoc basis when an appeal is received by the Tribunal. The chair of the panel will deal with the preliminary procedural issues such as setting up hearing dates.

The Tribunal normally holds its hearings at a location — usually a hotel or other community meeting place — in the municipality where the parent resides, within the jurisdiction of the school board involved in the appeal. This is part of the Tribunal's effort to make its processes as accessible as possible to parents.

The legal authority or "jurisdiction" of the Tribunal to hear appeals is defined by section 57 of the *Education Act*. Because the Tribunal is established by statute, its "jurisdiction"— that is, the limits of what subject matters it can make decisions on and any threshold criteria as to when it may deal with that subject matter — is defined by statute as well. The jurisdictional limits of the Tribunal will be discussed later in this chapter.

INITATING THE APPEAL: THE WHO, WHEN, WHAT AND HOW

Who can Appeal?

Under section 57(3) of the *Education Act*, only a parent or guardian may initiate an appeal to the Tribunal. This is because what the parent is appealing is the final decision of the school board, which has the right to accept or reject the recommendation of the Special Education Appeal Board.

Of note is the absence of any appeal rights for the students themselves.[4] While there seems to be no doubt that an adult student (*i.e.*, a student aged 18

3 *Ibid.*, s. 57(1.4) and (1.5).

4 Section 1(2) of the *Education Act* provides that the rights accorded to parents under the Act may be exercised by the pupil where the pupil is an adult. The Act does not define when a pupil becomes an adult. The Ministry of Education uses the age of 18 — the age specified under the *Age of Majority and Accountability Act*, R.S.O. 1990, c. A.7 — as the age at which a pupil will be deemed to be an adult; however, except as specifically stated in the statute and regulations, the rights of students under age 18 are exercised by their parents or guardian.

years or older) is able to appeal on his/her own behalf,[5] the same is not true of a student under 18 years of age. Usually, the student's parents will be in the best position to determine whether or not it is in the student's best interests to appeal the school board's decision and to take the steps necessary to do so.

The Supreme Court of Canada has recognized, however, that, in the special education context, children have rights and interests that are separate and distinct from those of their parents and therefore the parents' views of what is in the student's best interests will not always be conclusive of the question.[6] Accordingly, it is possible that in an appropriate case, a student — particularly a student over the age of 16 who has withdrawn from parental control or a student whose capacity to understand the desirability and consequences of an appeal is not questioned — could successfully persuade the Tribunal to allow him or her to proceed with an appeal to the Tribunal in the absence of his or her parents, based on legal arguments under the *Canadian Charter of Rights and Freedoms*.[7]

When Can an Appeal be Made?

The *Education Act* sets two criteria, both of which must be met before the parent can appeal to the Tribunal. Where either of these criteria has not been met, the Tribunal will not have the legal authority or jurisdiction to hear the parent's appeal.[8]

The first criterion relates to the timing of the appeal: the parent must have "exhausted" the appeal process set out in Ontario Regulation 181/98, *Identification and Placement of Exceptional Pupils*, before they can appeal to the Special Education Tribunal.

The appeal process set out in the regulation is "exhausted" after all the steps required in the regulation for appealing a decision of an Identification, Placement and Review Committee ("IPRC") have been completed. This means that the parent must have initiated an appeal of an IPRC decision[9] in a timely manner to a Special Education Appeal Board, must have co-operated

---

5 The Special Education Tribunal's Notice of Appeal form specifically contemplates that an adult student may file an appeal. See the Ontario Special Education (English) Tribunal's "Form A: Notice of Appeal", available online at http://www.oset-tedo.ca/eng/forms.html.

6 *Eaton v. Brant County Board of Education* (1997), 142 D.L.R. (4th) 385, [1997] 1 S.C.R. 241, at para. 77.

7 Section 15 of the Charter guarantees equal treatment under the law without discrimination on the basis of grounds, which include "age".

8 *J.C. & Toronto District School Board* (2008-06-06), File No. 2008-1 (Ont. Spec. Ed. (Eng.) Trib.); *I. & Toronto District School Board* (2006-12-18), File No. 59 (Ont. Spec. Ed. (Eng.) Trib.); *R. & Durham District School Board* (2004-05-19), File No. 39 (Ont. Spec. Ed. (Eng.) Trib.).

9 *J.F. & Near North District School Board* (2007-08-15), File No. 2007-01 (Ont. Spec. Ed. (Eng.) Trib.). In this case, the parents appealed after failing to attend an Identification, Placement and Review Committee meeting that was postponed

in setting up the Appeal Board by nominating a nominee to the Appeal Board and must have attended the Appeal Board's meeting.[10] Normally, the process will be "exhausted" (*i.e.*, completed) when the school board makes a final decision on the Appeal Board's recommendation since, as noted earlier, it is this decision that is the subject of the parent's appeal to the Special Education Tribunal.

There have been cases, however, where the Tribunal has held that the appeal process provided for in the regulation was exhausted, even though the full process set out in the regulation was not completed. This has occurred where the school board acted in a manner that effectively frustrated the parent's attempts to appeal the IPRC's decision by unreasonably failing to process the parent's appeal as required under the regulation.

For example, in one case, the Tribunal found that the appeal process was "exhausted" when the school board, on receipt of the Appeal Board's recommendation, decided to send the recommendation back to the Appeal Board for reconsideration rather than making a decision on it as required by the regulation.[11] Nothing in the regulation provides for sending the Appeal Board's recommendation back for reconsideration and the school board's actions were viewed by the Tribunal as an unreasonable delay of the parent's appeal.

In another case, the Tribunal found that the appeal process was "exhausted" when the school board failed to take any steps to set up the Special Education Appeal Board after receiving the parent's notice of appeal.[12] In this type of situation, the Tribunal will not permit the school board to rectify its failure to follow the process since this would, in turn, further delay the parent's appeal to the Tribunal. In this situation, the IPRC's decision is effectively the decision that is appealed to the Tribunal.

It will be important, therefore, for a school board, on receipt of an appeal, to be seen to be making reasonable efforts to move the appeal forward under the process set out in the regulation in a timely manner. Where the parent is having difficulty in finding or appointing a nominee to the Appeal Board, the school board should recommend that the parent contact the Ministry of

---

when they failed to attend. The Tribunal, therefore, found that the process had not been exhausted.

10 In *J.C. & Toronto District School Board*, *supra*, footnote 8, the parent initiated an appeal to a Special Education Appeal Board but, just prior to the scheduled meeting of the Appeal Board, notified the Appeal Board that, instead of participating in the Appeal Board process, she was going to appeal to the Tribunal. The Tribunal found that, in declining to participate in the Appeal Board meeting, the parent had failed to exhaust her appeal rights and that consequently, the Tribunal could not hear the appeal.

11 *J.K. & Halton District School Board* (2004-02-12), File No. 43a (Ont. Spec. Ed. (Eng.) Trib.).

12 *J.D. & Toronto District School Board* (2002-12-24), File No. 30 (Ont. Spec. Ed. (Eng.) Trib.).

Education for assistance. It is recommended that the school board ensure that all communications are made — or confirmed — in writing to the parent in order to be able to show the Tribunal what the school board has done to carry out its obligations under the regulation to set up the Special Education Appeal Board.

What Can be Appealed?

The second criterion that must be met before a parent can appeal to the Tribunal is that the appeal must relate to a decision by the school board on identification or placement with which the parent is dissatisfied. If there were no decision by the school board on identification or placement or if the parent were not dissatisfied with the school board's decision on identification or placement, then the Tribunal would have no jurisdiction to deal with the appeal.

An appeal on identification may be filed where the parent disagrees with either a decision that his/her child is or is not exceptional[13] or a decision on the particular category or definition of exceptionality applicable to the child.[14]

Most appeals relate to decisions relating to placement. As discussed in Chapter 5, "Placement", the Tribunal defines "placement" to include the special education programs or special education services involved in defining the placement.[15] Consequently, the Tribunal will permit appeals dealing with special education programs and services as long as those programs or services are involved in the definition of the placement;[16] however, the Tribunal found

---

13 *A. & Upper Canada District School Board* (2001-09-24), File No. 28 (Ont. Spec. Ed. (Eng.) Trib.).

14 See, for example, *L. & Board of Education for the City of Windsor* (1988-08-29), File No. 13 (Ont. Spec. Ed. (Eng.) Trib.); *P. & Nipissing Board of Education* (1986-07-18), File No. 9 (N.E. Reg. (Eng.) Spec. Ed. Trib.).

15 *J.T. & Peterborough Victoria Northumberland and Clarington Catholic District School Board* (2006-09-14), File No. 56 (Ont. Spec. Ed. (Eng.) Trib.).

16 An argument was made by school boards under *Special Education Identification Placement and Review Committees and Appeals*, R.R.O. 1990, Reg. 305, ss. 4 and 9 — the predecessor regulation to O. Reg. 181/98 — that the right of appeal placement did not include the right to appeal special education programs and services based on the language of the regulation that indicated that programs and services could not be the subject matter of appeals. Nevertheless, soon after the special education scheme was introduced, it was recognized that the issue of appropriate programs and services is often intimately intertwined with the issue of placement. In one of the first cases dealing with the special education scheme, the Ontario Divisional Court recognized that consideration of the nature and content of the programs and services offered in the placement was an essential component of determining whether or not the placement directed was appropriate. See *Dolmage v. Muskoka Board of Education* (1985), 15 D.L.R. (4th) 741 at p. 750, 49 O.R. (2d) 546 (Div. Ct.). See also Chapter 5, "Placement". Consequently, from fairly early on in its existence, the Tribunal has addressed special education programs and services in the course of deciding placement appeals where it has determined that the issue of the services or program provided to the student in the

that it had no jurisdiction to hear an appeal based on the parent's belief that the services outlined at the IPRC were not being provided — that is, a parent cannot appeal for the purpose of obliging the school board to prove that it is providing services in the placement.[17]

Some parents have attempted to appeal to the Tribunal about the procedures used by the school board in the IPRC process; however, the Tribunal does not have the authority to entertain an appeal relating to issues of "due process" or the procedures used by a school board in carrying out its obligations under the *Education Act* and regulations.[18] Where the parent mentions procedures followed by the school board in the appeal, the Tribunal will examine the issues raised by the parent to determine whether those issues are purely procedural in nature or whether they, in fact, relate to placement or identification. Where the issues are purely procedural and there is no disagreement over the decision on placement (or identification), the Tribunal will find that it had no jurisdiction to hear the parent's appeal.[19] But, where a "procedural issue" appealed by the parent does raise questions regarding placement, the Tribunal will find that it has jurisdiction to deal with the placement issue. For example, in a case where the school board's decision on placement was "regular class placement with resource assistance" with a recommendation of "resource support as deemed appropriate by school personnel," the parents argued that this did not provide sufficient detail to permit them to know what the placement was. The Tribunal agreed and found the decision on placement to be "lacking in such clarity and detail that the parents could not make an informed decision to determine if the proposed placement as described would meet the needs." On this basis, the Tribunal found that it had jurisdiction to hear the appeal.[20]

On occasion, where it is not clear to the Tribunal whether or not the issues raised by the parents in an appeal properly relate to the special education placement, the Tribunal may be obliged to hear the merits of the appeal to decide whether or not it does have jurisdictional in the matter. Thus, when the issue of Intensive Behaviour Intervention ("IBI") therapy was first raised before the Tribunal, the argument made on behalf of the parents was that IBI was either a special education placement or a special education service that the

---

placement were critical to the definition of the placement. See Chapter 5 for decisions of the Tribunal on placement where the Tribunal dealt with programs and services as part of the placement.

17 *T. & Toronto District School Board* (2006-10-30), File No. 60 (Ont. Spec. Ed. (Eng.) Trib.)

18 *G.T.K. & Simcoe County District School Board* (2006-02-16), File No. 51 (Ont. Spec. Ed. (Eng.) Trib.).

19 *L.W. & Toronto District School Board* (2008-05-03), File No. 2007-04 (Ont. Spec. Ed. (Eng.) Trib.). See also *T. & Toronto District School Board* (2006-10-30), File No. 60 (Ont. Spec. Ed. (Eng.) Trib.), to similar effect.

20 *D. & Windsor Essex Catholic District School Board* (2003-09-30), File No. 38 (Ont. Spec. Ed. (Eng.) Trib.).

child required as part of the placement. In these cases, the school boards objected that IBI therapy was not a special education placement or a special education service and that the Tribunal did not have jurisdiction in the case. In three of the cases, because of the way the appeal was framed, the Tribunal determined that in order to decide the jurisdictional question, it needed to hear the full case. In the end, the Tribunal decided that IBI was a therapy delivered under the direction of a clinical psychologist, whereas education is delivered by a teacher; the Tribunal concluded that IBI is not a special education service, program or placement and that it, therefore, did not have jurisdiction to make an order regarding the provision of IBI therapy as part of a child's educational placement.[21]

How is an Appeal Initiated?

An appeal to the Tribunal is initiated by sending a written request to appeal the identification and/or placement decision of the school board to the Secretary of the Tribunal.[22] This initial request need not follow a particular form; a letter or e-mail will suffice. As a practical matter, the request should provide full contact information, including full name, title if any, mailing address, telephone number(s) and, if available, facsimile number and/or e-mail address for the parents or guardian — or their representative, as the case may be — as well as the name of the child to whom the appeal relates and the name of the school board whose decision is being appealed. Finally, the written request should always be signed by the parents or guardian initiating the appeal.[23]

On receipt of the request, the Secretary of the Tribunal will notify the chair of the Tribunal and the school board that a request to appeal has been received and will send "Form A: Notice of Appeal" to the parent, along with a copy of the Special Education Tribunal Rules of Procedure.[24] The parent must fill out and file this Notice of Appeal with the Tribunal within 20 days of receipt of the form.[25] The form asks the parent to provide information regarding whether or not the process under the regulation has been exhausted, what the grounds of the appeal are and whether or not the parent is prepared to consider mediation. The parent is also required to attach a copy of the original IPRC

---

21 *C. & Simcoe County District School Board* (2003-09-15), File No. 34 (Ont. Spec. Ed. (Eng.) Trib.).

22 The address of the Special Education Tribunal can be found at the Tribunal's website: http://www.oset-tedo.ca.

23 Ontario Ministry of Education, *Special Education: A Guide for Educators* (Toronto: The Ministry, 2001), available online at http://www.edu.gov.on.ca/eng/general/elemsec/speced/guide.html.

24 Available online at http://www.oset-tedo.ca/eng/pdfs/rules.pdf.

25 Note that the Form A will be deemed to have been received by the parent five days after the date of mailing by the Secretary of the Tribunal: Rules of Procedure, rule 5.1a).

decision, the report of the Special Education Appeal Board and the letter from the school board advising of its decision on the Appeal Board's report. The Secretary of the Tribunal will forward the parent's Form A to the school board (or the school board's counsel).

On receipt of the Notice of Appeal, the school board has 10 days to fill out and file with the Tribunal a "Form B: Response to Notice of Appeal"[26] along with copies of the IPRC decision, the SEAB report and the decision of the school board on the Appeal Board's decision. Form B requires the school board to set out information as to whether or not the process under the regulation was exhausted and its position on the identification and placement of the student. The school board is required to set out in Form B whether there are any preliminary issues, including issues relating to jurisdiction.

PROCEDURAL RULES GOVERNING THE TRIBUNAL'S PROCESSES

Where a parent or guardian appeals an identification or placement decision, the Tribunal must hold a hearing,[27] even when that hearing is to determine whether or not the Tribunal has jurisdiction to hear the appeal.

Section 57(2) of the *Education Act* allows the Lieutenant Governor in Council to make regulations concerning, among other things, the practices and procedures to be followed by the Special Education Tribunal in holding a hearing; however, no such regulations have ever been made. This does not mean that there are no procedural rules that govern hearings before the Tribunal. The Tribunal's procedures are governed by both the *Statutory Powers Procedure Act*[28] ("*SPPA*") and the general rules of "natural justice" and "procedural fairness" applicable to administrative tribunals.

The *SPPA* sets out the minimum procedural rules that must be followed by a wide range of administrative tribunals in Ontario, including the Special Education Tribunal. These procedural rules are designed to ensure that uniform, minimum standards of procedural fairness are maintained, unless

---

26 Rules of Procedure, rule 7.5. The school board will also be required to send the documents (*i.e.*, the IPRC decision, the SEAB report and/or the school board's letter to the parent setting out the school board's decision) that the parent fails to send.

27 *Education Act*, s. 57(3).

28 R.S.O. 1990, c. S.22. By virtue of s. 3(1), the *SPPA* applies "to a proceeding by a tribunal in the exercise of a statutory power of decision conferred by or under an Act of the Legislature, where the tribunal is required by or under such Act or otherwise by law to hold or to afford to the parties to the proceeding an opportunity for a hearing before making a decision". Section 57(3) of the *Education Act* provides for an appeal of an identification or placement to the Special Education Tribunal and, specifically, states that the Tribunal must hold a hearing in respect of the identification or placement. Thus, the Tribunal is covered by the *SPPA*.

expressly waived by the parties.[29] The *SPPA* authorizes an administrative tribunal to make rules governing its own practices and procedures, provided that they are consistent with the *SPPA*.[30] The Special Education Tribunal has done so and these are set out in its Rules of Procedure.

In addition to the procedural rules set out in the *SPPA* and in its own rules, the Tribunal is also governed by general rules of natural justice or procedural fairness established by the courts. The *SPPA* was intended, in part, to codify some of these judge-made rules and, as a result, there is considerable overlap between the procedural rules established by the courts and the procedural rules set out in the statute; however, the overlap is not complete and there are some rules of natural justice or procedural fairness with which the Tribunal must comply that exist outside the *SPPA*.

In the discussion on the Tribunal's procedures that follows, we will identify both the statutory and the judge-made rules with which the Tribunal must comply in carrying out a hearing, as well as the Rules of Procedure that it has established for itself.

PRELIMINARY MATTERS

Format of the Hearing

The *SPPA* allows a tribunal to hold written, oral or electronic hearings to deal with preliminary issues and the hearing of the merits of the appeal. The Tribunal's Rules of Procedure permit a hearing to be conducted in any one of these formats or a combination of them.[31] The format to be selected in each case will depend on the circumstances of each case; normally, however, written or electronic hearings are used only to deal with procedural issues or situations where no evidence is to be called.

The Parties to the Hearing

Section 5 of the *SPPA* provides that the parties to a proceeding "shall be the persons specified as parties by or under the statute under which the proceeding arises or, if not so specified, persons entitled by law to be parties to the proceeding".

The Tribunal's Rules of Procedure specify that the parties to an appeal are the appellant and the school board whose decision is under appeal. "appellant" is defined by the rules as the adult pupil, or the parent or guardian who initiated the appeal.[32]

---

29 *SPPA*, s. 4(1). Section 4(1) allows the parties and the tribunal to consent to waive any procedural requirement set out in the *SPPA* or any other statute or regulation.

30 *SPPA*, s. 25.1.

31 Rules of Procedure, rule10.1.

32 Rules of Procedure, rule 3.3.

As noted earlier, the question still exists as to whether or not a student under 18 years of age can appeal a school board's identification or placement decision; however, where an appeal has been initiated by a student's parents, section 5 of the *SPPA* provides a possible route for the student to be granted party status at the hearing of the appeal, where the student can convince the Tribunal that he or she is "entitled by law" to be a party. The principles of natural justice outlined by the courts provide that an individual who could be negatively impacted by the decision of an administrative tribunal is entitled to notice of and to participate in the proceeding that leads to the decision.[33] Identification and placement decisions will be of direct interest to any student who is able to understand these concepts. Moreover, the student who is the subject of an appeal could be adversely affected by the outcome if his or her parent were taking a position that was contrary to the student's wishes. It is also relevant to note that the Supreme Court of Canada has recognized that the student's rights and interests in special education proceedings are separate and distinct from the rights and interests of his or her parents.[34] These factors suggest that, at least where there is a divergence in views between the student and the parents or where the student is capable of expressing the desire to be a party, the student should be entitled to independent party status. The right to party status, however, is not automatic under section 5 of the *SPPA* and the student would be obliged to apply to the Tribunal for an order adding the student as a party.[35]

Notice of Hearing Dates

Section 6(1) of the *SPPA* requires that the parties to a proceeding must be given "reasonable notice" of the time and place of a hearing by the Tribunal. The period of notice that is "reasonable" will depend on the particular circumstances of the case. The content of the notice that is required depends on whether the hearing will be a written, oral or electronic.[36]

In some cases, the parties to a proceeding before the Special Education Tribunal may elect to deal with preliminary matters by way of a written or

---

33 In *MacCosham Van Lines (Canada) Co. v. Ontario (Minister of Transportation & Communications)* (1988), 11 M.V.R. (2d) 230, 66 O.R. (2d) 198 (Div. Ct.), at para. 33, Reid J. stated, "[T]here is a genuinely entrenched principle of administrative law that where natural justice requires it notice and an opportunity to respond must be given to persons who might be prejudiced by acts done under legislative authority notwithstanding that the legislation does not require it. . . . That principle is explicitly recognized in s. 5 of the S.P.P.A."

34 *Eaton v. Brant County Board of Education* (1997), 142 D.L.R. (4th) 385 at pp. 409-10, [1997] 1 S.C.R. 241.

35 In a case where parents with joint custody of the student disagree on the issue being appealed by the parent who initiated the appeal, s. 5 of the *SPPA* would also provide a route for the parent who is not the appellant to gain party status in the hearing and put his or her position forward.

36 *SPPA*, s. 6.

electronic hearing; however, the Tribunal will almost always hold an oral hearing to deal with the merits of the appeal, since it will be necessary to receive evidence from witnesses to determine the merits.

Section 6(2) and (3) of the *SPPA* requires that notice of an oral hearing must include the following:

- a reference to the statutory authority for holding the hearing (*i.e.*, section 57 of the *Education Act*);
- a statement of the time, place and purpose of the hearing; and
- a statement that, if a party notified does not attend at the hearing, then the Tribunal could proceed in that party's absence and the party will not be entitled to any further notice in the proceeding.

The place of the hearing will usually be a location within the geographic jurisdiction of the school board — normally, a meeting room will be arranged in a local hotel or government office to provide a venue for the hearing.

Initial Conference Call

Once the Tribunal has received the school board's Form B, the Secretary to the Tribunal will contact the parties to find a mutually convenient date on which the initial conference call can be held. According to rule 8.1 of the Tribunal's Rules of Procedure, this call must be held within 20 days of the receipt of the Form B.

The purpose of this initial conference call, which will include the parties (and/or their representatives), the secretary and the chair of the panel appointed to hear the appeal, is to review a number of preliminary and pre-hearing issues and to set the date for the hearing. Although the Tribunal's rules also provide for a pre-hearing conference, the initial conference call also serves as a pre-hearing conference.

During the call, the chair will confirm the identification of the parties to the appeal. The chair will canvas the issues to be raised by the parties, including any preliminary issues and the issues in dispute between the parties — the latter in order to clarify precisely what the parent is appealing and what the parent is seeking by way of remedy.

Where there are any preliminary issues that need to be decided before a hearing on the merits of the appeal itself — for example, jurisdictional issues — the chair will determine whether a hearing of the preliminary issues needs to be oral or can be held by teleconference or in writing. In the event of a hearing held orally or by teleconference, dates will be set for an exchange of positions in writing by the parties as well as the date(s) for the oral or teleconference hearing. In the event that the matter is to be dealt with by way of written submissions, the dates for the exchange of the submissions will be set.

Where there are no preliminary issues, dates will be set for the hearing and the exchange of pre-hearing disclosure between the appellant and the school board.

During the initial conference call, the chair will also ask the parties if they are willing to participate in a mediation of their differences. If so, then the parties could agree to have a member of the Special Education Tribunal who will not be on the hearing panel conduct the mediation or agree to have another mediator conduct the mediation.[37] Either way, dates will be set for the hearing sufficiently far off to permit the mediation process to run its course. Where the parties are able to resolve their issues in the mediation, the hearing dates will be cancelled.

Preliminary Motions or Objections

The Tribunal's Rules of Procedure permit preliminary motions to be made to the Tribunal prior to the hearing.[38] Therefore, should an issue arise following the initial conference call, either party may contact the Tribunal — usually by writing, so that the other party may be copied with the communication — to ask that the matter be dealt with. This may include a request for delay of the hearing or for production of documents that the party believes are necessary for a fair hearing from the other side.

The secretary of the Tribunal will set up a pre-hearing conference with the chair of the panel who will deal with the request or the motion in the first instance. This will take the form, initially, of a teleconference convened by the chair, who will attempt to see whether or not the issue can be resolved by mutual agreement. Dates will be set prior to the pre-hearing conference for the parties to exchange information. In the case of the party bringing the motion, that party will be required to set out the grounds for the motion and the remedy sought, to identify witnesses, if any, who will testify in respect of the motion, along with a summary of their evidence and to provide a list of documents to be provided to the Tribunal as part of the motion.

The responding party will be obliged, upon receipt of the moving party's materials, to set out its position on the motion in writing and provide a list of any witnesses who will be called in responding to the preliminary motion, along with a summary of their evidence, together with a list of any documents to be relied on in a hearing of the issue.

During the pre-hearing conference, the chair may discuss the issue with the parties to see whether or not it can be resolved informally and, if it cannot be resolved, then the chair will determine whether the motion should be resolved in a hearing prior to the hearing on the merits or whether it can be dealt with at the start of the hearing on the merits.

---

37 See Chapter 9, "Alternative Dispute Resolution: Mediation".

38 Rules of Procedure, rule 12.

Jurisdictional Issues

The preliminary issue most commonly dealt by the Tribunal relates to its jurisdiction to deal with the merits of the appeal. Some of the jurisdictional issues that can arise have been discussed earlier in this chapter, in the discussion under "Initiating the Appeal: The Who, When, What and How". These jurisdictional issues usually will be identified by the school board in Form B at the outset of the appeal process; however, these issues can be raised at any point during the proceeding and even after the Tribunal has given its decision. In the normal case, where a jurisdictional issue is raised at the outset of the process, the issue will be dealt with by the panel appointed to hear the appeal prior to the hearing on the merits, either by way of written submissions or oral or teleconference hearing. Where the issue is raised by the school board as a preliminary objection in the Form B or prior to the initial conference call, the dates for the hearing of the objection — which is usually an oral hearing — and for the exchange of information relating to the objection will be fixed during the initial conference call.

The Tribunal's Rules of Procedure recognize that the Tribunal has the authority to dismiss an appeal without a hearing on the merits where it decides that it has no jurisdiction as a preliminary manner.[39] The Tribunal may also decide to dismiss an appeal that is "frivolous, vexatious, or commenced in bad faith."[40] The Tribunal has not defined what this phrase means, but it is likely that this provision will apply only where it is clear or can be clearly demonstrated that the appeal is either lacking in merit and/or has been commenced for an improper motive, such as to harass the school board. While there are not, as of the date of writing, any decisions by the Tribunal dismissing an appeal under this rule, the type of case where the Tribunal might exercise its right to dismiss an appeal for being frivolous, vexatious or commenced in bad faith would include circumstances where a parent appeals following every IPRC, despite the fact that there has been no change in the student's condition that would justify a change in the student's identification or placement. It is noteworthy that the Tribunal may, of its own accord, without a request by the school board, decide, on receipt and review of an appeal that it appears to be frivolous, vexatious or made in bad faith or outside of the Tribunal's jurisdiction. In this event, the Tribunal would advise the parties of its view and provide them with an opportunity to address the issue in writing before deciding whether to dismiss the appeal or proceed to a hearing of the merits.[41]

---

39 Rules of Procedure, rule 20.

40 *Ibid.*, rule 20.1a)

41 *Ibid.*, rule 20.2 to 20.4.

Pre-hearing Disclosure

It is critical to a fair hearing of the appeal that each party understand the position that the other is taking in the hearing. Further, the Tribunal's rules require disclosure of the evidence that each side will call.[42]

The Rules of Procedure established by the Tribunal provide for disclosure of each party's position on the appeal in the Forms A and B exchanged between the parties. Should the allegations made by one party be lacking in specifics sufficient to permit the other party to understand the allegation being made, the Tribunal's Rules of Procedure provide that, at any point in the proceeding, the other party may apply to the Tribunal for an order for particulars, information or documents that will permit that party to obtain a clear understanding of the issues being raised in the appeal. Upon receipt of such an application, the Tribunal will hold a hearing — usually by way of teleconference — to hear both parties on the issue and then will decide what, if any, further disclosure must be made to the other party.[43]

It is a fundamental principle of natural justice — reflected in both the *SPPA* and the Tribunal's Rules — that, where one party in a hearing intends to put into the issue the good character, propriety of conduct or competence of another party, disclosure of the allegations to be made must be provided to the other party in advance of the hearing.[44]

As noted above, in the initial conference call, dates will be set for pre-hearing disclosure. This pre-hearing disclosure involves an exchange between the parties of their list of witnesses, together with a summary of what each witness is expected to say, a list of documents that each party will rely on and document books containing those documents. The date for disclosure by the parent will normally be 30 days prior to the first day of the hearing and, for the school board, 15 days in advance of the commencement of the hearing.[45]

Where a party wishes to call an expert witness at the hearing, that party must provide to the other party, at least 15 days prior to the anticipated date on which the expert witness would qualify, a statement of the expert's name, address, qualifications, a copy of the expert's resume and either a copy of the expert's report or a summary of the evidence that the expert will provide.[46]

The Tribunal's Rules of Procedure provide that a party who seeks to put into evidence a document that was not disclosed in the pre-hearing disclosure process may not put that document into evidence without the consent of the Tribunal and subject to any terms that the Tribunal may set for doing so.[47] Normally, the terms set by the Tribunal will be to permit the other party an adjournment, where it is necessary to deal with the surprise occasioned by the

42 *Ibid.*, rule 13.
43 *Ibid.*, rule 13.3.
44 *Ibid.*, rule 13.5.
45 *Ibid.*, rules 13.1 and 13.2.
46 *Ibid.*, rule 14.1
47 *Ibid.*, rule 13.4.

introduction of the undisclosed document. Further, the other party may be permitted to put into evidence documents not previously disclosed that respond to the undisclosed document in question. While the Tribunal does not have similar rules where a party seeks to call a witness whose name was not included in the pre-hearing disclosure, it is assumed that the Tribunal would grant a similar remedy if the calling of a previously undisclosed witness would cause an unfair surprise or other prejudice to the other party.

Similarly, if, at the hearing, a party's witness were to provide oral testimony that caught the other party by surprise because it was different than the summary of evidence to be given by that witness that was provided in the disclosure, then the other party could request an adjournment of the proceedings before cross-examining the witness. The Tribunal would hear argument from both sides and decide whether or not the adjournment would be granted.

Because surprise evidence may lead to adjournment of the proceedings, it is in the best interest of both parties — and for the student whom the appeal concerns — to ensure that the pre-hearing disclosure is complete. Co-operation is certainly highly desirable in special education proceedings, in which the tactical advantages of non-disclosure should be outweighed by the importance for all parties of ensuring that the best interests of the student are being served.

Securing the Attendance of Witnesses at the Hearing

A summons is a legal document that requires the recipient to attend at the hearing to give evidence and to bring with him or her any documents or things specified in the summons. The summons may cover any documents or things that are arguably relevant to the proceedings and admissible in evidence. The Tribunal's Rules of Procedure provide that a party may request the secretary of the Tribunal to have a summons issued by the chair of the Tribunal. The party who requests a summons will be responsible to serve the summons on the witness. To be effective in compelling a witness to attend, summonses must be served personally on a witness, along with the requisite "conduct money".[48]

Failure to comply with a properly served summons without lawful excuse can be grounds for arrest and the initiation of proceedings for contempt of the Tribunal.[49]

---

48 Conduct money includes a fixed amount that is intended as a modest stipend to the witness, along with an amount determined by a formula to cover travel expenses.

49 *SPPA*, ss. 12 and 13. What might constitute a lawful excuse for failure to comply with a summons is a complex question that may well warrant consultation with a lawyer. The question will be decided by the Tribunal, which may want to see the disputed documents, and/or question the person who failed to comply, before making its decision.

THE HEARING PROCESS

The hearing before the Tribunal is a formal, adversarial[50] proceeding. The parties to the hearing have a right to be represented by a legal representative,[51] if they so choose. The hearing will typically involve full examination and cross-examination of witnesses, including expert witnesses, and the parties will usually make legal argument concerning the decision that the Tribunal should reach. The details of how the hearing is conducted are described further under the heading "Overview of the Proceedings at the Hearing", *infra*.

It is important to understand that the hearing before the Tribunal is a hearing *de novo*. That is, the Tribunal does not merely review the decisions of the IPRC and the SEAB to determine whether or not errors have been committed and correct any errors; rather, the Tribunal hears all the evidence presented by the parties and comes to its own conclusion on identification and/or placement. This approach ensures that the Tribunal can take into account any changes in the pupil's circumstances between the time the SEAB decision is released and the time the hearing before the Tribunal begins.

Open versus Closed Hearings

In Ontario, the general rule is that tribunal hearings must be open to the public; however, where personal or financial information might be disclosed in the hearing that is of such a sensitive nature that privacy concerns regarding the information outweigh the importance of an open public hearing, an administrative tribunal may, at the request of one of the parties, order that the proceedings be closed. The Tribunal's Rules of Procedure, therefore, contemplate an exception to the general rule that a hearing should be open:[52]

> [I]ntimate financial or personal matters or other matters may be disclosed at the hearing of such a nature, having regard to the circumstances, that the desirability of avoiding disclosure thereof in the interests of any person affected or in the public interest outweighs the desirability of adhering to the principle that hearings be open to the public.

---

50 Generally, hearings before courts and administrative tribunals in common law jurisdictions such as Canada proceed on the "adversarial model" — that is, the parties are responsible to put before the decision-maker any evidence that is relevant to the decision. This is to be contrasted with the "inquisitorial model", where the adjudicator seeks out or participates in the calling of evidence.

51 The Tribunal's Rules define "representative" as either a lawyer or licensed paralegal appointed by the party to represent the party in the hearing. Following amendments to the *Law Society Act*, R.S.O. 1990, c. L.8, paid third-party advocates who are not either lawyers or licensed paralegals can no longer act for a party before the Special Education Tribunal.

52 *SPPA*, s. 9(1)(*b*). See also Rules of Procedure, rule 10.5.

Alternatively, where the testimony of only one or a small number of witnesses is expected to be sensitive, a request may be made to close the hearing only while particular witnesses testify.

Where a party wishes to request a closed or partially closed hearing, the appropriate course of action is to raise the issue as a preliminary matter at the outset of the hearing before the Tribunal begins to hear evidence or argument on the merits of the appeal. Each side will be given the opportunity to present arguments on the issue to the Tribunal. The Tribunal will then issue a decision on the matter and the hearing will proceed in accordance with the Tribunal's decision.

It should be noted that the Tribunal's policy in publishing its decisions is to "anonymize" decisions by using initials to identify the student and the student's parents. This policy is responsive to privacy rights and is motivated by a desire to "protect minor children"; recognizing that inevitably, an appeal will disclose "very sensitive and intimate" information about the child who is the subject of the appeal.[53]

Overview of the Proceedings at the Hearing

The Special Education Tribunal hearing will usually begin with introductory statements by the chair of the Tribunal. These introductory statements will include introduction of the members of the Tribunal, the Tribunal secretary and the court reporter transcribing the proceedings;[54] introduction of the parties; and an overview of the procedures that will be followed. The chair will usually ask whether there are any preliminary matters to be addressed and the parties can then discuss with the Tribunal how the preliminary matters should be dealt with. Sometimes preliminary matters are addressed immediately after introductory statements from the chair; sometimes the parties will deliver their opening statements before preliminary matters are addressed.

When preliminary issues are raised, the party raising the issue will proceed first. The other party will then have an opportunity to respond. Often, preliminary matters can be resolved solely on the basis of the submissions of the parties; however, in some cases, it may be necessary for the Tribunal to hear evidence before making its decision on the preliminary matters. Once the parties have presented their evidence and/or made their submissions, the members of the Tribunal will typically confer — sometimes a recess will be necessary for this purpose — and then advise the parties about how they will proceed.

[53] See the Ontario Special Education (English) Tribunal policy, "Anonymization of Tribunal Decisions", available online at http://www.oset-tedo.ca/eng/pdfs/anonymization.pdf.

[54] Proceedings of the Special Education Tribunal are always transcribed verbatim by a court reporter, so that a transcript can be made available to the Tribunal members and the parties.

In some cases, the Tribunal may request further written submissions before making its decision; in other cases, the Tribunal may make its decision on the preliminary matter right away. In still other cases, the Tribunal may reserve its decision on the preliminary matter and adjourn the hearing pending that decision. In yet other cases, the Tribunal may reserve its decision on the preliminary matter, continue with the hearing and release its decision at a later date.

Once any preliminary issues have been dealt with, each party will be asked to make an opening statement. The purpose of opening statements is to summarize each party's position, clarify the issues in dispute and the result being sought and, thereby, enable the Tribunal to place the parties' evidence in its proper context. The parents or guardian or their legal counsel, will be asked to present their opening statement first, followed by the school board or its legal counsel.

The next stage of the hearing is the presentation of evidence. The parents or guardian who initiated the appeal — or their legal counsel — will be expected to proceed first in calling and questioning witnesses to give evidence supporting their position.

As noted above, the Tribunal has the power to issue summonses to witnesses.[55] Each summons must be signed by the chair of the Tribunal, who is entitled to ask the requesting party to justify either the number of summonses requested or the particular witnesses summoned. A summons is not required for every witness. In practice, they are usually used only for witnesses who require a summons in order to obtain a leave of absence from their places of employment or who are unwilling (or potentially unwilling) to testify for the party who had the summons issued.

Evidence that is given at a hearing of the Special Education Tribunal must be given under oath or affirmation — that is, before giving evidence, each witness will be asked to swear or affirm that he or she will tell the truth.[56]

The party who called the witness — or that party's legal counsel — will have the first opportunity to question the witness. These questions must be non-leading questions; that is, the question cannot suggest the answer. For example, a question such as, "Then, did you tell the teacher you were dissatisfied?" is a leading question and cannot be asked at this stage of the proceeding. Non-leading questions usually take the form of "who/what/when/where/why" questions, which do not suggest to the witness how the question should be answered — for example, the examiner might ask the witness, "What did you say to the teacher?" to elicit the same information

---

55 *SPPA*, s. 12.

56 Technically, to give an oath, a person must swear on the Bible that he or she will tell the truth. An affirmation is a secular form of oath whereby a person promises to tell the truth after being advised of the penalties for perjury. Many administrative decision-makers now use affirmations instead of oaths, in recognition of the diverse religious beliefs of the persons coming before them.

covered by the leading question set out above. A party's examination of a witness whom that party has called to testify is referred to as "direct examination" or "examination-in-chief".

Once direct examination is completed, the school board — or its legal counsel — will be entitled to cross-examine the witness. Cross-examination is designed to achieve four main purposes: to obtain additional helpful evidence; to qualify or limit any adverse evidence that has been given; to impeach, contradict or minimize adverse evidence that has been given; and to undermine the credibility of the witness. In contrast with direct examination, leading questions can and will be asked during cross-examination.

Following cross-examination, the party who called the witness — or his or her legal counsel — will have a limited opportunity to ask additional questions of the witness. This final stage of questioning is known as "re-direct examination". Re-direct examination is limited to clarification of matters that arose for the first time in cross-examination; it cannot be used as an opportunity to repeat evidence already given or question the witness on entirely new areas not covered in examination-in-chief. Again, questions asked during re-direct examination cannot be leading questions.

The members of the Tribunal can ask a witness questions at any time in order to clarify any matters raised during questioning by the parties or to ensure that the witness's answer was understood;[57] however, the Tribunal usually will reserve its questions until the end of questioning by the parties. When this occurs, the parties will be given a further opportunity to question the witness on the evidence given in response to the Tribunal's questions.

Once each of the parents' or guardian's witnesses has been questioned in this manner, the school board — or its legal counsel — will have an opportunity to present its evidence. The school board's witnesses will undergo direct examination by the school board or its counsel, cross-examination by the parent and re-direct examination by the school board or its counsel and may also be subject to questioning by the Tribunal.

Once the school board has called all its witnesses, the parents or guardian — or their legal counsel — will have an opportunity to present reply evidence. Like re-direct examination, reply evidence is limited in scope to any matters that arose for the first time during the school board's evidence. Reply

---

[57] Members of the Tribunal should exercise restraint in asking questions of witnesses. In the adversarial system, it is up to the parties to bring forward the evidence the Tribunal requires in order to reach its decision. In *Majcenic v. Natale* (1967), 66 D.L.R. (2d) 50 at p. 65, [1968] 1 O.R. 189, the Ontario Court of Appeal emphasized the risks associated with active intervention by the decision-maker:

> When a Judge intervenes in the examination or cross-examination of witnesses, to such an extent that he projects himself into the arena, he of necessity, adopts a position which is inimical to the interests of one or other of the litigants. His action, whether conscious or unconscious, no matter how well intentioned or motivated, creates an atmosphere which violates the principle that "justice not only be done, but appear to be done".

evidence, however, may involve new witnesses and new documentary evidence where necessary in order to respond to the other party's position.

Finally, once all the evidence is completed, each party will have an opportunity to make a closing statement (sometimes called a "summary statement"). Again, the parents or guardian — or their legal counsel — proceed first, followed by the school board or its legal counsel. The closing statement allows each party to summarize the evidence, make legal argument — the applicable legal tests are discussed further under the heading "The Special Education Tribunal's Decision", later in this chapter — and generally try to persuade the Tribunal in favour of the outcome they are seeking.

Preventing Abuse of Process

The Special Education Tribunal has wide powers to control its proceedings in order to prevent abuse of process. Some examples of the Tribunal's powers include the following:

- The Tribunal has authority to exclude evidence or limit a witness's testimony, on the basis that it is "unduly repetitious".[58]
- The Tribunal can reasonably limit examination or cross-examination of witnesses where it is satisfied that the examination or cross-examination "has been sufficient to disclose fully and fairly all matters relevant to the issues in the proceeding".[59]
- The Tribunal has the authority to make whatever orders or give whatever directions it "considers proper to prevent abuse of its processes".[60]
- The Tribunal has authority to make any orders or give any directions it considers necessary to maintain order at the hearing, including the authority to call for the assistance of a peace officer where its orders or directions are disobeyed.[61]

PROVIDING EVIDENCE TO THE TRIBUNAL

Earlier in this chapter, we have noted that the proceedings before the Special Education Tribunal are adversarial proceedings. That is, the Tribunal is not permitted to seek out evidence on its own;[62] rather, it is the responsibility

---

58 *SPPA*, s. 15(1).
59 *Ibid.*, s. 23(2).
60 *Ibid.*, s. 23(1).
61 *Ibid.*, s. 9(2).
62 The adversarial nature of Special Education Tribunal proceedings was highlighted in the seminal *Eaton* case, in which the Ontario Court of Appeal criticized the Tribunal for conducting its own literature search and relying in part on the results of that search in reaching its decision: *Eaton v. Brant County Board of Education*

of the parties to ensure that all relevant evidence is presented to the Tribunal during the hearing.

The evidence presented to the Special Education Tribunal will normally take two forms: first, evidence may be presented through the *viva voce* (*i.e.*, in person, oral) testimony of witnesses; second, evidence may be presented through documents introduced during testimony of the witnesses.

Documents may be submitted to the Tribunal in three ways: they may be introduced as evidence during the questioning of witnesses; they may be admitted by agreement at the outset of the hearing, subject to further proof; or, where both parties intend to refer to many of the same documents, the parties may agree on a joint book of documents that can be introduced at the beginning of the hearing. Where the parties intend to utilize one or both of the latter two methods, the documents will generally be submitted during or immediately after opening statements.

The Special Education Tribunal is not strictly bound by the rules of evidence applicable in a court of law.[63] Nevertheless, it is important to have an understanding of the rules of evidence in order to appreciate what limits there are on admissibility of evidence and how those limits will affect the presentation of a case to the Tribunal.

Competence of Witnesses

One issue that can arise in proceedings before the Special Education Tribunal is whether a particular witness is "competent" to give evidence — that is, capable of understanding the nature of the oath or affirmation, capable of understanding what it means to tell the truth and the importance of doing so, and/or of observing events, recalling those events and communicating them to the decision-maker. Competence is most likely to be an issue in proceedings before the Tribunal where the student is to be called as a witness.[64]

Under Canadian law, witnesses are presumed to be competent unless proven otherwise;[65] however, both age and disability may provide grounds for challenging a witness's competence. Where the competence of a particular

---

(1995), 123 D.L.R. (4th) 43, 27 C.R.R. (2d) 53 (Ont. C.A.), revd on other grounds 142 D.L.R. (4th) 385, [1997] 1 S.C.R. 241

63 *SPPA*, s. 15.

64 There may be good reason in some cases to avoid calling the student who is the subject of the appeal, if at all possible. Many younger children find the process of testifying before a tribunal very intimidating, particularly when they are being asked to contradict the views of authority figures such as parents, teachers and other school officials. Nevertheless, the Supreme Court of Canada's decision in *Eaton, supra*, footnote 62, suggests that the student has a right, independent of his or her parents, to express his or her views concerning the issues under appeal. Moreover, there may be cases in which calling the student as a witness is necessary in order to ensure that the Tribunal has all the relevant facts before it in making its decision.

65 *Evidence Act*, R.S.O. 1990, c. E.23, s. 18(1).

witness is challenged, the decision-maker — in this case, the Special Education Tribunal — must inquire into the competence of the witness and rule on the issue before the witness can give his or her evidence.[66]

Section 18.1 of the *Evidence Act* provides that, where the competence of a person under 14 years of age is challenged, a court may admit the evidence when the court is satisfied that the person is able to communicate the evidence and understand the nature of the oath or affirmation and that person testifies under oath or affirmation. Where the person does not understand the nature of the oath or affirmation, the evidence may still be admitted where the person understands what it means to tell the truth and promises to do so. Further, even where the person does not understand what it means to tell the truth, the court could still admit the evidence if it were satisfied that the evidence was sufficiently reliable.[67]

Many children understand the importance of telling the truth at a reasonably young age and may, therefore, be competent to give evidence. The authors are aware of children as young as eight years old who have been found to be competent to give sworn evidence. Certainly, most adolescent children will have sufficient understanding of the importance of truth-telling to be competent witnesses. Nevertheless, where an objection to competence is raised, the Tribunal will need to question the child in order to satisfy itself that the child has the necessary understanding to be a competent witness.

The *Evidence Act* also contemplates that persons under the age of 18 may be permitted to give their evidence under special conditions when it will assist them to give complete and accurate testimony. Examples of such special conditions include testifying on videotape or behind a screen or similar device. Similarly, a witness who is younger than 18 may be accompanied by a support person while giving evidence. Limits may also be placed on cross-examination of a person under the age of 18 where cross-examination would be likely to adversely affect the witness's ability to give evidence or would otherwise be contrary to the best interests of the witness.[68]

Ontario Regulation 181/98 gives students aged 16 and over the right to be present at and participate in both IPRC and SEAB proceedings, thereby implicitly recognizing that students in this age group are competent to participate in special education proceedings;[69] however, where any person under the age of 18 is called as a witness and the other party objects, the Tribunal will need to hear arguments from both sides and make a determination of whether or not the witness is competent. It may be that setting conditions on the testimony or the circumstances in which it is given — *i.e.*, by closing the part of the hearing where the witness testifies or by allowing

---

66 *Ibid.*, s. 18(2) and (3).

67 *Ibid.*, s. 18.1(1) to (3). Notably, s. 18.2 further provides that the evidence of a person under 14 need not be corroborated by other evidence in order to be relied upon.

68 *Ibid.*, ss. 18.3 to 18.6.

69 O. Reg. 181/98, s. 5.

a support person to be present while the witness testifies — will be sufficient to address any concerns about the witness's competence; however, there may be significant questions concerning the weight that should be assigned to the witness's evidence, particularly where the witness testified under special conditions.

Disabilities that interfere with an individual's ability to understand the importance of telling the truth or his or her ability to observe, recall or communicate information, may also call into question the individual's competence to give evidence. Determining the competence of an individual with a disability can be a complex task, sometimes requiring expert evidence concerning the individual's capabilities.

In special education proceedings, circumstances are likely to arise in which a potential witness is both a child and has a disability. In these cases, complex questions may have to be resolved concerning what evidence the witness is competent to give and what weight should be assigned to his or her evidence. These questions will have to be determined by the Tribunal, following submissions from the parties, based on the particular facts of the case.

Admissibility

The Special Education Tribunal is given considerable latitude under the *SPPA* to determine what evidence will be admitted at the hearing.[70] Although the courts have developed a number of rules governing the admissibility of evidence, the Tribunal is not bound by the rules of evidence that apply in courts of law. As a result, the Tribunal may admit evidence that would not be admissible in court; however, like a court, the Tribunal will listen to arguments about the weight to be accorded to such evidence and will determine the appropriate weight when making its final decision.

Section 15(2) of the *SPPA* does place two restrictions on the scope of the evidence that may be admitted by the Tribunal: first, the Tribunal may not admit evidence that would be inadmissible in court because it is "privileged" (*i.e.*, protected from disclosure) under the laws of evidence; and second, the Tribunal may not admit evidence that is rendered inadmissible under the *Education Act* or any other statute. These restrictions will be discussed later in this chapter under the heading "Privileged Information".

Relevance and Weight

The main factor that the Special Education Tribunal will consider in determining whether or not evidence should be admitted is whether the evidence is relevant to the issues before the Tribunal. Evidence is relevant where it tends to prove or disprove facts that are in dispute.

---

[70] *SPPA*, s. 15.

In considering relevance, the Tribunal will balance the value of the evidence in proving key matters in dispute — often referred to as its "probative value" — against the prejudice or harm that could be caused to a party or other person if the evidence were admitted. Extremely prejudicial evidence that is of dubious or limited assistance to the Tribunal will often be excluded.

The question of whether or not evidence is relevant should be distinguished from the question of what weight should be given to it. The concept of "weight" describes the importance or significance accorded to a piece of evidence in reaching a particular factual conclusion. A witness's evidence may be relevant, yet may be given little weight, because of circumstances such as the witness's limited direct knowledge of or involvement in events, questions about the witness's competence or credibility, the existence of a preponderance of evidence to the contrary and many other factors.

It is not uncommon for tribunals such as the Special Education Tribunal to take a broad view of what is relevant. Often, the degree of relevance of a particular piece of evidence will not be clear until all the evidence has been presented. Accordingly, the Tribunal may decide to admit the evidence and reserve its decision on the relevance of the evidence and the weight it should be given until the hearing has concluded.

Privileged Information

Section 15(2) of the *SPPA* prohibits the Tribunal from admitting evidence that is "privileged" (*i.e.*, protected from disclosure) under the laws of evidence or evidence that is rendered inadmissible under the *Education Act* or any other statute.

Privilege Under Evidence Law

The law of evidence recognizes a number of different categories of "privileged" communications that cannot be the subject of evidence in legal proceedings, unless the party for whose benefit the privilege is imposed agrees to waive it. The most common categories of privilege include solicitor-client privilege, which protects communications between a client and his or her lawyer, as well as litigation privilege, which protects communications with third parties that were made for the dominant purpose of preparing for actual or anticipated litigation, and settlement privilege, which protects communications made in the course of good faith efforts to resolve a dispute where litigation has been commenced or is contemplated.[71]

---

[71] Notably, settlement privilege may protect mediation discussions from disclosure in litigation, provided that litigation has been commenced or was in contemplation at the time the mediation was held; however, parties to mediation are nevertheless well-advised to confirm any understanding about confidentiality in a written agreement.

In addition to the categories of privilege discussed previously, the common law recognizes that privilege may extend to other communications that meet all four of the following criteria:[72]

- the communications must originate in a confidence that they will not be disclosed;
- this element of confidentiality must be essential to the full and satisfactory maintenance of the relationship between the parties;
- the relationship must be one that, in the opinion of the community, ought to be sedulously fostered; and
- the injury that would be caused to the relationship by disclosure of the communication must be greater than the benefit thereby gained for the correct disposal of the litigation.

This latter type of privilege is often referred to as "case-by-case" privilege, because the question of whether or not the above criteria are met — with the result that the communication is privileged — must be determined on a case-by-case basis.

Significantly, the fourth criterion listed above grants a court a wide discretion to override the confidentiality of the communication in the interests of the administration of justice. Accordingly, it is often quite difficult in practice to establish that a communication is "privileged" under this test.

Privilege Under the Education Act

As noted above, section 15(2) of the *SPPA* also prohibits the Tribunal from admitting any evidence that is rendered inadmissible under its governing statute, the *Education Act*. Section 266(2) of the *Education Act* creates a privilege for the contents of the Ontario Student Record ("OSR"):

> 266(2) A record is privileged for the information and use of supervisory officers and the principal and teachers of the school for the improvement of instruction of the pupil, and such record,
>
> (a) subject to subsections (2.1), (3), (5), (5.1), (5.2) and (5.3), is not available to any other person; and
>
> (b) except for the purposes of subsections (5), (5.1), (5.2) and (5.3), is not admissible in evidence for any purpose in any trial, inquest, inquiry, examination, hearing or other proceeding, except to prove the establishment, maintenance, retention or transfer of the record,
>
> without the written permission of the parent or guardian of the pupil or, where the pupil is an adult, the written permission of the pupil.

At first blush, the result of this provision appears to be that the documents in the student's OSR are not admissible in proceedings before the Special

[72] See John Henry Wigmore, *Wigmore on Evidence in Trials at Common Law*, vol. 8, rev. by John T. McNaughton (Boston: Little, Brown and Co., 1961), at p. 527, para. 2285, as quoted in *Slavutych and Board of Governors of the University of Alberta (Re)* (1975), 55 D.L.R. (3d) 224 at p. 228, [1976] 1 S.C.R. 254 *sub nom. Slavutych v. Baker*. See also *R. v. Gruenke* (1991), 67 C.C.C. (3d) 289, [1991] 3 S.C.R. 263; *M. (A). v. Ryan* (1997), 143 D.L.R. (4th) 1, [1997] 1 S.C.R. 157.

Education Tribunal without parental consent. This result, however, is widely perceived as problematic, because it would allow the parents/guardian unilaterally to control what OSR material is before the Tribunal, even if that material were before the IPRC when the original identification/placement decision was made.[73]

There are a number of arguments that can be made to counter the proposition that OSR documents are not admissible before the Tribunal without parental consent. One such argument is that, by appealing the school board's decision, the parents or guardian must be taken to have waived any privilege that might apply to the OSR documents, at least to the extent necessary to allow the school board to make a full and fair response to the appeal.[74]

Another argument flows from the fact that the very reason that many OSR documents relevant to the special education process are obtained or compiled is for use in that process. Section 32(*c*) of the *Municipal Freedom of Information and Protection of Privacy Act*[75] ("*MFIPPA*"), permits the disclosure of personal information "for the purpose for which it was obtained or compiled or for a consistent purpose". Section 53(1) then provides that the *MFIPPA* prevails over the confidentiality provisions of any other Act unless the other Act specifically says that it does not. Thus, the *MFIPPA* "trumps" section 266 of the *Education Act* and any OSR documents to which this argument applies may be disclosed before the Tribunal.[76]

A similar argument can be made in support of the proposition that, quite apart from the admissibility of OSR documents, the teache1rs and school board personnel involved in obtaining, compiling, reviewing or using those documents can give oral evidence about their contents before the Tribunal. Section 266(10) of the *Education Act* allows a person to disclose the contents of OSR documents "as may be required in the performance of his or her duties". A teacher or other school board representative who discloses such informa-

---

73 The authors note that s. 266 was enacted before the special education scheme was introduced. Arguably, the provision is no longer responsive to the diverse array of administrative proceedings carried on under the *Education Act* and needs to be reviewed by the Legislature.

74 Many tribunals and courts take the view that, where evidence that would otherwise be privileged relates to a matter placed in issue by the party protected by the privilege, the opposing party is entitled to sufficient disclosure of the evidence to ensure that it can make a full and fair response to the issue raised. In such cases, however, the decision-maker may place limits on disclosure to ensure that it does not go any further than necessary in order to ensure fairness to the other party. Although the authors are not aware of a case in which this issue has arisen before the Tribunal, the same principles would seem to apply in such a case.

75 R.S.O. 1990, c. M.56.

76 The authors note that, thus far, this argument does not appear to have been tested before the Tribunal or the courts; however, it appears consistent with the approach arbitrators have taken to this issue, which is discussed further in Chapter 6, "The Identification, Placement and Review Committee".

tion in the context of testifying in support of the school board before the Tribunal is surely acting "as may be required in the performance of his or her duties".

Hearsay Evidence

"Hearsay evidence" is evidence given by a person who did not observe events firsthand, but rather is relying on an account of events provided by another person — for example, if a parent were to give evidence of what he or she was told by the student about the student's experiences in the classroom or about classroom observations reported by the teacher, then the evidence would be hearsay evidence.

Hearsay evidence is generally inadmissible in court for the purpose of proving the truth of the position being put forward. There are two main reasons for this. First, the courts generally require the parties to put forward the "best evidence" in support of their case. Hearsay evidence is not the best evidence of what transpired; evidence from witnesses with firsthand knowledge is far more persuasive. Second, hearsay evidence is viewed as unreliable because of the absence of any opportunity to cross-examine the person who provided the original account of events. Without the opportunity for cross-examination, it is not possible to draw any conclusions about the credibility of the person who provided the information.

Although hearsay evidence is generally inadmissible in court, there are a number of specific situations in which hearsay may be admitted.[77] In addition, the Supreme Court of Canada has held that, even in court proceedings, in some very limited circumstances, hearsay evidence may be admitted where the party putting forward the evidence can establish that the evidence is both reasonably necessary and reliable.[78]

The Supreme Court has also recognized that, because of the special challenges young children may face in giving evidence, hearsay evidence may also be admissible in some exceptional cases involving child witnesses;[79] however, even in these cases, hearsay evidence is very much the exception, rather than the rule, and direct evidence will always be preferable.

Despite the fact that hearsay evidence is generally not admissible in court, all tribunals covered by the *SPPA*, including the Special Education Tribunal, can admit hearsay evidence, subject to a later assessment of the weight it should be given. In this way, the Tribunal can ensure that it has the fullest possible evidentiary record before it when it makes its decision. Where the hearsay evidence is not corroborated through other evidence or the truth of

---

77 For example, under s. 35(2) of the *Evidence Act*, records made in the "usual and ordinary course of business" are exempted from the hearsay rule, provided that certain statutory preconditions are met.

78 *R. v. Khan* (1990), 59 C.C.C. (3d) 92, [1990] 2 S.C.R. 531; *R. v. Smith* (1992), 94 D.L.R. (4th) 590, [1992] 2 S.C.R. 915.

79 *R. v. F. (W.J.)* (1999), 178 D.L.R. (4th) 53, [1999] 3 S.C.R. 569.

the evidence is in dispute, the Tribunal may decide to give little or no weight to the hearsay evidence in reaching its final decision. Accordingly, even though the Tribunal can admit hearsay evidence, it is generally preferable to rely on firsthand evidence rather than hearsay evidence.

Expert Evidence

As a general rule, witnesses are not permitted to give evidence in a court of law about their opinions — particularly their opinions concerning the disposition of the issues in dispute in the litigation. There is one significant exception, however, to the prohibition on opinion evidence. The courts will permit a qualified expert to give opinion evidence concerning matters within his or her area of expertise, provided that the evidence is: relevant to an issue in the case; necessary to assist the decision-maker, in the sense that it concerns matters outside the experience of a lay person and the decision-maker cannot reach a decision without the benefit of the evidence; otherwise admissible; and given by a properly qualified expert.[80]

Proceedings before the Special Education Tribunal will often involve evidence from numerous experts. Physicians, psychiatrists, psychologists, audiologists, speech-language pathologists, speech-language therapists, physiotherapists, occupational therapists and educators specializing in education of children with special needs are but a few of the kinds of experts who may be called as witnesses by either party to give evidence about the appropriate identification and/or placement of the student.

In many cases, these experts will have prepared reports or assessments and these reports or assessments will have been relied on by the IPRC and/or the SEAB to support a particular identification or placement. On appeal, the individuals who prepared these reports or assessments will often be called as witnesses to elaborate on or explain their conclusions.

In some cases, classroom teachers and others who deal with the student on a daily basis may also be able to provide expert evidence to the Tribunal. With respect to identification as an "exceptional pupil",[81] the classroom teacher will not necessarily have the expertise to provide an opinion on whether the student has "behavioural, communicational, intellectual, physical or multiple exceptionalities" or what category of exceptionality applies; however, the teacher may be able to provide an expert opinion about whether the student appears to "need placement in a special education program". A teacher may also be able to give evidence about proposed placements and what special education programs and services can be delivered in the various placements. Depending on the circumstances and the teacher's particular expertise, the teacher may even be able to provide an expert opinion concerning the student's

---

80 *R. v. Mohan* (1994), 114 D.L.R. (4th) 419, [1994] 2 S.C.R. 9.

81 The definition of an "exceptional pupil" is found in s. 1(1) of the *Education Act*.

learning style and progress (or lack of progress) in the regular class or in a particular placement.[82]

Although expert evidence is a legitimate and often a necessary part of an appeal to the Tribunal, both the school board and the parents should be cautious of being drawn into a contest of opposing experts. Each party should carefully consider the implications of the expert witnesses they call and the manner in which they handle the expert witnesses called by the other party. For example, it may be that teachers and other school board personnel who will be working with the student in the placement proposed by the school board have valuable expertise to share with the Tribunal; however, being examined and cross-examined in contentious legal proceedings can inject an adversarial note into the student-teacher relationship. Both parties must remember that the purpose of the special education appeal process is to ensure that the student's educational needs and best interests are met and keep that objective uppermost in their minds when dealing with the expert evidence submitted to the Tribunal.

Where a party does wish to call a witness as an "expert witness", the Tribunal's rules provide that notice must be given to the other party at least 15 days before the expert witness is expected to testify and to serve on the other party and file with the Tribunal a statement setting out the name, address and qualifications of the witness, a copy of the witness' resume and either the report of the witness or a written outline of what the witness's evidence will be.[83] It is important to note that the Tribunal will not automatically accept the witness as an "expert" unless both parties agree. Normally, the party calling the witness will state, at the outset, the area of expertise that the witness has and ask questions of the witness — usually about his or her qualifications and work — to establish that the witness has expertise in the area claimed. If the other party were to continue to challenge the expertise of the witness, then the other party could cross-examine the witness on the issue of his or her expertise. Following this process, the Tribunal will give its decision as to whether or not it will accept the witness as an expert and, if so, in what areas it recognizes the witness' expertise.

THE SPECIAL EDUCATION TRIBUNAL'S DECISION

Timing

At the conclusion of the hearing, a Special Education Tribunal will usually "reserve" its decision. This means that the Tribunal will not issue its decision

82 It may be appropriate to distinguish here between the student's classroom teacher — who knows the student and is able to observe the student in the classroom — and the student's special education teacher — who may not know the child well, but will understand how the placements work. Each of these teachers may bring different expertise to the appeal process.

83 Rules of Procedure, rule 14.1.

right away, but will take some time to consider the matter and prepare a decision in writing. In contrast to IPRC and SEAB decisions, there is no time limit within which the Tribunal must issue its decision.

In some cases, particularly where there is some specific urgency with respect to the student's placement, the Tribunal may make its order verbally at the end of the hearing and then issue written reasons at a later time.

Weighing the Evidence

As part of the decision-making process, the Tribunal will have the task of sorting through the evidence and making findings with respect to any material facts that are in dispute. This task will require the Tribunal to decide what weight should be assigned to various items of evidence and is often referred to as "weighing the evidence".

Where expert evidence has been presented, the Tribunal may have to decide between conflicting expert opinions. In weighing the expert evidence, the Tribunal will consider factors such as the relative expertise of the various witnesses, whether they had an opportunity to observe or examine the student and, if so, the extent of those observations or examinations and the degree of the expert's objectivity.

The Legal Test

Once the Tribunal has weighed the evidence and made its findings of fact, the Tribunal must apply the appropriate legal test to those facts in order to reach its decision on identification and/or placement.

In dealing with identification, the question before the Tribunal is whether or not the expert evidence supports a finding that the student is an "exceptional pupil" because of "behavioural, communicational, intellectual, physical or multiple exceptionalities . . . such that he or she is considered to need placement in a special education program".[84]

The question before the Tribunal on a placement appeal is somewhat more complex. In the *Eaton* decision, the Supreme Court of Canada confirmed that the legal test to be applied by the Tribunal in reviewing placement is whether or not, from the student's perspective, the placement is in his or her best interests. In determining the student's best interests, some weight is to be given to parental preferences — parental preferences, however, are not determinative. The court said:[85]

> We cannot forget, however, that for a child who is young or unable to communicate his or her needs or wishes, equality rights are being exercised on his or her behalf, usually by the child's parents. Moreover, the requirements for

[84] *Education Act*, s. 1(1), definition "exceptional pupil". This issue is discussed further in Chapter 4, "Identification and Exceptionality".

[85] *Eaton v. Brant County Board of Education* (1997), 142 D.L.R. (4th) 385, [1997] 1 S.C.R. 241, at para. 77.

respecting these rights in this setting are decided by adults who have authority over this child. For this reason, the decision-making body must further ensure that its determination of the appropriate accommodation for an exceptional child be from a subjective, child-centred perspective, one which attempts to make equality meaningful from the child's point of view as opposed to that of the adults in his or her life. As a means of achieving this aim, it must also determine that the form of accommodation chosen is in the child's best interests. A decision-making body must determine whether the integrated setting can be adapted to meet the special needs of an exceptional child. Where this is not possible, that is, where aspects of the integrated setting which cannot reasonably be changed interfere with meeting the child's special needs, the principle of accommodation will require a special education placement outside of this setting. For older children and those who are able to communicate their wishes and needs, their own views will play an important role in the determination of best interests. For younger children, and those like Emily, who are either incapable of making a choice or have a very limited means of communicating their wishes, the decision-maker must make this determination on the basis of the other evidence before it.

Reasons

By virtue of section 17(1) of the *SPPA*, a tribunal must give its decision and order and the underlying reasons in writing. Where the tribunal has given a verbal decision at the end of the hearing, it will subsequently confirm its decision in writing and will provide its reasons at that time.

In the case of the Special Education Tribunal, it normally reserves its decision and does not provide an oral decision at the end of the hearing. Its rules provide that it will issue its decision within 90 days of the completion of the hearing.[86]

Once the Tribunal's written decision is completed, the Tribunal must give a copy of the decision, including the reasons, to each party who participated in the hearing.[87] Usually the secretary of the Tribunal will forward the decision to the parties by regular mail or by courier.[88]

It is important to note that, particularly where there are unresolved preliminary issues, the Tribunal may issue a number of separate decisions in a single appeal. Depending on the circumstances, these decisions may either be issued separately at different times during the litigation or consolidated into a single decision issued at the end of the litigation. Regardless of which of these courses of action is followed, the decisions will all be issued in accordance with the statutory rules described above.

---

86 Rules of Procedure, rule 16.1.

87 Depending on the student's age, it may also be prudent for the Tribunal to give its decision to the affected student, whether or not the student was a party.

88 *SPPA*, s. 18(1).

REMEDIES AVAILABLE

The Special Education Tribunal is given broad remedial powers under section 57(4) of the *Education Act*:

> 57(4) The Special Education Tribunal shall hear the appeal and may,
> (a) dismiss the appeal; or
> (b) grant the appeal and make such order as it considers necessary with respect to the identification or placement.

In other words, the Tribunal may dismiss the appeal and confirm the identification and/or placement decision of the school board.

Where a parent is seeking to change a placement to a different placement, it is not likely that the appeal will succeed when the child is succeeding in the current placement. In one such case, the Tribunal stated, "On the first issue, the child's present success in school confirms to this Tribunal that the child's current placement is in the child's best interests."[89]

Alternatively, the Tribunal may grant the appeal and set aside the identification or placement decision or both. Where the Tribunal grants the appeal, it may substitute its own identification and/or placement decision for that reached by the IPRC or the school board (following an appeal to the SEAB). It may also make any further or other order it considers necessary with respect to the identification and/or placement.

There have been cases in which the Tribunal has ordered a placement different from what was proposed by either the parents or the school board.[90] For example, in one case,[91] the parents sought to have the student identified as "multi-handicapped" and placed in a regular Kindergarten or grade 1 class in her neighbourhood school, with the assistance of a teacher's aide and other support staff as required. The school board argued that the IPRC's decision, identifying the student as "trainable retarded"— a category of exceptionality that is now called "developmentally disabled" — and directing that she be

---

89 *D.M. & Simcoe County Board of Education* (1993-04-02), File No. 17 (Ont. Spec. Ed. (Eng.) Trib.).

90 *Y. v. X. X. District School Board* (2002-02-18), File No. 31 (Ont. Spec. Ed. (Eng.) Trib.). In this case, the parent sought a gifted class placement for her son who was moving into secondary school under a school board that did not offer self-contained gifted classes at the secondary level. The IPRC had determined that the student should be placed in a regular class placement with enrichment opportunities. The parent sought to have the student transported to a neighbouring school board that offered a self-contained gifted class in the secondary level. During the hearing, the Tribunal heard evidence that, at one of the school board's secondary schools, gifted students were congregated in their grade 9 classes and were delivered programming that was specifically enriched for them. The Tribunal felt that this third option would meet the student's needs and so ordered a placement in what it described as a "gifted congregated (clustered) program".

91 *L. & York Region Board of Education* (1985-09-10), File No. 7 (Ont. Spec. Ed. (Eng.) Trib.).

placed in a special school for the trainable retarded, should be confirmed. The Tribunal accepted the parents' position that the student should be identified as "multi-handicapped", but rejected both the parents' proposed placement and the school board's proposed placement. Instead, the Tribunal directed that the student should be placed in another school that already offered a class for multi-handicapped students and had specialized services and staff available on a regular basis to assist such students.

Similarly, in another case,[92] the parents submitted that the student should be provided with "teacher's aide fluent in cued speech in the regular classrooms, a resource withdrawal teacher fluent in cued speech, and a speech pathologist, 'until it is demonstrated that [his] needs have significantly changed'". The school board submitted that "the provision of a non-cueing resource withdrawal teacher, assisted by a teacher's aide who is fluent in cueing" was an appropriate placement.

However, the Tribunal observed that: "Evidence called by both parties through several witnesses caused the Tribunal to examine the student's overall needs beyond the positions of the parties taken in their written submissions".[93] In the end result, the Tribunal ordered the following:[94]

> 1. the student continue in a regular class for about 50 per cent of each school day with the assistance of a cueing teacher's aide/interpreter; and
> 2. the Board provide a teacher of the deaf for the student for approximately 50 per cent of each school day.
>
> . . . . .
>
> 3. the Board ensure that an effective mechanism be established to co-ordinate the various aspects of the student's program; and
> 4. that the Board establish an effective mechanism for the continuous assessment of the student and the evaluation of the student's program.

The Tribunal's decision may also include recommendations concerning special education programs and special education services. These recommendations are not binding on the school board, but must be considered by the principal in developing and/or reviewing the pupil's IEP.[95]

In yet another case,[96] the parents requested the Tribunal to make a number of specific orders with respect to the program to be provided to their child, who was autistic. The parents' request included:

---

[92] *O. & Wentworth County Board of Education* (1987-06-05), File No. 12 (Ont. Spec. Ed. (Eng.) Trib.).

[93] *Supra*, at p. 20.

[94] *Supra*, at p. 21. The Tribunal also specified, at p. 20 of its decision, that the special education class contemplated by item 2 must provide for "(i) language, speech and social skills development, auditory training and the development of independent work habits; (ii) resource support for the student's regular class placement; (iii) ongoing support from a speech pathologist".

[95] O. Reg. 181/98, ss. 6(6)(*b*) and 7(3)(*b*).

[96] *D.B. & Sudbury Catholic District School Board* (1999-09-21), File No. 26 (Ont. Spec. Ed. (Eng.) Trib.).

- clinical in-service training for the teachers and the educational assistant in the method of behaviour modification and education in the disorder of autism;
- an educational assistant with training in modification and specific knowledge of PDD/autism assigned to the student for 100% of the school day; and
- a speech pathologist with knowledge and experience in PDD/autism overseeing her program and the involvement of an occupational therapist, also with knowledge and experience in PDD/autism.[97]

The school board responded that these were programming matters that were not properly the subject of an appeal; however, in its decision, the Tribunal recommended a number of specific programming outcomes:[98]

> - the [student] must receive daily instruction in language skills from a trained educational assistant
> - in the development of the I.E.P. benchmarks and appropriate activities and resources must be specified
> - in planning and implementing this special education program, and services including the necessary in-service for staff, in particular the educational assistant, the Board should avail itself of the services and expertise of [a specified doctor] and his staff at [a specified institution]
> - the selection of the teacher and the educational assistant who work with the [student] must be done with great care
> - the selection of materials and the training of staff must become a high priority of the Catholic Board to ensure that the [student] has a successful school experience.
> - the placement for the [student] be in a life skills program with appropriate integration.

More recently, since articulating clearer statements that special education programs and services can form part of placement, the Tribunal has made orders regarding the provision of programs and services. In one case, where the parent was seeking a full time regular class placement with a full time Educational Assistant at all times, the Tribunal ordered a placement that provided for part-time withdrawal to a special education class, with regular class for the balance of the school day. With respect to the special education program and services to be provided in the regular class, the Tribunal ordered as follows:[99]

> The program in the regular grade 8 class for the child will be delivered by the classroom teacher, and assisted by a special needs assistant as necessary for a minimum of 50 percent of the time that child is in the regular classroom. The instructional level will be identified by the classroom teacher in the IEP for the school year until further assessment is completed.

---

97 *Supra*, at p. 2.

98 *Supra*, at p. 20.

99 *I. & Toronto District School Board* (2005-11-17), File No. 46c (Ont. Spec. Ed. (Eng. Trib.), at p. 22.

In one of the cases already referenced, the Tribunal found that it had jurisdiction to consider the parents' request for "a resource withdrawal teacher fluent in cued speech", even though the requirement of fluency in cued speech related to the special education programs and services available in the placement, rather than to the placement *per se*.[100] In another case,[101] the Tribunal ordered the school board to purchase a special education program for the student, who was gifted, from the co-terminus school board.

As the above examples illustrate, the Tribunal exercises broad remedial jurisdiction in dealing with identification and/or placement appeals. This broad discretion provides the Tribunal with the flexibility it requires in order to address the circumstances of individual cases.

LEGAL COSTS

Order-in-Council 1382/97, which established the Special Education Tribunal, also authorized the Tribunal to order a party to pay certain costs associated with appeal proceedings. The Order-in-Council stated as follows:[102]

> Pursuant to s. 36(2)(*b*) of the *Education Act*, the Tribunals are hereby authorized to fix the maximum costs assessable against a party in respect of,
>
> (a) the fees of expert witnesses subpoenaed to attend the hearing;
> (b) the fees of witnesses subpoenaed to attend the hearing;
> (c) counsel fees of counsel for the parties; and
> (d) the travelling and living expenses of the parties, counsel for the parties and of any witnesses, that are incurred for the purpose of attending a hearing.
>
> The said Tribunals are also authorized to assess such other costs of the hearing as they find appropriate, other than the remuneration and expenses of the members of the Tribunal, against one or other of both the parties, regardless of success at the hearing, and for such purpose the Tribunal may, but need not, require the parties to speak to the matter of costs prior to or at the conclusion of the hearing.

The provisions of the Order-in-Council dealing with costs were based on the authority to fix costs set out in section 36(2)(*b*) of the *Education Act*. This provision has been repealed[103] and replaced by section 57(2)(*c*), which requires that costs issues be dealt with by regulation. No such regulation has been created.

---

[100] *O. & Wentworth County Board of Education*, *supra*, footnote 92, at pp. 2-5.

[101] *G.R. & Carleton Roman Catholic Separate School Board* (1988-12-16), File No. 14 (Ont. Spec. Ed. (Eng.) Trib.).

[102] O.C. 1382/97, dated June 25, 1997.

[103] Notably, the fact that the costs provisions of the Order in Council may no longer be valid does not affect the validity of the Order in Council as a whole.

EFFECT OF THE SPECIAL EDUCATION TRIBUNAL'S DECISION

Section 57(5) of the *Education Act* provides that the decision of a Special Education Tribunal is "final and binding on the parties to the decision". This provision has a number of important implications.

Section 57(5) states that the Tribunal's decision must be considered final. This means that, once it has released its decision, the Tribunal cannot reopen it. It cannot amend or revise its decision, except to correct a "typographical error, error of calculation or similar error".[104] Similarly, once the Tribunal has rendered its decision on a particular set of facts, the issues underlying the decision generally cannot be re-litigated by the same parties before another Tribunal or in any other forum. Note, however, that this does not preclude parents from appealing a subsequent IPRC decision. Even though the issue may be the same, the underlying facts will have changed.

There is no direct appeal to the courts from the Special Education Tribunal's decisions; however, there is one set of circumstances in which the Special Education Tribunal's decision can be reviewed by the courts. Where a party is dissatisfied with the Tribunal's decision, that party can apply to the Divisional Court of the Ontario Superior Court of Justice for judicial review of the Tribunal's decision; however, in the event of judicial review proceedings, the statutory admonition in section 57(5) that the Tribunal's decision is "final and binding on the parties to the decision" will be viewed as a signal that the Legislature intended the courts to defer to the Tribunal's decision. As a result, judicial review will be available only on certain narrowly circumscribed grounds.[105]

Section 57(5) also states that a decision of the Tribunal is binding on the parties. In other words, the decision has the force of law and must be implemented by the parties.[106] By virtue of section 19(1) of the *SPPA*, the Tribunal's decision can be filed in a court of law, with the result that it is enforceable as though it were an order of the court.[107] Accordingly, the Tribunal's decision must be implemented by the parties in accordance with its terms.

---

[104] *SPPA*, s. 21.1. See also *Chandler v. Alberta Assn. of Architects* (1989), 62 D.L.R. (4th) 577, [1989] 2 S.C.R. 848, the leading Canadian authority on the doctrine of *functus officio*.

[105] Judicial review proceedings are discussed in greater detail in Chapter 13, "Review by the Courts".

[106] It may be open to the parties to agree to not implement the Tribunal's decision, but rather to implement some other agreed upon course of action; however, such an agreement should be consistent with the educational best interests of the student.

[107] *SPPA*, s. 19(1).

12

The Human Rights Process

INTRODUCTION

As we noted in Chapter 2, "The Legal Framework", special education law is part of and subject to human rights law. The special education regime provided for under the *Education Act*[1] and the regulations[2] can be viewed as a form of legislated "special program" designed to accommodate students with disabilities and assist them to achieve an equal opportunity to benefit from education. The fact that a special statutory scheme has been created to provide for the accommodation of students with disabilities in the education system does not mean, however, that the implementation of that statutory scheme is insulated from review under the *Human Rights Code*[3] (the "Code"). In fact, virtually every aspect of special education decision-making may be reviewed under the Code to ensure that any decisions or actions taken are consistent with the requirements of human rights law.

Over the past few years, it has become increasingly common for students and their parents or guardians to utilize the human rights process to raise issues about the manner in which the Ontario Government, school boards, or particular schools or school personnel are carrying out their special education responsibilities. The practice of challenging special education decision-making under the Code is now sufficiently well-entrenched that it must be considered an established feature of the legal landscape for dealing with special education in this province. Not only are human rights challenges "here to stay", but it can be expected that they have increased in number as a result of changes to the Code that took effect in 2008, which have created a more streamlined and expeditious process for bringing human rights disputes before the Human Rights Tribunal of Ontario ("the HRTO") and have conferred new powers on the HRTO to deal with the cases before it.

1 R.S.O. 1990, c. E.2.
2 For example, *Identification and Placement of Exceptional Pupils*, O. Reg. 181/98.
3 R.S.O. 1990, c. H.19.

As a result of the increased use of the human rights process to challenge special education decision-making, special education administrators need to have at least a basic understanding of the human rights process. This chapter focuses on the practical considerations involved in human rights proceedings and on the procedures followed by the HRTO in dealing with human rights disputes.

COMPARING THE SPECIAL EDUCATION AND HUMAN RIGHTS REGIMES

The *Education Act* and the Code create overlapping or complementary statutory schemes with respect to accommodating the special needs of students with disabilities; indeed, the HRTO has expressly recognized that the *Education Act* and the Code serve a common purpose or goal with respect to accommodating students with disabilities:[4]

> I find that the statutory scheme for special education has as its central purpose the accommodation of children with special needs, including those with disabilities, so that they are able to receive the benefits of education available to others (see *Eaton*, para. 68). With respect to the provision of education services to children with disabilities, therefore, it has the same goal as the Code. In the words of the Board, "special education is all about finding the appropriate accommodation for students with disabilities".

Initially, human rights proceedings were most common with respect to special education issues that did not clearly fall within the four corners of the special education regime under the *Education Act*. At one time, the Ontario Human Rights Commission was often willing to decline to deal with special education issues, particularly identification and placement issues, finding that such issues ought to be dealt with by special education tribunals pursuant to the *Education Act*.[5] Because of the commission's position in this regard, those human rights cases that did go forward tended to involve novel issues or perceived gaps in the special education regime.

Over time, however, the commission began to take a greater interest in the policy issues arising from the accommodation of students with disabilities in the education system[6] and began to demonstrate a greater willingness to

---

4 *Campbell v. Toronto District School Board*, 2008 HRTO 62, at para. 42.

5 Prior to the June 2008 amendments to the Code, s. 34(1)(*a*) conferred a discretion on the commission to decline to deal with a complaint "that could or should be more appropriately dealt with under an Act other than this Act". This provision has now been repealed.

6 For example, in September 2004, the commission-approved guidelines — see Ontario Human Rights Commission, *Guidelines on Accessible Education* (Toronto: The Commission, 2004), available online at http://www.ohrc.on.ca/en/resources/Guides/AccessibleEducation. The commission has also developed a number of other publications dealing with accommodation of disability in the education system, also available online at http://www.ohrc.on.ca/en/issues/disability.

proceed with special education-related complaints. The commission also developed a strong interest in the "safe schools" provisions of the *Education Act*,[7] their impact on students with disabilities and their relationship to special education.[8] School boards began to experience an increase in the frequency of special education-related human rights proceedings, as well as an expansion in the range of issues being raised in such proceedings. This trend continued to the point that human rights proceedings were quite commonplace in the special education area, even before the human rights process was changed to provide for easier access to the HRTO.

Although the *Education Act* and the Code are overlapping and complementary statutory schemes, they are not identical statutory schemes. The statutory schemes have different strengths and weaknesses, both generally and in relation to specific kinds of issues or disputes, and lead to different outcomes or remedies. Generally speaking, parties are discouraged from using both statutory schemes, either at the same time or one after the other.[9] It will, therefore, be necessary to consider which process is best-suited to deal with a particular issue or dispute before proceedings are commenced.

In previous chapters, we have described the statutory scheme available under the *Education Act* for dealing with special education issues. The purpose of this chapter is to describe the processes that will be followed where such issues are raised in the context of a human rights proceeding.

RECENT CHANGES TO THE HUMAN RIGHTS PROCESS

In the previous section, we referred to the Ontario Human Rights Commission. Until June 30, 2008, the commission was responsible for intake, processing, investigation, mediation and litigation of human rights complaints; however, a number of significant changes were made to the dispute resolution procedures under the Code, effective July 1, 2008.[10] Human rights proceedings, formerly called "complaints", are now called "applications". While the commission still plays a role in human rights proceedings, it no

---

7 *Education Act*, ss. 300 to 316.

8 See Ontario Human Rights Commission, *The Opportunity to Succeed: Achieving Barrier-Free Education for Students with Disabilities* (Toronto: The Commission, 2003), available online at http://www.ohrc.on.ca/en/resources/discussion_consultation/ConsultEduDisablty2/pdf.

9 See *Campbell v. Toronto District School Board*, *supra*, footnote 4, where the HRTO held that it would be an abuse of process to allow the re-litigation of issues already litigated in front of the Special Education Tribunal, finding, at para. 58, that doing so would "violate principles of judicial economy, consistency, finality and the integrity of the administration of justice" and "improperly place the [HRTO] in the position of an appellate court with respect to the decision of an expert tribunal, acting within its jurisdiction as part of a comprehensive scheme for the accommodation of special education students".

10 The amendments to the Code were made pursuant to the *Human Rights Code Amendment Act, 2006*, S.O. 2006, c. 30.

longer plays the role of "gatekeeper" of the human rights system. Individuals who feel their human rights have been infringed now have "direct access" to the HRTO. This means that they can file their own applications directly with the HRTO and are no longer dependent on a government body like the commission with respect to the processing of the case. It also means they are directly responsible for complying with all of the requirements of the HRTO's Rules of Procedure with respect to the processing and litigation of human rights applications. This can, at times, be a complex and time-consuming task.

The change to a "direct access" model of human rights dispute resolution has resulted in more applications being litigated before the HRTO more quickly than was the case when the commission was responsible for administering the human rights system. As a result, school boards may find themselves facing a significantly increased volume of special education-related human rights litigation in the future. That having been said, as of the date of this writing, both the "direct access" model and the HRTO's Rules of Procedure are still relatively new and untested. The true extent of the practical impact they will have is not yet fully known.

Later in this chapter, we describe the procedures applicable to new applications filed with the HRTO from July 1, 2008 onwards.[11] The discussion focuses primarily on the requirements of the Code and the HRTO's Rules of Procedure. Case law, however, is developing under the new statutory scheme, and should also be reviewed whenever dealing with proceedings under the Code.

THE HUMAN RIGHTS TRIBUNAL OF ONTARIO

Composition of the HRTO

Section 32 of the Code provides for the continuation of the Human Rights Tribunal of Ontario.[12] Whereas two Special Education Tribunals have been established under the *Education Act* — a Special Education Tribunal (English) and a Special Education Tribunal (French) — the HRTO provides services in both English and French.[13]

The Code empowers the Lieutenant Governor to appoint the members of the Tribunal.[14] The legislation specifically requires that members are to be

11 Separate procedures applied to complaints originally filed with the Ontario Human Rights Commission prior to June 30, 2008, which were transferred to the HRTO during specified transitional windows: see the Code, s. 53(3) and (5). Given that these transitional windows have now closed, however, we have not discussed the applicable procedures here.

12 The HRTO's name in French is the "Tribunal des droits de la personne de l'Ontario": Code, s. 32(1).

13 HRTO Rules of Procedure, available online at http://www.hrto.ca/hrto/sites/default/files/New%20Applications1/RulesOfProcedure.pdf. See rules 1.11 and 3.8.

14 Code, s. 32(2).

appointed using a competitive process and that the criteria to be applied are to include:[15]

1. Experience, knowledge or training with respect to human rights law and issues.
2. Aptitude for impartial adjudication.
3. Aptitude for applying the alternative adjudicative practices and procedures that may be set out in the Tribunal rules.

The Code requires the Lieutenant Governor to appoint a Chair (who is so designated in the Order-in-Council appointing him or her) as well as one or more Vice-Chairs and to appoint one of the Vice-Chairs as the Alternate Chair.[16] Over 20 Vice-Chairs and a similar number of additional Members have been appointed to the HRTO.[17]

The Code authorizes the Chair to appoint panels of one or more members to exercise and perform the powers and duties of the HRTO.[18] Most often, the HRTO sits in "panels" comprised of a single member.

Communicating with the HRTO

Parties to proceedings before the HRTO are required to communicate with the HRTO through the Registrar.[19] The Registrar's office is located at the HRTO's offices in Toronto. The Registrar's contact information changes from time to time; current contact information can be obtained from the HRTO's website.[20]

HRTO's Location and Hearing Locations

The HRTO's main office is in Toronto. The Registrar determines the location of all in-person hearings in accordance with the HRTO's policies.[21] The HRTO has issued a "Practice Direction on Hearings in Regional Centres", which states that the HRTO will hold hearings in Toronto, Kingston, London, North Bay, Ottawa, Sarnia, Sault Ste. Marie, Sudbury, Timmins, Thunder Bay and Windsor and may hold hearings in other locations in order to accommodate Code-related or other needs of the parties or their witnesses.[22]

---

15 *Ibid.*, s. 32(3).
16 *Ibid.*, s. 32(6) and (7).
17 A full current listing of the members of the HRTO can be found online at http://www.hrto.ca.
18 Code, s. 33.
19 HRTO Rules of Procedure, rule 1.12.
20 As of the date of this writing, the Registrar for new applications is Richard Hennessy. Mr. Hennessy's contact information is available online at http://www.hrto.ca/hrto/?q=en/node/19.
21 HRTO Rules of Procedure, rule 3.6.
22 Human Rights Tribunal of Ontario, "Practice Direction on Hearings in Regional Centres" (Toronto: The Tribunal, 2008), available online at http://www.hrto.ca/

Language of Proceedings, Interpretation Services and Accommodation of Participants

The HRTO conducts its proceedings in English, French or bilingually. A party wishing that some or all of a proceeding be conducted in French is required to notify the Registrar as soon as possible.[23]

On request, the HRTO will also provide sign language interpretation services and other language interpretation services.[24] The HRTO has issued a practice direction that states that it will provide language interpretation or sign language interpretation services where such services are required to participate fully in the process. Again, requests for such services are to be made to the Registrar as soon as possible.[25]

The HRTO's Rules of Procedure also recognize that parties, representatives and witnesses may be entitled to accommodation of Code-related needs.[26] The HRTO has issued a "Policy on Accessibility and Accommodation", which provides for accommodation of special needs in accessing HRTO services and in participating in proceedings before the HRTO.[27] Requests for accommodation can be made at any time, but ideally, should be raised as soon as possible so that they can be addressed in a timely manner.[28]

---

hrto/?q=en/node/60. A request for a change in location of a hearing should be in writing and made to the Registrar as soon as possible.

23 HRTO Rules of Procedure, rule 3.8.

24 *Ibid.*, rule 3.9.

25 *Ibid.*, rules 3.8 and 3.9. The HRTO's "Practice Direction on Requests for Language Interpretation" provides:

> Where a party requires language interpretation or sign language interpretation services in order to participate fully in a hearing or mediation, and makes a request that the Tribunal provide such services, the Tribunal will provide for interpretation services to be available to the requesting party at the hearing and/or in the mediation conference.
>
> Requests for language interpretation or sign language interpretation services must be made to the Registrar as soon as possible.

See Human Rights Tribunal of Ontario, "Practice Direction on Requests for Language Interpretation" (Toronto: The Tribunal, 2008), available online at http://www.hrto.ca/hrto/?q=en/node/54.

26 HRTO Rules of Procedure, rule 2.1. For example, accommodation may be required for disability-related needs.

27 See Human Rights Tribunal of Ontario, "Policy on Accessibility and Accommodation" (Toronto: The Tribunal, 2008), available online at http://www.hrto.ca/hrto/sites/default/files/Resources/AccessibilityAndAccommodation.pdf.

28 The Application (Form 1) and Response (Form 2), which are to be filed with the HRTO by the parties under the HRTO Rules of Procedure, include a question regarding accommodation needs, which is designed to ensure that accommodation requests are addressed at an early stage of the process; however, the Policy on Accessibility and Accommodation states that accommodation issues can be raised at any point in the proceedings, including during a hearing before the HRTO, in which case they will be directed to the Registrar.

REPRESENTATIVES

The Human Rights Legal Support Centre

One of the stated objectives underlying the introduction of "direct access" to the HRTO was to create a dispute resolution process that was straightforward and user-friendly and that any citizen of Ontario could navigate without the need for legal representation. As will be seen in the discussion later in this chapter, the reality of the "direct access" model is not so straightforward. While the complexity of the process varies from case to case, there are numerous forms to fill out and procedural rules to follow before the parties even get to the hearing stage. The hearings themselves are reasonably formal legal proceedings. Witnesses (including expert witnesses) are called and cross-examined. Complex legal issues must often be addressed. Where a finding of discrimination is made, significant remedies can be awarded. Accordingly, while it is not necessary for them to do so, parties to human rights proceedings often find that it is in their best interests to be represented by legal counsel or a representative.

In an effort to address this reality and to respond to critics who argued that the reforms undermined access to justice for human rights claimants, the Ontario Government established the Human Rights Legal Support Centre ("HRLSC").[29] The HRLSC is a publicly funded organization that is independent of — but accountable to — the Ontario Government.[30] Its role is to provide support services to individuals who wish to file a human rights application.[31] These support services include legal and non-legal advice, as well as assistance and legal services in relation to human rights applications and related proceedings.[32]

In keeping with the fact that the services provided by the HRLSC are publicly funded, the Code requires the Board of Directors of the HRLSC: to act in a "financially responsible and accountable manner"; to act in good faith with a view to the objects of the HRLSC, which include "establish[ing] and administer[ing] a cost-effective and efficient system for providing support services, including legal services, respecting applications to the [HRTO]" and "establish[ing] policies and priorities for the provision of support services based on its financial resources"; and to "exercise the care, diligence and skill of a reasonably prudent person" in doing so.[33]

---

29 Code, s. 45.11.

30 Code, s. 45.11(5).

31 See Ontario Human Rights Legal Support Centre, "Getting Legal Help From the Centre" (Toronto), available online at http://www.hrlsc.on.ca/en/legalhelp.htm.

32 Code, s. 45.13(1). It will be noted that the HRLSC's services are available *only* to individuals who believe their human rights have been violated and are considering filing an application with the Tribunal. Its services are *not* available to individuals or organizations who are named as respondents to human rights applications.

33 Code, s. 45.12 as well as s. 45.14(8) and (9).

Given the emphasis in the legislation on financial responsibility and accountability, it was widely anticipated that the HRLSC's services would be made available primarily or exclusively to individuals who lacked the resources to retain their own counsel.[34] So far, the HRLSC has not been engaging in any means testing to screen potential applicants on the basis of need; however, they do engage in a critical assessment of the merits of the application and will not necessarily provide representation in every case about which they are consulted.

Identifying a Representative to the HRTO

The HRTO's Rules of Procedure provide that parties to proceedings before the HRTO may be self-represented or they may be "represented by a person licensed by the Law Society of Upper Canada or by a person authorized to provide legal services in accordance with the *Law Society Act* and its regulations and by-laws".[35] In practice, this means that a party's representative must be a lawyer or licensed paralegal professional.

An applicant, respondent or other participant in a human rights proceedings who chooses to obtain legal representation is required to identify the representative and provide the representative's contact information in the initial filings with the HRTO (discussed later in this chapter). The representative's Law Society of Upper Canada registration number must be provided so that the HRTO can verify that the representative is appropriately licensed.

Where a representative's contact information changes, the representative is required to so advise the HRTO as well as all parties and their representatives as soon as possible.[36] In addition, where a representative who is "on record" for a party ceases to represent that party, the representative is required to notify the HRTO and all parties of this fact immediately.[37]

DELIVERY AND FILING OF DOCUMENTS

In the course of proceedings before the HRTO, the parties to those proceedings will be called upon to deliver documents to the other parties and file those documents with the HRTO. The requirements for delivery and filing

---

[34] This would have been a significant change in access to the human rights dispute resolution system, since individuals were able previously to file complaints with the commission and, where the commission referred the complaint the HRTO, Commission counsel would assume carriage of the case before the HRTO. While the commission's interests and the complainant's interests were not always aligned, nevertheless, the case would be carried by Commission counsel at no cost to the complainant.

[35] HRTO Rules of Procedure, rule 1.14.

[36] *Ibid.*, rule 1.13.

[37] *Ibid.*, rule 1.15.

of documents are reviewed in here and the specific documents that may be required are reviewed later in this chapter.

Delivery to the Parties or Other Affected Persons

With the exception of the Form 1, "Application" and Form 2, "Response", all documents are to be delivered to the other parties, their representatives and any other persons identified who may be affected by the proceedings before they are filed with the HRTO.[38] The Application and Response are filed directly with the HRTO, reviewed by the HRTO and then delivered by the HRTO to the other party or parties and any affected persons.[39]

A document that must be delivered to the other parties, their representatives and other affected persons may be delivered in any one of the following ways:

- Hand delivery, in which case receipt is deemed to have occurred when the document is given to the party or left with a person at the party's last known address.
- Regular, registered or certified mail, in which case receipt is deemed to have occurred on the 5th day after the postmark date.
- Courier, in which case receipt is deemed to have occurred on the second day after the document was given to the courier.
- Facsimile transmission — although consent is required to deliver by facsimile a document which is longer than 20 pages — in which case receipt is deemed to have occurred when the sender receives a facsimile confirmation sheet. If a facsimile confirmation sheet were to indicate a time after 5:00 p.m., then the document would be deemed to have been received the following day.
- E-mail, where the party or person receiving the document has consented to e-mail delivery, in which case receipt is deemed to have occurred on the day sent or, if the e-mail were sent after 5:00 p.m., on the following day.
- Any other way agreed on by the parties or directed by the HRTO.[40]

A party who is delivering a document pursuant to the Rules of Procedure — other than a Form 1, "Application", or Form 2, "Response" — is required

---

38 *Ibid.*, rule 1.20.

39 *Ibid.*, rules 6.2, 6.4, 8.1 and 8.4.

40 *Ibid.*, rules 1.22 and 1.23. As of the time of this writing, the Tribunal had released proposed changes to the Rules for consultation that would limit the maximum size of attachments to a single e-mail to 10mb: Human Rights Tribunal of Ontario, "Notice: Consultation of Proposed Amendments to the Rules of Procedure Governing Applications Under the Human Rights Code, Part IV" (Toronto: The Tribunal, March 31, 2010), available online at http://www.hrto.ca/hrto/sites/default/files/Whats%20New/s34RuleChanges.pdf.

to prepare a Form 23, "Statement of Delivery", for each party or person to whom the document is delivered. Form 23 is a brief form confirming delivery of the document and stating how the document was delivered. Form 23 must be filed with the HRTO when the document is filed with the HRTO or, where the document is not being filed with the HRTO, no later than two days after the deemed date of delivery.[41]

Where a party fails to deliver a document or materials to another party or person as required by the Rules, that party can face adverse consequences. The HRTO may refuse to consider the document or materials altogether or it may take any other action it considers appropriate in the circumstances.[42]

Filing Documents with the HRTO

When filing a document with the HRTO, it is customary to include a cover letter. The cover letter should be addressed to the Registrar and should make clear what is being filed and by whom. It should also include the following information, which is required under rule 1.16 of the HRTO's Rules of Procedure:

> a) name of the Applicant and Respondent in the Application;
> b) name of the person filing the document and, if applicable, his/her representative's name;
> c) mailing address, telephone number and, if available, e-mail address and facsimile number of the person filing the document or his/her representative; and
> d) Application file number, if available.

A document can be filed with the HRTO, along with a Form 23, "Statement of Delivery", if required, in any of the following ways:

- Facsimile transmission to the HRTO's fax number, in which case filing is deemed to take place when the sender receives a fax confirmation sheet. If the fax confirmation sheet indicates a time after 5:00 p.m., then filing is deemed to have occurred the following day.
- Hand delivery, courier, or regular, registered or certified mail to the HRTO at its mailing address, in which case filing is deemed to have occurred on the date of receipt stamped on the document by the HRTO.
- E-mail, in which case filing is deemed to have occurred when the sender receives an e-mail confirmation from the HRTO. If the e-mail confirmation indicates a time after 5:00 p.m., then filing is deemed to have occurred the following day.
- As directed by the HRTO.[43]

---

41 HRTO Rules of Procedure, rules 1.20 and 1.23.

42 *Ibid.*, rule 5.6.

43 *Ibid.*, rule 1.19. At the time of this writing, the HRTO has released proposed changes to the Rules for consultation, which would require the filing of either an

Filing Deadlines and Other Time Limits

The HRTO's Rules of Procedure often require documents to be filed or other actions to be taken within a specified number of days. The reference to days generally refers to calendar days rather than business days or working days. The number of days is calculated by excluding the first day and including the last day. Where the time limit for filing a document or taking some other action expires on a holiday, the time limit is extended to the next day that is not a holiday.[44]

Missing a time limit may not be fatal, as the HRTO has a broad discretion to extend a time limit and to provide relief with respect to a failure to comply with the Rules (such as allowing late filing of a document);[45] however, it is always preferable to be proactive and request an extension of a deadline in advance rather than wait until the deadline has passed to ask to be relieved from the consequences.[46] As long as the request and an explanation of the reasons for the request are provided in writing, the HRTO is often willing to provide a brief extension of a filing deadline.

APPLICATIONS, RESPONSES AND REPLIES

Applications By and On Behalf of Individuals

Who Can File an Application?

Section 34(1) of the Code provides that any person who believes that any of his or her rights under the Code have been infringed can make an application to the HRTO. An application can be made by a person on his or her own behalf, or it can be made jointly by two or more persons who are entitled to make their own applications, or it can be made by a person or organization on behalf of another person who is entitled to make his or her own application with that person's consent.[47]

---

electronic version or two copies of any bound document or any document greater than 20 pages in length: Human Rights Tribunal of Ontario, *op. cit.*, footnote 40.

44 HRTO Rules of Procedure, rules 1.8 to 1.10. "Holiday" is defined in rule 1.4 to mean "any Saturday, Sunday, or other day on which the [HRTO's] offices are closed". This latter reference will include most government holidays.

45 *Ibid.*, rules 1.7a), 5.1 and 5.2.

46 While the HRTO does have broad powers to provide relief, it is under no obligation to do so. It may decline relief or impose terms on the party or person seeking relief. Rule 5 of the HRTO Rules of Procedure also sets out a number of adverse consequences that can follow in cases where a there is a failure to comply with the Rules, such as a failure to comply with specified time limits.

47 See s. 34(1), (4) and (5) of the Code; however, in the case of two or more persons who file applications jointly, the HRTO may direct that one or more of the applications be considered in a separate proceeding: Code, s. 34(4); HRTO Rules of Procedure, rule 1.7e).

Where a potential applicant lacks the legal capacity to file his or her own application, another person may be entitled at law to "stand in the shoes" of that person and exercise his or her right to file an application.[48] For example, a parent or guardian may file a human rights application on behalf of a student who is a minor.[49] Similarly, a litigation guardian or substitute decision-maker (who may be, but need not be, a parent) may file an application on behalf of a student who is no longer a minor but who does not have the mental capacity to do so on his or her own behalf. In such cases, the application is filed under section 34(1) of the Code as if it had been filed by the student in question him- or herself.

In addition, there may situations where a person or organization wishes to file an application on behalf of another person. For example, an advocacy group may file an application on behalf of a particular student with special needs. In this situation, the application is to be filed under section 34(5) of the Code and the person filing the application must obtain the consent of the person who is the subject of the application. In the case of a student who is a minor or who otherwise lacks capacity to provide consent, the student's parent, guardian or other representative would provide consent on the student's behalf.

The HRTO has issued two application forms applicable to applications filed under section 34(1) or (4) (applications by a person or by someone entitled at law to stand in that person's shoes or by two or more persons) and applications filed under section 34(5) (applications on behalf of another person), respectively. Only Form 1, "Application", is used in the former case; both the Application and Form 4, "Application Filed on Behalf of Another Person" are used in the latter case.[50] The information required in order to complete these forms is discussed in more detail later in this chapter.

---

48 The HRTO has issued a practice direction for dealing with this situation: see Human Rights Tribunal of Ontario, "Practice Direction on Applications to the Human Rights Tribunal of Ontario on Behalf of Another Person Under Section 34(1) OR 34(5) of the Human Rights Code" (Toronto: The Tribunal, 2008), available online at http://www.hrto.ca/hrto/?q=en/node/62.

49 The HRTO's practice direction, *ibid.*, defines a minor as "someone who is less than eighteen (18) years of age". As noted elsewhere, the Supreme Court of Canada has recognized in the special education context that children have rights and interests which are separate and distinct from those of their parents: *Eaton v. Brant County Board of Education* (1997), 142 D.L.R. (4th) 385, at pp. 409-10, [1997] 1 S.C.R. 241. It is possible that, in an appropriate case, a student — particularly a student over the age of 16 who has withdrawn from parental control or is living independently — could successfully persuade the HRTO to allow him or her to proceed with an application in the absence of his or her parents. Since young people in Ontario have the right to leave home and be free from discrimination in housing at the age of 16, their legal rights would be undermined if they were denied the right to file an application independently.

50 HRTO Rules of Procedure, rule 6.1.

The Timing of an Application

The Code imposes a flexible one-year time limit on applications filed by or on behalf of individuals. Section 34(1) states that an application is to be filed within one year after the incident to which the application relates or, where there was a series of incidents, within one year after the last incident in the series.[51] This time limit must be considered a flexible one in light of section 34(2), which authorizes the HRTO to allow a person to apply after the expiry of the one-year time limit where the HRTO "is satisfied that the delay was incurred in good faith and no substantial prejudice will result to any person affected by the delay".

The Application

A person filing an application on his or her own behalf must file a Form 1, "Application", while a person filing an application on another person's behalf must file a Form 4, "Application Filed on Behalf of Another Person" (which, in turn, requires the filing of a Form 1 as well as Form 4).[52] In this section, the two forms are referred to separately by form number; however, elsewhere in this chapter, where we have used the term "Application", the reference is generally a reference to the Form 1, which is filed in both types of proceeding.

Form 1 and the Form 4 each contain a number of detailed questions. The applicant must complete each of these questions before filing the form(s) with the Tribunal.[53]

Form 1 requires full contact information for the person(s) filing the application and his or her representative, if any, including full name, mailing address, telephone number(s) and, if applicable, facsimile number and/or e-mail address. When there is a change in the contact information of the applicant or the applicant's representative, the HRTO and all the other parties and their representatives are to be notified as soon as possible.[54]

---

[51] Section 34(1) of the Code states that a person may apply to the HRTO within these time frames. The same requirement is extended to applications by two or more persons, or by a person or organization on behalf of another person, by virtue of the wording of s. 34(4) and (5). Section 34(4) requires that the persons filing a joint application must each be entitled to make an application under s. 34(1), and s. 34(5) requires that a person or organization may only make an application on behalf of a person who is entitled to make an application under s. 34(1). Since one of the preconditions for making an application under s. 34(1) is that the application must be filed within the one-year time limit, the time limit applies to applications under s. 34(4) and (5) as well. For greater certainty, s. 34(8) states that an application under s. 34(5) shall be made within the time-period required under s. 34(1), and s. 34(9) states that s. 34(2) shall apply to an application on behalf of another person under s. 34(5).

[52] HRTO Rules of Procedure, rule 6.1.

[53] *Ibid.*

[54] *Ibid.*, rule 1.13. It is important that contact information be accurate and be kept up-to-date, as the HRTO has the authority to proceed and finally determine an

Form 4 contains a number of additional questions regarding contact information for the person filing the application and the person who is the subject of the application. Form 4 is divided into three separate sections, and the applicant is to fill out the section applicable to the proceeding in question. One section deals with applications on behalf of minors; one section deals with applications by a litigation guardian or substitute decision-maker; and one section deals with other applications on behalf of another person. The last of these sections includes a consent, which is to be signed by the subject of the application, authorizing the applicant to make the application on his/her behalf.

Form 1 requires the applicant to identify the ground of discrimination and type of discrimination alleged as well as the location where and date when the alleged discrimination occurred. When the application is being filed more than one year after the last event, the applicant must explain the reason for the delay in filing. The purpose of this question is to assist the HRTO to determine whether or not the delay was incurred in good faith, which is one of the preconditions for acceptance of an application filed beyond the statutory time limit.[55]

The applicant is required to "give details of every incident of discrimination [the applicant] wants to raise at the hearing". It is important for the applicant to be thorough in describing the incidents relied on because the applicant may not be permitted to present evidence or make submissions with respect to a fact or issue that was not raised in the application.[56]

Form 1 requires the applicant to explain how the events described affected him or her and to identify the remedy he or she is seeking from the HRTO. The applicant is asked to indicate whether he or she will agree to try mediation. The form also contains a number of other questions designed to elicit information about possible grounds for dismissing or deferring the application (discussed further in this chapter).

Form 1 requires the applicant to list any documents that he or she has in his or her possession that are "important" to the application, to provide an explanation as to why they are important and to identify whether or not they are privileged.[57] The applicant is also asked to identify any documents in the possession of the respondent(s) that are "important" and explain why they are important. The applicant is only required to identify "important" documents at this stage; they need not be attached to the form when it is filed with the Tribunal.

---

application without further notice to any person who cannot be contacted according to the contact information that person provided to the HRTO: rule 5.4.

55 The Code, s. 34(1).

56 HRTO Rules of Procedure, rule 5.7. The HRTO does have the discretion to allow evidence or submissions in such a case where it is satisfied that there would be no substantial prejudice and no undue delay in the proceedings.

57 The concept of privilege is explained in Chapter 11, "The Final Appeal".

Similarly, Form 1 asks the applicant to list any witnesses who may be called at the hearing and explain why each witness' testimony is important to the application. The witness list and witness information provided by the applicant is considered confidential. When the HRTO reviews the Form 1 (as discussed later in this chapter), it will exclude this information from the form before delivering the form to the respondent(s).[58]

Both Form 1 and Form 4, where applicable, must be signed by the person filing the application. By signing Form 1 and Form 4, the signatory declares that, to the best of his or her knowledge, the information found in the form is complete and accurate. By signing Form 1, the applicant further acknowledges that information about the application may have to be disclosed in certain listed circumstances.

At the same time the applicant files a Form 1 or Form 4, the applicant must also file a Supplemental Form dealing with the type of discrimination being alleged. In cases involving special education, a Form 1-C, "Goods, Services, or Facilities", will typically be required.

HRTO Review of the Application and Delivery to Respondent(s)

The HRTO's Rules of Procedure specifically require that the Application must be complete. An Application is considered "complete" when it "provide[s] the information requested in every section of the Application form and . . . set[s] out all the facts that form the substance of the allegations of discrimination including the circumstances of what happened, where and when it happened, and the names of the person(s) or organization(s) alleged to have violated the Applicant's rights under the *Code*".[59]

Upon receipt of an Application, the HRTO will review the form to determine whether or not it complies sufficiently with the Rules to be processed. Where the HRTO is of the view that the Application is not sufficiently complete, the HRTO may send it back to the applicant with an explanation as to how it is incomplete. When the HRTO sends the Application back, the applicant has a period of 20 days to complete the form and resubmit it to the HRTO.[60] When the Application is resubmitted, the HRTO will review it again and, if it decides that the Application is complete, the HRTO will treat the Application as if it was complete on the day it was originally filed for the purpose of deciding whether or not it was filed within the statutory time limit sent out in section 34(1) of the Code.[61] If the Application still does not comply

58 HRTO Rules of Procedure, rule 6.7.
59 *Ibid.*, rules 6.1 and 6.2.
60 *Ibid.*, rule 6.4.
61 *Ibid.*, rule 6.5.

with the Rules after being resubmitted, the HRTO may decline to deal with the Application.[62]

Where the HRTO is of the view that an Application is complete and accepts the Application for processing, the HRTO will redact the witness information and send the Application form to the respondent(s).[63] If the HRTO is unable to contact a respondent due to inaccurate contact information, the HRTO may advise the applicant that it would not be proceeding against the respondent(s) in question.[64]

Before sending the Application to the respondent(s), the HRTO will consider whether or not there is any argument that the application is outside of its jurisdiction; if so, the HRTO may initiate a process to determine whether or not it had jurisdiction over the application.[65]

Responding to an Application

The Application filed with the HRTO will identify one or more respondents who are alleged to have discriminated against the applicant. In many cases, the applicant will name an organizational respondent as well as one or more individual respondents.[66] In cases involving special education, the school board will typically be named as the organizational respondent, while individual administrators, principals, teachers or other school board personnel involved with the student may be named as individual respondents.

School board or school personnel who receive an Application from the HRTO should take steps to respond to it immediately. The HRTO's processes are complex and the timelines for responding are short. The receipt of an Application means that formal litigation has been commenced and it is important to get legal counsel involved as soon as possible.

A person or organization named as a respondent to an application must file a Form 2, "Response", in order to respond to the Application.[67] It is important for every respondent to file a Response because, according to rule 5.5, if a respondent fails to do so, the HRTO can:

---

62 *Ibid.*, rule 5.3.

63 *Ibid.*, rules 6.6a) and 6.7.

64 *Ibid.*, rule 6.6b).

65 *Ibid.*, rule 6.6c).

66 The HRTO has issued an information bulletin on naming respondents that states: "If you believe a person engaged in discrimination while they were acting on behalf of an organization, you may want to name both the person and the organization. However, if the individual was acting in the regular course of their employment or duties, you may not need to name the individual as a separate respondent in addition to the organization." See Human Rights Tribunal of Ontario, "Information Bulletin: Naming Respondents" (Toronto: The Tribunal, 2008), available online at http://www.hrto.ca/hrto/sites/default/files/Resources/IB-NamingRespondents.pdf.

67 HRTO Rules of Procedure, rule 8.1.

a) deem the Respondent to have accepted all of the allegations in the Application;
b) proceed to deal with the Application without further notice to the Respondent;
c) deem the Respondent to have waived all rights with respect to further notice or participation in the proceeding;
d) decide the matter based only on the material before the Tribunal.

It is not always necessary for each respondent to an Application to file his or her own Response; it is often appropriate to file a collective Response on behalf of all respondents. A collective Response, however, may not be appropriate where there is a real or potential conflict of interest between the respondents.[68]

The Response Form

Form 2 contains a number of detailed questions, each of which must be answered by the respondent.[69] The Response must be completed and filed with the HRTO not later than 35 days after the Application was sent to the respondent by the HRTO.[70]

Form 2 requires full contact information for the respondent and the respondent's representative, if any, including full name, mailing address, telephone number(s) and, if applicable, facsimile number and/or e-mail address. Where there is a change in the contact information of the respondent or the respondent's representative, the HRTO and all the other parties and their representatives are to be notified as soon as possible.[71] The Response also invites the respondent(s) to identify other persons who should be respondents to the application or who may be affected by the application and to provide contact information for those persons.

There are three situations in which a respondent is not required to provide a full Response to the allegations in the Application. A full Response need not

[68] Conflict of interest is a complex topic that is beyond the scope of this work and should be discussed in each case with legal counsel. For present purposes, it will suffice to note that, where it appears that the respondents wish to pursue significantly different strategies in responding to the Application or where it appears that a respondent has conducted him- or herself in a manner that is significantly at odds with organizational norms and requirements, there may be a real or potential conflict of interest, which will preclude a collective response on behalf of all respondents. Where an actual or potential conflict of interest exists vis-à-vis one or more respondents, however, it may still be possible for the other respondents to file a collective response.

[69] HRTO Rules of Procedure, rule 8.2.

[70] *Ibid.*, rule 8.1.

[71] *Ibid.*, rule 1.13. As noted earlier, it is important that a respondent's contact information be accurate and up-to-date, as the HRTO has the authority to determine an application without further notice to any party who cannot be contacted according to the contact information they provided to the HRTO: see rule 5.4.

be filed where the respondent alleges that the issues in dispute in the Application are the subject of:[72]

a) a full and final signed release between the parties, or
b) a civil court proceeding requesting a remedy based on the alleged human rights infringement, or
c) a complaint filed with the Ontario Human Rights Commission.

These are all situations in which the applicant will be barred from proceeding with the application. Accordingly, rather than filing a full Response, the respondent is only required to attach to the Response form a copy of the applicable release, statement of claim or court decision, or complaint filed with the commission or its decision.[73] The HRTO may still direct the respondent to file a complete Response where the HRTO considers it appropriate to do so.[74]

In all other situations, the respondent must respond to each allegation in the Application, indicating what allegations the respondent agrees with, what allegations the respondent disagrees with and any additional facts that the respondent intends to rely on. The Response also asks the respondent to indicate which exemptions under the Code the respondent is relying on, if any. It is important to be thorough in completing this portion of the Response, because a respondent may not be permitted to present evidence or make submissions with respect to a fact or issue that was not raised in the Response.[75]

The Response asks the respondent whether or not the respondent agrees to mediation, as well as a number of questions designed to elicit information about possible grounds for dismissing or deferring the application (discussed further later in this chapter). The respondent is also asked how it (they) first became aware of the events described in the Application and how it (they) responded initially. Organizational respondents are asked to indicate whether they have any internal human rights policies and procedures in place, whether those procedures were utilized by the applicant, and, if so, what the outcome was.

Like the Application, the Response requires respondents to list any documents in their possession that are "important" to the application, to provide an explanation why they are important and to identify whether or not

---

72 *Ibid.*, rule 8.2. The last of these situations will likely decrease in significance with the passage of time, as the commission ceased processing complaints on behalf of individuals on June 30, 2008. As of the date of this writing, the HRTO has announced proposed changes to its Rules for consultation that would add to this list issues that fall within exclusive federal jurisdiction: Human Rights Tribunal of Ontario, *op. cit.*, footnote 40.

73 HRTO Rules of Procedure, rule 8.2.

74 *Ibid.*

75 *Ibid.*, rule 5.7. The HRTO does have the discretion to allow evidence or submissions where it is satisfied that there would be no substantial prejudice and no undue delay in the proceedings.

they are privileged.[76] Respondents are also required to identify any documents in the possession of the applicant that are "important" and explain why they are important. Generally speaking, the respondent is only required to identify "important" documents at this stage; they need not be attached to the Response when it is filed with the Tribunal. There are a few documents, however — such as any policies an organizational respondent might have in place dealing with the subject matter of the Application — that do have to be attached to the Response when it is filed with the HRTO.

The Response also requires respondents to list any witnesses who may be called at the hearing and explain why each witness' testimony is important to the Application. The witness list and witness information provided by respondents is considered confidential. When the HRTO reviews the Response (discussed further later in this chapter), it will exclude this information from the form before delivering the Response to the applicant and any other persons named in the Response.[77]

The Response must be signed by each respondent. In the case of a collective Response on behalf of a group of respondents, this can be done by attaching a separate signature page for each respondent or by having one person sign on behalf of all respondents. By signing the Response, each respondent declares that, to the best of his or her knowledge, the information found in the form is complete and accurate and acknowledges that information about the Response may have to be disclosed in certain listed circumstances.

HRTO Review of the Response and Delivery to the Applicant

Like the Application, the Response must be complete. To be considered "complete", the Response must "provide the information requested in each section of the Form 2, respond to each allegation set out in the Application, and . . . include any additional facts and allegations on which the Respondent relies".[78]

Upon receipt of the Response, the HRTO will review the form to determine whether or not it is complete. When the HRTO is of the view that the Response is not complete, the HRTO may send it back to the respondent with an explanation as to how it is incomplete. If the HRTO sends the Response back, the respondent has a period of 20 days to complete the form and resubmit it to the HRTO.[79] If the Response is resubmitted, the HRTO will review it again and, if it then decides that the Response is complete, the HRTO

---

76 The concept of privilege is explained in Chapter 11, "The Final Appeal".

77 HRTO Rules of Procedure, rule 8.6.

78 *Ibid.*, rule 8.2. This requirement does not apply in the three exceptional situations identified in rule 8.2 in which a respondent is not required to file a complete response. These exceptional situations were previously discussed.

79 *Ibid.*, rule 8.3.

will treat the Response as if it was complete on the day it was originally filed.[80] If the Response still does not comply with the Rules after it has been resubmitted, the HRTO can proceed as if no Response had been filed.[81]

When the HRTO is of the view that a Response is complete and accepts the Response for processing, the HRTO will redact the witness information and send the Response to the applicant and any other respondent or affected person identified in the Response.[82]

The Applicant's Reply

Following the delivery of the Response, the person(s) who filed the Application may file a Reply in Form 3.[83] In the Reply, the applicant may only address new matters that were raised in the Response.[84] Where new matters have been raised in the Response, it is important to file a Reply, since failure to do so may preclude an applicant from presenting evidence or making submissions with respect to that matter at the hearing.[85]

The Reply must be completed, delivered to all the parties and any person or organization identified as an affected person in the Response, and filed with the HRTO no later than 14 days after the Response was sent to the applicant.[86]

Applications by the Ontario Human Rights Commission

In the previous section, the process to be followed when a person wishes to make a human rights application, either on his or her own behalf or on behalf of another person, was reviewed. The Code also contemplates applications to the Tribunal by the Ontario Human Rights Commission.

As noted above, as a result of the legislative reforms that took effect in 2008, there has been a significant shift in the role and responsibilities of the Ontario Human Rights Commission. For the most part, the commission is now involved in promoting awareness of human rights, human rights policy-making, and prevention of discriminatory practices;[87] however, as will be clear from this section and the section on interventions later in this chapter, the commission still plays a significant role — or, at least, has the potential to play a significant role — in human rights litigation in the province.

Section 35 of the Code provides that the commission may make its own application to the HRTO where two preconditions are met. First, the

80 *Ibid.*, rules 8.4 and 8.5.
81 *Ibid.*, rule 5.3.
82 *Ibid.*, rules 8.4 and 8.6.
83 *Ibid.*, rule 9.1.
84 *Ibid.*, rule 9.2.
85 *Ibid.*, rule 5.7; however, the HRTO has a discretion to allow evidence or submissions on the matter in question where it is satisfied that there would be no substantial prejudice and no undue delay in the proceedings.
86 *Ibid.*, rule 9.3.
87 The commission's functions are described in the Code, at s. 29.

commission must be of the opinion that it is in the public interest to make the application. Second, the commission must be of the opinion that an order under section 45.3 could provide an appropriate remedy.[88] The remedies available from the HRTO are discussed further later in this chapter. For present purposes, it will suffice to note that an order under section 45.3 is essentially a public interest remedy designed to promote compliance with the Code and prevent future discriminatory practices.[89]

The Code expressly states that the commission's decision to file its own application does not affect a person's right to file an application with respect to the same matter.[90] Where the commission and a person file an application with respect to the same matter, the applications are to be dealt with together unless the HRTO determines otherwise.[91]

The commission had a similar authority to file its own complaints prior to the amendments which came into effect in 2008, but rarely utilized this authority. Given the ease with which the commission can intervene in individual applications as a party with full participatory rights (discussed further later in this chapter), it seems likely that commission will often prefer that approach. Nevertheless, the prospect of a commission application remains available as a means to address human rights policy issues in the absence of an individual applicant who wishes to bring the matter forward.[92]

Commission Applications

Where the commission opts to file its own application, it must complete a Form 7, "Application by Commission", and file it with the HRTO.[93] There is no statutory time limit applicable to a Commission Application. While this may seem surprising at first blush, it likely reflects the fact that a Commission Application is directed towards a policy issue, rather than a series of events or set of facts occurring at a particular point in time.

The Form 7 requires detailed contact information for the commission, the respondents — whether organizational or individual respondents — and any other affected persons.[94] The commission must state what the grounds of discrimination are and the social area in which discrinimation is alleged to

[88] *Ibid.*, s. 35(1). Under the former human rights process, the commission had initiated its own complaints against school boards and the Ministry of Education. Under the current process, the commission has continued to bring applications in the area of disability discrimination and may do so in the future in the educational context.

[89] *Ibid.*, s. 45.3.

[90] *Ibid.*, s. 35(3).

[91] *Ibid.*, s. 35(4).

[92] The commission has recently filed applications against a number of public transit authorities.

[93] HRTO Rules of Procedure, rule 12.1.

[94] HRTO must be notified of any changes in this contact information as soon as possible: *ibid.*, rule 1.13.

have occurred (for example, employment or services). It must list the facts and issues that it wishes to address, the material facts on which it will rely and explain why it is in the public interest that the application be filed. The commission must also state what remedies it will be seeking and indicate whether or not it will agree to participate in mediation.

The Form 7 also requires the commission to list any documents on which it intends to rely; however, those documents need not be attached when the Application by Commission is filed with the HRTO. The commission must also list any documents in the possession of the respondent(s) or any third parties that may be relevant to the matter.

The Form 7 must be signed, thereby signifying that to the best of the signatory's knowledge, the information in the form is complete and accurate.

As in the case of an individual application, a Commission Application must be complete.[95] In order to be considered "complete", a Commission Application must:[96]

> a) include a statement why, in the opinion of the Commission, the Application is in the public interest;
> b) set out the issues the Commission wants to address;
> c) set out all the material facts upon which the Commission intends to rely; and
> d) set out the remedies the Commission is seeking.

A Commission Application is not subject to initial review for completeness by the HRTO before it is delivered to the respondent; rather, it is to be delivered by the commission directly to the respondent and any other affected persons identified in the Form 7 and then filed with the HRTO.[97]

Response to a Commission Application

Any respondent to a Commission Application and any person identified as an affected person in a Commission Application may respond by filing a Form 8, "Response to Commission Application".[98]

The Response to Commission Application form requires a respondent to provide detailed contact information for the respondent and the respondent's representative.[99] The form asks the respondent to state its position on each of the issues and material facts set out in the Commission Application, to set out any material facts on which it will rely, to provide a response to the remedies sought by the commission and to indicate whether or not the respondent is prepared to participate in mediation.

---

[95] *Ibid.*, rule 12.1.

[96] *Ibid.*, rule 12.2.

[97] *Ibid.*, rule 12.1.

[98] *Ibid.*, rule 12.3.

[99] The HRTO must be notified of any changes in this contact information as soon as possible: *ibid.*, rule 1.13.

In addition, the respondent must list any documents in its possession, in the possession of the commission or in the possession of any other person, which are "important" to the Response. These documents need not be attached to the Response when it is filed with the HRTO.

The Response to Commission Application form must be signed, thereby signifying that to the best of the signatory's knowledge, the information in the form is complete and accurate.

Like the Commission Application, the Response to Commission Application form must be complete. To be considered "complete", the Response must:[100]

> a) include a statement setting out the position of the Respondent or affected person in respect of each of the issues and material facts set out in the Commission Application;
> b) set out all of the material facts upon which the Respondent or affected person intends to rely; and,
> c) include a response to the remedies requested by the Commission.

There is no initial review by the HRTO of a Response to Commission Application form. The Response must be completed, delivered to the commission and any other party or identified affected person named in the Commission Application form and filed the Tribunal not later than 60 days after the delivery of the Commission Application.[101]

Amendments and Withdrawals

Amending Filings

Once the Application, Response and Reply have been filed with the HRTO, a party may find it wishes to amend its filings. The HRTO has fairly broad discretion to allow a party to amend its filings.[102] Typically, a request to amend filings will be made by filing a Form 10, "Request for an Order During Proceedings". The procedure for making a request for an order during proceedings is discussed later in this chapter.

While each case will turn on its particular facts, the HRTO will often be prepared to grant an amendment, as long as the HRTO is satisfied that the amendment will not cause prejudice to the other parties.

Withdrawal of Applications

The HRTO's Rules of Procedure also contain a special procedure that must be followed to withdraw an application that has been filed with the

---

[100] *Ibid.*, rule 12.4.

[101] *Ibid.*, rule 12.3. The HRTO may be prepared to grant a brief extension of the timeframe for response, upon submission of a written request with reasons by the respondent: see rule 5.2.

[102] *Ibid.*, rule 1.7c).

HRTO where the withdrawal has not come about as a result of a settlement. The applicant must deliver and file Form 9, "Request to Withdraw" and any respondent or other affected person may respond by delivering and filing Form 11, "Response to a Request for an Order During Proceedings" no later than 14 days after the Request to Withdraw was delivered. Where a Response to the Application has already been filed, the Application may be withdrawn with the permission of the HRTO and the withdrawal may be subject to such terms as the HRTO may deem appropriate.[103]

INTERVENTION BY THE COMMISSION AND OTHER AFFECTED PERSONS

Generally speaking, the parties to a human rights application are the person(s) who filed the Application and the person(s) named in the Application as respondent.[104] Both the Code and the HRTO's Rules of Procedure contemplate intervention by the commission and other affected persons in proceedings before the HRTO.

Intervention can take different forms. A person or organization may be permitted to intervene as a party, in which case that organization or person has the right to participate in the proceedings in the same way and to the same extent as any other party. Alternatively, a person or organization may be permitted to intervene on a more limited basis. For example, intervenors may be permitted to intervene only for the purpose of making submissions to the HRTO on a particular issue or set of issues.

As discussed further on in this chapter, where the applicant consents, the commission has a right to intervene in the proceedings as a party pursuant to section 37(2) of the Code. In all other cases, a person or organization seeking to intervene must file Form 5, "Request to Intervene", and the other parties to the proceeding are given an opportunity to respond.[105] Based on the material submitted, the HRTO will determine whether the intervention will be permitted, the extent to which the intervenor will be entitled to participate in the proceeding, whether or not any terms will be imposed on the intervenor's participation and, if so, the nature and extent of those terms.[106]

---

[103] Code, s. 34(10) and HRTO Rules of Procedure, rule 10.

[104] Code, s. 36. Note that, in the case of an application under s. 34(5) (application on behalf of another person), it is not the person who has commenced the application, but the person on whose behalf the application was commenced who is considered a party to the proceedings. In the case of a Commission Application, the commission is automatically a party and need not intervene to attain party status.

[105] HRTO Rules of Procedure, rules 11.2, 11.4, 11.7 and 11.9.

[106] *Ibid.*, rule 11.1.

Intervention by the Commission

Section 37 of the Code addresses the circumstances in which the commission may intervene in an application before the HRTO. Section 37(1) states that the commission may intervene in any application before the HRTO, but also contemplates that the HRTO may impose terms on the commission's intervention that reflect the role and mandate of the commission.[107] Section 37(2) states that the commission may intervene *as a party* — that is, with full participatory rights — where the applicant consents to intervention as a party.[108]

The Code authorizes the commission to require the HRTO to disclose to it copies of all Applications and Responses filed with the HRTO.[109] The commission has exercised this authority and therefore receives copies of all Applications and Responses. This enables the commission to monitor proceedings at the HRTO and determine whether or not to intervene in those proceedings.

Commission Intervention with Consent

Where the commission has obtained the applicant's consent to intervene in an application, then the commission is required to file a Form 6, "Notice of Commission Intervention (with Consent)", which includes a consent that must be completed by the applicant.[110] The Notice of Commission Intervention must be delivered to the parties and any identified affected persons and then filed with the HRTO.[111] The Notice of Commission Intervention must be complete and must include a statement of the issues the commission wants to address as well as set out the commission's position (if any) on each of the issues raised in the Application and Response, all the material facts on which the commission will rely, the remedies that the commission is seeking and the terms on which the commission is seeking to intervene.[112]

The Code and the HRTO Rules of Procedure contemplate that, provided the applicant consents, the commission has a statutory right to intervene as a party. Notably, the Rules require the commission to provide the parties and the HRTO with "Notice of Intervention", not with a "Request to Intervene" (as is the case in other circumstances where intervention is being sought). No input or response is invited from the respondent(s) concerning the commission's intervention as a party or otherwise.

---

[107] Code, s. 37(1).
[108] Code, s. 37(2).
[109] Code, s. 38.
[110] HRTO Rules of Procedure, rule 11.11.
[111] *Ibid.*, rule 11.12.
[112] *Ibid.*, rule 11.13.

Commission Intervention without Consent

Where the applicant is not willing to consent to the commission's intervention as a party, the commission may still make a Request to Intervene. In such a case, the commission is required to complete a Request to Intervene, deliver it to the parties and any identified affected persons and file it with the HRTO.[113]

A Request to Intervene by the Commission must include the same information required in a Notice of Intervention by the Commission — namely, a statement of the issues the commission wants to address, the commission's position (if any) on each of the issues raised in the Application and Response, all the material facts on which the commission will rely, the remedies that the commission is seeking and the terms on which the commission is seeking to intervene. In addition, the Request to Intervene by the commission must include an explanation of how the issues the commission wishes to address relate to the commission's role, mandate and the public interest.[114]

Any party may respond to the Request to Intervene by filing Form 11, "Response to a Request for an Order During Proceedings", no later than 21 days after the Request to Intervene was delivered.[115] The Response must be delivered to the commission, all other parties, and any identified affected person, and filed with the HRTO.[116]

The HRTO has considerable flexibility to conduct its process in any manner it considers to be fair, just and expeditious in the circumstances.[117] In the majority of cases, the HRTO will be able to deal with Requests to Intervene based on the written material filed, without the necessity of an in-person hearing. The HRTO typically issues brief written decisions regarding preliminary matters such as intervention. In the case of a Request to Intervene, the decision will be delivered to the proposed intervenor and the parties.

---

[113] *Ibid.*, rule 11.7.

[114] *Ibid.*, rule 11.8.

[115] *Ibid.*, rule 11.9.

[116] *Ibid.*, rule 11.10.

[117] Section 40 of the Code provides that the HRTO "shall dispose of applications . . . adopting the procedures and practices provided for in its rules or otherwise available to the [HRTO] which, in its opinion, offer the best opportunity for a fair, just and expeditious resolution of the merits of the applications". Section 41 further states that Part IV of the Code and the HRTO Rules of Procedure "shall be liberally construed to permit the [HRTO] to adopt practices and procedures, including alternatives to traditional adjudicative or adversarial procedures that, in the opinion of the [HRTO], will facilitate fair, just and expeditious resolutions of the merits of the matters before it". See also HRTO Rules of Procedure, rules 1.1, 1.6, 1.7 and 3.5.

Intervention by Other Persons or Organizations

The HRTO Rules of Procedure also contemplate that persons or organizations other than the commission may seek to intervene in an application filed with the HRTO. In many cases, potential intervenors will be affected persons identified in the Application or Response. A person or organization who is identified as an affected person who wishes to participate in the proceeding must file a Request to Intervene within 35 days of delivery of the Application or Response. If this does not occur, the HRTO is entitled to proceed without further notice to that person or organization.[118]

In addition to affected persons identified in the Application or Response, any person or organization with an identifiable interest and/or expertise in the issues before the HRTO may be a potential intervenor. For example, an advocacy organization such as an Association for Community Living may seek to intervene in a human rights proceeding involving special education to make representations to the HRTO on some issue or issues arising in the proceeding.

Any person (including an affected person) who wishes to intervene in an application is required to file a Form 5, "Request to Intervene".[119] This is the same form that the commission is required to file when it is seeking to intervene without consent. In the case of a Request to Intervene filed by a person or organization other than the commission, each question on the Request to Intervene must be completed. The request must describe the issues the person or organization wants to address and explain the proposed intervenor's interest in the issue(s) and its expertise, if any, regarding the issues. It must also set out the proposed intervenor's position, if any, on each of the issues raised in the Application and Response and any material facts on which the proposed intervenor will rely.[120] Once completed, the Request to Intervene must be delivered to all parties and all identified affected persons and filed with the HRTO.[121]

Any party wishing to respond to a Request to Intervene may do so by filing a Form 11, "Response to Request for an Order During Proceedings". The Form 11 must be delivered to the proposed intervenor, all other parties as well as any other affected persons and filed with the HRTO no later than 21 days after the Request to Intervene was delivered.[122]

As in the case of a Commission Request to Intervene, the HRTO may utilize any procedure to deal with the request that it considers fair, just and expeditious in the circumstances.[123] Most often, preliminary matters such as

118 HRTO Rules of Procedure, rule 3.14.
119 *Ibid.*, rule 11.2.
120 *Ibid.*, rule 11.3.
121 *Ibid.*, rule 11.2.
122 *Ibid.*, rules 11.4 and 11.5.
123 See footnote 117.

requests for intervention will be determined based on the written material filed and a brief written decision will be issued by the HRTO.

EARLY DISMISSAL AND DEFERRAL

There are a number of situations in which an application that has been filed may be dismissed or deferred by the HRTO in the early stages of the process, either at its own initiative or at the request of one of the parties. The HRTO must dismiss the application where the application falls outside its jurisdiction[124] or where the application is barred because the applicant has previously filed a civil proceeding or a human rights complaint covering substantially the same subject matter.[125]

The HRTO also has a discretion to dismiss the application where it finds that the substance of the application has been appropriately dealt with in another proceeding. The HRTO has a discretion to defer consideration in other situations, as well, such as where there are other legal proceedings pending.

Early Dismissal: Appropriately Dealt with in Other Proceeding

The Code confers a discretion on the HRTO to dismiss an application, either in whole or in part, when it is of the opinion that another proceeding has appropriately dealt with the substance of the application.[126] The HRTO has recognized that it may exercise its discretion to dismiss an application where the facts underlying the application have been appropriately dealt with in a proceeding before the Special Education Tribunal.[127] Another situation in which the HRTO will often exercise its discretion to dismiss an application is where some or all of the issues in dispute have been the subject of a settlement and release between the parties in the context of other proceeding.[128]

---

[124] HRTO Rules of Procedure, rules 6.6c) and 13. For a discussion about the jurisdiction to resolve special education issues at the Human Rights Tribunal versus the Special Education Tribunal, see *Sigrist and Carson v. London District Catholic School Board*, 2010 HRTO 1062. The discussion in the case is based on a case characterized as "transitional"; that is, it began under the previous complaints regime, not under the current legislation. The arguments about jurisdiction will, no doubt, continue in the coming years.

[125] Code, ss. 34(11), (12) and 53(8); HRTO Rules of Procedure, rules 6.2, 6.3 and 8.2. As of the date of this writing, the HRTO has released proposed changes to its Rules for consultation that would introduce a process of summary hearings to determine whether an application should be dismissed in whole or in part because "there is no reasonable prospect of success": Human Rights Tribunal of Ontario, *op cit.*, foonote 40.

[126] Code, s. 45.1, HRTO Rules of Procedure, rule 22.1.

[127] *Campbell v. Toronto District School Board*, 2008 HRTO 62, at paras. 66-9.

The Application form asks the applicant whether the facts underlying the application are part of another proceeding and whether that proceeding is still in progress. Where the underlying facts are part of another proceeding, the applicant is required to attach to the Application form a copy of the document that commenced the other proceeding. Where there was another proceeding and it has been completed, the applicant is asked to explain why he or she believes the other proceeding did not deal appropriately with the substance of the application.

The Response form asks the respondent to indicate whether the respondent is seeking early dismissal on the basis that another proceeding has appropriately dealt with the substance of the application and, if so, to explain why. A respondent who alleges that some or all of the issues in dispute have been the subject of a full and final signed release can request early dismissal without filing a full Response.

The Rules specifically provide that the parties will be given an opportunity to make oral submissions before the HRTO dismisses an application on the basis that another proceeding has appropriately dealt with the substance of the application.[129]

Deferral

The Code also allows the HRTO to defer consideration of an application in accordance with its Rules of Procedure.[130] The Rules allow the HRTO to defer consideration of an application on its own initiative, at the request of the applicant or any other party.[131]

Deferral at the Applicant's Request

Rule 7 contemplates that an applicant may file an application and, at the same time, ask the HRTO to defer consideration of the application on the basis that there are other proceedings pending dealing with the subject matter of the application.[132] The Application form asks the applicant whether or not other proceedings are pending and to indicate whether he or she is requesting the HRTO to defer the application until the other proceeding is completed. If so, the applicant must provide identifying information regarding the other legal proceeding, and provide a copy of the document that commenced the

---

[128] See, for example, *Dunn and Sault Ste. Marie (Re)*, 2008 C.L.L.C. ¶ 230-041, 2008 HRTO 149.

[129] Code, s. 43(2), HRTO Rules of Procedure, rule 22.2.

[130] Code, s. 45.

[131] HRTO Rules of Procedure, rule 14.1.

[132] *Ibid.*, rule 7.1. The HRTO will, however, dismiss the application rather than consider the request for deferral where the proceedings in question are civil proceedings that bar an application by virtue of s. 34(11) of the Code: see rule 7.2.

proceeding to the HRTO with the application.[133] The HRTO will not defer consideration of an application without first giving the parties and any affected persons the opportunity to make submissions on the request for deferral.[134]

Where the HRTO has granted a request to defer an application pending completion of another legal proceeding, the applicant must make a request to the HRTO no later than 60 days after completion of the other proceeding if the applicant wishes the HRTO to proceed with the application.[135] The request is made by filing a Form 10, "Request for an Order During Proceedings", which must include the date that the other legal proceeding concluded and a copy of the decision or order.[136]

Deferral in Other Cases

As noted, the HRTO may also defer consideration of an application at its own initiative or at the request of one of the parties.[137] Most often, this will occur where there are other legal proceedings pending or underway but the applicant has not requested deferral; however, neither the Code nor the Rules place any limitation on the range of circumstances in which an application may be deferred.

Where the HRTO intends to defer consideration of an application at its own initiative, the HRTO must give the parties notice of its intention and an opportunity to make submissions.[138] The Response form asks the respondent to indicate whether or not it is asking the HRTO to defer the application pending the outcome of another legal proceeding. Where a respondent wishes to request deferral at a later stage of proceedings, or another party wishes to request deferral, it will be necessary to file a Form 10, "Request for an Order During Proceedings".[139]

Where an application has been deferred pending the outcome of other legal proceedings, the HRTO may require the application to proceed at its own initiative.[140] On the other hand, where a party wishes the HRTO to proceed with the application, the party must make a request to proceed with the HRTO no later than 60 days after completion of the other proceeding.[141] The request is made by filing a Request for an Order During Proceedings, which must include the date that the other legal proceeding concluded and a copy of the decision or order.[142]

---

133 *Ibid.*, rule 7.3.
134 *Ibid.*, rule 7.4.
135 *Ibid.*, rule 7.5.
136 *Ibid.*, rules 7.5, 14.3, 14.4 and 19.
137 *Ibid.*, rule 14.1.
138 *Ibid.*, rule 14.2.
139 *Ibid.*, rules 14.2 and 19.
140 *Ibid.*, rule 14.5.
141 *Ibid.*, rule 14.3.

EXPEDITED PROCEEDINGS AND INTERIM REMEDIES

In some cases, a person filing an application may feel that he or she (or, if a parent, his or her child who is a student) will suffer some harm if required to wait for the proceedings to run their course or if steps are not taken to preserve or restore the *status quo* pending the outcome of the proceedings. In the former case, the applicant may make a request to expedite the proceedings. In the latter case, the applicant may seek an interim remedy from the HRTO while the proceedings are underway.

Expedited Proceedings

An applicant who believes that the circumstances require an urgent resolution of the issues in dispute may file Form 14, "Request to Expedite Proceeding".[143] The form must describe:[144]

a) any urgent circumstances that may affect the fair and just resolution of the merits of the Application;
b) the harm that would result if the request is denied; and
c) whether the other parties consent to the request.

The Form 14 is to be filed directly with the HRTO at the same time as the Application form. It will be delivered to the respondent(s) and any other identified affected persons by the HRTO along with the Application.

Any party or affected person who wishes to respond to the Request to Expedite Proceeding may do so by delivering and filing Form 15, "Response to Request to Expedite Proceeding". The form must be filed not later than seven days after it was sent or as the HRTO directs.[145] In most cases, the HRTO will deal with these requests based on the written material and provide its decision to the parties.

---

142 *Ibid.*, rules 14.3, 14.4 and 19. Presumably, at this point, the respondent(s) may ask the HRTO to dismiss the application on the basis that the other proceeding has appropriately dealt with the substance of the application. The respondent(s) may need to file a Request for an Order During Proceedings to place this issue before the HRTO.

143 *Ibid.*, rule 21.1. At the time of this writing, the HRTO has released proposed changes to its Rules for consultation that would make significant amendments to the Rules respecting requests to expedite proceedings: Human Rights Tribunal of Ontario, *op cit.*, footnote 40.

144 HRTO Rules of Procedure, rule 21.2. Rule 21.2 suggests that an order expediting proceedings is to be the exception rather than the rule. The HRTO will require proof of urgent circumstances beyond the general desirability of having the matter disposed of as quickly as possible, as well as proof that harm will result if the request were denied. The final requirement in rule 21.2c) implies that the applicant is expected to have sought the consent of the other party or parties before making the request.

145 *Ibid.*, rule 21.3.

It is not uncommon for parents who apply to the HRTO regarding special education issues to seek an expedited hearing before the HRTO; however, the HRTO has stated as follows:[146]

> The desirability of dealing expeditiously with a claim that a student is not receiving proper education services is self-evident. However, whether such a claim warrants expediting the Tribunal's regular processes must be assessed on a case-by-case basis. It has been the Tribunal's experience that it receives a significant number of complaints about the schooling of young students — if all were expedited, the Tribunal's resources would be heavily weighted in favour of dealing with these cases at the expense of many other applications before it.

In considering the criteria set out above for determining whether or not to expedite an application in cases involving special education issues, the HRTO has also considered the following:

- How much time has passed since the occurrence of the events that give rise to the application and the request to expedite?[147]
- How complex are the issues and is it appropriate to require the respondents to prepare their Responses in an abridged fashion?[148]
- Is the child currently in school or has the child's attendance been limited or has the child been excluded?[149]
- Is there any expert evidence that, as a result of the school board's allegedly discriminatory actions, there is ongoing harm to the child?[150]

Interim Remedies

An applicant may also ask the HRTO to order an interim remedy that will remain in place while the proceedings are pending. An example might be an

---

146 *Haughton v. Toronto District School Board*, 2009 HRTO 655, at para. 8. In the *Haughton* case, the parent complained that her son was being discriminated against in the provision of educational services on the basis of disability. She also alleged that he had been physically abused and that the school board was failing to investigate this. As a result, she withdrew her son from school. The HRTO found that an expedited hearing was unlikely to resolve the parent's issue, which was to compel the school board to act on her complaint that her son had been physically abused.

147 *Haughton*, *supra*, at para. 10. See also *Nye v. Hamilton-Wentworth District School Board*, 2009 HRTO 1205.

148 *Haughton*, *supra*, footnote 146, and *Nye v. Hamilton-Wentworth District School Board*, *supra*.

149 *Griffiths v. Toronto District School Board*, 2009 HRTO 545. In this case, a child with autism, whose behaviours were extremely aggressive, was limited to one hour of school a day as the school struggled to find a way to meet his needs safely. The parent successfully sought to have her application expedited after providing evidence from a developmental pediatrician that the continued absence from school was causing the child to regress developmentally.

150 *Griffiths v. Toronto District School Board*, *supra*.

order requiring a school board to take action, or refrain from taking action, while the legality of that action is under scrutiny by the HRTO.

An applicant seeking an interim remedy is required to complete Form 16, "Request for Interim Remedy". The form is to be delivered to the other parties along with the completed Application form before it is filed with the HRTO.[151]

The Rules state that the HRTO has a discretion to grant an interim remedy in cases where it is satisfied that the following three criteria exist:[152]

a) the Application appears to have merit;
b) the balance of harm or convenience favours granting the interim remedy requested; and,
c) it is just and appropriate in the circumstances to do so.

With this test in mind, the Rules provide that Form 16 must include the following information:[153]

a) a detailed description of the order sought;
b) one or more declarations signed by persons with direct first-hand knowledge detailing all of the facts upon which the Applicant relies; and
c) submissions with respect to the merits of the Application, the balance of harm or convenience and why an interim remedy would be just and appropriate in the circumstances, in accordance with the Rule 23.2.

Any other parties or affected persons who wish to respond to the Form 16 must do so by delivering and filing with the HRTO a Form 17, "Response to Request for Interim Remedy", not later than seven days after the Form 16 was delivered.[154] The Response to Request for Interim Remedy must also include one or more declarations signed by persons with direct first-hand knowledge detailing the facts on which the respondent relies as well as submissions with respect to the merits of the underlying application, the balance of harm or convenience and reasons why an interim remedy would not be just and appropriate in the circumstances.[155]

One interim remedy that the HRTO will generally grant, on the request of a parent who has brought an application on behalf of his or her child, is to anonymize the name of the child and parent(s) in its decisions. This means that the names of the student and the parent will be referred to in any written decisions by only their initials in order to provide a measure of confidentiality and privacy for the student.[156]

---

[151] HRTO Rules of Procedure, rule 23.1. At the time of this writing, the HRTO has released proposed changes to the Rules governing interim remedies for consultation: Human Rights Tribunal of Ontario, *op cit.*, footnote 40.

[152] HRTO Rules of Procedure, rule 23.2.

[153] *Ibid.*, rule 23.3.

[154] *Ibid.*, rule 23.4.

[155] *Ibid.*, rule 23.5.

[156] *C.M. v. York Region District School Board*, 2009 HRTO 735. In this case, the parent sought a publication ban. The HRTO denied this request on the basis that the

A parent who seeks as an interim remedy essentially the same remedy being requested as a resolution of the application — *e.g.*, that the student be provided on an interim basis with the accommodations that the parent has requested as a final remedy — will face an uphill battle obtaining interim relief. This is because the granting of the final remedy as an interim order effectively means that the HRTO will be obliged to determine the merits of the dispute within the context of the interim relief hearing.[157] The HRTO is unlikely to do this, except perhaps in exceptional circumstances.

REQUEST FOR AN ORDER DURING PROCEEDINGS

It is not uncommon for issues to arise during the course of proceedings before the HRTO — but before the hearing itself — that necessitate an order or ruling from the HRTO. These issues may range from straightforward housekeeping matters — such as adding or removing a party or correcting the proper legal name of a party — to complex and significant procedural matters — such as the scope of disclosure of documents required. The order sought will usually apply to the parties, but there may also be cases where the order may apply to a person who is not a party — for example, where a party seeks an order requiring a third party, such as a physician, to disclose documents that are relevant to the proceeding.

Subject to a few specified exceptions, the HRTO uses one set of forms to deal with all pre-hearing procedural matters.[158] A party who wishes to request the HRTO to make an order must deliver and file Form 10, "Request for an Order During Proceedings".[159] A party wishing to respond to the Request for an Order During Proceedings must deliver and file Form 11, "Response to a Request for an Order During Proceedings" within 14 days of delivery of the Form 10.[160]

The Request for an Order During Proceedings must:[161]

---

circumstances of the case were not such as to outweigh the fundamental principle of open and transparent decision-making that is critical to a free and democratic society. As of the date of this writing, the HRTO has proposed changes to the Rules for consultation that would codify this practise by providing that the HRTO will use initials to indentify any children under age 18, the next friend of children under age 18, or any other participants if necessary to protect the identity of children: Human Rights Tribunal of Ontario, *op cit.*, footnote 40.

157 *Griffiths*, *supra*, footnote 149.

158 HRTO Rules of Procedure, rule 19. Rule 19.1 provides that a verbal request for an order may be made in the course of the hearing; however, a written request for an order is required to raise an issue for determination prior to the hearing.

159 *Ibid.*, rule 19.2. The Form 10 must be delivered to all parties and to all identified affected persons or organizations that have an interest in the request. Where a request is for an order with respect to a person who is not a party, the form must also be delivered to the third party as well: rules 19.2 and 19.3.

160 *Ibid.*, rule 19.6.

161 *Ibid.*, rules 19.4 and 19.5. The purpose of requirements such as those set out at

a) describe the order requested;
b) contain reasons for the request, including any facts relied on and submissions in support of the request;
c) where the order requested is for production of a document(s) a copy of the party's written request for the document(s) and the responding party's response, if any, must be attached to the Form 10;
d) include the documents relied on in support of the request, if any;
e) indicate whether the requesting party wishes the Tribunal to deal with the matter in writing, in person, or electronically; and,
f) indicate whether the consent of another party has been obtained as to any term of the order sought or as to the manner in which the request should be dealt with.

The Response to a Request for an Order During Proceedings, in turn, must include:[162]

a) the responding party's position on the order(s) requested and the whether the Request for Order should be dealt with in writing, in person, or electronically;
b) identify which facts in the Request for Order are accepted and which are disputed. Where the order requested is for production of documents the responding party must attach the written response to the request, if any;
c) reasons and any submissions in support of the responding party's position;
d) any additional facts relied on by the responding party; and,
e) include any documents not included in the Request for Order upon which the responding party intends to rely.

The HRTO has the discretion to determine whether the Request for an Order During Proceedings will be dealt with in writing, in person or electronically.[163] It is not bound to proceed in accordance with the parties' preferences, but rather will be guided by its statutory responsibility to adopt procedures and practices that offer the best opportunity for a fair, just and expeditious resolution of the merits.[164] On the other hand, the HRTO is not permitted to dispose finally of an application that is within its jurisdiction without affording the parties an opportunity to make oral submissions.[165] Accordingly, while straightforward matters will often be dealt with in writing or electronically, in-person hearings will be required in some cases.

When an in-person hearing is required, the HRTO will set a date for the hearing and notify the parties.[166] The HRTO has the authority under its Rules of Procedure to schedule hearing dates with or without consultation with the parties, as the HRTO considers appropriate.[167] However, usually the HRTO will engage in some consultations with the parties regarding hearing dates before doing so.

---

c) and f) is to encourage parties to co-operate and engage in constructive problem-solving before seeking the assistance of the HRTO.

162 *Ibid.*, rule 19.6.

163 *Ibid.*, rules 19.7 and 3.5.

164 Code, s. 40.

165 *Ibid.*, s. 43(2) and HRTO Rules of Procedure, rule 3.5.

166 HRTO Rules of Procedure, rule 19.7.

167 *Ibid.*, rule 3.4.

The HRTO generally endeavours to make its decisions on preliminary matters in a timely manner so as not to delay unduly the next steps in the process. Straightforward matters can often be addressed quite quickly; however, in the case of more complex preliminary matters and those that may result in a final disposition of the application, the HRTO may require more time to make its decision and compose its reasons.[168] In either case, the HRTO's usual practice is to provide the parties with a written decision outlining the determination it has made and the underlying reasons.

MEDIATION AND SETTLEMENTS

After the Application, Response and any Reply have been filed and any preliminary matters arising from the parties' initial filings have been addressed, the next major step in the human rights process is mediation.

The HRTO does not have a positive obligation under its Rules of Procedure to offer mediation services.[169] In practice, however, the HRTO strongly encourages mediation and will usually hold a mediation in any case in which both parties have expressed a willingness to try mediation.[170] The HRTO also has the authority to offer mediation at its own initiative in cases where the parties do not express a willingness to try mediation.[171] Since mediation is voluntary, however, the HRTO will not force an unwilling party to attend mediation.

Where the parties have agreed to try mediation, either in their initial filings or following further inquiries from the HRTO, the Registrar will issue a Notice of Mediation advising the parties of the date and location of the mediation. The Registrar's office will not typically consult with the parties before setting the initial date for the mediation.[172] When a party is unavailable to attend the mediation on the date in question, the party is required notify the Registrar within five days of receiving the Notice of Mediation and provide five alternative dates within 8 to 12 weeks of the date of the Notice.[173] Beyond that five-day period, the HRTO will reschedule a mediation "where a party or their representative is unavailable for a valid reason such as: being out of the province or country, a previously arranged appointment that cannot be

---

168 Section 43(2) of the Code requires the HRTO to provide written reasons for any decision that may finally dispose of an application.

169 HRTO Rules of Procedure, rule 15.1.

170 Both the Application and Response forms contain a question asking whether or not the party in question will agree to mediation.

171 HRTO Rules of Procedure, rule 15.1.

172 The HRTO has the authority to schedule dates with or without consultation with the parties, as the HRTO considers appropriate: *ibid.*, rule 3.4.

173 See Human Rights Tribunal of Ontario, "Information Bulletin: Scheduling of Hearings and Mediations, Rescheduling Requests, and Requests for Adjournments" (Toronto: The Tribunal, 2008), available online at http://www.hrto.ca/hrto/sites/default/files/Resources/IB-Scheduling.pdf, at p. 3.

changed, [or] a previously scheduled court/tribunal appearance", but not "merely because the scheduled date is inconvenient for the parties or their representative".[174]

Mediations will generally be held in the Regional Centre nearest to the parties' location.[175] Requests to move a mediation to an alternate location will not generally be granted unless there are Code-related reasons for the request.

The applicant, a representative of the organizational respondent with authority to settle on the organization's behalf,[176] and every individual respondent should attend the mediation. Legal counsel representing the parties should also be present. Affected persons or organizations who are participating in the matter and additional support persons or advisors may also attend the mediation, although limitations may be placed on their participation in some cases.

Mediation is a confidential process. Confidentiality is viewed as essential to facilitating the full and frank discussion, which is essential for mediation to be successful. The HRTO requires every person who attends the mediation to sign a confidentiality agreement before the mediation commences.[177] In addition, the HRTO's Rules of Procedure explicitly state that all matters disclosed during mediation are considered confidential and may not be raised in proceedings before the HRTO or in other proceedings, except with the permission of the person who gave the information.[178]

The HRTO utilizes a "rights-based" approach to mediation. The mediator, a Vice-Chair or member of the HRTO who will not be assigned to hear the case, will ask the parties questions about their respective positions and will often provide feedback to the parties on the strengths and weaknesses of their case in view of the rights protected and the remedies available under the Code. The mediator's role is to propose options and assist the parties to find a mutually satisfactory resolution, not to impose an outcome on the parties.

Where the parties are successful in reaching a settlement at mediation, they will be expected to set their agreement out in writing and sign the agreement before the mediation concludes. The settlement agreement must include language requesting the HRTO to issue a consent order disposing of the application in accordance with the settlement and confirming that the parties are waiving their right to make oral submissions.[179] The parties will

---

174 *Ibid.*, at p. 2.

175 The Regional Centres are Toronto, Kingston, London, North Bay, Ottawa, Sarnia, Sault Ste. Marie, Sudbury, Timmins, Thunder Bay and Windsor: See Human Rights Tribunal of Ontario, "Practice Direction on Hearings in Regional Centres" (Toronto: The Tribunal, 2008), available online at http://www.hrto.ca/hrto/?q=en/node/60.

176 HRTO Rules of Procedure, rule 15.3.

177 *Ibid.*, rule 15.2.

178 *Ibid.*, rule 15.4.

179 *Ibid.*, rule 15.6.

also be asked to complete a Form 25, "Settlement", which essentially restates these terms.[180] A settlement of an application that is agreed to in writing and signed by the parties is binding on the parties.[181]

Where the mediation is not successful, the mediator will request the parties to complete and sign a case management checklist at the end of the mediation.[182] This checklist is discussed further in the next section; for present purposes, it suffices to note that parties should come to mediation prepared to complete the checklist in case the matter cannot be resolved.

SCHEDULING THE HEARING

Where the parties do not participate in mediation or where mediation is attempted but is unsuccessful, the parties will be required to go through a case management checklist to assist the HRTO with the scheduling of the hearing. This checklist includes a number of questions designed to assist in managing the next steps of the proceeding — for example, the parties are asked for an estimate of the duration of the hearing, how many witnesses they intend to call, whether any expert witnesses will be called, whether they anticipate any preliminary matters and the like. They are also asked to provide information concerning their availability during the time period when the hearing will likely be scheduled.

After reviewing the case management checklist, the HRTO may schedule a case management conference where it feels that doing so is necessary or appropriate to discuss the next steps for dealing with the application. Alternatively, the HRTO may schedule a summary hearing to address discrete issues or preliminary or procedural matters prior to the scheduling of the hearing.[183]

Otherwise, the HRTO will issue a Confirmation of Hearing to the parties, setting out the dates, start times and location of the hearing. The HRTO has stated that it will endeavour to schedule hearings such that they begin approximately four to five months after the mediation date or, where no mediation is held, approximately four to five months after the expiry of the timeframe for filing a Reply.[184]

As in the case of mediations, once hearing dates are set the HRTO will consider requests to reschedule hearing dates for legitimate reasons, but not for reasons of convenience. Where a party is unavailable for some or all of the

---

180 There is a process for dealing with failure to comply with settlement agreements: see the Code, s. 45.9(3) and the HRTO Rules of Procedure, rule 24.

181 Code, s. 45.9(1).

182 See Human Rights Tribunal of Ontario, *op. cit.*, footnote 173, at p. 2.

183 *Ibid.*

184 *Ibid.*, at p. 2. It remains to be seen whether or not the HRTO will be able to continue to meet these scheduling goals, as they are already dealing with a very large volume of applications.

hearing dates, that party must contact the Registrar within five days of receiving the Confirmation of Hearing and provide five alternative dates on which the party is available within 16 to 22 weeks from the date of the Confirmation of Hearing. The HRTO will contact the other parties and attempt to obtain mutually agreeable dates. In instances where the parties are unable to agree on dates, the HRTO will set dates without agreement of the parties.[185]

PRE-HEARING DISCLOSURE

Previously in this chapter, we discussed the requirement to list "important" documents and the names of potential witnesses in the Application and Response forms. As the commencement of the hearing approaches, the parties are subject to more extensive disclosure obligations. The timing of these obligations is generally tied to the date of the Confirmation of Hearing, unless some other timetable for disclosure has been ordered by the HRTO.

Disclosure of Documents

There are two stages to the parties' documentary disclosure obligations. The first stage involves disclosure of all arguably relevant documents in a party's possession. The second stage involves disclosure of documents that the party actually intends to rely on at the hearing.

"Arguably Relevant" Documents

The parties' first set of disclosure obligations involves the listing of all arguably relevant documents and the exchange of copies of all such documents that are not privileged. "Arguable relevance" is a very broad concept that encompasses all documents that tend to prove (or disprove) some fact in issue in the proceeding.

The parties are expected to disclose all such documents that are in their possession, even when they are unfavourable and will not be relied on at the hearing. Requiring full disclosure well in advance of the hearing is seen to be beneficial for a number of reasons. It ensures the parties have a common understanding of the documentary evidence that may be relevant to the case. It assists the parties to better understand the merits of their respective positions and consider whether they should revisit the possibility of settlement or proceed with the hearing. It avoids surprises during the hearing and the resulting delays in the hearing process. It also increases the likelihood that all of the relevant evidence will be brought before the HRTO, thereby enhancing the HRTO's ability to make accurate findings of fact.

---

[185] *Ibid.*, at p. 2. Rule 3.4 allows the HRTO to schedule hearing dates with or without consultation with the parties, as the HRTO considers appropriate: HRTO Rules of Procedure, rule 3.4.

The only arguably relevant documents that do not have to be disclosed are documents for which privilege is claimed.[186] These documents must still be listed and the basis for the privilege claimed explained, so that the other party can consider whether or not there is any reason to dispute the privilege claim.[187]

The specific requirements in the Rules of Procedure are as follows. Not later than 21 days after the HRTO sends a Confirmation of Hearing to the parties, each party must deliver the following material to every other party:[188]

a) a list of all arguably relevant documents in their possession. Where a privilege is claimed over any document the party must describe the nature of the document and the reason for making the claim; and,
b) a copy of each document contained on the list, excluding any documents for which privilege is claimed.

In addition to delivering this material to the other parties, each party must file one or more Statement(s) of Delivery (Form 23) with the HRTO, confirming that delivery has taken place.[189] It is not necessary to file the list of documents or the copies thereof with the HRTO at this point.

Documents on Which a Party Intends to Rely

The parties' second set of disclosure obligations involves disclosure of those documents on which each party actually intends to rely at the hearing. These disclosure obligations must be completed not later than 45 days prior to the first scheduled day of the hearing, unless the HRTO orders otherwise.[190]

Each party must deliver to every other party a list of the documents on which the party intends to rely and either a copy of each document on the list or confirmation that each document has already been provided at the first stage of disclosure. A Statement of Delivery must be filed with the HRTO verifying that such delivery has occurred.[191]

In addition, each party must file with the HRTO the list of documents on which it intends to rely and a copy of each document contained on the list.[192]

---

[186] The concept of privilege is explained in Chapter 11, "The Final Appeal".

[187] Where a party wishes to dispute a claim of privilege, it would normally do so by filing a Form 10, "Request for an Order During Proceedings". Ideally, such a dispute would be raised and resolved by the HRTO before the second set of disclosure obligations arise under rules 16.2 and 16.3.

[188] HRTO Rules of Procedure, rule 16.1. The HRTO will not usually extend this deadline, even where the date of the hearing is changed.

[189] *Ibid.*

[190] *Ibid.*, rules 16.2 and 16.3. In some cases, the HRTO (usually in consultation with the parties) will develop a schedule for disclosure of documents that may differ from what the Rules ordinarily require.

[191] *Ibid.*, rule 16.2.

[192] *Ibid.*, rule 16.3.

Confidentiality

Sometimes, parties to human rights proceedings will be concerned that documents disclosed during the process will be shared with others or used for some other purpose. A parent may be concerned that medical documentation about an identified student will become public knowledge or be shared with administrators or teachers who would not ordinarily have access to it. A school board may be concerned that confidential board documents will be shared with other parents, used in parallel litigation, or even shared with the media.

The HRTO has addressed these concerns by providing in the Rules of Procedure that parties and their representatives may not use documents obtained under the Rules for any purpose other than the proceeding before the HRTO.[193] Any breach of this provision is considered unlawful and will be subject to sanctions appropriate to the circumstances of the breach.

Failure to Disclose and Disclosure Disputes

It is very important that a party's pre-hearing disclosure be thorough and complete. The HRTO's Rules state that a party may not rely on or present to the HRTO any document that was not included in the document list, delivered to the other parties or filed with the HRTO, unless the party obtains the HRTO's permission to do so.[194] In the absence of a compelling explanation for the omission, the HRTO's permission may not be forthcoming. Thus, failure to disclose a document prior to the hearing can significantly undermine a party's ability to present its case at the hearing.

Of course, there will be situations where legitimate differences of opinion will arise about the relevance of documents, the validity of a claim of privilege, or the completeness of the disclosure provided. When the parties cannot resolve these issues between themselves, it may be necessary for one party to make a request for an order during proceedings to obtain a ruling from the HRTO clarifying whether or not disclosure is required.[195]

Ideally, disclosure issues should be addressed as early as possible in the process, preferably before the commencement of the hearing. If the issue is raised sufficiently in advance of the hearing, the HRTO may be able to deal with outstanding disclosure disputes early enough to avoid delay of the hearing on the merits.

Disclosure of Witnesses and Witness Statements

At the same time they deliver and file the list of documents they intend to rely on and copies of those documents, the parties are required to deliver and

193 *Ibid.*, rule 3.3.
194 *Ibid.*, rule 16.4.
195 *Ibid.*, rule 19.

file a witness list and witness statements. These latter steps must be completed no later than 45 days prior to the first scheduled day of hearing, unless the HRTO orders otherwise.[196]

The Rules of Procedure state that, prior to the above-noted deadline, each party must deliver a witness list to every other party and file it the HRTO. The witness list must include the name of every witness whom the party intends to present to the HRTO and must also include a brief statement summarizing the witness' expected evidence.[197]

Additional requirements apply to expert witnesses. Expert witnesses are individuals with specialized expertise who are being called to provide an opinion to the HRTO on an issue or issues in dispute. In a human rights proceeding involving a special education issue, expert witnesses might include a medical expert (a general practitioner or specialist treating a student) or educational expert.

The names of any expert witnesses to be called must be included on the witness list.[198] A copy of the expert witness' curriculum vitae must accompany the witness list. In instances where the expert witness has prepared a written report, a copy of that report must accompany the witness list; otherwise, a full summary of the expert witness' proposed evidence must be provided.[199] This additional information will allow the other party to consider whether there is any basis to challenge the witness' expertise or the admissibility of his or her proposed evidence.[200]

The above material must be filed with the HRTO, along with a Statement of Delivery reflecting delivery to each other party.[201] A party who fails to comply with the foregoing requirements with respect to a witness or expert witness may not call that witness at the hearing, unless the party obtains the HRTO's permission to do so.[202] In the absence of a compelling explanation for the omission, the HRTO's permission may not be forthcoming.

THE HEARING

Following the disclosure stage, the next stage in the process is an in-person hearing before the HRTO. The Code requires the HRTO to give the parties an opportunity to make oral submissions before it finally disposes of an application.[203] Accordingly, the HRTO will always hold an in-person hearing

---

196 *Ibid.*, rule 17.1. Again, the HRTO would normally order an alternate schedule after consulting with the parties.
197 *Ibid.*, rules 17.1 and 17.2.
198 *Ibid.*, rule 17.1.
199 *Ibid.*, rule 17.2.
200 The principles applicable to the admissibility of expert evidence are discussed in Chapter 11, "The Final Appeal".
201 HRTO Rules of Procedure, rule 17.1.
202 *Ibid.*, rule 17.4.
203 Code, s. 43(2). See also the HRTO Rules of Procedure, rule 3.5.

to deal with the merits of an application; however, as discussed later in this chapter, the HRTO has a number of tools at its disposal to streamline the hearing process in order to ensure that the hearing takes place as efficiently and expeditiously as possible.

The HRTO's Procedural Powers

The Code requires the HRTO to dispose of applications "by adopting the procedures and practices . . . which, in its opinion, offer the best opportunity for a fair, just and expeditious resolution of the merits of the applications".[204] In furtherance of this statutory mandate, the Code also authorizes the HRTO to make procedural rules that provide for alternatives to traditional adjudicative or adversarial procedures and enable the HRTO to streamline the hearing process as well as ensure that it has the necessary material before it to reach a fair and just resolution of the case.[205]

The Rules of Procedure developed by the HRTO pursuant to this statutory authority expressly authorize the HRTO to determine its own procedures and use procedures other than traditional adjudicative or adversarial procedures.[206] The Rules also empower the HRTO to exercise a number of unique procedural powers in order to provide for the fair, just and expeditious resolution of any application.[207] For example, the HRTO may:[208]

> g) determine and direct the order in which issues in a proceeding, including issues considered by a party or the parties to be preliminary, will be considered and determined;
> h) define and narrow the issues in order to decide an Application;
> i) make or cause to be made an examination of records or other inquiries, as it considers necessary;
> j) determine and direct the order in which evidence will be presented;
> k) on the request of a party, direct another party to adduce evidence or produce a witness when that person is reasonably within that party's control;
> l) permit a party to give a narrative before questioning commences;
> m) question a witness;
> n) limit the evidence or submissions on any issue;
> o) advise when additional evidence or witnesses may assist the Tribunal;
> p) require a party or other person to produce any document, information or thing and to provide such assistance as is reasonably necessary, including using any data storage, processing or retrieval device or system, to produce the information in any form;
> q) on the request of a party, require another party or other person to provide a report, statement, or oral or affidavit evidence;

[204] Code, s. 40.
[205] *Ibid.*, s. 40.
[206] HRTO Rules of Procedure, rule 1.6.
[207] *Ibid.*, rule 1.7.
[208] These powers may generally be exercised on the request of a party or at the HRTO's own initiative, except where the Rules specifically state that they may only be exercised on the request of a party. See the HRTO Rules of Procedure, rule 1.5.

r) direct that the deponent of an affidavit be cross-examined before the Tribunal or an official examiner.[209]

In addition, the Code contemplates that a party to an application may request the HRTO to appoint a person to conduct an inquiry prior to or during proceedings. The HRTO may grant this request where it is satisfied that:[210]

(a) an inquiry is required in order to obtain evidence;
(b) the evidence obtained may assist in achieving a fair, just and expeditious resolution of the merits of the application; and
(c) it is appropriate to do so in the circumstances.

Where the HRTO grants a request for an inquiry, the person appointed to conduct the inquiry is granted significant investigatory powers. At the end of the inquiry, the person conducting the inquiry is to prepare a report and submit it to the HRTO and the parties.[211] The report itself will not become evidence in the proceeding unless it is formally introduced into evidence, introduced by agreement or the HRTO so directs.[212]

Thus, the HRTO has very significant procedural powers that allow it to take a very active role in determining what evidence is before the Tribunal. At one end of the spectrum, this may involve limiting the material that the parties wish to present. At the other end of the spectrum, it may involve requiring the parties to produce additional material that the HRTO considers would be of assistance in resolving the matter. The extent to which the HRTO will use these powers will depend on the circumstances of individual cases and the decision-maker's procedural preferences.

Pre-Hearing Matters

Adjournments and the Consequences of Non-Attendance

On occasion, as the hearing date approaches, a party may find that it wants or needs to seek an adjournment from the HRTO — that is, an order temporarily postponing the hearing to a future date. The HRTO has stated that its approach to scheduling hearing dates "is designed to give the parties a fair opportunity to find suitable dates" and that it "discourages adjournment requests, and will only grant adjournments in extraordinary circumstances such as illness of a party, witness or representative".[213]

A party seeking an adjournment should contact the Registrar as soon as possible. Where possible, the party should contact the other party or parties

[209] HRTO Rules of Procedure, rule 1.7g) to r).
[210] Code, s. 44. See also the HRTO Rules of Procedure, rule 20.
[211] Code, s. 44(14); See also the HRTO Rules of Procedure, rule 20.6.
[212] HRTO Rules of Procedure, rule 20.7.
[213] Human Rights Tribunal of Ontario, "Information Bulletin: Scheduling of Hearings and Mediations, Rescheduling Requests, and Requests for Adjournments" (Toronto: The Tribunal, 2008), available online at http://www.hrto.ca/hrto/sites/default/files/Resources/IB-Scheduling.pdf.

prior to contacting the Registrar, attempt to obtain consent, and obtain some alternative dates. Those alternative dates must fall within five months of the date of the Confirmation of Hearing. The party making the request should then contact the Registrar, provide the reason for the request and, where applicable, advise the Registrar that the other party has consented and provide the alternative dates that have been agreed upon. The HRTO will not automatically grant the adjournment where all parties consent; consent is merely one factor that the HRTO will consider in deciding whether or not to grant the adjournment.

The Rules impose strict consequences on a party who has been notified of a hearing but fails to attend. In such a case, the HRTO may:[214]

> a) proceed in the party's absence;
> b) determine that the party is not entitled to further notice of the proceedings;
> c) determine that the party is not entitled to present evidence or make submissions to the Tribunal;
> d) decide the Application based solely on the materials before it;
> e) take any other action it considers appropriate.[215]

Accordingly, a party who has made an adjournment request and whose request has been denied by the HRTO should make every effort to attend the hearing on the scheduled date.

Case Assessment Directions

As noted above, the HRTO has considerable flexibility to conduct its proceedings in a manner that will ensure the fair, just and expeditious resolution of human rights applications.[216] In conjunction with this authority, the HRTO may issue a Case Assessment Direction to the parties in any case where it considers it appropriate to do so. The Case Assessment Direction may address any matter that, in the opinion of the HRTO, will facilitate the fair, just and expeditious resolution of the application. Among other things, a Case Assessment Direction may also include directions made pursuant to rules 1.6 and 1.7 (discussed earlier).[217]

Rule 18.1 does not require the HRTO to seek any input from the parties before issuing a Case Assessment Direction. Rule 18.2 states, "At the hearing parties must be prepared to respond to any issues identified in the Case Assessment Direction and to proceed in accordance with the directions set out in the Case Assessment Direction." It is not clear how much latitude a party may have to challenge the content of a Case Assessment Direction; however,

---

214 See the HRTO Rules of Procedure. Where the adjournment request is on short notice, the party making the request must contact the Registrar by telephone or e-mail.

215 HRTO Rules of Procedure, rule 3.13.

216 *Ibid.*, rules 1.1, 1.6 and 1.7.

217 *Ibid.*, rule 18.1.

when a party does wish to challenge some aspect of a Case Management Direction, that party should ensure that it comes prepared to do so at the outset of the hearing.

Summonses

Another issue that will often need to be addressed before the hearing is whether it is necessary to request the HRTO to issue one or more summonses to potential witnesses. A summons to witness is an order of the HRTO that compels a witness to attend the hearing to give oral evidence. The summons may also compel the witness to bring specified documents to the hearing and produce them in evidence. A witness who fails to attend a hearing in accordance with a summons can be subject to arrest, although this rarely happens in practice.

In many cases, a formal summons to witness will not be necessary because a witness will agree to attend the hearing, testify and produce relevant documents in advance of the hearing. In some cases, a party may need to call a witness who is sympathetic to another party or otherwise reluctant to testify on behalf of the party who wishes to call him or her. In such a case, the party intending to call the witness may need to request a summons in order to compel the witness' attendance. In yet other cases, a summons may be required primarily to obtain records relevant to the hearing — for example, records held by a third party, such as police records or bank records, or records that are ordinarily covered by legal or ethical confidentiality requirements, such as medical records or records from a student's Ontario Student Record.

The HRTO has developed a "Summons to Witness" form (Form 24). At the request of a party, the HRTO will provide a signed and sealed version of the form, which may then be filled out by the party.[218] The party seeking to call the witness is then responsible for delivering the summons to the witness.[219] Once the summons has been delivered, the witness is legally required to appear at the hearing.

The HRTO will not engage in any scrutiny of the propriety of the summons at the time it is requested; however, in some cases, there may be grounds to challenge a summons. Where the description of the documents to be produced is vague or overly broad or if the summons would compel testimony or disclosure of documents that are irrelevant or privileged, the summons may be subject to challenge. Where a party or a witness intends to challenge a summons, the issue should be raised with the HRTO as early as possible, either by filing a Form 10, "Request for an Order During Proceedings", or by raising the issue verbally before the HRTO, so that the matter can be addressed without unduly delaying the hearing.

---

[218] HRTO Rules of Procedure, rule 3.1.

[219] *Ibid.*, rule 3.2.

Notice of Constitutional Question

In some cases, a party may wish to raise a constitutional issue in the course of a proceeding before the HRTO. In the special education context, this would usually involve a challenge to the Code or to actions taken by a school board or government body under the *Canadian Charter of Rights and Freedoms*.

A party intending to raise a constitutional issue must file a Notice of Constitutional Question with the HRTO as soon as the circumstances requiring the notice become known and no later than 15 days prior to the date on which the question will be argued before the HRTO.[220] The requirement to provide a Notice of Constitutional Question arises from section 109 of the *Courts of Justice Act*,[221] and the Notice must be in the form required under the Rules of Civil Procedure or a substantially similar form.[222] The Notice must be delivered to the Attorney General of Canada and the Attorney General of Ontario.[223] The purpose of this requirement is to provide the Attorneys General with an opportunity to intervene and make submissions with respect to the constitutional issue.

At the Hearing

Open versus Closed Hearing

Hearings of the HRTO are generally open to the public; however, the HRTO may be asked to make an order to protect the confidentiality of personal or sensitive information. The HRTO has a broad discretion to make such an order when it considers that it is appropriate to do so.[224]

Because the general rule is that hearings are to be open to the public, it can be expected that the HRTO will make the least restrictive order that will adequately protect the confidential information in question. In some cases, the confidential information may permeate the entire proceeding to such a degree that it will be necessary to close the hearing altogether. In other cases, only the testimony of one or a small number of witnesses will be sensitive and it may be sufficient to close the hearing only when those witnesses are testifying. In yet other cases, less restrictive measures — such as excluding a particular person from the room during testimony or referring to a party or witness only by his or her initials in the HRTO's decision — may be sufficient to address the underlying confidentiality concern.

Where a party wishes to request a closed or partially closed hearing, the request should ideally be raised prior to the hearing or particular witness'

220 *Ibid.*, rule 4.1.
221 R.S.O. 1990, c. C.43.
222 Rule 4.11 of the *Rules of Civil Procedure*, R.R.O. 1990, Reg. 194, requires that the Notice be in Form 4F — a form created under the Rules for this purpose.
223 HRTO Rules of Procedure, rule 4.1.
224 *Ibid.*, rules 13.10 and 13.11.

testimony using a Form 10, "Request for an Order During Proceedings". When this is not possible, a request for a fully closed hearing can be raised orally at the outset of the hearing, before the HRTO has commenced hearing any evidence or argument. A request for a hearing to be closed during a specific witness' testimony can be raised orally or using a Form 10 at any time before the HRTO has commenced hearing that witness' testimony.

As discussed earlier, it is unlikely that a closed hearing will be ordered in a case simply because it raises issues pertaining to a child. It is more likely that the HRTO will use initials to protect the identity of any children involved.[225]

Recording of Proceedings

The HRTO does not normally record or transcribe its proceedings.[226] Accordingly, it is customary for the Chair, Vice-Chair or member presiding over the case, as well as the parties, to take their own notes of the proceeding, either longhand or on a computer. It is important to take thorough and detailed notes of everything that occurs during the hearing, as those notes will be invaluable in preparing questions for witnesses and submissions and in verifying what transpired during the hearing should that become an issue at some later stage in the proceeding or at the stage of reconsideration or judicial review.

Mediation/Adjudications

In cases where it considers it appropriate to do so, the HRTO may engage in mediation at the outset of the hearing. This may occur at the parties' request or at the HRTO's initiative. However, if this occurs, the understanding will be that, if the matter cannot be resolved, the "mediator" will continue on to adjudicate the application. The parties will be required to sign an agreement reflecting that understanding before the mediation commences.[227]

Order of Proceedings

Generally speaking, the order of proceedings before the HRTO is quite similar to the order of proceedings before the Special Education Tribunal.[228] The presiding Chair, Vice-Chair or member will typically begin the proceedings with some introductory comments. These comments may include introductions by the participants and a brief overview of the procedures to be followed. The presiding member of the HRTO may also ask whether there

---

225 *C.M. v. York Region District School Board*, 2009 HRTO 735.
226 HRTO Rules of Procedure, rule 3.7.
227 At the time of this writing, the HRTO has released proposed changes to its Rules for consultation that would codify this practice: Human Rights Tribunal of Ontario, *op cit.*, footnote 40.
228 See Chapter 11, "The Final Appeal", for further details.

are any preliminary matters that need to be addressed. Where there are outstanding preliminary matters, it is important to raise them with the HRTO at this point in the process so that the HRTO can determine when and how any such issues will be addressed.

At the outset of the hearing, the parties may be asked to provide an opening statement. Not all HRTO decision-makers request opening statements, but it is advisable to prepare one in case it is requested. Usually, the opening statement will be relatively brief. The purpose of the opening statement is to summarize the party's position, identify the issues in dispute and outline the result being sought. It is typical for the applicant to be asked to provide his or her opening statement first, followed by those of the respondent(s) and any other parties participating in the hearing.

In many cases, the next step will be to deal with any preliminary matters. In some cases, preliminary matters may be dealt with immediately, before any opening statements. Frequently, however, preliminary matters will be dealt with following opening statements. Typically, the party raising a preliminary issue is expected to present its position first and any other parties would then have an opportunity to respond. The HRTO will typically try to deal with such matters as expeditiously as possible, so as to avoid delays in the hearing process.

Following any opening statements and preliminary matters, the HRTO will then proceed to deal with the merits of the case. It is not uncommon for there to be discussion at the outset regarding evidentiary matters. In some cases, the parties may be able to agree on a statement of facts and provide it to the HRTO. Alternatively, it may be possible to admit some documents on agreement — thereby avoiding the need to introduce the documents formally through a witness' testimony — or even to enter a joint book of documents. Any agreements of this kind will assist in streamlining the process and will be welcomed by the HRTO.

Subject to any directions from the Tribunal to the contrary, the applicant will usually be expected to proceed first in presenting his or her evidence. For each witness, the same sequence is followed: the party calling the witness will conduct a "direct examination" or "examination-in-chief" of the witness, then any opposing parties have an opportunity to cross-examine the witness and finally, the party who called the witness will have a limited opportunity to re-examine the witness. The HRTO will also have an opportunity to question each witness and will usually allow the parties to ask further questions arising from its questions. This pattern will be followed for each witness called by the applicant. The respondent and any other parties will then have the opportunity to call their witnesses and the same pattern will be followed for each of their witnesses, until all the witnesses' testimony is complete.[229]

---

[229] For further detail regarding these processes, see Chapter 11, "The Final Appeal".

When the witnesses' testimony is complete, each party will be provided with an opportunity to make a closing argument. Closing argument usually includes a summary of the evidence in support of a party's position, as well as submissions regarding the findings of fact that the HRTO should reach based on the evidence. Closing arguments usually include legal argument regarding how the principles of human rights law apply to the evidence, and submissions concerning the result that the HRTO should reach. Usually, the applicant will present his or her closing argument first, followed by that of the respondent(s) and any other parties. The applicant will have a brief opportunity to reply after the other parties have presented their closing statements.

We have described above the order of proceedings in a "typical" proceeding before the HRTO. As previously discussed, however, the HRTO has considerable flexibility to depart from this "typical" process when it believes that doing so would promote a fair, just and expeditious resolution of the matter.[230] The HRTO can direct the order in which issues will be considered and the order in which evidence will be presented or witnesses called. It can and often will decided to take the lead in questioning the witnesses and will provide the parties with an opportunity to ask supplementary questions after its questioning of a witness is complete. It can limit evidence or submissions on any issue; it can also require a party to call additional evidence. The HRTO's flexibility in determining the procedure to be followed creates some uncertainty concerning how hearings will be conducted from one case to the next. Whatever process is followed, however, the HRTO will be mindful of its obligation to ensure that the parties are provided with a fair hearing and can be expected take steps to mitigate any potential unfairness as a result of its procedural choices.

Evidence

In Chapter 11, "The Final Appeal", we provided an in-depth discussion of the basic rules of evidence that apply in proceedings before the Special Education Tribunal. These same rules apply in proceedings before the HRTO and, therefore, that discussion will not be repeated here.

While the rules of evidence applicable in proceedings before the HRTO are generally the same as those applicable before the Special Education Tribunal, the HRTO's Rules of Procedure expressly authorize it to regulate the evidence presented. It can question witnesses. It can require parties to call witnesses or produce documents they did not intend to call. It can limit the number of witnesses called or limit the scope of their testimony and can determine the order in which witnesses will testify.

It should also be noted that the Code expressly allows the HRTO to draw an adverse inference where a party fails to comply — either in whole or in part — with an order of the HRTO requiring it to produce a document,

[230] See HRTO Rules of Procedure, rule 1.7.

information or a thing or provide assistance to produce the information in any form, provide a statement or oral or affidavit evidence or present evidence or produce witnesses that are reasonably within the party's control.[231] This means that the HRTO can assume that the reason the party did not comply is that the evidence in question would have harmed the party's case. Depending on the circumstances, an adverse inference of this kind can be very damaging.

DECISION AND REMEDIES

The Code expressly states that the HRTO may not finally dispose of an application without providing written reasons for its decision.[232] Consistent with this requirement, the HRTO will always provide written reasons for its decision on the merits of an application. The reasons will usually include a statement of the issue, a review of the evidence, the HRTO's findings of fact, an analysis of how the Code and the applicable case law applies to those facts and, where the HRTO finds that a violation of the Code has occurred, an analysis of the appropriate remedy and the HRTO's order with respect to remedy.

In most cases, when the hearing has concluded, the HRTO will "reserve" its decision — that is, it will not advise the parties of its decision immediately, but will take some time to consider the matter, weigh the evidence, make its decision and prepare its reasons. In some exceptional cases, the HRTO may provide the parties with a "bottom line" decision and then provide its written reasons at a later time. In either case, the HRTO will send the decision and/or reasons to the parties and their representatives.

The HRTO has broad remedial jurisdiction where it finds that a violation of the Code has occurred. The remedies available differ somewhat between individual applications and Commission applications; therefore, these two scenarios have been addressed separately.

Individual Applications

On an individual application under section 34 of the Code — whether filed by a single individual, jointly by two or more individuals or by one individual on behalf of another — the HRTO can order any party to the application to provide any of the following remedies:

- Monetary compensation for loss arising out the infringement, including compensation for injury to dignity, feelings and self-respect.[233] This may include reimbursement of any monies lost or expended as a result of the infringement. For example, in a special education case where an identified student was withdrawn from the board and enrolled in private school, a claim might be made for

[231] Code, s. 43(9).
[232] *Ibid.*, s. 43(2).
[233] *Ibid.*, s. 45.2(1).

tuition fees, and/or accommodation or transportation costs incurred as a result. It may also include damages for injury to dignity, feelings and self-respect and, in more extreme cases, compensation for psychological harm arising out of the infringement.

- Non-monetary restitution for loss arising out of the infringement, including restitution for injury to dignity, feelings and self-respect.[234] "Restitution" is a broad term that generally describes anything it may be equitable to require in order to redress the wrong that has occurred and restore an individual to the position he or she was in before the loss or injury occurred.[235] Restitution can include a variety of different remedies and the appropriate form of restitution will depend on the nature and legal context of the breach. It may include a wide range of non-monetary remedies, such as requiring the school board to place a student in a particular setting or to reverse a decision that has been successfully challenged.
- An order directing any party to do anything that, in the opinion of the HRTO, the person ought to do to promote compliance with the Code. Such an order can relate to future practices and can also be made by the HRTO even if it has not been requested by one of the parties.[236] This provision covers what are often referred to as "public interest" remedies. These are remedies designed to promote the public interest in preventing future discrimination and ensuring compliance with the Code rather than to redress specific losses incurred by the applicant. A public interest remedy may include a direction to an organizational or individual respondent to do (or not do) something with respect to future practices.[237] An example might be an order requiring a school board to provide certain training to its staff or amend a policy or develop an implementation plan for providing enhanced programs, services or accommodations in the future.

Commission Applications

In the case of a Commission application, the only order that the HRTO can make is a public interest order — that is, an order directing a party to do anything that, in the opinion of the HRTO, the party ought to do to promote compliance with the Code.[238] This is not surprising when one considers that a Commission application is only permitted under the Code where it is in the public interest to make such an application and a public interest remedy would

---

234 *Ibid.*
235 See, for example, *Fuller v. Daoud* (2001), 40 C.H.R.R. D/306 (Ont. Bd. Inq.).
236 Code, s. 45.2(1).
237 *Ibid.*, s. 45.2(2).
238 *Ibid.*, s. 45.3.

provide an appropriate remedy.[239] As in the case of individual applications, a public interest remedy ordered in the context of a Commission application may include a direction to an organizational or individual respondent to do (or not do) specific things with respect to future practices.[240]

Referral to the Commission

In addition to the foregoing, the HRTO has the authority to refer matters arising out of a proceeding to the commission where the HRTO is of the view that they are matters of public interest or are otherwise of interest to the commission.[241] This is potentially significant, as the commission has a broad authority to conduct inquiries where it believes it is in the public interest to do so.[242] As of the date of this writing, the HRTO has yet to exercise this authority and it is unclear whether — or in what circumstances — it would do so.

Legal Costs

One area that is currently the subject of some controversy concerns the HRTO's authority to award one party to reimburse the other for legal costs incurred in relation to the proceedings. This issue is of particular interest to respondents, for while applicants have access to free legal representation through the HRLSC, both individual and organizational respondents must generally bear their own legal costs.

Prior to the 2008 amendments to the Code, the HRTO had a very limited authority to award costs. It could only order the Ontario Human Rights Commission to pay a respondent's costs and then only where the HRTO dismissed the complaint and found that the complaint was either trivial, frivolous, vexatious or made in bad faith or had otherwise caused undue hardship to the respondent.[243] Since the commission had carriage of the complaint prior to the amendments,[244] it followed that the commission should be held responsible to pay the respondent's costs where the commission had pursued a trivial, frivolous, vexatious or bad faith complaint to hearing or otherwise caused undue hardship to the respondents.

---

239 *Ibid.*, s. 35(1).

240 *Ibid.*, s. 35(2).

241 *Ibid.*, s. 45.4.

242 *Ibid.*, s. 31.

243 Section 41(4) of the pre-amendment version of the Code dealt with the HRTO's authority to award costs.

244 Prior to the amendments, the commission had the authority to decline to deal with a complaint that was trivial, frivolous, vexatious or made in bad faith under s. 34(1)(*b*). In addition, under s. 36, the commission had a discretion as to whether a complaint would be referred to the HRTO for a hearing and was only to refer a complaint to the HRTO where "the procedure is appropriate and the evidence warrants an inquiry".

The current version of the Code is silent on the issue of costs. The silence of the legislation has generated some controversy concerning whether or not the HRTO has the authority under the remedial provisions described above to order a party to reimburse another for some or all of its legal costs. Early on, however, in a case dealing with a matter referred to the HRTO by the commission prior to the legislative changes, but heard by the HRTO at a time when its new powers were in effect, the HRTO ruled that it has no jurisdiction to award costs.[245] It remains to be seen whether this case will be the "last word" on the issue of the HRTO's authority to award costs or whether there will be any further litigation of this issue in the future.

RECONSIDERATION

The final step in any proceeding before the HRTO is reconsideration. A party who is dissatisfied with a decision of the HRTO may seek reconsideration of the HRTO's decision.[246] Indeed, doing so is generally a prerequisite to challenging the HRTO's decision by way of an application for judicial review.[247] In addition to dealing with a reconsideration request from a party, the HRTO may also reconsider one of its decisions on its own initiative.[248]

Request for Reconsideration by a Party

A party seeking reconsideration of a decision of the HRTO must deliver and file Form 20, "Request for Reconsideration", within 30 days of the date of the decision. The Request for Reconsideration must include the reasons for the request, including the basis on which the HRTO is asked to grant the request, submissions in support of the request and the remedy or relief sought.[249]

A party to whom a Request for Reconsideration is delivered is not required to file a Response unless the HRTO directs that a Response is to be filed. Where such a direction is made, the responding party must file Form 21, "Response to Request for Reconsideration". The Response to Request for Reconsideration must include complete written submissions in support of the position.[250] The HRTO is not permitted to grant a Request for Reconsideration without giving the parties an opportunity to make submissions.[251]

---

245 *Dunn v. United Transportation Union, Local 104*, 2008 HRTO 405.

246 Code, s. 45.7(1) and (2). As of the date of this writing, the HRTO has released proposed changes to the Rules respecting requests for reconsideration for consultation: Human Rights Tribunal of Ontario, *op cit.*, footnote 40.

247 See Chapter 13, "Review by the Courts".

248 Code, s. 45.7 (2).

249 HRTO Rules of Procedure, rules 26.1 and 26.2.

250 *Ibid.*, rule 26.4.

251 *Ibid.*, rule 26.6.

In most cases, requests for reconsideration will be dealt with exclusively by way of written submissions.[252] The test for granting reconsideration is a difficult test to meet. The Rules state that the HRTO should *not* to grant reconsideration *unless* it is satisfied that one or more of the following four criteria have been met:[253]

a) there are new facts or evidence that could potentially be determinative of the case and that could not reasonably have been obtained earlier; or
b) the party seeking reconsideration was entitled to but, through no fault of its own, did not receive notice of the proceeding or a hearing; or
c) the decision or order which is the subject of the reconsideration request is in conflict with established jurisprudence or Tribunal procedure and the proposed reconsideration involves a matter of general or public importance; or
d) other factors exist that, in the opinion of the Tribunal, outweigh the public interest in the finality of Tribunal decisions.

Where the HRTO decides that it is appropriate to reconsider its decision, it may do one of two things: It may make a decision on the substance of the matter without requesting further submissions from the parties; alternatively, it may determine a procedure for rehearing all or part of the matter.[254]

The HRTO has issued a "Practice Direction on Reconsideration" to guide applicants and respondents through the reconsideration process.[255] This practice direction should be consulted when dealing with an Application for Reconsideration.

Reconsideration at the HRTO's Initiative

As noted, the HRTO also has authority to reconsider one of its decisions on its own initiative, "where it considers it appropriate and advisable to do so". Where the HRTO takes this step, it must determine a procedure for rehearing the matter that will provide the parties with an opportunity to make submissions.[256]

---

252 *Ibid.*, rule 26.7. The HRTO has discretion under rule 26.7 to adopt a procedure other than written submissions where it considers it appropriate to do so.
253 *Ibid.*, rule 26.5.
254 *Ibid.*, rule 26.8.
255 The Human Rights Tribunal of Ontario, "Practice Direction on Reconsideration" (Toronto: The Tribunal, 2008), available online at http://www.hrto.ca/hrto/?q=en/node/56.
256 HRTO Rules of Procedure, rules 26.9 and 26.10.

13

Review by the Courts

INTRODUCTION

There is a limited range of circumstances in which a party to proceedings before a tribunal — *e.g.* a school board, parent or guardian, or student — dealing with a special education issue who is dissatisfied with the procedure followed or the decision reached may apply to the courts for review of the tribunal's decision.[1] These proceedings are referred to as judicial review proceedings.

In this chapter, we discuss both the procedures for initiating judicial review proceedings and the grounds for judicial review that are available. The discussion focuses primarily on judicial review of the Special Education Tribunal (the "Tribunal"); however, in light of the frequency with which special education issues are now arising in human rights proceedings, we have also included a few brief comments on judicial review of the Human Rights Tribunal of Ontario (the "HRTO").

REVIEW OF IPRC AND SEAB DECISIONS

In most cases, the courts will refuse to review the decisions of an Identification, Placement and Review Committee ("IPRC") or a Special Education Appeal Board ("SEAB"). The *Education Act*[2] and O. Reg. 181/98[3] provide for broad rights of appeal from the IPRC to the SEAB and from the SEAB to the Tribunal. These broad appeal rights provide an opportunity for review and correction of any procedural or substantive errors that may have occurred at an earlier level. As a matter of general principle, the courts will almost always conclude that judicial review proceedings are premature until the party seeking the review has exhausted any statutory appeal rights that are available.[4] Accordingly, judicial review proceedings usually cannot be

1 See also Chapter 11, "The Final Appeal".
2 R.S.O. 1990, c. E.2.
3 *Identification and Placement of Exceptional Pupils.*
4 *Harelkin v. University of Regina* (1979), 96 D.L.R. (3d) 14, [1979] 2 S.C.R. 561.

commenced until the case has proceeded to the Special Education Tribunal and the Tribunal has issued its decision.

It is possible that a case could arise in which the errors occurring at the IPRC or SEAB level were so fundamental to the Tribunal's jurisdiction or of such a serious nature that appeal rights would not provide an adequate remedy — for example, in a case where the IPRC refused to allow the parents to participate or the SEAB held a hearing without notice to the parents, or where there was a reasonable apprehension of bias at the IPRC or at the SEAB level, a court might be persuaded to deal with the judicial review without requiring the matter to proceed to the Tribunal. Nevertheless, such cases will be extremely rare and, more often, the parties will be required to exhaust their internal remedies before seeking the assistance of the courts.

THE PROCEDURE FOR JUDICIAL REVIEW

Once the Tribunal has issued its decision, if one of the parties believes that the Tribunal has committed a procedural or substantive error, that party could apply for judicial review of the Tribunal's decision.

In this chapter, we discuss the procedural rules that apply to judicial review proceedings in Ontario. The grounds for judicial review are discussed later in this chapter.

Commencing an Application for Judicial Review

In Ontario, judicial review proceedings are generally dealt with by the Divisional Court of the Superior Court of Justice.[5] The Divisional Court is a specialized branch of the Superior Court, which usually sits in panels comprised of three Superior Court judges.[6]

Judicial review proceedings are commenced by filing a legal document called a Notice of Application for Judicial Review with the Divisional Court.[7] After it has been filed, the Notice of Application must be served on all other parties to the judicial review proceedings.[8] Generally, the parties to the judicial

---

5 *Judicial Review Procedure Act*, R.S.O. 1990, c. J.1 ("*JRPA*"), s. 6(1).

6 *Courts of Justice Act*, R.S.O. 1990, c. C.43 ("*CJA*"), s. 21(1). Section 6(2) of the *JRPA* permits judicial review by a single judge of the Superior Court of Justice in cases involving a high degree of urgency. In order to bring an application under s. 6(2), the party seeking to do so must persuade the judge that "the case is one of urgency and that the delay required for an application to the Divisional Court is likely to involve a failure of justice". This is a very strict test, which is rigorously enforced by the judiciary, even where both parties have consented to a hearing before a single judge. As a result, judicial review proceedings before a single judge of the Superior Court are available only in exceptional circumstances.

7 *JRPA*, ss. 2 and 6(1); *Rules of Civil Procedure*, R.R.O. 1990, Reg. 194, rule 68.01.

8 *Rules of Civil Procedure*, rule 38.06.

review proceedings will be the same parties who participated in the proceedings before the Special Education Tribunal.[9]

The *Judicial Review Procedure Act* ("*JRPA*") contemplates that, in certain cases, the tribunal under review may participate in judicial review proceedings.[10] However, the courts have placed strict limits on the role an administrative tribunal may play in judicial review proceedings challenging its own decisions[11] and generally discourage tribunals from participating in such proceedings.[12]

---

9 See Chapter 11, "The Final Appeal".

10 *JRPA*, s. 9(2).

11 The leading case concerning the extent of an administrative tribunal's role in judicial review proceedings challenging its own decisions is *Northwestern Utilities Ltd. v. Edmonton (City)* (1978), 89 D.L.R. (3d) 161, [1979] 1 S.C.R. 684. In the *Northwestern Utilities* decision, the Supreme Court of Canada emphasized that an administrative tribunal should not participate as a party in a proceeding in which one of its own decisions is being challenged. Rather, the tribunal's role in such a proceeding should be limited to intervention as an *amicus curiae* ("friend of the court") and even then, should be very narrowly circumscribed. This approach is designed to protect the real and perceived impartiality of the tribunal's decision making. Mr. Justice Estey stated, at pp. 178-9 D.L.R.:

> . . . active and even aggressive participation [in judicial review proceedings] can have no other effect than to discredit the impartiality of an administrative tribunal either in the case where the matter is referred back to it, or in future proceedings involving similar interests and issues or the same parties. The Board is given a clear opportunity to make its point in its reasons for its decision, and it abuses one's notion of propriety to countenance its participation as a full-fledged litigant in this Court, in complete adversarial confrontation with one of the principals in the contest before the Board itself in the first instance.
>
> It has been the policy in this Court to limit the role of an administrative tribunal whose decision is at issue before the court, even where the right to appear is given by statute, to an explanatory role with reference to the record before the Board and to the making of representations relating to jurisdiction: [citations omitted].
>
> . . . . .
>
> Where the parent or authorizing statute is silent as to the role or status of the tribunal in appeal or review proceedings, this Court has confined the tribunal strictly to the issue of its jurisdiction to make the order in question: [citations omitted]. Arguably, the court relaxed these requirements somewhat in *C.A.I.M.A.W., Local 14 v. Paccar of Canada Ltd.* (1989), 62 D.L.R. (4th) 437, [1989] 2 S.C.R. 983, where the Supreme Court confirmed that a tribunal has standing to explain the record, to show that it had jurisdiction to embark on the inquiry and to show that it had not lost jurisdiction in the course of interpreting its powers.

12 For example, in *Great Atlantic & Pacific Co. of Canada Ltd. v. Ontario (Human Rights Commission)* (1993), 109 D.L.R. (4th) 214, 13 O.R. (3d) 82 (Div. Ct.), the court expressed its disquiet with the decision-maker's request to participate in the judicial review proceedings arising from her decision. Due to the exceptional circumstances of the case, which included allegations of personal bias against the decision-maker, the court permitted her to participate; however, when the bias

Despite these restrictions, it is common practice to serve the Notice of Application on the tribunal as well as the parties. This ensures that the tribunal is aware of the proceedings and has an opportunity to assert any participatory rights that it may be entitled to exercise. In addition, when the tribunal is served with the Notice of Application, it is required to file the record of proceedings (discussed further later on in this chapter) with the Divisional Court.[13] This step may be important in ensuring that the appropriate material is before the court. Thus, in cases involving judicial review of the Special Education Tribunal, the Notice of Application should usually be served upon the Tribunal as well as the parties.

The party filing the Notice of Application for Judicial Review must also serve a copy of it on the Attorney General for Ontario.[14] The Attorney General has an institutional interest in overseeing administrative tribunals in the province, including the Special Education Tribunal. As such, the Attorney General has a right to intervene in any judicial review proceeding, if he or she chooses to do so. In practice, the Attorney General will rarely become involved unless the issues in dispute have a public aspect that transcends the purely private interests of the parties, such as an important issue of legislative policy or tribunal governance or a constitutional issue, such as an issue under the *Canadian Charter of Rights and Freedoms*.[15]

Anyone — including the tribunal or the Attorney General — who is served with a Notice of Application for Judicial Review and wishes to defend against the application must file a legal document called a Notice of Appearance.[16] The Notice of Appearance informs the Divisional Court that the person filing it wishes to be notified of further steps in the proceeding and to participate in the hearing.

The Divisional Court charges a fee both for commencing and for responding to a Notice of Application for Judicial Review. These fees are subject to change from time to time. As of the date of this writing, the filing fee for a Notice of Application for Judicial Review was $181 and the filing fee for a Notice of Appearance was $102.[17]

Constitutional Issues

When the Notice of Application for Judicial Review raises a constitutional issue, such as an issue concerning the constitutional validity of legislation or an

---

objection was ultimately upheld, the decision-maker was held jointly and severally liable for costs.

13 *JRPA*, s. 10.

14 *JRPA*, s. 9(4).

15 For a further discussion of the Attorney General's role in Charter and other constitutional cases, see the discussion later in this chapter under the heading "Constitutional Issues".

16 *Rules of Civil Procedure*, rule 38.07.

17 *Superior Court of Justice and Court of Appeal — Fees*, O. Reg. 293/92.

issue under the Charter, the party raising the issue must serve a Notice of Constitutional Question on the other parties and on the Attorney General of Canada and the Attorney General of Ontario.[18] Both Attorneys General have a discretion as to whether or not to intervene in the proceeding. One or both Attorneys General are likely to intervene in any case involving an important constitutional issue.[19] Where they do intervene, they have full rights to adduce evidence and make submissions concerning the constitutional question.[20]

The Material Before the Court

The starting point for the judicial review proceedings is the record of proceedings before the Special Education Tribunal. Where a Notice of Application for Judicial Review is served on the Tribunal, the Tribunal is required to file the record of proceedings with the Divisional Court.[21] In most cases, the record will consist of the following:

- the notice of appeal to the Special Education Tribunal;
- the IPRC and SEAB decisions appealed to the Tribunal;
- any documentary evidence submitted to the Tribunal, which will usually include any documents that were part of the record before the IPRC and/or the SEAB;
- a transcript of the oral evidence before the Tribunal, if one has been prepared; and
- the written decision and reasons of the Tribunal.[22]

Sworn affidavit evidence will sometimes be put before the Divisional Court on an application for judicial review to identify and explain the record. Affidavit evidence may also be submitted to supplement the record in exceptional cases. Generally, supplementary affidavit evidence is only permissible to show a breach of procedural fairness (discussed further below)

---

[18] *CJA*, s. 109.

[19] For example, the Attorney General for Ontario — as well as the Attorneys General for Quebec and British Columbia — intervened in the ground-breaking decision, *Eaton v. Brant County Board of Education* (1997), 142 D.L.R. (4th) 385, [1997] 1 S.C.R. 241, a case involving judicial review of the Special Education Tribunal, because of the important issues raised concerning the application of s. 15 of the Charter. Attorneys General from provinces other than Ontario are more likely to intervene at the Supreme Court of Canada when the decision is expected to have an impact in their own provinces.

[20] *CJA*, s. 109(4).

[21] *JRPA*, s. 10.

[22] See the *Statutory Powers Procedure Act*, R.S.O. 1990, c. S.22, s. 136(1), s. 20. Generally speaking, in the absence of a statutory requirement to do so, a tribunal is not required to prepare a transcript of its proceedings: see, for example, *C.U.P.E., Local 301 v. Montreal (City)* (1997), 144 D.L.R. (4th) 577, [1997] 1 S.C.R. 793; however, where the tribunal does so, the transcript may form part of the record of proceedings.

or to show that there was a complete absence of evidence on a point that was essential to the decision.[23]

The documentation on which each party wishes to rely in judicial review proceedings — including both the record of proceedings and any affidavit evidence — must be served on the other parties and filed with the Divisional Court well in advance of the hearing.[24]

Prior to the hearing, each party will also be required to prepare written legal argument, known as a factum. The factum must be served on all other parties and filed with the Divisional Court in advance of the hearing.[25]

The Hearing

The hearing before the Divisional Court will be conducted on the basis of the documentary material filed by the parties. This material will include any affidavits that have been filed. It is very rare for any oral evidence to be presented.

At the hearing, each party will be expected to present an oral argument setting out the basis for its position. The party seeking judicial review will present its oral argument first. The responding party or parties will then present its oral argument. The party seeking judicial review will then have an opportunity to reply to any new matters raised for the first time during the argument by the responding party.

Judicial review proceedings are formal legal proceedings. The parties must follow the procedural steps required under the *Rules of Civil Procedure*. The legal principles involved are reasonably complex. As a result, the parties will usually find that it is very much in their interest to be represented by legal counsel familiar with administrative law principles.

The Court's Decision

In many cases, the Divisional Court will decide the case on the day of the hearing and issue a brief decision called an "endorsement". An endorsement sets out the court's "bottom-line" decision, but generally includes no reasons or only very brief reasons.

In other cases, the Divisional Court will "reserve" its decision — that is, it will not issue its decision immediately but will take time to prepare a full judgment with written reasons and will then provide the judgment to the parties. Where the Divisional Court reserves its decision, it can take anywhere from a few days to many months before its judgment is released.

---

23 See, for example, *Keeprite Products Ltd. v. Keeprite Workers' Independent Union* (1980), 114 D.L.R. (3d) 162, 29 O.R. (2d) 513 (C.A.), leave to appeal to S.C.C. refused 35 N.R. 85*n*; *Securior Investigations and Security Ltd. v. Ontario (Labour Relations Board)* (1985), 18 D.L.R. (4th) 151, 50 O.R. (2d) 570 (Div. Ct.).

24 *Rules of Civil Procedure*, rule 68.04.

25 *Ibid.*

To date, few judicial review applications in special education matters have reached the Divisional Court; however, one can expect that the court would likely reserve its decisions in many of these cases due to the complexity, sensitivity and importance of the issues involved.

Reimbursement for Legal Costs

The Divisional Court's usual practice is to award the "costs" of the judicial review proceeding to the successful party. These "costs" usually will not constitute full compensation for the expenses associated with the litigation; rather, the court will often fix costs at the hearing based on written material submitted by the parties. The size of the costs award will depend on a number of factors, including the length of the hearing as well as the complexity and importance of the issues raised.[26] Occasionally, the court may also consider the relative ability of the parties to pay and whether or not it was reasonable for the applicant to seek judicial review.

Further Appeal Rights

A party who is dissatisfied with the Divisional Court's decision may seek leave (or permission) to appeal the decision to the Ontario Court of Appeal.[27] Where the Court of Appeal grants leave and hears the case, a further level of appeal is possible — again with leave — to the Supreme Court of Canada.[28]

THE GROUNDS FOR JUDICIAL REVIEW OF SPECIAL EDUCATION TRIBUNAL DECISIONS

There are two broad categories of grounds for judicial review of the Special Education Tribunal's decisions. First, the Tribunal's decision can be judicially reviewed on the basis that the Tribunal committed a breach of procedural fairness. Second, a court may consider whether or not the Tribunal had the legal power or jurisdiction to make the decision in question and, if so, whether its reasoning or the conclusions it reached should be judicially reviewed.

Within each of these broad categories, a number of separate grounds for judicial review can be identified. It is to a discussion of these grounds of judicial review that we now turn.

Procedural Fairness

The first general category of judicial review that may be available is a challenge to the procedures or process followed by the Special Education

---

26 *Rules of Civil Procedure*, rule 57.
27 *CJA*, s. 6(1)(*a*); *Rules of Civil Procedure*, rule 61.
28 *Supreme Court Act*, R.S.C. 1985, c. S-26, s. 40(1).

Tribunal — or, in rare cases, an IPRC or SEAB — in the course of reaching its decision. That is, a party may seek judicial review of an interim or final decision of the Tribunal on the basis that the Tribunal did not comply with the rules of procedural fairness.

Standard of Review of Procedural Issues

When reviewing the procedures followed by an administrative tribunal such as the Special Education Tribunal, the courts will show little deference to the tribunal.[29] The courts will give some deference to the tribunal's own choice of procedures when considering the extent of the procedural safeguards that are required in order to provide procedural fairness to the parties.[30] They will also give some deference to the procedural rulings of a tribunal with statutory authority to control its own processes.[31] Ultimately, however, the tribunal's decision could be overturned if, in the court's view, the parties were not treated fairly during the proceedings.[32]

Procedural Fairness: General Principles

Every administrative tribunal in Ontario has a duty to treat the parties that come before it in a procedurally fair manner.[33] This is often referred to as

---

29 See, for example, *C.U.P.E. v. Ontario (Minister of Labour)* (2003), 226 D.L.R. (4th) 193, [2003] 1 S.C.R. 539, where the Supreme Court held that questions of procedural fairness are questions for the courts to resolve and do not attract judicial deference.

30 In *Baker v. Canada (Minister of Citizenship and Immigration)* (1999), 174 D.L.R. (4th) 193, [1999] 2 S.C.R. 817, at paras. 21-28, the Supreme Court said that the tribunal's own procedural choices was one factor to be considered in determining the level of procedural fairness required, but it was a factor that should be given "important weight".

31 The Special Education Tribunal has the statutory authority to control its own processes, pursuant to s. 25.0.1 of the *SPPA*, and has referenced this authority in rule 2.3 of its Rules of Procedure, available online at http://www.oset-tedo.ca/eng/pdfs/rules.pdf. In *VIA Rail Canada Inc. v. Canada (Transportation Agency)* (2007), 279 D.L.R. (4th) 1 at p. 6, [2007] 1 S.C.R. 650 *sub nom. Council of Canadians with Disabilities v. VIA Rail Canada Inc.*, the court noted that procedural rulings of a tribunal with authority to control its own processes are entitled to "considerable deference".

32 See Ian R. Dick, "Procedural Choices and Natural Justice (A Distinction Without a Deference)", in Michael H. Morris and Andrew Pinto, *The 3rd Annual National Forum Administrative Law and Practice* (Toronto: Osgoode Professional Development, September 2007). The author discusses some of apparently contradictory Supreme Court of Canada and Ontario Court of Appeal decisions dealing with the scope of review of the procedural choices and procedural rulings of a tribunal with authority to control its own processes. It is hoped that some clarification will be forthcoming from the Supreme Court in due course.

33 *Nicholson v. Haldimand-Norfolk (Region) Board of Police Commissioners* (1978), 88 D.L.R. (3d) 671, [1979] 1 S.C.R. 311.

the "duty of fairness". The content of the duty of fairness varies from tribunal to tribunal, depending on the interplay among a number of factors. The relevant factors include the following:

- *The nature of the decision being made and the process followed in making it*: The more adversarial and formal the proceeding, and the closer the process resembles that of a court of law, the higher the standards of procedural fairness that will be applied.
- *The nature of the statutory scheme*: The statutory scheme will often contain provisions that signal the degree of deference intended by the Legislature. For example, a higher standard of procedural fairness may be imposed where the legislation states that the tribunal's decision is a final decision than where a full appeal is available under the statute.
- *The importance of the decision for the individuals involved*: The greater the impact of the decision on individual rights, the higher the standard of procedural fairness that will be required.
- *The legitimate expectations of the parties*: Where the tribunal has published rules or guidelines establishing the procedures it will follow or has otherwise undertaken to follow particular procedures, the parties will be entitled to expect that those procedures will be followed.
- *The choices of procedure made by the tribunal itself*: The tribunal will generally be accorded some leeway to establish its own procedures, in light of its expertise and institutional constraints.[34]

The Special Education Tribunal

Applying the above principles to the Special Education Tribunal, it can be expected that a high standard of procedural fairness will be required. The Tribunal holds full, adversarial, court-like hearings, involving examination and cross-examination of witnesses and legal argument. Section 57(5) of the *Education Act* provides that its decisions are "final and binding on the parties to the decision". Proceedings before the Special Education Tribunal can have a considerable impact on the parties involved — particularly the student whose educational future and legal right to appropriate special education programs and services will be at stake. Accordingly, high standards of fairness will be imposed on the Tribunal. The Tribunal has established its own Rules of Procedure and, while the courts may pay some deference to those Rules and the Tribunal's application of those Rules in individual cases, they will supervise the Tribunal's procedures to ensure that the Tribunal complies with its own Rules and provides the parties with a fair process.

[34] These factors were set out in *Baker v. Canada (Minister of Citizenship and Immigration)*, *supra*, footnote 30, at paras. 21-28.

The Statutory Powers Procedure Act

In the previous section, we noted that the content of the duty of fairness varies from tribunal to tribunal. In Ontario, the issue is simplified somewhat by the enactment of the *Statutory Powers Procedure Act*[35] ("*SPPA*"). The Special Education Tribunal is covered by the *SPPA* and must comply with its terms.[36]

The *SPPA* was initially enacted as a uniform code of minimum procedural rules to be followed by tribunals covered by the statute. As a result of successive amendments over the years, the *SPPA* now functions more like a template that a tribunal can use to develop procedural rules appropriate to its mandate. The statute still provides a uniform set of procedural rules, but tribunals now have the flexibility to "opt in" to many of those rules by incorporating them into their own procedural rules.

The Special Education Tribunal has made its own Rules of Procedure that set out important procedural requirements in a number of areas, including the following:

- who is entitled to be a party to the hearing;
- what type of hearing should be held;
- whether the hearing should be open or closed to the public;
- how much advance notice of the hearing must be given;
- who should receive the notice;
- what information should be included in the notice;
- the right to representation at the hearing;
- the availability of mediation;
- what steps the Tribunal can take before the hearing to facilitate an effective, expeditious and accessible hearing process;
- what pre-hearing disclosure is required and at what stages of the process;
- the presentation and admissibility of evidence;
- what information must be included in the Tribunal's decision;
- whether reasons for decision must be given; and
- what powers the Tribunal has to control its processes and prevent abuse of process.

---

35 R.S.O. 1990, c. S.22.

36 By virtue of s. 3(1), the *SPPA* applies to "a proceeding by a tribunal in the exercise of a statutory power of decision conferred by or under an Act of the Legislature, where the tribunal is required by or under such Act or otherwise by law to hold or to afford to the parties to the proceeding an opportunity for a hearing before making a decision". Section 57(3) of the *Education Act* provides for an appeal of an identification or placement to the Special Education Tribunal and specifically states that the Tribunal must hold a hearing in respect of the identification or placement. Thus, the Tribunal is clearly covered by the *SPPA*.

Where the Special Education Tribunal has failed to comply with the procedural requirements set out in its own Rules of Procedure, the Divisional Court may set aside the Tribunal's decision on judicial review. Although a matter of some debate in legal circles, the prevailing view seems to be that a tribunal's decision may be set aside on procedural grounds, even where there is no positive proof that the procedural irregularity caused actual prejudice to the party who commenced the judicial review proceedings.[37]

Common Law Rules of Procedural Fairness

In addition to the procedural rules set out in the *SPPA* and their own procedural rules, administrative tribunals such as the Special Education Tribunal are also subject to myriad "common law"— that is, court-made — rules of procedural fairness. To some extent, these common law rules overlap with the procedural requirements set out in the *SPPA* and the tribunal's own procedural rules; however, the common law rules may also cover procedural issues that are not specifically addressed in the statute or the tribunal's rules.

A full discussion of the common law rules of procedural fairness is beyond the scope of this book; however, the rules can be divided into the following two broad categories:

- *The right to be heard*: A party affected by the decision of a tribunal is entitled to adequate notice of the case that must be met and a full and fair opportunity to respond. The *SPPA* and the Tribunal's Rules of Procedure cover certain aspects of this rule — such as the tribunal's obligation to give formal notice of the hearing and the nature of the hearing that will be held.[38] This rule, however, can also have broader consequences than those addressed in the *SPPA* and the Tribunal's Rules. It means, for example, that the Tribunal must disclose to the parties any factual information that has come to its attention outside the hearing on which it intends to rely and must provide the parties with a full opportunity to respond to that information.
- *The right to an impartial hearing before an independent tribunal*: The members of the Tribunal must be free of actual bias. Examples of actual bias include a financial or business interest in the outcome of the case or a personal or familial relationship with one of the parties. The members of the Tribunal also must conduct themselves in a way that does not give rise to a reasonable apprehension of bias. In

37 See, for example, *Kane v. University of British Columbia (Board of Governors)* (1980), 110 D.L.R. (3d) 311, [1980] 1 S.C.R. 1105; *Milne v. Nipissing District Secondary School Athletic Assn.* (1998), 15 Admin. L.R. (3d) 126, 115 O.A.C. 363 (Div. Ct.).

38 *SPPA*, ss. 5.1, 5.2, 5.2.1 and 6.

determining whether or not a reasonable apprehension of bias exists, the courts will apply the following test:[39]

> [W]hat would an informed person, viewing the matter realistically and practically — and having thought the matter through — conclude. Would he think that it is more likely than not that [the decision-maker], whether consciously or unconsciously, would not decide fairly?

A reasonable apprehension of bias may arise, for example, where an individual sitting on the Tribunal has been involved in the case at an earlier stage of the proceedings, is employed by one of the parties, runs a private school providing specific special education programs and services, has publicly expressed opinions favourable — or unfavourable — to one of the parties or the party's position in the proceeding or has conducted himself or herself in such a way during the proceeding as to give rise to a reasonable belief that he or she has prejudged the outcome of the proceeding. The mere fact that a Tribunal member has expertise or experience in special education matters, however, does not give rise to a reasonable apprehension of bias.

The Tribunal's Decision

In addition to reviewing the procedures followed by the Special Education Tribunal, the Divisional Court may also review the substance of the Tribunal's decisions. Substantive review may include consideration of whether the Tribunal had the legal authority or jurisdiction to make the decision in question and review of both the reasoning employed by the Tribunal and the conclusions it reached. Substantive review of the Tribunal's decision is available on a much more limited basis than the procedural review discussed in the preceding section.

Judicial Deference and the Standard of Review Analysis

The courts generally exercise deference when reviewing the substance of administrative tribunals' decisions. This deference is based on a recognition that the reason the Legislature establishes administrative tribunals and assigns certain decision-making functions to them is to take advantage of the specialized expertise that they can bring to bear on the decision-making process. An administrative tribunal will typically have more expertise than the reviewing court with respect to the particular issues assigned to it under the statutory scheme. As a result, it only makes sense that, as a general rule, the courts should bear in mind the tribunal's expertise and defer to its decisions.

---

39 *Canadian Arctic Gas Pipeline Ltd. (Re)* (1975), 65 D.L.R. (3d) 660 at p. 667, [1976] 2 F.C. 20 (C.A.), revd 68 D.L.R. (3d) 716, [1978] 1 S.C.R. 369 *sub. nom. Committee for Justice and Liberty v. Canada (National Energy Board)*; endorsed in *Baker v. Canada (Minister of Citizenship and Immigration)*, *supra*, footnote 30, at para. 46.

The courts, however, will not defer to an administrative tribunal in every case. Rather, the courts will conduct what is referred to as a "standard of review analysis" in order to determine the degree of deference to be paid to a tribunal's decision on the question at issue.[40] The standard of review analysis involves two steps:[41]

> First, courts ascertain whether the jurisprudence has already determined in a satisfactory manner the degree of deference to be accorded with regard to a particular category of question. Second, where the first inquiry proves unfruitful, courts must proceed to an analysis of the factors making it possible to identify the proper standard of review.

These factors include: the presence or absence of a privative clause; the purpose of the tribunal as determined by interpretation of enabling legislation; the nature of the question at issue; and the expertise of the tribunal.[42]

Where the standard of review analysis leads to the conclusion that deference should be paid to the tribunal's decision, the tribunal's decision will be upheld when it is reasonable (referred to as the "reasonableness" standard of review); otherwise, the tribunal's decision will be upheld only when it is correct (referred to as the "correctness" standard of review).[43] The Supreme Court has recently described the "reasonableness" and "correctness" standards, and their relationship to the concept of judicial deference, as follows:[44]

> Reasonableness is a deferential standard animated by the principle that . . . certain questions that come before administrative tribunals do not lend themselves to one specific, particular result. Instead, they may give rise to a number of possible, reasonable conclusions. Tribunals have a margin of appreciation within the range of acceptable and rational solutions. A court conducting a review for reasonableness inquires into the qualities that make a decision reasonable, referring both to the process of articulating the reasons and to outcomes. In judicial review, reasonableness is concerned mostly with the

---

40 *Dunsmuir v. New Brunswick* (2008), 291 D.L.R. (4th) 577, [2008] 1 S.C.R. 190. Until the *Dunsmuir* decision, the Supreme Court of Canada recognized three standards of review: "patently unreasonable" (or "patent unreasonableness"), "reasonableness" and "correctness". In *Dunsmuir*, however, the Supreme Court concluded that the "patently unreasonable" standard should be abandoned because there was no meaningful or principled basis for distinguishing a "patently unreasonable" decision from a merely "unreasonable" one. Moreover, as the majority recognized at para. 42:

> [E]ven if one could conceive of a situation in which a clearly or highly irrational decision were distinguishable from a merely irrational decision, it would be unpalatable to require parties to accept an irrational decision simply because, on a deferential standard, the irrationality of the decision is not clear *enough*. It is also inconsistent with the rule of law to retain an irrational decision. [emphasis in original]

41 *Supra*, at para. 62.

42 *Supra*, at para. 55.

43 *Supra*, at paras. 43-48.

44 *Supra*, at paras. 47, 48 and 50.

> existence of justification, transparency and intelligibility within the decision-making process. But it is also concerned with whether the decision falls within a range of possible, acceptable outcomes which are defensible in respect of the facts and law.
>
> . . . . .
>
> Deference is both an attitude of the court and a requirement of the law of judicial review. It does not mean that courts are subservient to the determinations of decision makers, or that courts must show blind reverence to their interpretations, or that they may be content to pay lip service to the concept of reasonableness review while in fact imposing their own view. Rather, deference imports respect for the decision-making process of adjudicative bodies with regard to both the facts and the law . . .
>
> . . . . .
>
> As important as it is that courts have a proper understanding of reasonableness review as a deferential standard, it is also without question that the standard of correctness must be maintained in respect of jurisdictional and some other questions of law. This promotes just decisions and avoids inconsistent and unauthorized application of law. When applying the correctness standard, a reviewing court will not show deference to the decision maker's reasoning process; it will rather undertake its own analysis of the question. The analysis will bring the court to decide whether it agrees with the determination of the decision maker; if not, the court will substitute its own view and provide the correct answer. From the outset, the court must ask whether the tribunal's decision was correct.

Given that there is relatively little jurisprudence dealing with the standard of review applicable to Special Education Tribunal decisions, the applicable standard of review — and thus the scope of substantive review available — will generally fall to be determined based on the second step of the analysis described above. With this in mind, we have discussed below the manner in which the standard of review analysis would likely be applied to the Tribunal's decisions.

The Presence or Absence of a Privative Clause

A privative clause is a provision in a statute that indicates that an administrative tribunal's decisions will not be subject to review in the courts. The existence of a privative clause does not exclude judicial review altogether, but is seen as an indication that the Legislature intended the courts to defer to the tribunal's decisions.[45]

Section 57(5) of the *Education Act* provides as follows: "The decision of the Special Education Tribunal is final and binding on the parties to the decision." Provisions like section 57(5) are often referred to by the courts as "finality" clauses. Although they are not considered full "privative" clauses,[46]

---

[45] See, for example, *Crevier v. Quebec (Attorney General)* (1981), 127 D.L.R. (3d) 1, [1981] 2 S.C.R. 220. See also *Dunsmuir, supra*, footnote 40, at para. 52.

[46] For an example of a "full" privative clause, see s. 116 of the *Labour Relations Act,*

they are viewed as a signal that the Legislature intended that a degree of deference should be paid to decisions of the tribunal within its core area of expertise.[47] The fact that the Legislature intended the Special Education Tribunal's decisions to be "final and binding" on the parties is a factor that indicates that the courts should pay some deference to the Tribunal's decisions.

Purpose and Expertise of the Special Education Tribunal

The Special Education Tribunal was established for the purpose of hearing and deciding appeals with respect to the identification and placement of exceptional pupils. The Tribunal's core area of expertise is fact-finding and adjudication in the special education context. In particular, it has been recognized that the Tribunal's primary area of expertise is in identifying exceptional pupils and placing such pupils into educational settings where special education programs and services appropriate to meet their needs can best be delivered. The Divisional Court and the Ontario Court of Appeal have confirmed that, within this core area of expertise, the Special Education Tribunal is entitled to judicial deference.[48]

The Nature of the Question at Issue

Another factor to be considered in determining the degree of deference that should be accorded to a decision of the Special Education Tribunal is the nature of the issue before the Tribunal. The Supreme Court has said that questions of fact, discretion and policy and questions of law that cannot be easily separated from policy issues will generally attract deference and be reviewed on a standard of reasonableness, while questions of law that are "of 'central importance to the legal system . . . and outside the . . . specialized area

---

1995, S.O. 1995, c. 1, Sch. A: "No decision, order, direction, declaration or ruling of the Board shall be questioned or reviewed in any court, and no order shall be made or process entered, or proceedings taken in any court, whether by way of injunction, declaratory judgment, certiorari, mandamus, prohibition, quo warranto, or otherwise, to question, review, prohibit or restrain the Board or any of its proceedings." See the discussion in *Dayco (Canada) Ltd. v. C.A.W.-Canada* (1993), 102 D.L.R. (4th) 609 at pp. 630-31, [1993] 2 S.C.R. 230.

47 *Dayco (Canada) Ltd. v. C.A.W.-Canada, supra*; *United Brotherhood of Carpenters and Joiners of America, Local 579 v. Bradco Construction Ltd.* (1993), 102 D.L.R. (4th) 402 at p. 413, [1993] 2 S.C.R. 316.

48 *Eaton v. Brant County Board of Education* (1994), 71 O.A.C. 69, 45 A.C.W.S. (3d) 879, at para. 10 (Div. Ct.), revd 123 D.L.R. (4th) 43, 22 O.R. (3d) 1 (C.A.), revd 142 D.L.R. (4th) 385, [1997] 1 S.C.R. 241. Although the Ontario Court of Appeal reversed the Divisional Court's decision, it agreed with the Divisional Court on this point. The degree of deference owed to the Tribunal was not an issue when the case reached the Supreme Court of Canada; however, the Supreme Court implicitly endorsed the principle of judicial deference to the Tribunal's decisions in upholding the original Tribunal decision.

of expertise' of the administrative decision maker will always attract a correctness standard".[49]

In this regard, at least four distinct categories of questions can be identified:

Jurisdictional Questions

No deference will be paid to a decision of the Special Education Tribunal on a question concerning the scope of its own statutory jurisdiction. The Tribunal must be correct in interpreting any provisions limiting or defining its jurisdiction.[50] If the interpretation is not correct, it can be reversed.

The jurisdiction of the Special Education Tribunal is defined in broad terms in section 57 of the *Education Act*. As a result, there will be relatively few circumstances in which the Tribunal will be called on to interpret provisions that define or limit its jurisdiction. Some examples of issues that could arise with respect to the scope of the Tribunal's jurisdiction include the following:

- issues concerning whether or not a particular child is a "resident pupil" to whom the identification, placement, review and appeal provisions of the *Education Act* and O. Reg. 181/98 apply;[51]
- issues concerning whether or not a particular individual who seeks to appeal qualifies as the pupil's parent or guardian;[52] or

---

49 *Dunsmuir*, *supra*, footnote 40, at para. 55, citing *Toronto (City) v. C.U.P.E., Local 79* (2003), 232 D.L.R. (4th) 385, [2003] 3 S.C.R. 77, at para. 62.

50 *Dunsmuir*, *supra*, footnote 40, at para. 59. See also *U.E.S., Local 298 v. Bibeault*, [1988] 2 S.C.R. 1048, 35 Admin. L.R. 153 *sub nom. Syndicat national des employés de la Commission scolaire régionale de l'Outaouais (C.S.N.) v. Union des employés de service, Local 298 (F.T.Q.)*; *Dayco*, *supra*, footnote 47.

51 Section 57(3) of the *Education Act* permits a parent or guardian to appeal the identification or placement of a pupil as an exceptional pupil. An "exceptional pupil" is defined in s. 1 as "a pupil whose behavioural, communicational, intellectual, physical or multiple exceptionalities are such that he or she is considered to need placement in a special education program" by an IPRC established — in most cases — by the school board of which the pupil is a resident pupil. Resident pupil qualifications are outlined in ss. 32 to 36.

52 Section 57(3) provides that only a parent or guardian of a pupil may appeal to the Tribunal. The term "parent" is not defined but, where there is a custody order in place, it will mean the parent or parents with legal custody of the student. Difficulties may arise where parents have joint custody and an agreement or order that educational decisions will be made jointly, yet the parents cannot agree. Schools may accept that either custodial parent can make decisions, but prudence may suggest that the parents seek judicial clarification. A "guardian" is defined in s. 1 of the *Education Act* as "a person who has lawful custody of a child, other than the parent of the child". Some school boards require guardianship to be supported by court-ordered change of custody, but the *Education Act* does not require a court order for custody to be lawful. In some cases, there may be an informal written permission from a parent that gives control over education decision-making to a trusted friend or relative while the parent focuses on a different family priority.

- issues concerning whether or not the parent or guardian has exhausted all rights of appeal under the regulations.[53]

Legal Questions of Central Importance and Outside the Tribunal's Area of Expertise

Similarly, little deference will be paid to decisions of the Special Education Tribunal on legal issues of "central importance" to the legal system or on legal issues that fall outside the core area of its specialized expertise.[54] The Tribunal's core area of expertise is fact-finding and adjudication in the special education context. With respect to issues outside this area, the Tribunal's decisions must be correct.

Some examples of issues with respect to which the Tribunal will be required to be correct include the following:

- interpretation of the Charter and other constitutional issues;
- interpretation of external statutes, such as the Ontario *Human Rights Code*;[55]
- interpretation of common law principles from outside the Tribunal's core area of expertise, such as the interpretation of a contract or a common law concept such as "good faith".

Legal Questions Within the Tribunal's Area of Expertise

Where the Tribunal is involved in determining issues within its core area of expertise (*i.e.*, special education) the courts will usually exercise a high degree of deference and the reasonableness standard will apply.[56] While the courts have often found ways to set aside decisions with which they disagree, a party who is seeking to persuade a court to set aside a decision by the Tribunal within its core area of expertise faces an uphill battle. This result is consistent with the view that the Tribunal should generally be accorded the "last word" with respect to special education matters and that resort to the courts should be discouraged in all but the most exceptional cases.

---

53 Section 57(3) of the *Education Act* also requires that a parent or guardian must have "exhausted all rights of appeal under the regulations" (*i.e.*, by appealing to the SEAB) before appealing to the Tribunal.

54 *Dunsmuir v. New Brunswick* (2008), 291 D.L.R. (4th) 577 at p. 579, [2008] 1 S.C.R. 190. See also *Eaton v. Brant County Board of Education* (1997), 142 D.L.R. (4th) 385, [1997] 1 S.C.R. 241.

55 R.S.O. 1990, c. H.19 (the "Code").

56 *Dunsmuir*, *supra*, footnote 54; *U.E.S., Local 298 v. Bibeault*, *supra*, footnote 50; *Dayco (Canada) Ltd. v. C.A.W.-Canada* (1993), 102 D.L.R. (4th) 609, [1993] 2 S.C.R. 230; *United Brotherhood of Carpenters and Joiners of America, Local 579 v. Bradco Construction Ltd.* (1993), 102 D.L.R. (4th) 402, [1993] 2 S.C.R. 316.

Factual Questions

The scope of judicial review is at its narrowest with respect to factual findings and credibility issues. It is generally recognized that decision-makers who actually hear and observe the witnesses as they testify are in the best position to judge their credibility and make factual findings. As a result, reviewing courts are extremely reluctant to intervene in the fact-finding process. Even where the reviewing court might have reached different factual conclusions based on the evidence presented, the court cannot overturn the tribunal's decision on that basis alone; rather, an administrative tribunal's decision will only be overturned for an error of fact where a complete absence of evidence on a point that was essential to the tribunal's decision has been demonstrated.[57]

A large part of the function entrusted to the Special Education Tribunal under the *Education Act* is fact-finding in the special education context. Many Tribunal decisions will be highly dependent on the factual findings reached. Given the very narrow scope for judicial review of findings of fact, the scope for judicial review of Tribunal decisions will, in many cases, be quite limited.

GROUNDS FOR REVIEW OF HUMAN RIGHTS TRIBUNAL DECISIONS

As discussed in Chapter 12, "The Human Rights Process", special education issues are now being raised more frequently in the context of proceedings under the Code and this trend will continue in the future as a result of the introduction in mid-2008 of "direct access" to the Human Rights Tribunal of Ontario ("HRTO"). A party wishing to challenge a decision of the HRTO may do so by way of a judicial review application. The same general procedure applies in the case of judicial review of an HRTO decision as in the case of judicial review of the Special Education Tribunal. Like decisions of the Special Education Tribunal, HRTO decisions can be reviewed on both procedural and substantive grounds. While the grounds for judicial review are generally quite similar, there are three important distinctions that merit further discussion.

First, any party to a proceeding before the HRTO has a right to seek reconsideration of the HRTO's decision.[58] The HRTO's Rules of Procedure provide that a request for reconsideration will only be granted in the following circumstances:[59]

---

57 *Toronto (City) Board of Education v. O.S.S.T.F., District 15* (1997), 144 D.L.R. (4th) 385, [1997] 1 S.C.R. 487, at paras. 37-8; *W.W. Lester (1978) Ltd. v. U.A., Local 740* (1990), 76 D.L.R. (4th) 389 at pp. 422-23, [1990] 3 S.C.R. 644.

58 Code, s. 45.7.

59 Rule 26.5 of the HRTO Rules of Procedure, available online at http://www.hrto.ca/

a) there are new facts or evidence that could potentially be determinative of the case and that could not reasonably have been obtained earlier; or
b) the party seeking reconsideration was entitled to but, through no fault of its own, did not receive notice of the proceeding or a hearing; or
c) the decision or order which is the subject of the reconsideration request is in conflict with established jurisprudence or Tribunal procedure and the proposed reconsideration involves a matter of general or public importance; or
d) other factors exist that, in the opinion of the Tribunal, outweigh the public interest in the finality of Tribunal decisions.

Although the grounds for reconsideration are reasonably narrow, a party will generally be required to exhaust the reconsideration procedure before seeking judicial review.

Second, like the Special Education Tribunal, the HRTO has issued its own Rules of Procedure that govern the proceedings before it. The Code confers considerable discretion on the HRTO to make its own rules[60] and expressly states that the rules "shall be liberally construed to permit the [HRTO] to adopt practices and procedures, including alternatives to traditional adjudicative or adversarial procedures that, in the opinion of the Tribunal, will facilitate fair, just and expeditious resolutions of the merits of the matters before it."[61] The Code also provides that the rules made by the HRTO will prevail over the *SPPA* where there is a conflict between them.[62] The HRTO's Rules of Procedure confer a number of innovative procedural powers on the HRTO that it may exercise at its own initiative.[63] The Code also contains the following unique language, limiting the circumstances in which the Tribunal may be subject to judicial review if it fails to follow its own procedural rules:[64]

> (8) Failure on the part of the Tribunal to comply with the practices and procedures required by the rules or the exercise of a discretion under the rules by the Tribunal in a particular manner is not a ground for setting aside a decision of the Tribunal on an application for judicial review or any other form of relief, unless the failure or the exercise of a discretion caused a substantial wrong which affected the final disposition of the matter.

Given the language of the Code, it can be expected that deference will be paid to the HRTO's procedural choices and that the HRTO will be accorded latitude with respect to the procedures it employs. Nevertheless, the courts will

---

hrto/sites/default/files/New%20Applications1/RulesOfProcedure.pdf. See *Campbell v. Toronto District School Board*, 2008 HRTO 423.

60 Code, s. 43. Section 43(2), however, provides that the HRTO's rules must ensure that an application that is within the jurisdiction of the HRTO will not be finally disposed of without affording the parties an opportunity to make oral submissions in accordance with the Rules and that an application may not be finally disposed of without written reasons.

61 *Ibid.*, s. 41.

62 *Ibid.*, s. 42.

63 HRTO Rules of Procedure, rules 1.5 to 1.7. See Chapter 12, "The Human Rights Process".

64 Code, s. 43(8).

supervise the HRTO's procedures to ensure that it provides the parties with a fair process.

Third, the Code also contains a unique provision dealing with substantive review of the HRTO's decisions.[65] Section 45.8 of the Code provides:[66]

> 45.8 Subject to section 45.7 of this Act, section 21.1 of the *Statutory Powers Procedure Act* and the Tribunal rules, a decision of the Tribunal is final and not subject to appeal and shall not be altered or set aside in an application for judicial review or in any other proceeding unless the decision is patently unreasonable.

The "patently unreasonable" standard of review has been described by the Supreme Court of Canada as an "extremely high standard", and a "strict" or "severe" test.[67] In order for a decision to be "patently unreasonable", it must be "clearly irrational".[68] The following passages illustrate the high standard that must be met to establish that a decision is "patently unreasonable":

> It is said that it is difficult to know what "patently unreasonable" means. What is patently unreasonable to one judge may be eminently reasonable to another. Yet any test can only be defined by words, the building blocks of all reasons. Obviously, the patently unreasonable test sets a high standard of review. In the Shorter Oxford English Dictionary "patently", an adverb, is defined as "openly, evidently, clearly". "Unreasonable" is defined as "not having the faculty of reason, irrational, not acting in accordance with reason or good sense". Thus, based on the dictionary definition of the words "patently unreasonable", it is apparent that if the decision the Board reached, acting within its jurisdiction, is not clearly irrational, that is to say evidently not in accordance with reason, then it cannot be said that there was a loss of jurisdiction. This is clearly a very strict test.[69]

---

65 Until the amendments to the Code took effect in 2008, the Code provided for a fairly broad right of appeal of HRTO decisions. Not only was that right of appeal removed, limiting parties who wished to challenge a HRTO decision to a judicial review application, but the Legislature built the highly deferential "patently unreasonable" standard of review into the legislation. Only a few months later, in *Dunsmuir v. New Brunswick* (2008), 291 D.L.R. (4th) 577, [2008] 1 S.C.R. 190, the Supreme Court of Canada concluded that the "patently unreasonable" standard should be eliminated in favour of two standards of review — reasonableness and correctness. Nevertheless, the "patently unreasonable" standard lives on in the Code. Whereas once there was a broad right of appeal of HRTO decisions, it is arguable that the HRTO's decisions are now entitled to greater deference than most other administrative tribunal decisions.

66 Section 45.6 is the reconsideration provision of the *Human Rights Code*. Section 21.1 of the *SPPA* deals with correction of typographical, calculation and other like errors.

67 *Toronto (City) Board of Education v. O.S.S.T.F., District 15* (1997), 144 D.L.R. (4th) 385 at p. 397, [1997] 1 S.C.R. 487; *Blanchard v. Control Data Canada Ltd.* (1984), 14 D.L.R. (4th) 289 at p. 302, [1984] 2 S.C.R. 476; *Canada (Attorney General) v. Public Service Alliance of Canada* (1993), 101 D.L.R. (4th) 673 at p. 690, [1993] 1 S.C.R. 941.

68 *Canada (Attorney General) v. Public Service Alliance of Canada, supra.*

69 *Supra*, at p. 690.

> [A] patently unreasonable defect, once identified, can be explained simply and easily, leaving no real possibility of doubting that the decision is defective. A patently unreasonable decision has been described as "clearly irrational" or "evidently not in accordance with reason" [citations omitted]. A decision that is patently unreasonable is so flawed that no amount of curial deference can justify letting it stand.[70]

REMEDIES AVAILABLE ON JUDICIAL REVIEW

Where the party seeking judicial review successfully persuades the Divisional Court that legitimate grounds for judicial review are present, the court will usually "quash" (*i.e.*, reverse, overturn or set aside) the decision. The Court will usually also send the decision back to the Special Education Tribunal or, less commonly, to a differently constituted Tribunal or to the IPRC or SEAB or, in the case of a judicial review of an HRTO decision, to the same or a different member of the HRTO. The purpose of sending the decision back to the original decision-maker or a different decision-maker on the same tribunal is to allow the tribunal to reconsider the matter in light of the court's decision. In some rare cases — such as where there has been a very serious breach of procedural fairness by the tribunal that calls its impartiality into question or where there has been a very long delay — the court may simply quash the decision and declare the proceeding to be at an end.[71]

In an appropriate case, the court may make a "declaration" regarding a party's legal rights or legal status. For example, the court may make a declaration regarding the category of exceptionality that applies to a student. The court may also direct the school board to take specific action. For example, the court may quash the school board's decision and order it to implement a particular placement; however, panels of the Divisional Court will often be reluctant to order that specific action be taken, as such an order is often seen as an undue incursion into the school board's special education decision-making.

It should also be remembered that, even where the Divisional Court finds that an application for judicial review is well-founded, the court has a discretion to refuse to make a remedial order. While the court will generally order a remedy, it may refuse to do so in exceptional cases — such as where there has been considerable delay in the process or where the issue between the parties no longer appears to be a "live" issue.

---

70 *Ryan v. Law Society of New Brunswick* (2003), 223 D.L.R. (4th) 577, [2003] 1 S.C.R. 247, *per* Iacobucci J., at para. 52.

71 See, for example, *Commercial Union Assurance v. Ontario (Human Rights Commission)* (1988), 47 D.L.R. (4th) 477, 20 C.C.E.L. 236 (C.A.), leave to appeal to S.C.C. refused 51 D.L.R. (4th) vii, 65 O.R. (2d) x.

IMPLEMENTATION OF THE JUDICIAL REVIEW DECISION

A decision of the Divisional Court is a binding legal decision and must be implemented in accordance with its terms. What those terms are will depend on the terms of the court's order. As noted above, implementation may involve referring the matter back to the Tribunal, the IPRC or the SEAB or, in the case of judicial review of a decision of the HRTO, to the HRTO. Alternatively, the court may make a declaration or direct the school board to take specific action — for example, to implement a specific placement — in which case that direction must be implemented by the school board.

The school board's implementation responsibilities may be suspended where leave to appeal is granted by the Ontario Court of Appeal. Generally, the fact that an appeal is filed does not relieve the parties from implementing the decision under appeal. In many cases, however, the parties will be able to reach an agreement that the Tribunal's decision need not be implemented pending the appeal. Where no agreement can be reached, there are some rare circumstances in which a party may be able to obtain an order called a "stay of proceedings", which will preserve the status quo while the appeal is underway.[72]

The test to obtain a "stay of proceedings" is an onerous one. In order to obtain a stay, the party seeking it must show: that there is a serious issue to be tried; it would suffer irreparable harm if the stay were not granted; and that the balance of convenience favours granting the stay.[73] Thus, while a stay may be available in some cases, those cases will be the exception, rather than the rule.

72 *Rules of Civil Procedure*, rule 63.02.

73 *RJR-MacDonald Inc. v. Canada (Attorney General)* (1994), 111 D.L.R. (4th) 385, [1994] 1 S.C.R. 311.

14

Discipline and Other Issues

INTRODUCTION

While discipline is currently considered to be one of a range of pedagogical tools to be used in teaching students to be a good citizens[1] it also carries a negative connotation. To be a successful pedagogical tool, discipline must be seen as "fair" when it is used — that is, when a student is disciplined for misconduct, the disciplinary response must be seen to be a just and appropriate response, having regard to the circumstances of the conduct.

[1] In Ontario, revisions were made in 2007 to the *Education Act*, R.S.O. 1990, c. E.2, its regulations and Ministry of Education Program/Policy Memoranda to redefine the approach that Ontario schools are to follow in disciplining students: *An Act to amend the Education Act in respect of behaviour, discipline and safety*, S.O. 2007, c. 14 ("Bill 212"); *Behaviour, Discipline and Safety of Pupils*, O. Reg. 472/07; *Access to School Premises*, O. Reg. 474/00; Ontario Deputy Minister of Education, "Policy/ Program Memorandum No. 128: The Provincial Code of Conduct and School Boards Codes of Conduct" (Toronto: Ministry of Education, 2007), available online at http://www.edu.gov.on.ca/extra/eng/ppm/128.html; Ontario Deputy Minister of Education, "Policy/Program Memorandum No. 144: Bullying Prevention and Intervention" (Toronto: Ministry of Education, 2009), available online at http://www.edu.gov.on.ca/extra/eng/ppm/144.html; and Ontario Deputy Minister of Education, "Policy/Program Memorandum No. 145: Progressive Discipline and Promoting Positive Student Behaviour" (Toronto: Ministry of Education, 2009), available online at http://www.edu.gov.on.ca/extra/eng/ppm/ 145.html. These revisions have shifted the focus away from using discipline to remove students who commit "infractions" from school in order to keep schools safe — an approach often referred to as "safe schools" — to using discipline as part of a range of strategies designed to change the behaviour of students who "engage in" inappropriate "activities" with the aim of teaching students to be respectful. These changes were prompted, at least in part, by concerns that the "safe schools" approach to discipline had a disproportionately negative impact on students who were disabled or from racialized communities. Anecdotal evidence collected by the Ontario Human Rights Commission prompted it to initiate a complaint against the Ontario Ministry of Education. This complaint was ultimately resolved by way of an extensive settlement in which the Ministry committed to make the changes that were put into place in 2007.

The purpose of the discipline is, after all, to change the student's behaviour — if discipline were perceived to be unfair or the student did not understand the purpose of the discipline, then it would not have the desired effect.

Particularly in the case of exceptional students, there will be circumstances in which discipline is not an effective pedagogical tool. For example, where, because of his or her disability, an exceptional student has no control over the behaviour that would prompt a disciplinary response, discipline will not change the student's behaviour.

Similarly, a student who is unable to understand that certain conduct is wrong will not understand from a suspension or expulsion that he or she must stop the conduct. This raises human rights issues because, in such situations, discipline gives rise to an adverse effect because of the student's disability — punishing the student cannot be expected to have the desired result of changing the conduct and, at the same time, a suspension or expulsion removes the student from the classroom where programs are delivered that may change the conduct. Therefore, it may be discriminatory to discipline an exceptional student in certain situations.

In this chapter, we will review the use of discipline in the context of special education and the human rights issues which must be taken into account.

HUMAN RIGHTS AND DISCIPLINE

The Supreme Court of Canada made clear in *Eaton v. Brant County Board of Education*[2] that "equal treatment" in education for students with disabilities does not necessarily mean treating them the same as non-disabled students. Identical treatment of a student whose disability precludes him or her from learning in the same way as students without disabilities will often disadvantage that student. For example, it would be discriminatory to place a student with a developmental delay in a regular class without any special education services, programs or accommodations and then expect that student to learn from the regular program presented in the class without any modification or alteration.

Similarly, a student's disability may render him or her incapable of learning from a suspension or expulsion or understanding that his or her behaviour is inappropriate and must change. The student may not be able to comprehend that biting, pinching, hitting or pulling hair is wrong; in fact, for some students with complex disabilities who have no formal communication system, biting, pinching, hitting or hair-pulling may be an effort to communicate frustration, upset or another emotion.

Where a student is unable make the connection between a suspension or expulsion and the inappropriate behaviour or activity that prompted the discipline or to understand from the suspension or expulsion that the student

---

2 (1997), 142 D.L.R. (4th) 385, [1997] 1 S.C.R. 241.

should change his or her behaviour, a suspension or expulsion would be discriminatory. The Ontario *Human Rights Code*[3] provides that a "requirement, qualification or factor" which, while being neutral on its face, has the result of adversely impacting a group identified by a prohibited ground, is discriminatory.[4] A provision in a statute or Code of Conduct requiring students to be suspended or expelled for certain behaviours will often have an adverse impact on students whose disabilities preclude them from understanding that a particular behaviour is inappropriate or from learning from the discipline imposed that they must change the inappropriate behaviour. In these cases, it will be necessary to accommodate the student's disability by finding a different way to "teach" the student that the behaviour in question is unacceptable and must be changed.

Sometimes, a question will arise as to whether or not a student is able to understand the consequences of his or her actions — and therefore, whether or not the student is entitled to accommodation in the form of being exempted from disciplinary responses to inappropriate behaviours. In such a case, an obligation exists on the part of the student (*i.e.*, the student's parent) to provide clear medical or psychological evidence that the student is unable to understand the consequences of his or her actions. In human rights law, the onus is on the person seeking accommodation to establish that he or she is entitled to accommodation and to co-operate in the search for accommodation.[5] A student (with his or her parents) should also co-operate in obtaining and providing to the school any psychological or psychiatric assessments that would assist the school in determining how to best work with the student to change the student's conduct.

Similarly where a student cannot control his or her actions because of a disability (*e.g.*, Tourette Syndrome), no disciplinary response will change the behaviours. In this type of situation, where the student fails to abide by a Code of Conduct, the school should accommodate the student's needs instead of imposing discipline. This will include considering whether or not there is any other way to help the student to learn to control the behaviour.

Where a question arises respecting the student's ability to control his or her actions, the onus, again, will be on the student or his or her parents to provide medical or psychological evidence that establishes this. In the event that a student is unable to control his or her conduct, it will be important that school staff and the student's classmates be educated about the student's disability and its consequences, in order to attempt to provide the student with an educational environment in which the student is understood and accepted. In this regard, it will be important that other students understand why they are disciplined for the conduct in question, while the student in question is not.

---

3 R.S.O. 1990, c. H.19.

4 *Ibid.*, s. 11.

5 These concepts are discussed further in the context of post-secondary education in Chapter 15, "Post-Secondary Education".

MITIGATING AND OTHER FACTORS

In Ontario, the principles of the *Human Rights Code* are reflected in the requirement that certain "mitigating factors" and "other factors" must be considered by a principal before making a decision to suspend or expel a student.[6] The three "mitigating factors" can be summarized in the following three questions:

- Does the student have the ability to control his or her actions?
- Does the student understand the foreseeable consequences of his or her actions?
- Does the student's presence in the school create an unacceptable danger to the safety or well-being of any person?

In any case where the answer to either of the first two questions is yes, discipline decision-makers must pause to consider whether or not the student would learn to change his or her inappropriate behaviour if the student were suspended or expelled. As noted above, where there is a different strategy available that will work better to change the student's behaviour — such as a behaviour management plan — then this strategy should be pursued.

For students with cognitive disabilities, the real challenge for an educator will often be to determine whether, in fact, the student is aware of what he or she is doing, whether the student does have the ability to control his or her impulses, and whether the student has the capacity to learn from the discipline. In such cases, again, it will be necessary to obtain information from and work with the student's psychiatrists, psychologists or other medical practitioners who are working with the student and the student's family in order to determine whether or not the normal discipline system must be adjusted or modified in order to address the student's particular disability. Given that the end goal is behaviour modification, it will be critical for the school to have as much information and support as possible from the medical and psychological experts who are working with the student. In this respect, parents and the student do have an obligation under human rights principles to co-operate in obtaining and sharing relevant information with the school board in order that the student's needs can be understood and met.

It is important to note that the fact that a student has a disability does not mean that the student cannot be disciplined where none of the mitigating factors exist. This was confirmed by the Ontario Divisional Court in *Jackson v. Toronto Catholic School Board.*[7] This case involved a student with special needs — including language impairment and behavioural issues — who brought a knife (a double-edged blade hidden within a silver pen) to school.

---

6 *Behaviour, Discipline and Safety of Pupils*, O. Reg. 472/07.

7 (2006), 50 Admin. L.R. (4th) 243, 143 C.R.R. (2d) 170 (Ont. S.C.J. (Div. Ct.)). While this case was decided prior to the recent Bill 212 amendments to the *Education Act*, it remains relevant because the mitigating factors have not changed.

The student, who was placed half-time in a language impairment class and half-time in a regular class, threatened another student with the knife during recess. The student had a record of increasingly aggressive behaviour. The evidence established that the principal had considered the three mitigating circumstances and concluded that: the student had the ability to control his behaviour; the student had the ability to foresee the consequences of his behaviour; and the student's continued presence in the school created an unacceptable risk. The student was given a limited expulsion from the school and, during this limited expulsion, was assigned to a language impairment class in another school. The student's parents appealed the expulsion to the board and, when that appeal was dismissed, applied to the Ontario Divisional Court for judicial review of the principal's decision. The court dismissed the judicial review application and upheld the principal's decision. The court determined that the principal had acted in good faith at all times, had proceeded fairly and had acted pursuant to his duties and responsibilities under the *Education Act* to maintain order and discipline and to ensure that the school was kept safe and secure for all its students. The fact that the student had a disability did not exempt the student from discipline where the student was able to understand the consequences of his actions and was able to control his behaviour.

If a student does have control over his or her behaviours and can make a connection between the inappropriate behaviour and the discipline of suspension or expulsion *and* if the suspension or expulsion will not disproportionately impact the student because of his or her disability, then it would be contrary to the *Human Rights Code* to treat the student differently just because she/he has a disability. It is only where the student's disability results in that student being disadvantaged by the suspension or expulsion in a way that a non-disabled student would not be disadvantaged that the decision-maker is obliged to consider whether or not a different strategy would be more effective or give rise to an equal result.

As part of the changes to Ontario's legislation that removed the mandatory consequences of certain conduct, a number of other considerations were codified in O. Reg. 472/07, in order to assist school administrators in determining whether a disciplinary response is appropriate or should be moderated. These other factors include the following:

- whether or not the activity for which the student may be — or is being — suspended or expelled was related to any harassment of the student because of his or her race, ethnic origin, religion, disability, gender or sexual orientation or to any other harassment;
- how the suspension or expulsion would affect the student's ongoing education;
- the age of the student;

- in the case of a student for whom an Individual Education Plan has been developed:
  - whether or not the behaviour was a manifestation of a disability identified in the pupil's Individual Education Plan;
  - whether or not appropriate individualized accommodation has been provided;
- whether or not the suspension or expulsion is likely to result in an aggravation or worsening of the pupil's behaviour or conduct.[8]

The following questions should be considered:

- was racial or other harassment a factor in the student's behaviour?
- has progressive discipline been attempted with this student?
- what would the impact of the suspension/expulsion be on the student's continued education?
- what is the student's age?
- would the suspension/expulsion likely worsen the student's behaviour?
- was the student's behaviour a manifestation of a disability?

In the case of students with disabilities, the answers to these questions will assist in determining whether or not the discipline process must be adjusted to accommodate the particular student. For example, if a student were goaded into a fight after being repeatedly teased about her disability, then this provocation would be a factor that would have to be considered and may moderate, lessen or even rule out discipline. While violence is never justified — except as is reasonably necessary for self defence or the defence of others — if a student were goaded into a violent action by the taunts of others, then care would have to be taken to ensure that this was taken into account and that those responsible for the harassment that generated the violent response were also disciplined appropriately.

Similarly, these other factors come into play when considering discipline for students who have been identified as exceptional because of behavioural issues or students whose disabilities include behavioural issues (*e.g.*, Fetal Alcohol Syndrome, autism or Oppositional Defiant Disorder). For example, a student may be able to understand from a one- or two-day suspension that his or her behaviour must change, but a suspension for a longer period may become counterproductive. This may be because the student will lose sight of the reason for the suspension if the period were longer or because the student is missing out on programming at school that is critical to the student's ability to be successful. In such cases, it will be particularly important for principals to consult with the health professionals (*i.e.*, psychiatrists and psychologists) who are working with the student in order to ensure not only that behaviour plans are appropriate, but that the discipline is appropriate to gain the desired

[8] O. Reg. 472/07, ss. 2 and 3.

ends. Where such a student is not being seen by a psychiatrist or psychologist, the school should recommend that parents arrange for this, in order to gain the best information possible on which to make discipline decisions.

RECORDING CONSIDERATION OF MITIGATING AND OTHER FACTORS

It is recommended that administrators dealing with issues of student discipline make careful notes that record that they have taken into account relevant considerations when dealing with student discipline. Written confirmation that appropriate considerations were taken into account in disciplining an exceptional student can become important if the discipline is challenged through appeal (in the case of an expulsion), in court or in an application to the Human Rights Tribunal of Ontario.

The fact that careful consideration has been given to all relevant factors should also be made clear to students and parents and should be set out in any letter sent confirming the discipline given to the student, whether that discipline is a suspension, expulsion or alternative discipline.

DEALING WITH STUDENTS WHO CANNOT CONTROL THEIR ACTIONS BUT POSE A THREAT TO SCHOOL SAFETY

Where the student cannot control or understand that his or her behaviours are inappropriate and those behaviours put the student or others at risk, what recourse does a principal have?

Increasingly, principals are facing the situations involving students with severe disabilities who do not understand the nature of their actions and whose behaviours have become so uncontrollable that their continuing attendance at school raises a real safety concern for other students or staff or even the student himself or herself. On occasion, the situation reaches the point where the safety risk is so serious that the student's continued attendance poses too high a risk of harm for the student, staff or other students. In this circumstance, suspensions or expulsions should not be used to remove the student from school, unless no other recourse is possible; however, there may be other options available to the principal.

In Ontario, section 265(1)(*m*) of the *Education Act* provides a course of action that is not considered to be disciplinary in nature. This provision permits a principal to exclude a "person" where safety issues arise that cause the principal to believe that the person's "presence in the school or classroom would be detrimental to the physical or mental well-being of the pupils".[9] In

9 Where a student's violent behaviours are directed at classroom staff rather than students, a concern for the mental well-being of the students who are observing the violent behaviour may nevertheless arise, in which case, s. 265(1)(*m*) of the *Education Act* could be triggered.

Bonnah (Litigation Guardian of) v. Ottawa-Carleton District School Board,[10] the Ontario Court of Appeal confirmed that a principal may rely on section 265(1)(*m*) of the *Education Act* to exclude a student in circumstances where the student's behaviour is posing a safety risk for staff or students. The fact that the behaviours that created the undue safety hazard are the result of the student's disability was not an issue in the *Bonnah* case, and there was no suggestion in the Court of Appeal's decision that either the *Human Rights Code* or section 15 of the Charter limited the use of section 265(1)(*m*) in the circumstances of that case.

It is a requirement that all students attending school not pose a safety risk to other students. Where a student is unable to comply with that requirement because of his or her disability, the only issue will be whether or not the student's needs can be accommodated without undue hardship. Where safety to students and others is a real risk as a result of disability, the student's needs may not be capable of accommodation; however, the obligation to accommodate will require that all possible efforts be made to reduce or manage the risk so that the student can return to school.

Therefore, a principal should consider exclusion only where there is no immediately available way to limit or contain the safety risk posed by the student. Further, where a student is excluded in circumstances where the behaviour creating the risk is a result of his or her disability, steps must be taken to try to get the student back into school safely as soon as possible. At the same time, the obligation to accommodate the student also means that the school board must attempt to continue to provide an education to the student while excluded.[11] This may be by way of a program of home instruction or an offer of a temporary alternative placement.[12]

In some cases, a student's disability precludes him or her from benefiting from a full day at school. Where a student's behaviour deteriorates as the day progresses and the student ceases to benefit from being at school, shortening the length of the student's day may constitute an appropriate accommodation

---

[10] (2003), 64 O.R. (3d) 454, 170 O.A.C. 248 (C.A.).

[11] Section 17 of the *Human Rights Code* provides that the right to equal treatment without discrimination under the Code is not infringed where a person with a disability is unable to fulfill the essential requirements attending the exercise of the right because of disability, provided that the needs of the person cannot be otherwise accommodated without undue hardship. It is an essential requirement that students attend school without creating an undue safety risk for others. A student whose disability results in a safety risk that cannot be addressed or contained by the means available to the school or school board can be excluded for as long as it reasonably takes to find the way to permit the student to attend school safely *but*, in the interim, the student will have to be accommodated by continuing to provide an education to the student to the extent possible.

[12] Section 265(1)(*m*) cannot be used, however, to place a student in a new placement recommended by the IPRC where the parents are appealing the IPRC's decision. In this instance, the original placement must continue until the appeal is abandoned, unless the parents agree to a new temporary placement.

for the student.[13] At the same time, there must be a goal to return the student to full time attendance, if possible.

---

[13] *Operation of Schools — General*, R.R.O. 1990, Reg. 298, s. 3(3).

15

Post-Secondary Education

INTRODUCTION

In previous chapters, we have focused on the special education regime that applies to students with special needs in the public education system. One of the indicators of the success of Ontario's special education system is the number of students with special needs who have successfully graduated from high school and progressed to post-secondary education. The student populations of colleges and universities across Ontario — and, indeed, across Canada — now include many individuals who benefited from special education programs and services at some point during their education.

It is difficult to do justice in a brief chapter to the complexity involved in accommodating students with special needs related to disability[1] at the post-secondary level. Any attempt to do so is made even more complex by the fact that Canadian law in this area is still evolving.[2] However, in light of the increasing number of students with special needs enrolling in post-secondary educational institutions, it is becoming ever more important for educators to understand the transitional issues that may arise when a student moves from secondary to post-secondary education, as well as the nature and extent of the accommodations that may be required at the post-secondary level.

1 We are mindful that Ontario's special education system also addresses the special needs of gifted students; however, for the most part, it is only students with other identifications and disabilities who will require accommodation at the post-secondary level. Accordingly, we have limited the discussion in this chapter to students with disabilities.

2 With the advent of "direct access" to the Human Rights Tribunal of Ontario in mid-2008 (discussed further in Chapter 12, "The Human Rights Process"), the Tribunal is now receiving quite a few applications from post-secondary students. One of the benefits of a new human rights system, therefore, may be the development of a useful body of case law to guide post-secondary institutions in decision-making about accommodation issues.

TRANSITION TO POST-SECONDARY EDUCATION

The transition from high school to post-secondary education can pose significant challenges for students with special needs. In addition to transitioning to a new and different educational environment, these students may be transitioning to new living arrangements and perhaps even a new community. They will often find themselves in a very different environment, sometimes far from home, subject to significant pressures and with little or no access to the personal and educational supports that they relied on during their high school years.

There is no routine information sharing between high schools and post-secondary educational institutions. Generally speaking, the choice is left to the student and his or her parent(s) whether to disclose information about special needs and seek accommodation at the post-secondary level. While motivated by important privacy considerations, a lack of information sharing can create a significant "disconnect" in the student's educational experience. A student with special needs who was succeeding in high school with all the supports available in that context may suddenly find him- or herself struggling to cope with the academic and other demands of university or college life.[3]

[3] A particularly dramatic example of the difficulties that can be caused by lack of information sharing is discussed in the report of the review panel appointed to inquire into the April 2007 Virginia Tech shooting. Seung Hui Cho, the student responsible for the shooting, had been diagnosed with psychiatric disabilities while in middle school following disturbing behaviours that suggested a propensity towards violence. During his middle school years, Cho progressed well enough in treatment that his doctor allowed him to stop taking his medications. In high school, he was provided with a number of accommodations with respect to his psychiatric disabilities — including curriculum and classroom accommodations — and achieved good grades. Against the recommendation of his guidance counsellor, who strongly recommended that he attend a small school close to home, Cho chose to attend Virginia Tech, a large school in another state. He did not disclose to anyone at Virginia Tech that he had been diagnosed or treated for a mental disability, nor did he disclose to anyone at Virginia Tech that he had received special education services during high school. He also did not seek any accommodations at Virginia Tech, so Virginia Tech did not become aware of his mental health issues in that way. This combination of circumstances gave rise to a volatile situation. At p. 38 of *Mass Shootings at Virginia Tech: April 16, 2007*, Report of the Independent Virginia Tech Incident Review Panel (G. Massengill, Chair) (Arlington: TriData Division, System Planning Corporation, 2007), available online at http://www.vtreviewpanel.org/report/index.html, the incident review panel stated:

> As Cho looked to the fall of 2003, he was preparing to leave home for the first time and enter an environment where he knew no one. He was not on any medication for anxiety or depression, had stopped counseling, and no longer had special accommodations for his selective mutism. Neither Cho nor his high school revealed that he had been receiving special education services as an emotionally disabled student, so no one at the university ever became aware of these pre-existing conditions.While the incident review panel acknowledged the privacy interests placed in the hands of the student, the ultimate decision of

Even where a student is willing to share information with a post-secondary institution, he or she may not have information to share. Students who were formally identified as exceptional pupils will have been referred for periodic assessments as part of the Identification, Placement and Review Committee process. These students will typically be in a position to share information about their exceptionality and assessment reports that can assist the post-secondary institution to understand their needs and develop appropriate accommodations. In contrast, students who were never formally identified but were accommodated on an informal basis typically will not have this information at their disposal.[4] When they are seeking accommodation at the post-secondary level, these students will need to obtain medical or other expert evidence[5] identifying their accommodation needs. In addition, following admission, both groups of students (those who have been formally identified and those who have not) can expect to be required to provide updated medical or expert evidence from time to time to support ongoing accommodations. Obtaining this evidence can be time-consuming and costly. For some students, fulfilling these requirements can delay their post-secondary education or place it out of reach altogether.[6]

While students with special needs face a number of challenges in making the transition from high school to college or university life, the challenges are

---

> whether or not to share information concerning disability or disabilities and past accommodation, the panel was also dismayed by the abundance of information suggesting that Cho was a risk to himself and/or others that had never been shared with Virginia Tech. This led the panel to recommend that there be full public debate about the prospect of requiring students to disclose such information, after admission, but prior to enrolment.

Of course, Cho's case is an extreme example of the difficulties that can arise when a student decides not to disclose his or her special needs or seek accommodation at the post-secondary level, and the authors by no means intend to suggest that all or even many students with special needs transitioning to post-secondary education present similar issues. Indeed, the most commonly needed accommodations include relatively straightforward matters such as extra time to write examinations, or note-taking assistance. Incidents like the Virginia Tech shooting do highlight, however, the potential value of consensual information-sharing between the sending and receiving educational institutions.

4 It has been suggested earlier in this book that one of the reasons it is important to initiate the formal identification process rather than proceeding informally is to ensure that the student is prepared for transition to post-secondary education in the future.

5 As discussed further later in this chapter, medical evidence should be required to support a student's accommodation request. In some cases, non-medical assessment evidence may be needed in addition to — or as an alternative to — the medical evidence, such as a psycho-educational assessment for a student with a learning disability or an ergonomic assessment for a student with a physical disability.

6 Bursaries and other forms of financial assistance may be available in some cases to assist with the costs associated with accommodation, either directly from the post-secondary institution the student is attending or through the Ontario Student Assistance Plan.

far from insurmountable. A proactive, problem-solving-oriented approach can be very helpful in ensuring the transition goes as smoothly as possible. The sooner the transition process begins and the more consultation there is between the student, the parents, the sending and receiving institutions, and any other stakeholders involved, the more likely it is that the transition will be successful.

In Ontario, the transition planning process is formalized for those students who have been identified as exceptional. Under O. Reg. 181/98, the Individual Education Plan of every exceptional student aged 14 years or over — other than those who are identified solely as gifted — must include a transition plan for the student's transition to (among other things) further education.[7] The principal is required to ensure that the transition plan is developed in consultation with the parent — and the student, if 16 years of age or over — and, where the principal judges it to be appropriate, with community agencies and post-secondary institutions as well.[8] The Ministry of Education has published a helpful resource guide that provides useful guidance with respect to the transition planning process.[9]

Most Canadian colleges and universities now have policies and procedures in place to accommodate students with disabilities. Most colleges and universities also provide support services to students with disabilities through a Disability Services Office or special needs office or similar department or office. The Disability Services Office can be a very useful source of information about the programs and services available for students with special needs, potential sources of funding with respect to assessment or accommodation costs and the steps that should be taken prior to admission to ensure that any accommodations required can be put in place as early as possible.

The Ministry of Education has recognized the importance of making contact with the post-secondary institution that the student wishes to attend at least a year prior to the transition:[10]

> Contact with postsecondary institutions a year in advance of a student's transition may help to ensure access for the student to program opportunities and allow time for the institution or department to arrange supports needed by the exceptional student.
>
> In some cases, informal arrangements for provisional acceptance of the student in a college or university program may be possible and may facilitate specific transition planning by both the student and the educational institution.

---

7 *Identification and Placement of Exceptional Pupils*, O. Reg. 181/98, ss. 6 and 7. See Chapter 7, "The Individual Education Plan", for further discussion of the requirements with respect to transition plans.

8 O. Reg. 181/98, ss. 6(6), (7) and 7(6).

9 Ontario Ministry of Education, *Transition Planning: A Resource Guide, 2002* (Toronto: The Ministry, 2002), available online at http://www.edu.gov.on.ca/eng/general/elemsec/speced/transiti/transition.html.

10 *Ibid.*, at p. 15.

Although the formal transition process ends once the student is admitted and enrolled in a post-secondary institution, the value of information-sharing and co-operation continues. An open and constructive dialogue between the student, his or her parents — at least where the student is not yet old enough to make his/her own information-sharing decisions — and the educational institutions involved can be very helpful in maximizing the likelihood that the accommodation process will be as successful as possible.

ACCOMMODATION IN POST-SECONDARY EDUCATION: THE GOVERNING PRINCIPLES

The Basic Obligation

An Ontario college's or university's legal obligation to accommodate its students with disabilities arises under the *Human Rights Code* (the "Code").[11] The Code requires equal treatment in the provision of educational services, without discrimination on the basis of disability.[12] Where a student has a disability that interferes with his or her ability to benefit from education, the Code requires the educational institution to provide accommodation to the point of undue hardship.[13]

Equal Treatment: Building Accommodation into Institutional Standards

What constitutes equal treatment in the provision of educational services? The principles established in *Eaton v. Brant County Board of Education*,[14] the seminal decision arising under Ontario's special education system, are equally applicable to post-secondary education:[15]

> The principal object of certain of the prohibited grounds is the elimination of discrimination by the attribution of untrue characteristics based on stereotypical attitudes relating to immutable conditions such as race or sex. In the case of disability, this is one of the objectives. The other equally important objective seeks to take into account the true characteristics of this group which act as headwinds to the enjoyment of society's benefits and to accommodate them. Exclusion from the mainstream of society results from the construction of a society based solely on "mainstream" attributes to which disabled persons will never be able to gain access. Whether it is the impossibility of success at a written test for a blind person, or the need for ramp access to a library, the discrimination does not lie in the attribution of untrue characteristics to the disabled individual. The blind person cannot see and the person in a wheelchair needs a ramp. Rather, it is the failure to make reasonable accommodation, to fine-tune society so that its structures and assumptions do not result in the relegation and banishment of

---

11 R.S.O. 1990, c. H.19.
12 *Ibid.*, ss. 1 and 11.
13 *Ibid.*, ss. 11and 17.
14 (1997), 142 D.L.R. (4th) 385, [1997] 1 S.C.R. 241.
15 *Supra*, at para. 67.

> disabled persons from participation, which results in discrimination against them.

The notion of building reasonable accommodation into existing social and institutional structures was subsequently reinforced in a groundbreaking employment case known as the *Meiorin*[16] case:

> Employers designing workplace standards owe an obligation to be aware of both the differences between individuals, and differences that characterize groups of individuals. They must build conceptions of equality into workplace standards. By enacting human rights statutes and providing that they are applicable to the workplace, the legislatures have determined that the standards governing the performance of work should be designed to reflect all members of society, in so far as this is reasonably possible. Courts and tribunals must bear this in mind when confronted with a claim of employment-related discrimination. To the extent that a standard unnecessarily fails to reflect the differences among individuals, it runs afoul of the prohibitions contained in the various human rights statutes and must be replaced. The standard itself is required to provide for individual accommodation, if reasonably possible. A standard that allows for such accommodation may be only slightly different from the existing standard but it is a different standard nonetheless.[17]

Although the *Meiorin* case arose in the employment context, the principles articulated in that case are applied in the context of educational services as well. Thus, it is now generally recognized that a post-secondary educational institution should ensure that the standards that govern its students — including admission standards, academic standards, standards of conduct, and the like — are consistent with human rights principles and provide for reasonable accommodation of students who are members of groups protected under the Code (including those with disability-related needs).

Justifying Institutional Standards

How can a post-secondary institution be sure that the standards governing its students are consistent with human rights principles and provide for reasonable accommodation? In the *Meiorin* case, the Supreme Court of Canada articulated a three-part test for determining whether or not a general standard (in that case, a workplace standard) can be justified under human rights legislation. First, the employer must establish that the standard was adopted for a purpose rationally connected to the performance of the job. Second, the employer must establish that the standard was adopted in an honest and good faith belief that it was necessary to the fulfillment of this legitimate purpose. Third, the employer must establish that the standard is reasonably necessary to the accomplishment of its legitimate purpose. In order to establish that the standard is reasonably necessary in this sense, the

---

16 *British Columbia (Public Service Employee Relations Commission) v. B.C.G.S.E.U.* (1999), 176 D.L.R. (4th) 1, [1999] 3 S.C.R. 3 ("*Meiorin*").

17 *Supra*, at para. 68.

employer is required to demonstrate that is impossible to accommodate individual employees without imposing undue hardship on the employer.[18]

The three-part *Meiorin* test is also applied, with necessary modifications, in the context of post-secondary education. The test is not always an easy one to meet. A recent Newfoundland and Labrador human rights case, *Harvey v. Woodford Training Centre Inc.*,[19] provides an example of the potential difficulties a post-secondary institution can face in justifying its institutional standards under the *Meiorin* test.

Harvey was admitted to Woodford Training Centre, a private training institution, as a student in the esthetics program. The institution required all applicants for admission to the esthetics program to provide a medical certificate stating that they were free of communicable diseases; however, there was no requirement to provide updated medical information following admission to the program. The medical certificate that Harvey provided to the institution upon admission stated that she had been diagnosed with Hepatitis C. In response, she was told that she could no longer continue in the program as a result of the "no communicable diseases" requirement. She subsequently filed a human rights complaint.

The Board of Inquiry found that the purpose of the "no communicable diseases"requirement was to prevent the exposure of the public and other students to the risk of communicable diseases; however, the institution had not conducted its own assessment of the need for the requirement. Furthermore, it took no steps to obtain updated medical evidence to ensure that esthetics students remained free of communicable diseases after they had been admitted to the program, which weakened its argument that the requirement was necessary. In fact, the evidence before the board indicated that the risk of transmission of communicable diseases by a student to another student or member of the public was extremely low to begin with, and could be further reduced by taking straightforward precautions such as wearing gloves.

The Board of Inquiry concluded that the institution had not given any meaningful consideration to whether or not there was a rational connection between the purpose of protecting students and members of the public and the

---

18 *Meiorin*, *supra*, footnote 16, at para. 54.

19 2009 CanLII 3756, [2009] N.L.H.R.B.I.D. No. 1 (Nfld. Bd. Inq.). Extrapolating from the language used in the *Meiorin* case, the Board of Inquiry stated, at para. 140, that a service provider is required to establish:

(1) that the service provider adopted the standard for a purpose rationally connected to the provision of the service;

(2) that the service provider adopted the particular standard in an honest and good faith belief that it was necessary to the fulfillment of that legitimate purpose related to the provision of the service; and

(3) that the standard is reasonably necessary to the accomplishment of that legitimate purpose related to the provision of the service. To show that the standard is reasonably necessary, it must be demonstrated that it is impossible to accommodate individuals sharing the characteristics of the claimant without imposing undue hardship upon the service provider.

requirement that students be free of communicable diseases at the time of admission. The board was, therefore, unable to find that the requirement was adopted in an honest and good faith belief that it was necessary to the achievement of its purpose. Further, because there was a very limited risk of transmission of Hepatitis C in the circumstances and because the institution had not given any meaningful consideration to accommodating Harvey, the board was not prepared to find that the requirement was reasonably necessary. The board observed that the "no communicable diseases" requirement amounted to an "absolute prohibition" on persons with Hepatitis C — or any communicable disease — entering the esthetics program, and stated that justifying an absolute prohibition "require[s] a foundation in medical science and not merely a lay person's belief, however sincere, that hepatitis c is an infectious disease with an unknown but potential risk of transmission".[20] Consequently, Harvey's allegations of discrimination were upheld.

While the facts in the *Harvey* case were unusual, they do highlight the reality that a post-secondary institution's standards will be subject to rigorous scrutiny in the event of a human rights challenge. This, in turn, underlines the importance of designing standards in a way that will withstand such scrutiny, reviewing those standards on an ongoing basis to ensure that they can still be justified, and keeping appropriate records of these processes so that the rationale for the standard can be explained in the event of a subsequent legal challenge.

HOW FAR IS TOO FAR? THE LIMITS ON THE DUTY TO ACCOMMODATE

As the discussion in the previous section illustrates, it can be challenging to develop institutional standards that will withstand human rights scrutiny. It can be even more challenging to apply those standards to individual cases. Many post-secondary institutions struggle with the question of how far they must go to accommodate the individual needs of their students with disabilities.

The obligation under the *Human Rights Code* to accommodate students with disabilities in post-secondary education is a broad and far-reaching obligation; however, it is not an unlimited obligation. The Code provides that accommodation is to be provided where this can be done without causing undue hardship.[21]

When the *Meiorin* case was initially released in 1999, there was some concern that the Supreme Court had replaced the already onerous "undue hardship" requirement with the even more onerous requirement to demon-

---

20 *Supra*, at para. 164.
21 Code, ss. 11 and 17.

strate that accommodation was "impossible". This concern arose from the terminology used by the court in articulating the third part of its test for justifying institutional standards. The court said that, to establish that the standard was "reasonably necessary", it was necessary to demonstrate that "it is impossible to accommodate individual employees sharing the characteristics of the claimant without imposing undue hardship upon the employer".[22] More recently, the Supreme Court clarified that the use of the word "impossible" in *Meiorin* was not intended to expand the scope of the duty to accommodate. The obligation remains an obligation to provide accommodation to the point of undue hardship.[23]

The Supreme Court has also recently clarified that all the steps taken to accommodate an individual are to be considered in determining whether or not accommodation has been provided to the point of undue hardship.[24] In other words, a post-secondary institution is not limited to considering whether or not the latest request for accommodation would result in undue hardship. The institution may consider whether all the accommodations provided from the outset of the accommodation process, viewed cumulatively, result in undue hardship.

The Code specifically identifies three factors that are to be taken into account when determining whether a particular accommodation would cause undue hardship: cost; outside sources of funding; and health and safety requirements.[25] Some commentators have argued that this list is exhaustive and prohibits the consideration of any other factors;[26] however, in decisions dealing with the scope of accommodation required, the Supreme Court of Canada has repeatedly demonstrated a willingness to consider a range of factors in addition to those specified in the Code.[27]

---

22 *Meiorin*, *supra*, footnote 16, at para. 33.

23 *Syndicat des Employé-e-s de Techniques Professionnelles et de Bureau d'Hydro-Québec, Section Locale 2000 v. Hydro-Québec* (2008), 294 D.L.R. (4th) 407, [2008] 2 S.C.R. 561.

24 *Supra*. See also *Syndicat des Employés de l'Hôpital Général de Montréal v. Centre Universitaire de Santé McGill* (2007), 277 D.L.R. (4th) 577, [2007] 1 S.C.R. 161 ("*McGill*").

25 Code, ss. 11 and 17.

26 See, for example, Ontario Human Rights Commission, "Policy and Guidelines on Disability and the Duty to Accommodate" (Toronto: The Commission, 2000) available online at http://www.ohrc.on.ca/en/resources/Policies/PolicyDisAccom2.

27 *Ontario (Human Rights Commission) v. Simpsons-Sears Ltd.* (1985), 23 D.L.R. (4th) 321, [1985] 2 S.C.R. 536; *Central Alberta Dairy Pool v. Alberta (Human Rights Commission)* (1990), 72 D.L.R. (4th) 417, [1990] 2 S.C.R. 489; *Central Okanagan School District No. 23 v. Renaud* (1992), 95 D.L.R. (4th) 577, [1992] 2 S.C.R. 970; *Chambly, Commission scolaire régionale v. Bergevin* (1994), 115 D.L.R. (4th) 609, [1994] 2 S.C.R. 525; *British Columbia (Public Service Employee Relations Commission) v. B.C.G.S.E.U.* (1999), 176 D.L.R. (4th) 1, [1999] 3 S.C.R. 3 ("*Meiorin*"); *McGill*, *supra*, footnote 24.

There are a number of factors that may be relevant to a post-secondary institution's assessment of undue hardship. A brief discussion of some of these factors has been provided here.

Cost

Cost is a factor that will often arise in considering whether or not potential accommodations for students with disabilities will give rise to undue hardship.

While human rights decision-makers recognize that cost is a legitimate factor in assessing whether or not a particular accommodation would cause undue hardship, they will scrutinize cost arguments with a critical eye. The Supreme Court of Canada has issued a caution regarding the dangers of being too willing to accept undue hardship arguments based on cost, particularly when put forward by government and other publicly-funded institutions:[28]

> While in some circumstances excessive cost may justify a refusal to accommodate those with disabilities, one must be wary of putting too low a value on accommodating the disabled. It is all too easy to cite increased cost as a reason for refusing to accord the disabled equal treatment. . . . I do not assert that cost is always irrelevant to accommodation . . . Government agencies perform many expensive services for the public that they serve.

In order to establish undue hardship based on cost, a post-secondary institution must be able to demonstrate, through tangible evidence, the cost associated with the accommodation in question and the adverse impact that absorbing that cost would have on the institution's financial well-being and/or the other services it provides.[29] The institution must also be able to prove that there were no cost-reduction alternatives or alternate sources of funding available to reduce or negate the hardship arising from the accommodation.[30]

---

28 *British Columbia (Superintendent of Motor Vehicles) v. British Columbia (Council of Human Rights)* (1999), 181 D.L.R. (4th) 385, [1999] 3 S.C.R. 868 ("*Grismer*"), at para. 41.

29 The Ontario Human Rights Commission has taken the policy position for many years that, in order to constitute undue hardship, the costs related to an accommodation must be "so substantial that they would alter the essential nature of the enterprise, or so significant that they would substantially affect its viability". See Ontario Human Rights Commission, *op. cit.*, footnote 25. This very high threshold of undue hardship never gained acceptance among human rights decision-makers and the commission no longer has statutory oversight over the human rights process. Nevertheless, the human rights case law makes it clear that, in order to establish undue hardship based on cost alone, it will be necessary to demonstrate that the cost involved would have a significant negative impact on the financial well-being of the institution. For a case in which cost-based undue hardship arguments failed because the evidence of cost was found to be overly impressionistic or speculative, see *VIA Rail Canada Inc. v. Canada (Transportation Agency)* (2007), 279 D.L.R. (4th) 1, [2007] 1 S.C.R. 650 *sub nom. Council of Canadians with Disabilities v. VIA Rail Canada Inc.*

30 *Grismer*, *supra*, footnote 28.

The challenges that a post-secondary institution may face in establishing undue hardship based on cost alone are illustrated by a 1993 British Columbia human rights decision, *Howard and University of British Columbia (Re)*.[31] Howard was a profoundly deaf individual. He attended the University of British Columbia as an undergraduate student and was provided with the services of an American Sign Language ("ASL") interpreter in the classroom at the university's expense. After completing his undergraduate degree, Howard sought to return to the university to work towards his teaching certificate. At that time, he learned that the university did not provide interpreters for post-graduate students.

The evidence at the hearing indicated that the cost of a full-time interpreter was approximately $40,000 per year. Howard explored various sources of funding, but was only able to obtain a one-time payment of $1,000 and a $2,000-per-year forgivable loan. In the absence of additional funding to cover the cost of a full-time interpreter, he was unable to continue with his education.

Howard filed a human rights complaint, and his complaint proceeded to the British Columbia Human Rights Council. The council agreed with Howard that, without the services of an ASL interpreter in the classroom, Howard was deprived of meaningful access to educational services. In the council's view, this constituted *prima facie* discrimination on the basis of disability and shifted the onus to the university to establish that providing Howard with an ASL interpreter (or funding for one) would cause undue hardship.

In support of its undue hardship argument, the university pointed to a number of potential consequences that could follow if it were required to accommodate Howard and other deaf students by providing them with ASL interpreter services. The council noted, however, that the $40,000 per year required to accommodate Howard constituted only a small fraction of the university's $700 million annual operating budget. The council also observed that the university's evidence concerning the impact of accommodating Howard was largely speculative:[32]

> The Respondent did not adduce any evidence to suggest that the operations of the University would be seriously affected if it provided the Complainant with an interpreter. There is no evidence to suggest the nature of its operation would fundamentally change or that it would cease to operate. Indeed, beyond Dr. Srivistava's speculations, there was no evidence at all about the potential economic impact of the requested accommodation. It is obvious, however, that making the accommodation would have some impact on the University's resources. The University would have to either reallocate funds or increase revenues. To raise revenues, it would either have to persuade the government to contribute more or raise tuition. Raising tuition fees would have an impact on other students. I calculate that with approximately 30,000 students enrolled,

[31] (1993), 18 C.H.R.R. D/353 (B.C.H.R.C.).

[32] *Supra*, at para. 62.

> each student would have to pay slightly more than $1.00 per year to fund each full-time interpreter. Alternatively, if funds were reallocated from other programs, there would be some impact on students whose programs were cut back. There was no evidence before me on the impact of such a reallocation.

Given the lack of tangible evidence, the university's undue hardship argument failed. The council not only ordered the university to provide Howard with interpreter services, but subsequently awarded him over $30,000 in damages for the three-year delay in his education that resulted from the university's refusal to provide interpreter services.

While the university was not successful in establishing undue hardship in *Howard*, it appears that this outcome resulted largely from shortcomings in the evidence presented. A post-secondary institution that rigorously analyzes the costs of potential accommodations and musters the tangible evidence necessary to demonstrate the negative impact those costs will have on the institution may find itself in a better position to establish undue hardship.

Safety

Safety is another factor that may provide the basis for an undue hardship argument. Tangible evidence of safety risks will be required.[33] In addition, both the magnitude of the risk and who bears it will be considered.[34] While it may be appropriate to allow the individual seeking accommodation to assume some risk, the point of undue hardship will be reached when an accommodation exposes the individual, other students, staff, or members of the public to undue risk.[35]

---

33 *Grismer*, *supra*, footnote 28. See also *Harvey v. Woodford Training Centre Inc.*, 2009 CanLII 3756, [2009] N.L.H.R.B.I.D. No. 1 (NL Bd. Inq.). In *Harvey*, the expert evidence submitted at the hearing did not substantiate the existence of a significant safety risk. Moreover, the evidence demonstrated that any risk that did exist could have been reduced to a negligible level by taking some very straightforward precautions. The board made clear in its decision that it would not have accepted that accommodating the complainant would cause undue hardship.

34 *Central Alberta Dairy Pool v. Alberta (Human Rights Commission)*, *supra*, footnote 27, at p. 439 D.L.R.

35 Safety issues have become a topical issue on university and college campuses in recent years as a result of a number of unfortunate incidents of on-campus violence at schools such as Dawson College and Virginia Tech. When dealing with a student who appears to be at risk of harming him- or herself or others, staff will often have to consider whether or not continuing to accommodate the student in the educational environment gives rise to an unacceptable safety risk. A full discussion of this topic is beyond the scope of this work, however many post-secondary institutions have developed sophisticated approaches to risk assessment and risk management in order to address these concerns.

Impact on Other Students

Another factor that may be relevant is the impact of the accommodation on other students' learning experience or learning environment.[36] While this argument was not successful in the *Howard* case, this was largely because of the lack of tangible evidence concerning the impact on other students.[37] Where a post-secondary institution can demonstrate, through tangible evidence, that a particular accommodation will have a significant negative impact on the programs and services available to other students, will impose significant costs on other students, or will have some other significant negative impact on the learning environment, then it may be able to establish undue hardship.

Integrity of Academic Standards

A final factor that may be relevant to the issue of undue hardship relates to the impact the accommodation will have on the integrity of the institution's academic standards or requirements.

Post-secondary institutions will often receive requests for accommodation with respect to the academic requirements of a course or program. Examples may include exemptions from entrance requirements, tutoring, note-taking, distraction-free testing environments, additional time to complete examinations or other evaluation requirements, alternative evaluation formats, course substitutions and exemptions from core courses. While many of these accommodations can be made without undermining the integrity of the institution's academic standards, some cannot. An accommodation that would fundamentally undermine the institution's academic standards or significantly alter the course or program requirements may give rise to undue hardship.

In considering the availability of undue hardship arguments of this kind, the institution should first ensure that the academic standards in question will withstand scrutiny under the *Meiorin* test described above. The institution will need to be able to demonstrate that it established the standard for a rational purpose, that it acted honestly and in good faith in doing so and that the standard that was chosen is necessary to accomplish the institution's purpose. The institution should not assume that a human rights decision-maker will always defer to academic judgments regarding the pedagogical justifications for specific academic requirements. To the contrary, where those requirements create barriers for students with disabilities, the institution should expect that the legitimacy of those requirements will be rigorously scrutinized.[38]

Assuming that the academic standards in question withstand this initial scrutiny, the institution will then have to demonstrate, through tangible

---

36 See, for example, *Lewis v. York Region Board of Education* (1996), 27 C.H.R.R. D/261 (Ont. Bd. Inq.).

37 *Howard, supra*, footnote 31.

38 See *Harvey, supra*, footnote 33.

evidence, why it cannot accommodate the student in the manner requested. This will usually involve proof that the accommodation requested would fundamentally alter the nature of the course or program or exempt the student from the requirement to demonstrate mastery of the subject-matter.

There are very few Canadian cases in which such arguments have been considered, but in the cases to date that have dealt with this issue, the educational institution was successful in establishing that it was not required to provide an accommodation that fundamentally altered course requirements. In *Harris v. Camosun College*,[39] the complainant was a first-year student in a criminology program. She claimed that she suffered from multiple chemical and environmental sensitivities and that she experienced difficulty in attending classes in certain classrooms because of her sensitivities to chemicals. In a number of instances, she was able to arrange appropriate accommodations with the course instructors; however, there were two courses in which the instructors insisted that Harris' physical presence in the classroom was an essential component of meeting the course objectives and they refused to provide the accommodations she was seeking.

The British Columbia Human Rights Tribunal carefully reviewed the instructors' rationale for insisting on Harris' physical presence in the classroom. In one class, the course objectives required the student to personally complete laboratory work. In the other course, the course objectives included development of skills through group interaction. In both cases, the Tribunal was satisfied that Harris' physical presence in the classroom was essential to meeting the requirements of the course. The Tribunal concluded that the college was not required to accommodate Harris in a manner that would fundamentally change or exempt her from meeting these course requirements.

A second decision dealing with this issue, *Grant MacEwan Community College v. Alberta (Human Rights Commission)*,[40] was not a disability case. It involved a claim by a student of Native Canadian ancestry that the evaluation requirements for a Life Management Skills Leader Training Course discriminated against her on the basis of her race, gender and ancestry.

The course outline for the course in question expressly stated that its main objective was to "demonstrate during daily group process, the interpersonal skills taught in the lesson, communicate empathy and concern for others, and describe personal growth achieved in the course."[41] The evaluation format was somewhat unusual — at the end of the program, the class, as a whole, voted on whether or not each student had demonstrated mastery of the skills required. The ultimate decision, however, rested with the instructor. On two separate occasions, the class voted that the complainant had not demonstrated the skills necessary to pass the course and the instructor agreed. Following an

---

39 (2000), 39 C.H.R.R. D/36 (B.C.H.R.T.).

40 (2000), 20 Admin. L.R. (3d) 271, 37 C.H.R.R. D/421.

41 *Supra*, at para. 30.

unsuccessful internal appeal, she filed a human rights complaint, alleging that the evaluation process was culturally biased and that she had failed because she demonstrated "typically Native characteristics".[42]

The Human Rights Panel that dealt with the matter at first instance upheld the complaint; however, the Alberta Court of Queen's Bench overturned that decision on judicial review. The court relied on the fact that the course outline specifically set out the skills students would be required to demonstrate in order to pass the course. Since the complainant had not demonstrated mastery of those skills, she did not deserve to pass the course. The court did not require the college to exempt the complainant from meeting the fundamental requirements of the course because of her Native Canadian ancestry.

Although the Canadian law in this area is not yet fully developed, the case law that does exist suggests that an educational institution will not be required to accommodate a student in a manner that would fundamentally alter course or program requirements. Further support for this notion can be found in a recent Supreme Court of Canada decision in which the court confirmed that the purpose of the duty to accommodate is not to completely alter the essence of the contract between the parties.[43] In the educational context, the contract is to deliver a particular course or program and an accommodation that fundamentally alters the nature of that course or program would seem to go beyond what the law requires.

THE ACCOMMODATION PROCESS

As a general rule, a student who is seeking academic or other accommodation is expected to initiate the accommodation process by making a request for accommodation.[44] Many post-secondary institutions now include information in the pre-admission package provided to potential applicants that encourages self-identification of any special needs requiring accommodation as early as possible so that accommodations can be arranged in a timely way. Further information is typically provided when students arrive on campus, as part of the registration process or the orientation process (or both) or from the institution's Disability Services Office.

Despite the efforts that post-secondary institutions make to emphasize the importance of early identification of accommodation needs, not all students will identify their special needs or seek accommodation. There are many

---

42 *Supra.* The Human Rights Panel cited, at para. 28, as examples of these "typically Native characteristics" that "many people of Native descent do not look others straight in the eye, are often silent, and do not express emotion or praise very well".

43 *Syndicat des Employé-e-s de Techniques Professionnelles et de Bureau d'Hydro-Québec, Section Locale 2000 v. Hydro-Québec* (2008), 294 D.L.R. (4th) 407, [2008] 2 S.C.R. 561, at para. 15.

44 See, for example, *Hannaford v. Douglas College* (2000), 37 C.H.R.R. D/336 (B.C.H.R.T.)

reasons for this. The student may be seeking a fresh start in a new environment, may wish to avoid real or perceived labeling or stigma associated with identifying him- or herself as a student with a disability who requires accommodation, or may simply wish to test his or her ability to cope with the new educational environment before seeking accommodation. In some cases, the student may lack the insight or maturity to understand the need for accommodation. In other cases, such as those involving mental illnesses, the student's disability may interfere with the student's judgment and ability to recognize that seeking accommodation is in his or her own best interest.

In light of these realities, it is not appropriate for a post-secondary institution to wait for formal notification of the existence of a disability in every case. Where there is objective evidence of disability, the institution should not "turn a blind eye" to that evidence. In such a case, it is often advisable to make proactive inquiries and to encourage the student to seek medical or other expert assistance in identifying his or her accommodation needs, so that the accommodation process can be initiated.

The earlier the need for accommodation is identified, the more likely it is that accommodations can be put in place in a timely manner. The timing of a request for accommodation is not determinative of its legitimacy. Even late requests for accommodation must be given serious consideration by the institution. The earlier the request is made, however, the more likely it is that any adverse academic or other consequences can be avoided.

Once the need for accommodation has been identified, the next step will be to require the student to provide medical or other expert evidence in order to enable the institution to understand the nature and extent of the student's accommodation needs. The student can be expected to co-operate with reasonable requests for medical or other expert evidence.[45] Requests for accommodation should be dealt with through a centralized process, involving impartial review by staff who have appropriate qualifications and expertise to evaluate such requests and the underlying medical or other expert evidence and are in a position to maintain appropriate confidentiality with respect to the supporting evidence provided. With these considerations in mind, many post-secondary institutions utilize their Disability Services Office or a similar department or office to review accommodation requests as well as supporting medical and other expert evidence and develop appropriate accommodation plans.

On receipt of medical or other expert evidence identifying the student's accommodation needs, it will be necessary to determine how those needs will be accommodated. Post-secondary institutions should be "sensitive to the various ways in which individual capabilities may be accommodated" and

---

[45] See, for example, *Harris v. Camosun College*, *supra*, footnote 39. It should be noted, however, that disagreements frequently arise with respect to whether a particular request is reasonable.

"innovative yet practical" when assessing potential accommodations.[46] Staff responsible for developing accommodation plans should endeavour to identify all the potential accommodations that may be available, what is involved in implementing those accommodations and whether implementation is possible without causing undue hardship. Appropriate records should be kept of all the potential accommodations considered and, where an accommodation was rejected on the basis that it would cause undue hardship, the reasons why.

The most successful accommodations are those that are agreed on by the institution and the student. Where an agreement is reached, the terms of that agreement should be set out in writing in an accommodation plan. The plan should be signed by all the relevant stakeholders. A written accommodation plan will assist in reducing the risk of future misunderstandings or legal disputes about the nature, extent or reasonableness of any accommodations provided.

Where an agreement cannot be reached concerning the accommodations that will be provided, a post-secondary institution should formulate an accommodation proposal that it believes is reasonable in the circumstances. A student seeking accommodation can be expected to co-operate with reasonable accommodation proposals by at least attempting the proposed accommodations. The student cannot insist on what the student considers to be a perfect or preferred accommodation.[47] Accordingly, the institution should communicate its proposal to the student in writing, remind the student of his or her duty to co-operate and urge the student to attempt the accommodation. Where the student maintains his or her refusal and the accommodation process is frustrated by the student's unreasonable refusal to co-operate, there will come a point at which the institution will be entitled to take the position that it has fulfilled its obligations toward the student.[48] Given the sensitivity and potential liabilities associated with taking this position, post-secondary institutions are well-advised to seek legal counsel before doing so.

Once an accommodation is in place, that accommodation should be reviewed periodically in order to ensure that it remains consistent with the student's accommodation needs.[49] In most cases, this review process should

---

46 *British Columbia (Public Service Employee Relations Commission) v. B.C.G.S.E.U.* (1999), 176 D.L.R. (4th) 1, [1999] 3 S.C.R. 3 ("*Meiorin*"), at para. 64.

47 *Central Okanagan School District No. 23 v. Renaud* (1992), 95 D.L.R. (4th) 577, [1992] 2 S.C.R. 970. See also *Syndicat des Employés de l'Hôpital Général de Montréal v. Centre Universitaire de Santé McGill* (2007), 277 D.L.R. (4th) 577, [2007] 1 S.C.R. 161, at para. 38, where the Supreme Court stated that "[t]he duty to accommodate is neither absolute nor unlimited" but rather requires "reasonable compromise". Again, however, disputes frequently arise concerning whether a particular proposal is reasonable.

48 *Central Okanagan School District No. 23 v. Renaud*, *supra*; *Harris v. Camosun College*, *supra*, footnote 39.

49 The accommodation should be reviewed at least once every academic year — and

involve a request for updated medical information. Where the student's condition has improved, some or all of the accommodations provided may no longer be needed. Where the student's condition has deteriorated, additional accommodations may need to be considered.

---

more often where there is medical evidence indicating that the student's needs have changed or there are other reasonable grounds to believe that this may be the case.

Index

Administrative Law Requirements
Canadian Charter of Rights and Freedoms, 10-11
constitutional requirements, 14
Minister of Education's obligations, 8-9
procedural fairness and natural justice, 11-12
review of administrative decisions, 12
school boards' obligations, 9
Special Education Tribunal's obligations, 9

Advocates
competency, 126
lawyers, paralegals and lay advocates, 121-123
regulation, 121-122
representation at informal meetings, 123
representation at IPRC, 124
representation at SEAB, 125, 149
representation at Special Education Tribunal, 125-126

Age Requirements, 81, 82, 106, 144, 158-159

Alternative Dispute Resolution. *See* Mediation

Appeal
(*See also* Judicial Review)
exceptionality, 138-139
grounds, 138
IPRC, 28, 137
notice of appeal, 143
parties, 144
placement, 139
placement pending, 73-74, 108-109
programs and services, 139-140
Special Education Appeal Board, 137-138
Special Education Tribunal, 134

Appeal — *continued*
standing, 137
time limitations, 140-143

Assessments, 28

Autism
ABA/IBI, 65-66
class size, 43
definition, 50
home instruction, 62
Policy/Program Memorandum 75, 140
Tribunal decision, 64-65

Behaviour
(*See also* Exceptionality)
class size, 42-44
definition, 49-50
safety risk, 277-279

Best Interests, 69-71, 102-103

Bill 82, 1-2

Blindness and Low Vision
class size, 44
definition, 54

Canadian Charter of Rights and Freedoms
Eaton v. Brant County Board of Education, 11, 68-71, 103
general, 4
implications for special education decisions, 10-11, 67

Child Welfare Law, 19

Class Size, 29, 42-44

Communication, 50

Constitution
linguistic rights, 14
separate school rights, 13-14

Consultation
Special Education Plan, 24

Courts
(*See also* Judicial Review)
final order of Special Education Tribunal, 192

Deaf
class size, 43
definition, 50-51
programs and services, 63
transportation, 31

Demonstration School, 29-30, 61
IPRC, 82, 104
referral of student from demonstration school to IPRC, 82

Developmental Disability
(*See also* Exceptionality)
class size, 43
definition, 53-54
Special Education Plan, 32

Discipline
human rights, 272-279
mitigating factors, 274-277
records, 277

Education Law
denominational, separate and dissentient school rights, 14
minority language instruction rights, 13-14
school boards' statutory obligations, 15

Environmental Sensitivity, 63

Equipment, 30
Special Education Plan, 30

Evidence at Special Education Tribunal
admissibility, 179
competence, 177-179
expert, 184-185
hearsay, 183-184
privilege, 180-183
relevance, 179-180

Exceptionality
(*See also under individual exceptionality headings)*
assessments, 28
categories, 49
Special Education Plan, 27

Exclusion, 277-278

Expulsion, 272-277

Fairness, 8-9, 64, 68, 111, 117, 125-126, 157-160

Fragile. *See* Medically Fragile Students

Gifted
class size, 43
definition, 47, 52-53
needs of student, 62-63

Hard of Hearing. *See* Deaf

Health Care Consent Act, 61

Health Support Services, 28

History of Special Education, 1

Home Instruction. *See* Placement

Human Rights Code
application to special education decisions, 16-19,67

Human Rights Commission
applications, 212-214
  remedies, 244-245
former role, 195-196
interventions, 217-218

Human Rights Legal Support Centre, 199

Human Rights Tribunal
applications, 203-208
  amendments, 215
  withdrawals, 215-216
attendance, 236-237
Case Assessment Directions, 237-238
constitutional issues, 239
costs, 245-246
decision, 243
deferral, 221-222
dismissal, 220-221
expedited proceedings, 223-224
hearing, 234-244
  evidence, 242-243
  open or closed, 239-240
  recording, 240
Human Rights Tribunal vs. Special Education Tribunal, 194-195, 220-221

Human Rights Tribunal — *continued*
information-sharing/disclosure, 200-203, 231-234
interventions, 219-220
location, 197
mediation, 228-230
members, 196-197
proceedings, 200-247
reconsideration, 246-247
referral to Commission, 245
remedies, 243-244
  interim, 224-226
replies, 212
representatives, 199-200
responses, 208-212, 214-215
rules of procedure, 198
  streamlining, 235-236
summonses, 238
timing, 203, 205, 230-231

Identification
current assessments for, 56
early identification, 27, 47
requirement for, 55

Identification, Placement and Review Committee
access to information, 84-85
appropriate programming prior to IPRC decision, 108-109
chair, 78-79
conduct, 84-85
decision, 102-107
  identification, 103
  implementation, 109
  placement, 103-105
electronic recording of meetings, 101-102
establishment of IPRC, 77-79
form, 88-89
information to be considered, 95-100
meetings —
  adjournments, 94
  agenda, 91-92
  closed meetings, 94-95
  notice, 85, 90-91
  parent/student representation, 93
  participants, 86-88

Identification, Placement and Review Committee — *continued*
meetings — *continued*
  procedures, 88-89,92-93
members, 77-79, 85
parent request to discuss decision, 107-108
procedures, 88-90
program and placement pending decision, 108-109
recommendations
  programs and services, 103-104
  student over 21, 106-107
record of proceedings, 101-102
referral of students, 79-84
  from a provincial/demonstration school, 82-83
  review referral, 83-84
  role of principal, 80-81
  role of parent, 82
representation, 124
residency of student, 79
review, 83-84, 105-106
students 21 or older, 106-107
time limits, 81, 82, 107-108

Individual Education Plan
contents, 111, 116-119
consultation, 115
development process, 114-116
IEP Resource Guide, 112
IPRC recommendations, 116
mandatory vs optional, 112-113
Ministry reviews, 112
Ministry standards, 112, 117-119
monitoring and review, 120
role of principal, 113, 114
special funding, 113
time limits, 119-120
transition plan, 116
use in IPRC review, 96-97

Integration Movement, 67-71

Intellectual Disability, 67
(*See also* Developmental Disability; Gifted; Mild Intellectual Disability)

Judicial Review
constitutional issues, 252-253

Judicial Review — *continued*
costs, 255
evidence, 253-254
further appeal, 255
grounds —
  Human Rights Tribunal
    procedural errors, 267-268
    substantive errors, 268-269
  Special Education Tribunal
    factual errors, 266
    jurisdiction, 264-265
    procedural errors, 255-260
    substantive errors, 260-264, 265
Human Rights Tribunal decisions, 249
implementation, 270
IPRC decisions, 249-250
notice, 252
parties, 250-252
pre-conditions (Human Rights Tribunal), 266-267
procedure, 250
record, 253-254
remedies, 269
SEAB decisions, 249-250
Special Education Tribunal Decisions, 249
standard of review, 256-269
timing of decision, 254

Language Impairment
(*See also* Communication)
class size, 43
definition, 51

Learning Disability
class size, 43
definition, 51-52

Low Vision. *See* **Blindness and Low Vision**

Mediation
advantages —
  general, 130-131
  special education, 131-133
  preparation to increase effectiveness, 134-135

Mediation
— *continued*
cost, 131
mediation process, 133
Special Education Tribunal, 134

Mild Intellectual Disability
class size, 43
definition, 53

Minister of Education, 24-25, 49

Multiple Disabilities
class size, 44
definition, 54-55

Municipal Freedom of Information and Protection of Privacy Act, 74-77

Non-Students, 32

Notice
IPRC meeting, 81, 90-91
SEAB meeting, 148

Ontario Student Record, 97-99
IEP, 120

Orthopaedic Disability. *See* Physical Disability

Parent Guide, 22
contents, 41-42

Parents
consent to placement, 72, 109
custodial, 86-87
IEP consultation, 115-116
parent representatives, 93, 123-126
parental preferences, 73-74, 103
participation in IPRC, 86-87
request for IPRC, 82
request to discuss IPRC decision, 107-108
separated parents, 86-87

Personnel. *See* Resources, human

Physical Disability
class size, 43-44
definition, 54

Placement, 29, 57-75
appeal of, 59, 61-62, 73-74
definition, 57-58
determination of. *See* Identification, Placement and Review Committee
effect of appeal on, 72-73
home instruction, 62,
implementation, 59, 72
needs of the student, 69-70, 69-71
notice, 81
parental preference, 80, 82
placement vs. programs and services, 59-60, 62-66
placement vs. promotion, 109
privacy. *See* Municipal Freedom of Information and Protection of Privacy Act
procedural fairness —
IPRC, 84-85, 89-90
program, 58
promotion, 73-74
provincial school, 61
Special Education Plan, 29
purchase of, 25, 62-63
range of placements, 58, 61, 62
recommendations, 59
review of. *See* Identification, Placement and Review Committee
role of IPRC, 77
Special Education Plan, 23, 25-26
standards, 66-67
transitional placement, 73-74, 108-109

Policy/Program Memoranda, 45-46, 74-75
autism, 45
bullying, 271
codes of conduct, 271
deaf or blind pupils, 45
early identification, 21, 27, 45, 47
expelled student programs, 75
health support services, 45
learning disabilities, 45
progressive discipline, 45
psychological testing/assessments, 45
residential schools for learning disabilities, 45
suspended student programs, 75

Post-Secondary
academic standards, 293-295
accommodation process, 295-298
cost, 290-292
duty to accommodate, 285, 288-290
impact on other students, 293
institutional standards, 285-288
safety, 292
transition, 282-284

Preparation
communication
(*See also* Notice), 169, 170, 171, 173
IPRC, 171-173
objectivity, 169, 173
records, 170-173, 174, 176-177
SEAB, 173-176
SET, 176-177

Principal
parent guide, 82
participation with IPRC, 87
referral to IPRC, 80-81
violent students, 277-278

Provincial School
referral of student to IPRC, 82-83

Regular Class. *See* Placement

Resources
equipment, 30
human, 30
services, 31, 32
transportation, 31

Review
(*See also* Identification, Placement and Review Committee)
administrative decisions, 12

School Boards
implementation of board decision following SEAB, 155-156
implementation of IPRC decision, 109
role in SEAB process, 153-154
segregation, 67-68

Services
definition, 58
purchase of, 62-63

Special Education Advisory Committee ("SEAC"), 31, 33-34
administrative support, 40
alternative members, 39
composition, 35-38
conduct of meetings,40
role of, 22, 26, 29, 30, 31, 33, 34-35, 39
term of office, 38-39

Special Education Appeal Board
administrative support, 146
decision/recommendation, 153-154
  implementation, 155-156
expenses, 146
fairness, 146-147, 151
fees, 146
meeting, 150-154
members, 145
notice, 148
timing, 147, 151-153
OSR, 149
participation, 148-149
preparation, 174-6
record from IPRC, 149
representatives, 149
school board decision, 153-154

Special Education Plan
amendments, 24-25
contents, 25-33
historical context, 22-23
maintenance and review, 24
multi-year plans, 22-23
persons not enrolled as students, 32
requirements, 121, 23-24
role of Minister, 24-25, 27
standards, 23, 26

Special Education Programs and Services
programs and services vs. placement, 57-66

Special Education Tribunal
appropriate placement, 66-67

Special Education Tribunal — *continued*
costs, 191
disclosure, 170-171
evidence, 186-187
  experts, 185
finality of decision, 192
grounds on appeal, 161
hearing, 164-191
identification decision, 188
initiating an appeal, 157-158
members, 157-158
notice, 166-167
parties, 158-159, 165-166
placement decision, 188-191
procedure, 164-165
programs and services, 162-163
reasons on decision, 187
remedies, scope of, 188-191
representatives, 163
scope of appeal, 161-163
timing, 159-161
timing of decision, 185-186
who can appeal, 158-159

Speech Impairment
class size, 43
definition, 51

Student
aged 21 or older, 106
participation in IPRC, 86, 93
participation at SEAB, 144
participation at Special Education Tribunal, 166

Suspension, 272-277

Teachers
Special Education Plan, 27, 30

Trainable Retarded. *See* Developmental Disability

Training/Staff Development, 30

Transition, 32, 73-74, 108-109
IEP, 116

Transportation
Special Education Plan, 30, 31